# The Trials & Tribulations of
# LITTLE RED
# RIDING HOOD

THE TRIALS & TRIBULATIONS OF

# LITTLE RED RIDING HOOD

EDITED BY JACK ZIPES

SECOND EDITION

ROUTLEDGE · NEW YORK & LONDON

Published in 1993 by

Routledge, Inc.
29 West 35 Street
New York, NY 10001

Published in Great Britain by

Routledge
11 New Fetter Lane
London EC4P 4EE

**Library of Congress Cataloging-in-Publication Data**

Zipes, Jack David.
    The trials and tribulations of Little Red Riding Hood : versions of the tale in sociocultural context / Jack Zipes. —2nd ed.
      p.  cm.
    Includes bibliographical references.
    ISBN 0-415-90834-5 (hardback) —ISBN 0-415-90835-3 (pbk.)
    1. Little Red Riding Hood (Tale)  2. Women—Folklore.  3. Rape—Folklore.  4. Short stories—History and criticism.  5. Rape in literature.   I. Title.
GR75.L56Z56  1993
398.21—dc20                           93-19319
                                         CIP

In Memory of Angela Carter

# ❋ *Table of Contents* ❋

# ❋ *Preface* ❋

IN 1983, WHEN *The Trials and Tribulations of Little Red Riding Hood* first appeared, it caused a great deal of commotion because my study was based on the premise that literary fairy tales were consciously cultivated and employed in 17th-century France to reinforce the regulation of sexuality in modern Europe. I also tried to demonstrate that the discourse on manners and gender roles in fairy tales has contributed more to the creation of our present-day social norms than we realize. A tale like *Little Red Riding Hood* was my case in point. Its unique history can reveal to what extent the boundaries of our existence have evolved from male phantasy and sexual struggle for domination. As part of our common heritage, the tale and its reception through history indicate the hidden power of the commonplace that we neglect or tend to repress. My book was an attempt to recall a repressed history in the hope that we will explore alternatives for the future.

To my surprise, the heated debate about the destiny and identity of Little Red Riding Hood has continued during the last ten years, brought on in part by my own study, but also because, I believe, the issue of rape and violence in our society has taken on immense proportions. It is because rape and violence are at the core of the history of *Little Red Riding Hood* that it is the most widespread and notorious fairy tale in the Western world, if not in the entire world.

The revised edition of *The Trials and Tribulations of Little Red Riding Hood* is an endeavor to strengthen and refine my argument, and it provides me with an opportunity to re-enter the debate about the significance of this fairy tale and fairy tales in general. I do not intend now to present the definitive history of *Little Red Riding Hood* or bring about closure to the debate about the girl's fate. After all, there is no end to her story: even though Little Red Riding Hood is constantly mutilated by the wolf and dies, she is always reincarnated in some retold form to mark shifts in our attitudes toward gender formation, sexuality, and the use of power. My intention is to reflect once again upon the cultural and political significance of Red Riding Hood's continual reappearance.

In the present edition of *The Trials and Tribulations of Little Red Riding Hood* I have included seven new versions. Alphonse Daudet's dramatic skit, *The Romance of Red Riding Hood* (1862), is a brilliant interpretation of the underlying sexual connotations of the tale, and it is a rare work that most critics, even specialists of French literature, have never read or appreciated. Pierre Cami's *Little Green Riding Hood* (1917) is a hilarious burlesque that recaptures the original emancipatory impetus of the folk tradition through word play. Olga Broumas's poem "Little Red Riding Hood" (1977) is an incisive answer to Anne Sexton and one of the first lesbian reappropriations of the literary tradition. Tanith Lee's gothic narrative, *Wolfland* (1983), reflects the outrage that many women feel about the violence that the protagonist of *Little Red Riding Hood* experienced and continues to experience. Anne Sharpe's *Not So Little Red Riding Hood* (1985) develops an innovative narrative strategy to suggest ways in which women can protect themselves from exploitation. Gwen Strauss's poem "The Waiting Wolf" (1990) is a highly sophisticated analysis of the manner in which men rationalize their urge to victimize women. And finally, Sally Miller Gearhart's remarkable tale, *Roja and Leopold* (1990), is a carnivalesque revision of the traditional *Red Riding Hood* tale that turns all the characters inside out and speaks out in the name of animal and gay/lesbian rights.

It is not by chance that most of the new and experimental versions of *Little Red Riding Hood* since 1983 have been written by women and are feminist. The confrontations and situations that women experience in our society have compelled them to reflect upon the initial encounter between wolf and girl that they may have heard, read, or seen as children. I shall have more to say about Little Red Riding Hood and our "rape culture" in the prologue, "Framing Little Red Riding Hood," and in the epilogue, "Re-Framing and Reviewing Little Red Riding Hood." Both have been added to this revised edition. The essay, "Re-Framing and Reviewing Little Red Riding Hood," was originally printed in my book *Don't Bet on the Prince* as "A Second Gaze at Little Red Riding Hood," and I have thoroughly revised it to include recent research on the history of the tale and fairy-tale illustrations. Finally, all the bibliographies and references have been updated to 1993 in an effort to provide readers with the latest news about Red Riding Hood's moves. Otherwise, my original social history, that is, "The Trials and Tribulations of Little Red Riding Hood," has not been changed, since I still believe in this version of the literary narrative's history, and all that has happened since 1983 appears to confirm my views.

Once again I want to thank the Graduate School of the University of Wisconsin–Milwaukee for awarding me a summer research grant in 1980, which helped make this book possible. I also want to express my gratitude to Merrilan Edwards, Don Biddison, Jessica Brown, and the rest of the Golda Meir interlibrary loan department of the University of Wisconsin–Milwaukee, who were most generous in providing me with assistance and invaluable material. In the preparation of the first edition I profited from the fine suggestions and editorial assistance of Jeanne Juster and Jenna Schulman, who were working for Bergin and Garvey at that time. In the production of the revised edition, I have benefited from the expertise of Stewart Cauley, Michael Esposito, and Mary Neal Meador. My daughter Hanna has afforded me the pleasure of her many new insights about Little Red Riding Hood through her re-enacting and re-defining the role in my study, and my wife, Carol Dines, has thoroughly grounded my insights by editing the new sections and translations of the book. Of course, Bill Germano is always on the scene somewhere, and I am most grateful that he was willing to guide and support the revised edition of this anthology.

If it had not been for *The Trials and Tribulations of Little Red Riding Hood*, I would never have met Angela Carter, and over the last ten years until her untimely death in 1992, she not only encouraged me to develop some of my fairy-tale projects, but she also made immense contributions in revising the entire genre and the manner in which we look at fairy tales today. It was somewhat fortuitous that, before I actually became acquainted with Angela Carter, I had written this book in her spirit, and it is now reappearing as a gesture to keep her spirit alive.

# Prologue: Framing Little Red Riding Hood

IN 1989, ALAN DUNDES, the renowned folklorist, published *Little Red Riding Hood: A Casebook* with ten different essays exemplifying different approaches to the folk narrative that gave rise to the literary tale of *Little Red Riding Hood*. His concluding essay, "Interpreting 'Little Red Riding Hood' Psychoanalytically,"[1] is a masterful summary of the immense scholarship that has sought to explain why we continually retell the adventures of Little Red Riding Hood, and it is also a powerful argument for using psychoanalysis in folklore research. However, since Dundes is concerned primarily with opening the eyes of folklorists to the multi-faceted aspects of the tale and its underlying sexual meanings, he sets a frame for understanding the tale that still needs modification, if we are going to grasp how an oral tale of the 17th century was transformed into a literary tale of rape and violence.

In fact, Dundes obfuscates the issue of both narrative and sexual violence because of his interest in infantile fantasy. Yet, there is a way of framing the origins of *Little Red Riding Hood* in which the theme of literary appropriation and sexual initiation can be linked to rape that, I believe, takes precedence over questions of infantile sexuality. It may not be the only way to frame the story of Little Red Riding Hood, but I want to use Dundes's provocative essay to clarify why it is still important to keep the frame of violence in studying the social history of *Little Red Riding Hood*. Otherwise, "her" history as female object will continue to be violated in the name of a scholarship dominated by men.

Dundes argues that neither folklorists nor psychoanalysts are aware of the possible Asian cognates of *Little Red Riding Hood*, and therefore, their interpretations of the tale have been misleading if not myopic. Using the research of the sinologist and sociologist Wolfram Eberhard, Dundes shows that there is an oral tale type

(AT 123) generally known as "The Wolf and the Kids" that circulated in Asia before or about the same time as the oral tale type
(AT 333), "The Glutton" (Red Riding Hood). A literary example
of this Asian tale type is Chang Mi's "Goldflower and the Bear,"
published in both the original and present edition of *The Trials and
Tribulations of Little Red Riding Hood*, in which a cunning young girl
tricks an ogre/monster/beast by threatening to defecate in bed and
saves her siblings.[2] Given the long oral tradition of cognate *Red
Riding Hood* tales in China, Korea, and Japan, Dundes maintains
that Western folklorists and psychoanalysts have been too Euro-
centric in their approaches and have worked with false premises by
using the literary tales of Charles Perrault or the Brothers Grimm
as their starting points. It is only by making use of the full panoply
of oral texts of *Little Red Riding Hood* in Asia, Africa, and Europe
that one can gain a sense of the major conflict of the narrative, the
common thread that runs through all the versions up to the present. For Dundes, the tale depicts

> essentially an inter-generational conflict between daughter and
> mother . . . we find tremendous antagonism between heroine
> and female foe. We begin with a mother sending a hapless girl
> away from the safety of the home. This enforced abandonment
> (cf. weaning) leads the girl to take her revenge by eating her
> grandmother's flesh. If one stops to think about it, one can see
> that breast-feeding constitutes a kind of eating of maternal flesh
> in order to obtain the necessary nourishing mother's milk. In
> oral versions of the tale the heroine eats the flesh and blood of
> her grandmother, an unquestionably oral, aggressive act on the
> part of the girl. Infantile regression is also signaled by the desire
> to defecate *immediately* after eating. Here we have a series of
> projective inversions or reversals.[3]

Certainly, if one accepts Dundes's combination of folkloristics
and psychoanalytical theory, his interpretation of the oral narrative paradigm makes sense. However, it makes sense only at the
risk of de-historicizing a Western narrative tradition and not focus-
ing enough on the connections between the oral and literary tradition. The fact is that there is absolutely no proof that the Asian
cognates influenced the basic tale type AT 333 of *Little Red Riding
Hood* or were even known in Europe. Almost all the oral versions
of *Little Red Riding Hood* show a remarkable unity in plot and structure that represent a socio-ethnic initiation ritual practiced by wom-
en in the southeastern region of France and northern Italy. Therefore, though it is important to consider psychoanalysis for a study

❀ 3 ❀

Prologue:
Framing
Little Red
Riding
Hood

of such tales like *Little Red Riding Hood*, Dundes's frame is skewed because of a false cross-cultural model that is not related to European peasant traditions in the 17th century, nor does he discuss the modes of sexuality or ritual that may have influenced the formation of the tale.

Robert Darnton's book *The Great Cat Massacre* argues against a psychoanalytic approach such as that used by Dundes in favor of a socio-historical method that examines folk tales as historical documents. Darnton's preference is for an ethnographical study that investigates the world views or *mentalités* of peasants as expressed through their oral tales. At one point, he uses *Little Red Riding Hood* as an example and interprets it as a warning tale about inexorable calamity that confronted peasants in 18th-century France. According to Darnton, the peasants lived in a harsh world, and one step in the wrong direction could bring about a tragedy. "If the world is cruel, the village nasty, and mankind infested with rogues, what is one to do? The tales do not give an explicit answer, but they illustrate with aptness of the ancient French proverb, 'One must howl with the wolves.'"[4]

Though Darnton is correct in insisting that we look at the material conditions that brought about distinct world views in folk tales, he ironically bungles the task he sets for himself in the area of his own expertise—history. Darnton bases his faulty interpretation of *Little Red Riding Hood* on the following tale that he allegedly translated from Paul Delarue's collection *Le Conte populaire français*:

> Once a little girl was told by her mother to bring some bread and milk to her grandmother. As the girl was walking through the forest, a wolf came up to her and asked her where she was going.
> "To grandmother's house," she replied.
> "Which path are you taking, the path of the pins or the path of the needles?"
> "The path of the needles."
> So the wolf took the path of the pins and arrived first at the house. He killed grandmother, poured her blood into a bottle, and sliced her flesh onto a platter. Then he got into her nightclothes and waited in bed.
> "Knock, knock."
> "Come in, my dear."
> "Hello, grandmother. I've brought you some bread and milk."
> "Have something yourself, my dear. There is meat and wine in the pantry."
> So the little girl ate what was offered; and as she did, a little

cat said, "Slut! To eat the flesh and drink the blood of your grandmother!"

Then the wolf said, "Undress and get into bed with me."

"Where shall I put my apron?"

"Throw it on the fire; you won't need it any more."

For each garment—bodice, skirt, petticoat, and stockings— the girl asked the same question; and each time the wolf answered, "Throw it on the fire; you won't need it any more."

When the girl got in bed, she said, "Oh, grandmother! How hairy you are!"

"It's to keep me warmer, my dear."

"Oh, grandmother! What big shoulders you have!"

"It's for better carrying firewood, my dear."

"Oh, grandmother! What long nails you have!"

"It's for scratching myself better, my dear."

"Oh, grandmother! What big teeth you have!"

"It's for eating you better, my dear."

And he ate her.[5]

According to Darnton this tale and its tragic ending was the most common version of its kind in the 17th century and signified the barbarous conditions of peasant life. But this statement is totally false. First of all, we frankly do not know what tale was the most "common" in the 17th century, and the tale that Darnton presents to his readers is, in truth, a truncated translation in which he has willfully omitted the happy ending in Delarue's original version.[6] In other words, Darnton, like Perrault, has violated the oral tradition by distorting a female perspective as expressed in the oral tale. Secondly, Darnton claims that the majority of the folk tales ended on a tragic note without citing the different collections that he examined. However, in the various French oral collections that I have used, the girl always tricks the wolf and escapes in the end.[7] In fact, in the very collection that Darnton purportedly used or misused to translate his oral tale, Paul Delarue printed a 19th-century version from Nivernais, included in my essay about the social history of "The Trials and Tribulations of Little Red Riding Hood," that has different components and ends on a happy note. Delarue and other French folklorists and critics have maintained that this version was probably the most typical, because folk tales with a happy ending are more prevalent in the oral tradition, whereas tragic and abrupt endings tend to stem from literature. For instance, Charles Joisten, another gifted French folklorist, collected a group of folk tales in the region of the Haut-Alpines during the 1950s, and he published thirteen different oral versions of *Little Red Riding Hood*, out of which eight portrayed the little girl saving herself. One of the more interesting tales reads like this:

❊ 5 ❊

*Prologue:
Framing
Little Red
Riding
Hood*

> Once there was a little girl in a village, and she was called Red Riding Hood because of the way she adorned her hair with a poppy flower.
> One Saturday afternoon, her mother sent her to her grandmother with a pot of honey and some cake. On her way she amused herself by listening to the song of birds and gathering nuts and flowers.
> But time passed so quickly that it soon became night, and she began to walk rapidly through the forest. However, she met the wolf, and the wolf asked her:
> "Where are you heading, my little girl?"
> "I'm taking a pot of honey and some cake to my grandmother who lives in the first house of the next village," she answered.
> So he asked her," What path are you taking?"
> "The *path of needles* to mend my dress which has a hole in it."
> The wolf left the little girl and took the *path of pins* which was shorter. When he arrived at the grandmother's house, he tapped at the door, "Tick-tock," and the grandmother said, "Pull the latch, turn the knob, and the door will open."
> Later, when Red Riding Hood arrived, he said to her, "Well, light the fire. There's some blood on the side of the chimney, and I want you to cook it."
> So Red Riding Hood lit the fire, put the pan on top, and poured the blood into it. While the blood was cooking, the wolf said to her:
> "Grubby grub, grub
> It's grandma's blood."
> "Ah!" the little girl said. "Did you hear, grandmother, what I heard?"
> "Oh, those are just the evil spirits in the chimney," the wolf responded.
> When the blood was cooked, Red Riding Hood ate a little of it, but she did not like the taste and stopped eating. Then she went and lay down beside the wolf, believing that he was her grandmother.
> "What a large head you have, grandma!" she said.
> "That's because of old age, my little one."
> "What large legs you have, grandma!"
> "The better to run, my child."
> "What long hair you have, grandma!"
> "That's because of old age, my child."
> "What big arms you have, grandma!"
> "The better to catch you with, my child."
> "What big teeth you have, grandma!"

"The better to eat you with, my child."

But he was still digesting the grandmother, and the little girl now knew it was the wolf.

"I want to go pee pee, grandma," she said.

"Make pee pee here," the wolf responded.

"Oh, but I've also got to make cacka, grandma."

"Make cacka here," the wolf responded.

"Oh, that will smell bad," the little girl said. "If you're afraid that I'll escape, tie a rope around me, and you can hold me."

So the wolf attached a rope to her, and the little girl went outside, where she took a small knife out of her pocket, cut the rope, and escaped.

The wolf ran after her in pursuit, but he met up with a hunter, who killed him. Then Red Riding Hood returned home to her mother and told her the story.

This tale was related to Joisten in July of 1952 by François Armand, sixty-six years old, in Clémence-d'Ambel, and it is significant for a variety of reasons. Told in a region where the majority of oral versions of *Little Red Riding Hood* have been found, that is, in the Southeast of France and the North of Italy, this tale retains most of the older motifs that date back to the 17th century such as the paths of pins and needles, the blood of granny, the defecation in bed, and the escape of the girl. At the same time it reflects the influence of the literary tradition—the name of the girl, the cake, the gathering of nuts and flowers, the pulling of the latch, and the killing of the wolf by a hunter. As a French regional tale, it is a fascinating combination of oral and literary motifs that reveals a great deal about ritual and culture in France as well as sexual fantasies. Moreover, it provides us with important clues about the origins of the oral and literary versions of *Little Red Riding Hood* that neither Dundes nor Darnton follow, even though they ask some important questions. As I have shown, the oral tale emanates from a region in Europe during the 17th century where sewing was a major home industry, and women told tales representative of their sexual and social initiation. And, interestingly, the 1952 tale collected by Joisten keeps alive older motifs from the seventeenth century and combines them with literary motifs from Perrault and the Grimms.

Neither Dundes nor Darnton take into consideration the perpetuation and preservation of the oral and literary tradition of *Little Red Riding Hood* in their studies. And, though there is some validity to their to very different approaches, they use false models to argue for their interpretations and thus distort the frame of the narrative tradition. However, the tale collected by Joisten is a corrective to their approaches, for it demands that we pay more attention to the historical intersection of the oral tradition with the literary.[8]

Though I have argued this point in the first edition of *The Trials and Tribulations of Little Red Riding Hood*, I want to reiterate and refine it in light of the recent counter-arguments of Dundes, Darnton, and others. In essence, I begin with the premise that the literary origins of all our canonical fairy tales in the West mark the culmination of an oral tradition in history but certainly not its end. As historical culmination, the literary fairy tale regulates an oral folk tale thematically and stylistically, possesses it, passes it off and on as its own, and thus does violence to it. Therefore, it is at the intersection of the oral with the literary that we can begin to trace the cultural significance of a fairy tale as it makes its mark through word of mouth and in print.

In the case of *Little Red Riding Hood* it is with the remembering and writing down of some oral version by Charles Perrault in 1696/97 and the publication of this tale with the en-gendered and loaded title, *Le Petit Chaperon Rouge*, that the history and destiny of the narrativized girl is conceived. That means, it is the collusion of the oral and literary traditions within the hands of Perrault that gave rise to further versions within the civilizing process of the Western world. It is from Perrault's version that we can look backward and forward in history. From all the evidence gathered by folklorists, ethnologists, and historians, we know that there was indeed a separate oral tradition, controlled by peasants and most likely by women, before Perrault adapted the story of the girl who went into the woods to visit her grandmother for an upper-class audience in France at the end of the 17th century. But once he appropriated it as his own, and in the name of a particular sex and social class, it became practically impossible for either oral storytellers or writers not to take into account his version, and thus storytellers and writers became the conveyors of both the oral and literary tradition of this particular tale. They debated her body, the fate of her body, who would control her destiny.

The crucial point here is that, though the debate was volatile and the discourse multi-faceted, Perrault fixed the ground rules and sexual regulations for the debate, and these were extended by the Brothers Grimm and largely accepted by most writers and storytellers in the Western world. My thesis is that Perrault transformed a hopeful oral tale about the initiation of a young girl into a tragic one of violence in which the girl is blamed for her own violation.

*Little Red Riding Hood* is thus the tale of a double violence. As Theresa de Lauretis has persuasively argued in her essay "The Violence of Rhetoric," the representation of violence cannot be understood unless we grasp the techniques and discursive strategies by which gender is constructed.[9] Perrault 's writing is en-gendered violence because he conceived a strategy that violated an oral (female) perspective and fostered notions of violence through this strategy by treating the girl in the tale as a sadomasochistic object. This argument is the impetus behind the social history that I presented in the first edition of this work. It laid the framework for my discussion of the different literary and oral versions of the tale. But the beginning of the frame was prompted by the contemporary appearances of Little Red Riding Hood in all sorts of forms in comic books, cartoons, greeting cards, plays, videos, films, and advertisements that prompted me to look back in history and make connections between the various cultural manifestations of the tale over the past three centuries.

What attracted me to *Little Red Riding Hood* in the first place was "her" commodified appearance as sex object, and how I was socialized to gaze at her gazing at me. Three ads from the United States, Germany, and France illustrate to what extent Red Riding Hood has become an iconic sign of the seducer, the femme fatale, who lures men and thus must bear the consequences of her heedless acts.

In the 1962 American ad for Hertz [Figure 1], first printed in *The New Yorker*, Red Riding Hood is a beautiful young woman with an inviting gaze. In the 1982 German ad for Renault [Figure 2], printed in *Der Stern*, the seductive Red Riding Hood has already lured the wolf. Finally, in the 1983 French ad for Johnny Walker printed in *100 Idées* [Figure 3], we are informed that without red, nothing will work. However, red is not only the color of Johnny Walker's red label, it is also the label of sin and blood. Here we have a girl who does not have the required sexual allure to entrap the wolf, and therefore, he will have nothing to do with her.

Of course, there are numerous modern versions like the playfully erotic *True History of Little Red Riding Hood and her Grandmother and the Big Bad Wolf* (1979) by Jacqueline Loumaye that reveal, as the cover illustration shows [Figure 4], that both grandma and granddaughter have a great amorous interest in the wolf and take great delight in sleeping with him.

Almost all the commodified forms of Little Red Riding Hood as sex object portray her as thoroughly grown-up and desirous of some

❀ 9 ❀

*Prologue:
Framing
Little Red
Riding
Hood*

**I'm on my way to Grandma's house..**

**riding in my little red *HERTZ***

**HERTZ**
RENT A CAR

FIGURE 1.

kind of sexual assignation with the wolf. At the same time, there are numerous illustrated books, records, and films for children that sanitize the sexual innuendos in an effort to cleanse the tale of its erotic components. Nevertheless, they always imply that, if Red Riding Hood herself had not strayed off the straight path to her grandmother's house, to domesticity, she would not have brought about the

## SO SIEHT CHARLOTTE MARCH DEN RENAULT 4.

### UND WIE SEHEN SIE IHN?

Renault veranstaltet einen großen Gestaltungs-Wettbewerb. Jeder kann mitmachen! Denn es wird in sechs verschiedenen Kategorien bewertet:
1. Karikatur, 2. Illustration, 3. Foto, 4. Foto aus Familien-Album, 5. Collage/Montage, 6. Kinder-Gemälde.
Lassen Sie Ihrer Phantasie freien Lauf. Einzige Bedingung: Der Renault 4 muß in Ihrem Kunstwerk eine Rolle spielen.
Jeder kann gewinnen: unter allen Teilnehmern werden fünf Renault 4 lje Kategorie einer) verlost und in der Kategorie 6 „Kinder-Gemälde" 10 Cross-Räder.

Und wenn Ihr Kunstwerk zu den lustigsten oder originellsten gehört, wird es mit Ihrem Namen und Ihrem Foto in der Zeitschrift „Stern" und der „Photo-Revue" abgedruckt. Und bei allen Renault-Händlern in Deutschland ausgestellt. Obendrein winken DM 5.000,- Veröffentlichungs-Honorar. Sie haben schon eine Idee?
Dann gehen Sie gleich zu einem Renault-Händler. Er hat die Teilnahmebedingungen. Oder schreiben Sie an Deutsche Renault AG, 5040 Brühl, Postfach.
Einsendeschluß ist der 10.8.1982.

◊ **RENAULT 4**
Das Auto für Leute mit Ideen.

FIGURE 2.

trouble she experiences. Whether sex or sanitized object, Red Riding Hood is compelled to assume responsibility for the "predatory acts" of her creators themselves and the assortment of wolves created in illustrations and narratives that are only too willing to eat her.

One can joke about this, as numerous cartoonists have,[10] and one can dismiss the tale of *Little Red Riding Hood* as only a fairy tale that, any way you look at it, has a good warning for girls when you consider how widespread rape is in our culture. However, the tale as it is

❊ 11 ❊

*Prologue:
Framing
Little Red
Riding
Hood*

Sans le Rouge rien ne va plus

Red Label

**Figure 3.**

used in most commodities and books today (and probably in oral versions as well) still reinforces the notion that "women want to be raped." As Diane Herman has pointed out in her important essay, "The Rape Culture," "the imagery of sexual relations between males and females in books, songs, advertising, and films is frequently that of a sadomasochistic relationship thinly veiled by a romantic facade. Thus it is very difficult in our society to differentiate rape from 'normal' heterosexual intercourse relations. Indeed, our cul-

L'histoire VRAIE du
# PETIT CHAPERON ROUGE
### de sa Mère-grand
### et du grand méchant Loup

Dessins de Jean-Lucas
Texte de Jacqueline Loumaye

FIGURE 4.

ture can be characterized as a rape culture because the image of heterosexual intercourse is based on a rape model of sexuality."[11]

There are few women these days who do not arrange their days
with the possibility in mind that they may be raped. "There is what
might be called a universal curfew on women in this country.
Whenever a woman walks alone at night, whenever she hitch-
hikes, she is aware that she is violating well-established rules of

❀ 13 ❀

*Prologue:*
*Framing*
*Little Red*
*Riding*
*Hood*

conduct and, as a result, that she faces the possibility of rape. If in one of these situations she *is* raped, the man will almost always escape prosecution and the woman will be made to feel responsible because she was somehow 'asking for it.'"[12] Written in 1974, this statement is still unfortunately true and might even be expanded to indicate that, even with strong social movements against sexual harassment, it does not matter when a woman leaves her house, she must be prepared for violence.

As I began writing this prologue, the police in the city of Minneapolis have finally arrested a man suspected of raping fourteen women during the past two years. During that time the women in this city became increasingly frightened, if not terrified, and were compelled to place pressure on the police to form a special investigation squad. Of course, those fourteen rapes were not the only ones committed in Minneapolis in the past two years. There has been a steady increase of violence. Women must constantly be on their guard, and it is not safe to walk the streets at night in unprotected areas.

But it is not only in real life that rape permeates the daily routines of women. It is in fiction, newspapers, journals, film, and TV. Again, as I began writing this prologue, one of the women lawyers of the TV series *LA Law* was being stalked by an unknown assailant. The stalker sent her three fairy-tale "gifts" threatening her life. The first one was a red hood with a note—"the better to eat you with"; the second, a glass slipper; the third, a bleeding heart from some animal. Ironically, the assailant turned out to be a "crazed" woman. But the gender of the assailant is not important here, for males have en-gendered this stalker, who like many female slashers, represents male violence more than any threat that women pose to other women. As figments of the male imagination, women slashers represent the male fear of women taking their lives into their own hands. What is crucial here is the fear *socially and culturally produced* by men and the fear that women feel in our society, the manifold ways in which they (and men, too) encounter the possibility of rape. And, in this particular TV case, a commonplace, we see how even fairy tales can be used for gruesome ends.

All this talk, my talk of rape and violence, is not an endeavor to incriminate *Little Red Riding Hood* in all the rapes throughout history. Nor do I want to ban or censor *Little Red Riding Hood* in any of its versions. I am more concerned about how an initiatory ritual concerning women has been played out in the genre of the fairy tale in the West, how and why it was transformed into a story of rape, and why we frame the tale as we do. In short, I am interested in the rhetoric of violence in and about *Little Red Riding Hood*, its history as neglected history, to understand how we are compelled to comply with narrative prescriptions that many contemporary authors have been trying to revise and reappropriate in the name of feminism. It is through the frame of "The Trials and Tribulations of Little Red Riding Hood" that, I hope, we can review and appreciate how writers and illustrators have brought about the necessity to re-frame the oral tale and restore some sense of a happy ending that ironically keeps all endings open.

## ❀ *Notes* ❀

1. See *Little Red Riding Hood: A Casebook* (Madison: University of Wisconsin Press, 1989), pp. 192–236.

2. Recently Ed Young has written and illustrated another fine adaptation of this oral tale for children: *Lon Po Po: A Red-Riding Hood Story from China* (New York: Putnam, 1989). Winner of the Caldecott Medal in 1990, this book has of course done away with all the scatological motifs, but it does retain the basic plot of the Asian cognate of *Little Red Riding Hood*.

3. Dundes, pp. 223–4.

4. Robert Darnton, *The Great Cat Massacre and Other Episodes in French Cultural History* (New York: Basic Books, 1984), p. 55.

5. Ibid., p. 10.

6. As the source of his translation, Darnton cites pp. 373–81 in volume I of Paul Delarue's *Le Conte populaire français*. However, I have looked high and low for the tale that he translated, and I cannot find it. There is only one oral version printed in Delarue's volume, and it is the one which I translated and included in the original edition of *The Trials and Tribulations of Little Red Riding Hood* and which has been reprinted in the main text of my social history.

7. I have used the following collections: A. Millien and P. Delarue, *Contes du Nivernais et du Morvan* (Paris: Erasme, 1953); Paul Delarue, *Le*

*Conte Populaire Français*, vol. 1 (Paris: Erasme, 1957); Charles Joisten, *Versions populaires Haute-Alpines des Contes de Perrault* (Gap: Ribaud Frères, 1959); Charles Joisten, *Contes Populaires du Dauphiné*, vol. 1 (Grenoble: Publications du Musée Dauphinois, 1971). In all these works, the majority of the *Red Riding Hood* tales end on a happy note. However, to tell the truth, the matter at hand is not a question of quantitative analysis. As Steven Swann Jones has pointed out, "From our familiarity with the prevalence of happy endings in folk fairy tales (they are in essence a definitional feature of that genre), it seems more reasonable to conclude, as Soriano does, that the motif of the heroine's scatological escape and happy ending are authentic components of the folktale in oral tradition (given the folk's proclivity for scatological humor, also, which is more pronounced than in the literary tradition's use), and that the abrupt endings with the heroine's death are either literary adaptations or oral tales of a different variety, moral tales designed to teach an explicit lesson." See "On Analyzing Fairy Tales: 'Little Red Riding Hood' Revisited," *Western Folklore* 46 (1987), 99.

8. For two exemplary studies concerned with the interaction of the oral and literary traditions, see Catherine Velay-Vallantin, *L'histoire des contes* (Paris: Fayard, 1992) and *La fille en garçon* (Caracassone: Garae/Hesiode, 1992).

9. Theresa de Lauretis, "The Violence of Rhetoric: Considerations on Representation" in *The Violence of Representation: Literature and the History of Violence*, eds. Nancy Armstrong and Leonard Tennenhouse (New York: Routledge, 1989), pp. 239–258.

10. Cf. Wolfgang Mieder, "Survival Forms of 'Little Red Riding Hood' in Modern Society," *International Folklore Review* 2 (1982), 23–41, and Hans Ritz, *Bilder vom Rotkäppchen: Das Märchen in 100 Illustrationen, Karikaturen und Cartoons* (Munich: Heyne, 1986).

11. Diane Herman, "The Rape Culture," in *Women: A Feminist Perspective*, ed. Jo Freeman, 3rd Ed. (Palo Alto: Mayfield, 1984), p. 21.

12. Andra Medea and Kathleen Thompson, *Against Rape* (New York: Farrar, Straus and Giroux, 1974), pp. 4–5.

*Les Contes de Fées de Perrault,* Paris, Emile Guérin, ca. 1895. Illustrator unknown.

# The Trials and Tribulations
❀ of Little Red Riding Hood ❀

LITTLE RED RIDING HOOD has never enjoyed an easy life. She began her career by being gobbled up by the wicked wolf. Later she was saved by an assortment of well-meaning hunters, gamekeepers, woodcutters, fathers, grandmothers, and fairies. Of course they all scolded her for being too carefree, and she obediently promised to mend her ways. However, she was not always compelled to be obedient and rely upon saviors. Using her wits, Little Red Riding Hood also managed to trick the wolf all by herself in many different ways. Sometimes she cut her way out of the wolf's dark belly and filled it with stones so that he would topple over dead. One time she shot him with an automatic, which she carried in her basket. It has always been difficult for Little Red Riding Hood to suppress her fear of the wolf especially when his lust ultimately forces him to bare his dreadful fangs. Yet, on a few occasions she does overcome her fear, realizes that the wolf himself is a victim of slander, and even decides to marry him. In other, more prudish, versions of her life, it is said that she prevented the wolf from laying his vulgar sexual paws on her and her granny.

As for her character, Little Red Riding Hood has been described as pretty and lovely, but too gullible and naive. Sometimes she has appeared vain and foolish, sometimes sassy and courageous. Much ado has been made about her fetish of the red hood or cap. Clearly her innocence in the story has been suspect. There is a touch of nonconformity and sexual promiscuity in her character. But whatever her reputation and destiny, she has always been used as a warning to children, particularly girls, a symbol and embodiment of what might happen if they are disobedient and careless. She epitomizes the good girl gone wrong, and her history appears to be an open-and-shut case. Yet, the hidden motives in the different

versions of her life suggest that she may be the victim of circum-
stantial evidence. Given the fact that the plot and signs have varied in the course of 300 years, there is something suspiciously
manipulative about the way Little Red Riding Hood has been
treated. She has suffered abuse after abuse, and it is time that the
true history of this seductively innocent girl be revealed.

### ❀ *Background: The Tale Prior to Perrault*

For a long time, anthropologists, folklorists, and historians maintained that the plot of Little Red Riding Hood had been derived from
ancient myths about the sunrise and sunset.[1] The red garment of
Little Red Riding Hood was associated with the sun, and the wolf
was considered to be the personification of darkness. From another
erudite perspective, the tale was regarded as an offshoot of legends
about swallowing, which hark back to Jonah and the whale.[2] Other
scholars equated the tale with traditional Manichean myths about
the forces of darkness seeking to engulf the purity of Christian
goodness.[3] Undoubtedly parallels may be drawn to ancient myths,
beliefs, and rituals, but recent research has proven rather conclu-
sively that Little Red Riding Hood is of fairly modern vintage. By
modern, I mean that the basic elements of the tale were developed
in an oral tradition during the late Middle Ages, largely in France,
Tyrol, and northern Italy, and they gave rise to a group of tales intended explicitly for children.[4] These warning tales were so widespread in France that they undoubtedly influenced Charles Perrault's literary version of 1697, which is generally considered to be
his own creation (Tale 1). Again, critical research has now amply
demonstrated that Perrault did not invent the plot and characters
of Little Red Riding Hood. Rather, he borrowed elements from popular folklore and recreated Little Red Riding Hood to suit the needs of
an upper-class audience whose social and aesthetic standards were
different from those of the common folk.

But, before we turn to Perrault's tale and consider his major accomplishments, it will be important to examine the "rowdy" oral
folk tradition that actually gave birth to the more "refined" bourgeois literary tale. Here the work of Marianne Rumpf,[5] Paul Delarue,[6] and Marc Soriano[7] is most useful for restoring our sense of
authentic history. Rumpf has revealed that one of the most common European warning tales (*Schreckmärchen* or *Warnmärchen*) in
the Middle Ages involved hostile forces threatening children who
were without protection. Either an ogre, ogress, man-eater, wild

❀ 19 ❀

The Trials
and
Tribulations
of Little Red
Riding Hood

*The Entertaining Story of Little Red Riding Hood*, York: J. Kendrew, ca. 1825.

person, werewolf, or wolf was portrayed as attacking a child in the forest or at home. The social function of the story was to show how dangerous it could be for children to talk to strangers in the woods or to let strangers enter the house. Rumpf argues that the original villain in French folklore was probably a werewolf, and that it was Perrault who transformed him into a simple, but ferocious, wolf. She supports her case with a wealth of historical material.

For instance, Rumpf points out that superstitious tales about were-wolves flourished more in France during early Christianity and the Middle Ages than in any other European country. There was a virtual epidemic of trials against men accused of being werewolves in the 16th and 17th centuries similar to the trials against women as witches.[8] The men were generally charged with having devoured children and having committed other sinful acts. There were literally thousands if not hundreds of thousands of such cases, and Rumpf cites some of the more notorious ones, culled from the work of the historians Rudolph Leubuscher and Wilhelm Hertz.[9] One of the most famous incidents took place in December 1521, and involved Pierre Bourgot and Michel Verdun, who stood trial in Besançon. They were convicted of having attacked and killed children after having assumed the shape of werewolves. Bourgot described his transformation and feats in great detail. He admitted to having killed a seven-year-old boy with his wolf's teeth and paws. However, he was chased away by a peasant, so that he never had time to eat his victim. Verdun admitted to having killed a small girl as she was gathering pears in a garden. However, he, too, was chased away before he could eat his victim. Four other attacks on small girls, which the two accused were supposed to have carried out, were mentioned in the same report, which included particulars as to the ages of the children and the places and dates of the incidents.[10] In certain areas of 16th-century France people of all ages became afraid to pass through fields or woods alone because of werewolves or wolves. Rumpf's major point—and one that should carry great weight—is that wherever oral versions of the *Little Red Riding Hood* tale were found later in the 19th and 20th centuries, they were primarily discovered in those regions where werewolf trials were most common in the 15th, 16th, and 17th centuries.

Perrault's literary tale of 1697 was probably derived from stories about werewolves that were circulating in Touraine when his mother grew up there. In 1598 there was the sensational case of Jacques Raollet, who was sentenced to death in Angers, Touraine, for attacking and killing children as a werewolf. His case was appealed at the Parliament of Paris, and Raollet was declared insane and placed in the Hospital Saint Germaine des Pres. This trial took place at a time when Perrault's parents and his nursemaid could have witnessed the events. Though we do not have concrete proof, the major authority on Perrault, Marc Soriano, tends to agree with Rumpf's general assertions:[11] Perrault knew oral folk versions of *Little Red Riding Hood* before he wrote his own fairy tale.

Soriano corroborates Rumpf's findings by demonstrating that Perrault took truncated elements from folklore to form his own creation. If we look at this independent oral tradition and its existence up through the present, a number of elements

> have continued to survive in spite of the celebrity of the text published in 1697: the motif of cruelty—probably a reflection of a "primitive structure"—the motif of the blood and flesh of the grandmother which are placed on the bread-bin and which the little girl is invited to eat; the motif of the "familiar animal"—a cat or bird (or mysterious voice) which informs the child of what she is eating; the episode of the "ritual undressing," a sort of strip-tease by Little Red Riding Hood, who each time she

takes off a garment asks the wolf where she should put it, which leads to an enigmatic or frankly menacing response from the ferocious animal; and finally, a "happy ending" of a particular type, built on the scatological overtone of the "tie which sets free": the little girl pretends that she urgently needs to relieve herself, a pretext to escape from the monster.[12]

All of these elements, which were expurgated or refined in Perrault's literary text, have been kept alive in an independent oral tradition, and, thanks to the research of Paul Delarue, it has been possible to reconstitute an integral text uniting most of the elements *not* employed in Perrault's tale, though Perrault was probably familiar with them. Delarue's version of *Little Red Riding Hood* was recorded in Nièvre, about 1885.[13] Entitled *The Story of Grandmother*, it reads as follows:

> There was a woman who had made some bread. She said to her daughter: "Go carry this hot loaf and a bottle of milk to your granny."
> So the little girl departed. At the crossway she met *bzou*, the werewolf, who said to her:
> "Where are you going?"
> "I'm taking this hot loaf and a bottle of milk to my granny."
> "What path are you taking," said the werewolf, "the path of needles or the path of pins?"
> "The path of needles," the little girl said.
> "All right, then I'll take the path of pins."
> The little girl entertained herself by gathering needles. Meanwhile the werewolf arrived at the grandmother's house, killed her, put some of her meat in the cupboard and a bottle of her blood on the shelf. The little girl arrived and knocked at the door.
> "Push the door," said the werewolf, "it's barred by a piece of wet straw."
> "Good day, granny. I've brought you a hot loaf of bread and a bottle of milk."
> "Put it in the cupboard, my child. Take some of the meat which is inside and the bottle of wine on the shelf."
> After she had eaten, there was a little cat which said: "Phooey! . . .
> A slut is she who eats the flesh and drinks the blood of her granny. "Undress yourself, my child," the werewolf said, "and come lie down beside me."
> "Where should I put my apron?"
> "Throw it into the fire, my child, you won't be needing it anymore."
> And each time she asked where she should put all her other

**Original artwork by Catherine Orenstein, 1990.**

clothes, the bodice, the dress, the petticoat, and the long stockings, the wolf responded:

"Throw them into the fire, my child, you won't be needing them any more."

When she laid herself down in the bed, the little girl said:

"Oh, Granny, how hairy you are!"

"The better to keep myself warm, my child!"

"Oh, Granny, what big nails you have!"

"The better to scratch me with, my child!"

"Oh, Granny, what big shoulders you have!"

"The better to carry the firewood, my child!"

"Oh, Granny, what big ears you have!"

"The better to hear you with, my child!"

"Oh, Granny, what big nostrils you have!"

"The better to snuff my tobacco with, my child!"

"Oh, Granny, what a big mouth you have!"

"The better to eat you with, my child!"

"Oh, Granny, I've got to go badly. Let me go outside."

"Do it in the bed, my child!"

"Oh, no, Granny, I want to go outside."

"All right, but make it quick."

The werewolf attached a woolen rope to her foot and let her go outside. When the little girl was outside, she tied the end of the rope to a plum tree in the courtyard. The werewolf became impatient and said: "Are you making a load out there? Are you making a load?"

When he realized that nobody was answering him, he jumped out of bed and saw that the little girl had escaped. He followed her but arrived at her house just at the moment she entered.[14]

By collecting the different but related independent oral folk tales that contain the same elements missing in the literary tale of Perrault, Delarue has proven that a vital oral tradition in France preceded the conception of Perrault's "civilized" *Little Red Riding Hood*. Moreover, Gottfried Henssen has shown that similar tales of warning spread throughout Europe and Asia, which reveal that Perrault might have been influenced in a number of different ways.[15] One of the most important discoveries is the fact that the independent oral tales lack the motif of the red riding hood or the color red. So much for the traditional interpretation of sunrise/sunset, or the Christian view of Manichean forces in combat!

The direct forebears of Perrault's literary tale were not influenced by sun worship or Christian theology, but by the very material conditions of their existence and traditional pagan superstition. Little children were attacked and killed by animals and grown-ups in the woods and fields. Hunger often drove people to commit atrocious acts. In the 15th and 16th centuries, violence was difficult to explain on rational grounds. There was a strong superstitious belief in werewolves and witches, uncontrollable magical forces of nature, which threatened the lives of the peasant population. Since antiquity, tales had been spread about vicious creatures in France, and they continued to be spread. Consequently, the warning tale became part of a stock oral repertoire of storytellers. Evidence indicates that the teller would grab hold of the child or children nearby when the final line in the well-known dramatic dialogue with the wolf was to be pronounced—"the better to eat you with!" We must remember that storytelling was a dynamic process, with give and take between narrator and listeners. But the child was not devoured by the teller, who was more interested in showing care for children, nor does it seem that the little girl was killed in any of the folk-tale versions. She shrewdly outwits the wolf and saves herself. No help from granny, hunter, or father!

Clearly, the folk tale was not just a warning tale, but also a celebration of a young girl's coming of age. This has been substantiated
in the recent study by Yvonne Verdier,[16] who convincingly demonstrates that the references to the pins and needles were related to
the needlework apprenticeship undergone by young peasant girls,
and designated the arrival of puberty and initiation into society in
specific regions of France where the oral tale was common: districts
of the Loire, Nièvre, Forez, Velay, and the Alps. The young girl
symbolically replaces the grandmother by eating her flesh and
drinking her blood. It is a matter of self-assertion through learning
and conflict. Unlike the literary versions, where the grandmother
is reified and reduced to a sex object, her death in the folk tale
signifies the continuity and reinvigoration of custom, which was
important for the preservation of society. As Verdier maintains,

> the tale effectively reveals the fact that women transmitted the
> physical capacity of procreation among themselves, even
> though the radical character of this transmission illuminates the
> conflictual aspect, a rivalry which ends in physical elimination,
> the relationship of women among themselves concerning this
> matter. Classified by the maturation of their bodies, women find
> themselves divided and unequal. Perhaps one can see here the
> principal source of the violence in their conflicts? There are a
> number of tales which develop this aspect of elimination in the
> relationships among women, whether they be among women of
> the same generation (recalling the theme of the "hidden fi-
> ancée") or among women of different generations: mother and
> daughter, step-mother and step-daughter, grandmother and
> granddaughter, old and young.
>     Moreover, it is remarkable that each successful conquest of
> physiological capacity concerning the female destiny is marked
> in the tale by the acquisition of technique which is the equiva-
> lent in the stage of learning, and even in a certain order—the
> proper order—in the society: needlework for puberty, kitchen
> for the proper procreative function, flushing out for the hour of
> birth. All this knowledge and technique are in the hands of
> women in the traditional peasant society. These are the true
> "cultural goods" which are opposed in the tale to the ways of
> "nature" (the wolf devours the grandmother in the flesh). This
> knowledge imparts the "domestic" vocation and its rights of war
> upon women, a function which again underlines the autonomy
> and power of women in regard to their own destiny in this tradi-
> tional peasant society.[17]

Although Verdier pays little attention to the werewolf aspect
and warning motif in her interpretation of the folk tale, her overall

perspective does not actually contradict the views of Delarue, Rumpf, and Soriano, but rather amplifies them and makes them more concrete. Whether the story is about initiation, warning, or both, one thing is clear: the folk tale celebrates the self-reliance of a young peasant girl.

❉ 25 ❉

*The Trials
and
Tribulations
of Little Red
Riding Hood*

❉ *Perrault's Transformation of the Tale*

Perrault, who appears to have had a low opinion of women and of the superstitious customs of the peasantry, changed all of this, and his "contaminated" upper-class version of the "pure" lower-class version makes the little girl totally helpless. Delarue maintains that

> the common elements which are lacking in the literary story are precisely those which would have shocked the society of his epoch by their cruelty (the flesh and blood of the grandmother devoured by the child), their puerility (the path of needles and the path of pins) or their impropriety (the question of the little girl about the hairy body of the grandmother). And it appears likely that Perrault eliminated them, while preserving a folk flavor and freshness in the tale which have made it an imperishable masterpiece.[18]

Perrault's changes were substantive both in style and content, and they demand an even closer look if we are to grasp the continual impulse of later writers to make free with the fate of Little Red Riding Hood. To begin with, Perrault wrote for both children and adults of the upper educated classes. The irony of his narration suggests that he sought to appeal to the erotic and playful side of adult readers who took pleasure in naughty stories of seduction. This irony was lost on younger readers, who could still enjoy the warning aspect of the tale and the play between the wolf and Little Red Riding Hood that has a didactic anti-climax in the *moralité*.

If we focus for a moment on the tale as written for children, the changes can be seen to reflect an appreciable difference in the way the upper classes, particularly the *haute bourgeoisie*, were coming to view children. We must bear in mind that, because of changes in the socialization process, the term "child" as separate from "adult" was in the process of assuming a new meaning. As Philippe Aries has demonstrated in *Centuries of Childhood*,[19] an independent children's literature and culture were being developed to civilize children according to stringent codes of class behavior. Thus it is no

**French Postcard, Paris, ca. 1900. Illustrator A. Billon. Collection of Jack Zipes.**

surprise that the character of the little girl in Perrault's literary tale is totally different from the one in the oral tradition. The "peasant girl" is forthright, brave, and shrewd. She knows how to use her wits to escape preying beasts. Perrault's Little Red Riding Hood is pretty, spoiled, gullible, and helpless. The moral of the tale does nothing to alter her character or to suggest what would improve her character; it simply warns children to be more alert and to beware of strangers. The elaborate details added by Perrault to the oral tale all contribute to the portrait of a pretty, defenseless girl, who moreover may have been slightly vain because of her red hood. Exactly why Perrault added the red hood is not clear. However, we know that red was generally associated at the time with sin, sensuality, and the devil.[20] As a present from a doting grandmother, it refers directly to the child's "spoiled nature," and Perrault obviously intended to warn little girls that this spoiled child could be "spoiled" in another way by a wolf/man who sought to ravish her. Accustomed to being the center of attention, Little Red Riding Hood stops to listen to the wolf and tarries in the woods. The child seeks to amuse herself, and she ends her short life by being the object of the wolf's amusement.

Perrault's great artistic achievement consisted in his appropriating folk motifs, imbuing them with a different ideological content, and stylizing the elements of the plot so that they would be more acceptable for upper-class audiences of children and adults. Whereas the oral tale referred directly to actual conditions in the country faced by peasants and villagers, Perrault's literary version assumed a more general aspect. It talked about vanity, power, and seduction, and it introduced *a new child*, the helpless girl, who subconsciously contributed to her own rape. Gone are the alleged cruelty and coarseness of the oral tale. However, the refined elements of the literary tale contributed to an image of Little Red Riding Hood which was to make her life more difficult than it had ever been.

Perrault's historical contribution to the image of Little Red Riding Hood is a contradictory one, and it must be viewed in light of French social history and Perrault's own personal prejudices. On the one hand, he is responsible for shaping folklore into an exquisite literary form and endowing it with an earnest and moral purpose, the influencing of behavior of children in a tasteful way. On the other, he set rigorous standards of comportment, which were intended to regulate and limit the nature of children's development. This contradictory position was also evident in the works of French writers of fairy tales, like Prechac, L'Héritier, D'Aulnoy, Murat, de la Force, and scores of others during Louis XIV's reign:[21] they sought to civilize children to inhibit them, and as a result they contributed to a socially perverted configuration of natural growth. This is not to argue that Perrault and his contemporaries had nefarious plans and conspired to fill children's heads with illusions. On the contrary, despite his ironic attitude toward folklore and his double intention of writing for children and adults with moral fervor and charm, Perrault sincerely intended to improve the minds and manners of young people.

In the preface to his *Contes en Vers* (1695), Perrault argued that people of good taste recognized the substantial value of the tales. And he repeated this argument in the 1697 dedication to Elizabeth-Charlotte d'Orléans in *Histoires ou contes du temps passé*:

> They all contain a very sensible moral which can be discovered more or less according to the degree of perception of the reader. Moreover, as nothing can stamp the vast scope of a mind but the elevating power of great things and the degrading power of little things, one will no longer be surprised that even the Princess whom Nature and education have made acquainted with everything that is most elevated, does not disdain to take pleasure from trifles (stories). It is true that these tales present a picture of what happens in the inferior families where the

praiseworthy impatience of instructing children make them imagine stories devoid of reason to prepare these same children who still lack reason. Yet, who but those persons whom heaven has destined to lead the people is most suited to learn how the children live?[22]

It is apparent from his statements that Perrault composed his narratives to set standards and models of refined virtuous behavior for the children of his time. More precisely, he was interested in contributing to the prevalent discourse on *civilité* through the fairy tale. Here it is important to understand the cultural and political input of large sectors of the bourgeoisie in France if we are to grasp Perrault's role in "civilizing" the folk tale and transforming it into a literary tale for upper-class children. The French aristocracy of the 16th and 17th centuries displayed a unique capacity to adopt and use the best elements from other classes. The nobility provided access to its circles for a select group of reliable people of the third estate; these circles expanded as the need arose to secure aristocratic rule throughout the nation. Perrault was among the fortunate members of the *haute bourgeoisie* to be honored by the court.[23] He was a high royal civil servant, one of the first members of the *Académie Française*, a respected polemicist, and a significant figure in literary salons. Moreover, he endorsed the expansive political wars of Louis XIV, and believed in the exalted mission of the French absolutist regime to "civilize" Europe and the rest of the world. Perrault supported the "manifest destiny" of 17th-century France not only as a public representative of the court but privately in his family; he was also one of the first writers of children's books who explicitly sought to "colonize" the internal and external development of children in the mutual interests of a bourgeois-aristocratic elite.

The interaction between the French nobility and bourgeoisie must be carefully studied if one is to grasp the socio-genetic import of literary fairy tales for children in Western culture. Norbert Elias makes this connection clear.

> Both the courtly bourgeoisie and the courtly aristocracy spoke the same language, read the same books, and had, with particular gradations, the same manners. And when the social and economical disproportionalities burst the institutional framework of the *ancien régime*, when the bourgeoisie became a nation, much of what had originally been the specific and distinctive social character of the courtly aristocracy and then also of the courtly bourgeois groups, became, in an ever widening move-

ment and doubtless with some modification, the national character. Stylistic conventions, the forms of social intercourse,
affect molding, esteem for courtesy, the importance of good
speech and conversation, articulateness of language and much
else—all this is first formed in France within courtly society,
then slowly changes, in a continuous diffusion, from a social
into a national character.[24]

❀ 29 ❀

*The Trials
and
Tribulations
of Little Red
Riding Hood*

By the time Perrault had begun writing his fairy tales, the major
crises of the Reformation, which had been manifested drastically in
the massive witch hunts between 1490 and 1650, had been tempo-
rarily resolved, and they resulted in greater rationalization and regulation of social and spiritual life. This civilizing process coincided
with an increase in socio-economic power by the bourgeoisie, particularly in France and England, so that the transformed social,
religious, and political views represented a blend of bourgeois-aristocratic interests. The *homme civilisé* was the former *homme cour-
teois*, whose polite manners and style of speech were altered to include bourgeois qualities of honesty, diligence, responsibility, and
asceticism. To increase its influence and assume more political control the French bourgeoisie was confronted with a twofold task: to
adapt courtly models in a manner which would allow greater *lais-
sez-faire* for the expansion and consolidation of bourgeois interests;
and to appropriate folk customs and the most industrious, virtuous,
and profitable components of the lower classes to strengthen the
economic and cultural power of the bourgeoisie. In this regard the
French bourgeoisie was indeed a middle or mediating class, although its ultimate goal was to become self-sufficient and to make
the national interests identical with its own.

One way of disseminating its values and interests and of sublimi-
nally strengthening its hold on the civilizing process was through
literary socialization. Since childhood had become more distinct as
a phase of growth and was considered as the crucial base for the
future development of individual character, special attention was
now paid to children's manners, clothes, books, toys, and general
education. Numerous books, pamphlets, and brochures appeared in
the 16th and 17th centuries dealing with table manners, natural
functions, bedroom etiquette, sexual relations, and correct speech.[25]
The most classic example was Erasmus of Rotterdam's *De civilitate
morum puerilum* (*On Civility in Children*, 1530). Also important
were the works of Giovanni della Casa (*Galateo*, 1558); C. Calviac
(*Civilité*, 1560); Antoine de Courtin (*Nouveau traité de civilité*,

1672); François de Callieres (*De la science du monde et des connoissances utiles à la conduite de la vie*, 1717); and LaSalle (*Les Règles de la bienséance et de la civilité chrétienne*, 1729). It was impossible for a member of the aristocratic or bourgeois class to escape the influence of such manuals, which became part of the informal and formal schooling of all upper-class children. Coercion by members of high society to act according to *new* precepts of good behavior increased, so that the codes of dress and manner become extremely stringent and hierarchical by the end of the 17th century. Though not conspired, the rational purpose of such social pressure was to bring about an internalization of social norms and mores so that they would appear as second nature or habit. Yet, self-control was actual social control, and it was a mark of social distinction not to "let go of oneself" or to "lose one's senses" in public. As Elias has noted, the system of standardization and social conditioning had assumed fairly concrete contours with multi-level controls by the mid-17th century.

> There is a more or less limited courtly circle which first stamps the models only for the needs of its own social situation and in conformity with the psychological condition corresponding to it. But clearly the structure and development of French society as a whole gradually makes ever broader strata willing and anxious to adopt the models developed above them; they spread, also very gradually, throughout the whole of society, certainly not without undergoing some modification in the process.
>
> The passage of models from one social unit to another, now from the centers of a society to its outposts (for example, from the Parisian court to other courts), now within the same political-social unit (within France or Saxony, from above to below, or below to above), is to be counted, in the whole civilizing process, among the most important individual movements. What the examples show is only a limited segment of these. Not only the eating manners but also forms of thinking and speaking—in short, of behavior in general—are molded in a similar way throughout France, even if there are significant differences in timing and structure of their patterns of development.[26]

Within the French civilizing process, Perrault's tales provided behavioral patterns and models for children which were intended to reinforce the prestige and superiority of bourgeois-aristocratic values and styles. Like the civilizing process itself, the tales also perpetuated strong notions of male dominance, and here it is important to take Perrault's own biases into account. In her *Introduc-*

*❋ 31 ❋*

*The Trials
and
Tribulations
of Little Red
Riding Hood*

*tion aux contes de Grimm et Perrault*, Lilyane Mourey has aptly demonstrated how Perrault portrayed women in his tales:

> The concept of "morality" assumes here a very particular value mixed with irony and satire. Perrault argues for the total submission of the woman to her husband. Feminine coquetry (which is only the privilege of the dominant class) disturbs and upsets him: it could be the sign of female independence. It opens the way for the amorous conquest which endangers one of the fundamental values of society—the couple, the family. As we have seen, the heroines of the tales are very pretty, loyal, dedicated to their household chores, modest and docile and sometimes a little stupid insofar as it is true that stupidity is almost a quality in women for Perrault. Intelligence could be dangerous. In his mind as in that of many men (and women) beauty is an attribute of woman just as intelligence is the attribute of man. [27]

If *Little Red Riding Hood* is studied in light of Perrault's personal prejudices and the male-dominated civilizing process, the *underlying* history of the tale and its reception, as it spread throughout western Europe and America in its changing literary form, assumes greater significance than the history of the original oral tale. *Little Red Riding Hood* is a projection of male phantasy in a literary discourse considered to be civilized and aimed at curbing the natural inclinations of children. The changes made in the discourse about the fictional helpless girl dubbed Little Red Riding Hood—her discipline and punishment—indicate real shifts, conflicts, and ruptures in the Western civilizing process.

❋ *The Grimms' Modification of Perrault's Version*

Perrault's tale of *Little Red Riding Hood* had an unusually successful reception in the 18th century. In fact, it was one of the few literary fairy tales in history which, due to its universality, ambivalence, and clever sexual innuendoes, was reabsorbed by the oral folk tradition. That is, as a result of its massive circulation in print in the 18th and 19th centuries and of the corroboration of peasant experience, it took root in oral folklore and eventually led to the creation of the even more popular Grimms' tale, which had the same effect. Perrault's tale was translated into English in 1729 and was constantly reprinted by itself (e.g., by Robert Samber, 1729; Tale 2), in chapbooks and broadsheets, and in collections of children's tales. Eventually it made its way to America, where it became extremely popular (see, e.g., Tale 3).[28] In Europe the translations were made later in the 18th century; for instance, the first German translation appeared in 1790. But we must remember that everyone in the aristocracy and bourgeoisie read French or had French nursemaids, so the Perrault tale became extremely well known, particularly as a clever didactic tale for children just when it had been deemed necessary to rear children more prudently and prudishly. However, for the Grimms the tale was still too cruel, too sexual, and too tragic. They felt it necessary to clean it up for the bourgeois socialization process of the 19th century and adapted it to comply with the emerging Biedermeier or Victorian image of little girls and proper behavior.

Contrary to the general assumption of most "Grimm scholars," the Grimms' version was neither old Germanic nor told by some lovable old woman named Maria from Hessia. Heinz Rölleke has clearly established that the story was told to the Grimms between 1811 and 1812 by Marie Hassenpflug.[29] She came from a family with a German and French Huguenot background and was raised in the "French spirit."[30] Marie began contributing stories to the Grimm collection as early as 1808, and it appears that various members of the Hassenpflug family, steeped in the French cultural tradition, exercised a great influence on the Grimms. In addition, the Grimms were familiar with Ludwig Tieck's verse play *Leben und Tod des kleinen Rotkäppchens* (1800; Tale 4), which was based on Perrault's story, and they were probably exposed to the original story themselves during their youth. Finally, a close comparison by Harry Velten[31] of the Perrault and Grimm tales has shown that the original source of the Grimms' tale was the Perrault version. In sum, when the Grimms revised *Little Red Riding Hood* to *Little Red Cap* for their collection of 1812 (Tale 6), they were consciously working within a bourgeois literary tradition, and the significant changes they made reflect the social transformations in how children were viewed and reared. Furthermore, there is some indication that the Grimms were writing a "political" fairy tale, which, ironically, may have been anti-French in tone. But before we plunge into the politics of *Little Red Riding Hood*—or *Little Red Cap*, as she was dubbed in German—let us examine how the Grimms, following Perrault's example, further cleaned up for the bourgeois a tale emanating from the French peasant tradition.

As is generally known, the major change made by the Grimms in their version of *Little Red Cap* was the happy ending. Here the Grimms borrowed a motif from the folk tale *The Wolf and the Seven*

❋ 33 ❋

The Trials
and
Tribulations
of Little Red
Riding Hood

*Little Red Riding Hood Album*, ca. 1900. Collection of Jack Zipes.

*Kids.* A hunter saves Little Red Cap and her granny, and they proceed to fill the wolf's belly with stones. When the wolf tries to jump up and escape, the stones cause his death. Yet the Grimms were not content to kill the wolf just once. They added an anti-climatic moral. Some time after the first incident, another wolf accosts Little Red Cap in the woods. This time she runs directly to granny, who gives her instructions on how to trick the wolf so that he drowns. Obviously, the Grimms found the Perrault ending too cruel and too sexual. However, what is most significant is that Little Red Riding Hood as Little Red Cap is transformed even more into the naive, helpless, pretty little girl who must be punished for her transgression, which is spelled out more clearly as disobedience and indulgence in sensual pleasures. As in Perrault's story, the girl cannot save herself. Whereas Perrault kills her, the Grimms have her saved, first by a male hunter or gamekeeper and, second, by a shrewd grandmother. Without their protection, she is lost and unable to cope with *foreign* or strange elements in her surroundings. Yet, we must reconsider why she was placed in this dilemma in the first place, for it is never by chance that she encounters the wolf. That is, beginning with the folk tale, the wolf is *sent* to teach her and the audience a lesson. Her degradation and punishment set an example. Symbolically linked to the devil, the wolf is a powerful agent, but he was not necessarily used to punish "sinners" in the folk tradition. The wolf was crucial in archaic thinking as a representative of the human wild side, of wilderness. He was more a hazard of nature linked to sorcery and part of organic nature. The moral lesson, which the wolf brings with him, was both Christian and male and was first introduced by Perrault. The Grimms added some vital elements at the beginning of their narrative, which reinforced the didactic emphasis. Little Red Cap is *instructed* by her mother to behave and walk a *straight* path to her grandmother's cottage, and the girl promises to obey her mother. This "contract" is broken when Little Red Cap is tempted by the sensuous delights of the forest. For this—her indulgence in sensuality and her disobedience—she must be punished. The implicit and explicit notions of childhood and child rearing in this tale were an elaboration of bourgeois expectations, which Perrault consciously incorporated into the folk version. Then, more than a century later, the Grimms reacted to the civilizing process in Germany by making more changes. They eliminated the cruelty and sexuality from the tale, demanded that the child repress her own sensuality, and obligated her to meet the normative standards of responsibility set by adults. Little Red Cap was compelled to become eminently rational in her anti-climactic adventure.

Michel Foucault has referred to the process Red Riding Hood undergoes as a "pedagogization of children's sex," which had become typical especially among the middle classes in the 19th century. It was

> a double assertion that practically all children indulge or are prone to indulge in sexual activity; and that, being unwarranted, at the same time "natural" and "contrary to nature," this sexual activity posed physical and moral, individual and collective dangers; children were defined as "preliminary" sexual beings, on this side of sex, yet within it, astride a dangerous dividing line. Parents, families, educators, doctors, and eventually psychologists would have to take charge, in a continuous way, of this precious and perilous, dangerous and endangered sexual potential: this pedagogization was especially evident in the war against onanism which in the West lasted nearly two centuries.[32]

Clearly, what had formerly been a frank oral tale about sexuality and actual dangers in the woods became, by the time the Grimms finished civilizing and refining *Little Red Cap*, a coded message about rationalizing bodies and sex. Open sexual games and encounters were frowned upon throughout the 19th century. Hence, disciplinary measures had to be taken against all the Little Red Riding Hoods and Little Red Caps of the world.

However, in the Grimms' version, Red Riding Hood is not only punished and reprieved for trying to express her imagination and sexuality; there is also a political cutting edge to the discipline of the story. Far-fetched though it may seem, *Little Red Cap* was also a commentary on the French invasion of the Rhineland during the Napoleonic Wars. Hans-Wolf Jäger has argued[33] that the Grimms collected their tales at a time (1806–1811) when Kassel and the Rhineland were occupied by French troops. Although the French had been welcomed at the beginning of the century, the Germans came to resent French domination and expressed great relief and joy after the retreat of Napoleon's troops in 1813. According to Jäger, the Grimms recorded *Little Red Cap* during the French occupation and infused it with a remarkable combination of anti-French and anti-Enlightenment notions. The stark opposites of woods and path, nature and school make this apparent. The wolf exploits the unsuspecting nature of the innocent child. He plays upon her latent aversion to ordered and regulated normality and points seductively to the freedom of the colorful and musical woods. Thus, the conflict between freedom/wilderness/nature on the one hand versus school/straight path/order on the other is set up very early in the narrative to illustrate a socio-political situation.

Jäger documents his argument by pointing out how the French invaders had become associated with wolves in the German literature of the times. He demonstrates that the Grimms were familiar with Ludwig Tieck's verse drama *Leben und Tod des kleinen Rotkäppchens* (1800; Tale 4). It was Tieck who actually introduced historical and political motifs which were to find their way into the Grimms' version. First, Tieck created the gamekeeper or hunter, who does not save Little Red Cap but who does manage to kill the wolf. Here it must be emphasized that the German word *Jäger* (gamekeeper or hunter) was associated with the police. That is, the *Jäger* was hired by the feudal lord to protect his property from poachers and intruders. Second, Tieck made the stylish French *chaperon* into a cap (*Käppchen*) and drew parallels to the mode of wearing Republican or Jacobinite caps in honor of the French Revolution. Furthermore, the wolf incorporated a double identity: the French revolutionary who comes to liberate German youth and/or the French oppressor who comes to destroy the virtues of Germany. Little Red Cap symbolized the innocent German youth who is at first drawn by revolutionary enthusiasm to the French and is then repulsed by the actual cruelty and barbarism of the Revolution. Jäger sums up Tieck's drama by asserting that it could be rewritten this way:

Whoever—whether it be to keep in fashion or through the carelessness of youth—identifies too much with the idea of revolution will ultimately be seized and destroyed by the revolution itself. Or, dabbling with progress and revolution in a fashionable and harmless way produces an event which reveals the bitter truth about harmlessness and good-naturedness. This message which plays upon the rebellion of Little Red Cap against her parents and the authorities as well as upon the familial pedagogical and general political problem in the play is derived from the consensus of those times which recalls the saying, the revolution eats its own children.

Tieck himself distances himself from this message of his play and remains without a position and without judgement. It can be assumed that the Grimms, who mention Tieck's fairy-tale drama in the note to their own edition of their tale, understood the play upon the "red cap" and "wolf" and drew a connection to a Jacobinite, a Frenchman, and a revolutionary as givens and that they associated the major ideas discussed above in context with their tale. Their own warning tale does not eliminate the associations. It warns against being seduced and having youthful careless relations with the corrupter.[34]

Evidently there are very few children or even adults today who read the Grimms' version of *Little Red Cap* as a depiction of how guileless German youth were swallowed by wicked France and then saved by the keepers of German absolutism. Nevertheless, Jäger's socio-historical explanation of why the Grimms made certain changes is in keeping with their tendency to sanitize and render bourgeois the tales for middle-class audiences. Their narration of *Little Red Cap* is fundamentally a justification of law and order and against individual autonomy and imagination. The reverence to be shown toward mother, grandmother, and male gamekeeper demanded by the tale is absolute. Salvation comes only in the form of a male patriarch who patrols the woods and controls the unruly forces of nature—both inner and outer.

It is not by coincidence that once the Grimms' version of *Little Red Cap* came into being, it virtually dwarfed Perrault's version because of the prudent and puritanical modifications. Though it is difficult to collect comparative statistics regarding the circulation of the tales by Perrault and the Grimms in the 19th century, we do know that the Grimms' collection took second place only to the Bible as the most widely read book in Germany. In addition, most literary variations and translations in Europe and North America appear to be based on the Grimms' tale.[35] At the very least, they show signs of having been influenced by the Grimms' story. This is not to say that Perrault's version is not widely known and distributed, but it points to the fact that the Grimms were able to alter the tale ideologically to satisfy the morals and ethics of the emerging bourgeoisie in the 19th century more thoroughly than the 17th-century Perrault, and to comply more with the general Victorian taste which was rampant in Western culture up through the 20th century. In essence, they were able to project a notion of maidenhood or childhood that was closer than Perrault's to middle-class ideas of child rearing and child behavior.

If we look at the numerous translations and adaptations of *Little Red Riding Hood* in France, Germany, England, and the United States from the date of the Grimms' version—that is, shortly before the rise of the Holy Alliance and the Restoration—until the outbreak of World War I, it is interesting to note how uniform the tale remains, conforming either to the Perrault or Grimm paradigm. If changes are made, the modifications indicate prudery at work. Many writers of the 19th and early 20th centuries believed that Perrault and Grimm were too cruel, and they were afraid that children might be upset by the sexual undertones and violence in the original versions. References to Little Red Riding Hood being touched or swallowed were deleted. More stress was placed on obedience. Many bowdlerized versions indicated a Victorian-minded censorship,[36] which feared that Little Red Riding Hood might some day break out, become a Bohemian, and live in the woods with the wolf. Thus, consciously and subconsciously, more clamps were put on Riding Hood in these stories. However, Riding Hood did break out, and her various rebellions are indicative of the real changing social views of children, women, and political and sexual domination in the 20th century.[37] But before we analyze the radical changes of the 20th century, let us consider some of the more salient translations and adaptations of the 19th century, as examples of how middle-class morality triumphed in this fairy tale.

❀ *The 19th and Early 20th Centuries*

Throughout the 19th and early 20th centuries the tales of Perrault and Grimm came to play a crucial role in the socialization process of France and Germany. Moreover, these tales were translated and adapted so frequently that they became part of the standard literary building blocks for children of all social groups in Europe and America. Up through World War I there were various prose and dramatic adaptations of Perrault's *Little Red Riding Hood* in France.[38] One of the earliest dramatizations is the opera *Le Petit Chaperon Rouge*, with music by Adrien François Boieldieu and text by Marie E. G. M. Théaulon de Lambert.[39] This sentimental musical play experienced numerous successful productions during 1818 and 1819 in France and Germany, and eventually made its way to England and America. If Théaulon's libretto is significant at all, it is simply because it indicates the direction most adaptations would take for the next hundred years. Red Riding Hood becomes the model of virtue in danger of being molested and in need of male protectors to rescue her. In this melodramatic opera, set in the Middle Ages, Count Roger falls in love with a virginal country maiden named Rose d'Amour, who wears a red cap as talisman. Count Roger's intentions are honest, even though the maiden is beneath his class, and he must woo the girl in disguise as a shepherd named Alain because of a feud with his neighbor the Baron Rodolphe, who is known as the wolf because of his proclivity to prey upon his subjects, especially the females. Baron Rodolphe is angry at Count Roger, who has constantly refused to marry the baron's sister Baroness Zélinde, who in actuality has long had a relationship and child with another man. This is only one of many intrigues in the play; most important, of course, is Baron Rodolphe's plot to seduce the young Rose d'Amour, who has caught his fancy. He intends to seduce her when she carries some food to her sick spiritual father, the holy hermit, who lives in the woods. As long as Rose d'Amour wears her red cap, a magical virtuous force, she will be protected. However, the baron is also versed in black magic and threatens to compromise her virtue. Count Roger rushes to the rescue along with the hermit.

The hermit reveals that Rose d'Amour is actually the illegitimate daughter of the baron's sister, whom the hermit had raised as his own daughter to protect the good name of the Baroness Zélinde. This disclosure makes the baron stop short for fear of incest, and it appears that he will turn over a new leaf when he gives his blessings to the forthcoming marriage of Count Roger and Rose d'Amour.

Such a convoluted plot demonstrates to what extent writers would go to transform *Little Red Riding Hood* into a bourgeois morality play. To be sure, this opera was intended primarily for adults of the upper classes; however, all social groups were influenced by the new moral and political order of sexuality in *Little Red Riding Hood* through picture broadsheets and chapbooks at the beginning of the 19th century. Right about this time the Dutch publisher Rynden began printing picture sheets of Perrault's fairy tales in French and Flemish, and he was soon followed by other printers in Europe.[40] Generally speaking, slight changes were made to stress the notion of *obedience*. Otherwise the pictures were serious renditions of the tale, clearly intended to serve as a warning to young girls who might be seduced by "men-wolves." The figure of the wolf is often clothed as a gentleman or even a soldier. The situation has nothing more to do with actual hazards of country living but more with town life, obedience, and general seduction of women by sly debonair men, a theme which had become common by the end of the 18th century. Many illustrations depict the mother pointing her finger at Red Riding Hood, as if to reprimand the child for the "crime" she is about to commit. The meeting with the wolf is usually portrayed more like a tête-à-tête than a dangerous encounter. The illustrations seek to establish the little girl's complicity in the ensuing violence. Gustav Doré's famous etchings of 1867 show a Red Riding Hood fascinated by the wolf, looking at him somewhat seductively from the bed. Obviously, if she were not gullible and disobedient, she could prevent the rapacious wolf from carrying out his designs.

This possibility did, in fact, occur to some French writers in the 19th century. Charles Marelle stresses the notion of obedience in *The True History of Little Golden-Hood* (1888; Tale 11), which was printed in English by Andrew Lang in 1890[41] and adapted by the American James Baldwin in 1898.[42] Marelle changes the name of the little girl to Blanchette, and then has her chastised for talking to the wolf; but neither she nor granny is touched by the beast. Blanchette is saved by her "gold-and-fire-coloured hood," representative of her sensuality, which she must learn to curb. Here the modifications of Perrault's tale are tailored to accommodate 19th-century strictures of purity, and female figures are used extensively to enforce an essentially male-oriented sexual pedagogization. Despite the clever twists, Marelle's tale never succeeded in superseding Perrault's classic in France, perhaps because it suggested that women were capable of fending for themselves.

Before World War I there was another curious endeavor to transform Perrault's tale along these lines. Émilie Mathieu wrote *Le Nouveau Chaperon Rouge* (*The New Red Riding Hood*) in 1908, remolding it into a sentimental moralistic tale with a realistic setting. The story takes place in 1780, and Mathieu describes in some detail the customs and life of the village Morvan (in Nivernais, a region known for its folklore about werewolves, wolves, and little girls), providing background for the actions of a poor grandmother and her ten-year-old granddaughter. On the brink of starvation, the grandmother Monique prays to God for help, and the kind village priest listens to the imploring granddaughter and helps the two establish a small bakery. The granddaughter dons a costume that has a magic effect on prospective buyers, mainly because of her angelic disposition. People begin calling her Little Red Riding Hood, and she diligently helps the grandmother expand the business. Then one day, after having sold bakery goods in a neighboring village, Little Red Riding Hood returns home through the woods and discovers two robbers about to ambush a rich farmer. Paying no heed to the danger, she saves the farmer's life, and he not only rewards her with money but more or less guarantees that her virtue will be rewarded. Several years later, after she has become the "prettiest, most industrious, and gentlest girl of the village," the son of the rich farmer marries her. Despite the fact that the tale depicts an old woman and young girl as valiant, the narrative reads like a pious manual on how to rear the exemplary "good little girl." Red Riding Hood does everything she is told and has a kind heart. Typical of many heroines of the late-19th and early-20th centuries, she assumes the form of a little angel who willingly sacrifices herself to protect others, young and old. The tale is in this regard a fine example of the ambivalent social attitude toward women's role which was developing at this time: *women were expected to be strong and self-sufficient, yet dependent and self-denying.* Written by a female, the new quality in *The New Red Riding Hood* is the mixed message, a result of the changing code of civilization in the Western world, which now allowed the idealized girl to act out her own denial instead of being denied by the wolf. Here we can see how, in France, discipline and punishment had become fully internalized by the end of the 19th century.

In 19th-century Germany the Grimms' version of *Little Red Cap* remained as dominant as Perrault's was in France. There was little call to change it, and, if it was altered, it was generally made more Christian and sweeter for youngsters to digest. The Grimms themselves, particularly Wilhelm, kept changing and censoring all their tales so that the wolf in *Little Red Cap* is referred to as an "old sinner" by 1857. However, the most classically saccharine alterations were made not by the Grimms but by Ludwig Bechstein, whose *Deutsches Märchenbuch* was published in 1845 and achieved immediate popularity, though it never vied with the Grimms' household tales for first place in the hearts of German readers. In 1853 Bechstein included *Little Red Cap* in his anthology,[43] and it is evident that the Grimms' story was his model. Although he sought to make his tales more witty, pungent, and folksy than those of the Grimms, Bechstein's mannered style and didactic intentions generally transformed them into cute narratives bordering on puerility. This is the case in his version of *Little Red Cap*, which is loaded with diminutives and harmless jokes. Otherwise Bechstein remained loyal to the Grimms and the bourgeois literary tradition.

Three other significant German versions reveal just how strongly the bourgeois civilizing process was making itself felt in the Red Riding Hood fairy tales. Gustav Holting embroidered his *Little Red Cap* (1840) by amply describing the idyllic nature of the little girl's village and by setting her on a pedestal as a model of virtue and beauty. But once she encounters the wolf, she commits the sin of confiding things to him which are not his concern. Her fate is sealed, and Holting follows Perrault by having the *sinful* wolf swallow the girl in the end. In Moritz Hartmann's version of *Little Red Cap* (1869), she is more gullible than disobedient. So the author treats Riding Hood with disdainful irony and shows her pity after the wolf swallows her: "But it would be a very sad story if it were to end this way, and there would be no justice on earth if wolves were to eat little Red Riding Hoods without being punished."[44] Therefore, the hunter/gamekeeper is sent to the rescue. And he also rides to the rescue in Ernst Siewert's naturalist and pious play *Little Red Cap* (c. 1880). Though Little Red Riding Hood has a devout belief in God and convinces her parents that He will protect her on her way to visit her sick grandmother, she is also stupid enough to believe the wolf when he tells her that he is a doctor and can help her grandmother. As in the Bechstein version, Little Red Riding Hood is duped—and swallowed. Fortunately there is a price on the wolf's skin, and the hunter saves granny and granddaughter. It is interesting that the German versions in the 19th century stress patriarchal governance more than the French; the latter tend to leave Red Riding Hood in the bed she has made for herself. Erotic play and seduction appear to capture the imagination of the French, whereas the Germans are more concerned with law and order.

In England and America, sweet, innocent, and helpless Little Red Riding Hood suffered through hybrid adventures. That is, the

*Little Red Riding Hood,* New York: Golden Press, 1948. Illustrator
Elizabeth Orton Jones.

Perrault and Grimm versions were often mixed together, and,
whether the plot was developed in verse, prose, theatrical scenes,
or illustrations, there was a general tendency to make Little Red
Riding Hood into a Victorian middle-class lass whose virtue is
threatened because she forgets to control her sensual drives and
disobeys her good super-ego mother. Ironically, the 19th century

began with a Gothic persiflage of *Little Red Riding Hood* for adults. *The Wolf-King* (1801; Tale 5) was untypical of English and American versions in that it was a critique of M. G. Lewis's ballad *The Water King* and was written mainly for a sophisticated adult audience.[45] The traditional features of the Perrault version were exaggerated and mocked, and the gory details were used to titillate and shock the reader rather than provide a real warning for children. The tradition of parody can be seen in two other remarkable adaptations. F. W. N. Bayley included a farcical *Little Red Riding Hood* with social commentary in his *Comic Nursery Rhymes* (1846; Tale 7). Its end effect was not much different from Perrault's tale, for Little Red Riding Hood is punished because she is idle and careless. In "Ye True Hystorie of Little Red Riding Hood; or, The Lamb in Wolf's Clothing" (1872; Tale 10), by Alfred Mills, bedlam and confusion are the results of careless actions by a vain Red Riding Hood and her lamb, who follows her to granny's house in a wolf's skin. Mills used the traditional story to poke fun at political issues of the day, and Thomas Nast, the famous German-American illustrator, supplied appropriate illustrations.[46]

As I have indicated, the parodies of *Little Red Riding Hood* in the 19th century were the exceptions. For the most part the English and American adaptations printed after the horror story of 1801 were tame and prudent. The language was gilded, and the incidents were carefully transformed so that atrocities could be avoided, although harsh lessons were still conveyed so that children would at least learn to control their carnality. The major accomplishments of the translations and adaptations in England and America up through World War I were to shift most of the blame for Little Red Riding Hood's "rape" on to the girl herself. Her idleness, vanity, and negligence are stressed; she is treated as an accomplice in crime. The direction of this fairy-tale discourse about female indulgence in sin had been set by Perrault, expanded by the Grimms, and fully executed by a host of English and American writers.

The historical evolution of the literary *Red Riding Hood* parallels a development of sexual socialization in Western society. The socioreligious shifts in the late Middle Ages gave way to an obsession with sex and the body, an obsession that demanded new codes of governance and deployment of sexual energies. The family became

> an agency of control and a point of sexual saturation: it was in the "bourgeois" or "aristocratic" family that the sexuality of children and adolescents was first problematized, and feminine

sexuality medicalized; it was the first to be alerted to the potential pathology of sex, the urgent need to keep it under close
watch and to devise a rational technology of correction. It was
this family that first became a locus of the psychiatrization of
sex. Surrendering to fears, creating remedies, appealing for rescue by learned techniques, generating countless discourses, it
was the first to commit itself to sexual erethism. The bourgeoisie
began by considering that its own sex was something important,
a fragile treasure, a secret that had to be discovered at all costs.
It is worth remembering that the first figure to be invested by
the deployment of sexuality, one of the first to be "sexualized,"
was the "idle" woman. She inhabited the outer edge of the
"world," in which she always had to appear as a value, and of the
family, where she was assigned a new destiny charged with con-
jugal and parental obligations.[47]

There was the good "idle" woman as housewife, who could easily
become hysterical, and there was the bad "idle" woman as prosti-
tute, who could reap chaos. Each one is reflected in the trials of Little Red Riding Hood in America and England. Let us look at six
classical examples of the Victorian mode.

Richard Henry Stoddard's *The Story of Little Red Riding Hood*
(1864; Tale 9) is literally drenched with Christian sentimentality.
The girl of this verse melodrama is daddy's darling, and she sets a
standard that all little girls of the 19th century were expected to
emulate: she is kind, diligent, and obedient. Not only does she help
a wasp, a bird, and an old woman, but she also defends the wolf at
one point. Of course, this is almost her undoing, for wolves are
treacherous parasites. In contrast, everyone else is hard-working in
the poem, especially Little Red Riding Hood, who is saved by the
good fairy because she demonstrates that she is *not idle*. Stoddard
constantly stresses the notions of idleness as sin and obedience as
virtue. Neither girl nor granny is sexually molested, so the story
ultimately pays great tribute to the Protestant ethic.

This is also true of an anonymous verse translation written
toward the end of the 19th century. Here we are told that Little
Red Riding Hood is instructed by her mother not to loiter on her
way to her sick Grandma. Then in the very next stanza we learn:

> But the pretty flowers that in the wood
>   Bloomed gay and bright on either hand,
> So lured the maiden to gaze and pluck
>   That she quite forgot the strict command.[48]

From this point on, after succumbing to the wiles of outer
nature, Little Red Riding Hood is guilty of a heinous crime:

she "idly" chats with the wolf, and her *idleness* leads to her grand-mother's death and her own near rape. Typical of many Victorian versions, the Perrault story is mixed with the Grimm narrative so that Little Red Riding Hood is saved by woodcutters and learns a hard lesson:

> To her mother's words, ever after this,
>     Red Riding Hood gave better heed;
> For she saw the dreadful end to which
>     A disobedient act may lead.[49]

It is obvious from this verse adaptation that the entire story con-cerns the regulation of a child's sexuality and the internalization of social norms set by adults. To live, a child had to live *properly*, restraining natural instincts according to rules established by adults. To disobey these rules or to indulge one's sensual drives for pleasure meant death.

This is also the message of another hybrid prose version, by Sabine Baring-Gould, one of the leading late Victorian collectors of fairy tales.[50] In his *Little Red Riding Hood* (1895; Tale 12), *idleness* is again Red Riding Hood's downfall. She forgets her wise mother's commands and almost pays for her negligence. This time it is her father, the forester, who rescues her and kills the "cunning and cruel beast"; he bursts into verse at its happy end to preach the les-son of the tale:

> A little maid
> Must be afraid
> To do other than her mother told her.
> Of idling must be wary,
> Of gossiping must be chary,
> She'll learn prudence by the time that she is older.[51]

The tale reeks of sentimentality, and it is quite evident that Rid-ing Hood can be "daddy's darling" only if she learns to toe the line. The image of Red Riding Hood is that of a helpless, foolish, pretty little thing, whose potential will be wasted unless she learns to dis-cipline herself.

As I have mentioned, throughout the 19th century the Perrault version was generally garnished and transformed into a tale with more delicacy and ornateness, primarily for children of the upper class; this was also the case with the Grimms' tale. Most important was the inoffensive tone. Care was taken not to offend the fragile sensibilities of the child or to contradict the sexual and social taboos set up by adults. The Grimms' tale needed less revision than Perrault's, since it was a product of the 19th century—though it, too, was toned down. The swallowing and regurgitating of granny and Riding Hood was considered too prurient by many translators and publishers; thus, intimate intercourse with the Wolf was avoided, and the wolf himself was made less ferocious.

By far one of the cleanest and daintiest versions of the *Riding Hood* pattern in the 19th century was the operetta for juveniles by George Cooper and Harrison Millard.[52] Not only did they introduce a fairy queen and her court into the story, but the wolf is a former fairy who was transformed into a wicked beast because of her evil ways. Needless to say, vulgarity is avoided, innocence blessed, as fairies swarm through the woods to protect their ward. Though granny is eaten (offstage), not a hair on Riding Hood's head is touched. In fact, when the fairy queen intervenes and saves Riding Hood as the wolf is on the verge of devouring her, she is overly mild: after reprimanding the wolf, she exiles him to a cave deep in the woods, and teaches Riding Hood the usual lesson of good behavior:

> Arise, sweet girl, whom we have saved from harm,
>   Still round thy way we weave our mighty charm.
> Still may thy mem'ry live in glowing story,
>   Thy name still be each child's delight and glory.
> With dance and song, we'll bear thee to thy home
>   Then to the hills and valleys we must roam
> To shield the good and innocent from harm.[53]

The only way Little Red Riding Hood can protect herself is by not being herself, or rather by being "good," which means denying her instincts for pleasure. Only if she remains obedient, innocent, and defenseless will she be saved. Otherwise her fate might resemble that of the wicked fairy's—to be transformed into a wolf with a gluttonous appetite. Obviously the swallowing of Little Red Riding Hood by the wolf amounted to a loaded warning for children in the 19th century. To become at one with the wolf was to become a transgressor, a nonconformist, a predatory beast with no control of one's appetite. In the operetta by Cooper and Millard the wolf is described as insatiable and depraved. Such depravity (like masturbation, nymphomania, sexual promiscuity) was continually associated with disease, and with the devil, particularly from the 19th century up through the present. In the immortal case of Riding Hood, her memory continued to live "in glowing story" as predicted in the operetta. In fact, by the 1890s Schultz and Company of

❀ 47 ❀

The Trials
and
Tribulations
of Little Red
Riding Hood

*Star Soap Nursery Rhymes,* Zanesville, Ohio, ca. 1890. Illustrator
unknown.

Zanesville, Ohio, had already employed Riding Hood as the cover girl for advertisements of Star soap, which used nursery rhymes to convey two morals:

> MORAL I
> If in this world secure you'd be,
>     From danger, strife and care,
> Take heed with whom you keep company,
>     And how, and when, and where.

> MORAL II
> And cleanly you should ever be,
>     And cheerful; never mope.
> To accomplish both, my child, you must
>     Use ever our STAR SOAP.[54]

Two other exceedingly clean Victorian versions of *Little Red Riding Hood*, and perhaps the most fascinating, were written by two prim and proper ladies, Miss Thackeray (Anne Isabella Ritchie) and Mrs. Harriet Louisa Childe-Pemberton. Both sought to write true-romance stories in a moralistic and realistic mode, and in so doing they exemplified the manner in which women writers of the 19th century contributed to their own oppression and circumscription.

Miss Thackeray's *Little Red Riding Hood* of 1866 is a 72-page tale about Patty and Rémy, first cousins of upper-class families, who fall in love. However, their families are vying for the inheritance of the eccentric grandmother Madame Capuchon, and blood has been spilled. Rémy, of French extraction, is something of a playboy, who at first wants only to seduce and marry his English cousin Patty because she will probably be the sole heiress of the grandmother. Yet, her angelic innocence is so powerful that the "wolf" Rémy mends his ways and wins the trust of Patty, her parents, and even the grandmother to boot. Virtue is rewarded here in elegant fashion because both Patty and Rémy are obedient and follow the dictates of upper-class breeding.

In Mrs. Childe-Pemberton's long version of 1882, *All my Doing; or, Red Riding-Hood over again*, we are presented with the opposite example: disobedience leads to a catastrophe, and it is obvious that the heroine's lack of virtue precludes her eventual "reward" of a bourgeois marriage. Here the first-person narrator is a spinster, who tells her niece her own life story in the form of the *Little Red Riding Hood* fairy tale because her niece does not believe that fairy tales can be morally instructive. The plot is superbly contrived: Pussy, a heedless young woman, is sent to live with her rich grand-

❀ 49 ❀

*The Trials
and
Tribulations
of Little Red
Riding Hood*

mother in hopes that she might learn some proper manners and provide company for her grandmother. Before her departure, Pussy is given a great deal of advice about being cautious, considerate, and trustworthy. Yet, by her own account, Pussy was already too spoiled to heed the sage counsel. During her train ride she speaks to a suspicious-looking stranger who manages to win her confidence. This elderly man steals her money and then pretends to want to help her when they arrive at her destination. Later, after Pussy is settled in the luxurious manor house of her grandmother, she encounters the con man again and foolishly invites him to the manor house when nobody is there. Eventually, he robs the house and causes granny to suffer a stroke and Pussy's suitor, Herbert, to lose a leg during his pursuit of the criminal. At the end of this first-person narrative Pussy confesses that she was to blame for the tragedy that befell her grandmother and Herbert. Or, as the subtitle of the story states, it was "all my doing." Pussy, like all traditional heroines of *Little Red Riding Hood* stories, is responsible for her own downfall and for the rapaciousness of wolflike creatures. The accusatory tone and moralistic message of this elaborately constructed fairy tale, which keeps within the bounds of a male discourse, are similar to most of the *Little Red Riding Hood* tales in 19th-century England, which insisted that girls clean up their acts, become doll-like angels, or else receive the punishment they deserve: a self-induced rape and murder.

These morals and messages were bought wholesale in Europe and America during the 19th century. However, Riding Hood's story began to undergo some important changes after World War I, reflecting gradual shifts in child rearing and sexual roles. Moreover, the male-dominated civilizing process was now faced with strong opposition from organized labor and women's movements, which were to leave their marks on the fairy-tale discourse about Riding Hood's fate.

❀ *Revisionism and Radicalism Since World War I*

The period from 1919 to 1945 generated only the first cracks in the traditional cultural pattern inscribed in the plot of the fairy tale. (Here we must bear in mind that the Perrault and Grimm versions remained dominant during this time and are dominant even now.) There were various interesting revisions during the interwar period which were printed or broadcast by the mass media, and many of these are now lost or difficult to find. I want to discuss eight different adaptations—from France, Germany, England, Ireland, and America—which I have been able to uncover. What is striking about these versions of *Little Red Riding Hood* by Caroline Thomason, Charles Guyot, Joachim Ringelnatz (Tale 14), Milt Gross (Tale 15), Walter de la Mare (Tale 16), Johnny Gruelle, Edith A. O. Somerville (Tale 17), and James Thurber (Tale 18) is that they were not written expressly for children. With the exception of Thomason's and Gruelle's stories, it is evident from their debunking irony that the primary audience was to be mature— which, to be sure, is generally the case when authors write so-called children's books intended for children. After all, the distribution of children's books has always depended first on the reception they receive by publishers, educators, librarians, and parents. Consequently, it was expected, as we have seen in the 1801 Gothic persiflage, that the irreverence shown to the traditional *Riding Hood* would begin first with adults.

Charles Guyot's *The Granddaughter of Red Riding Hood* (1922) addresses the entire question of readers' reception in a most amusing manner. From Guyot's point of view, it is difficult to predict how children as readers will react to stories. Thus he begins his own story-within-a-story by refuting Perrault, insisting that another ending would have been preferable to the tragic one. So he relates *his* new version, ostensibly to a little boy as a test case. In contrast to Perrault's, Guyot's Riding Hood is saved, grows up to be a grandmother, and sends her own granddaughter to the woods to lure the old wolf into a trap. Instead of killing the wolf, who has become feeble by this time, the grandmother takes pity on him (after intercession by the kind granddaughter), and the wolf is kept as pet and watchdog in the house. So ends the main story, but there is a comment in the frame. The fictional boy who hears this new version would have preferred that the wolf eat Little Red Riding Hood. It would appear that the narrator's intentions and expectations are proven wrong. Yet, this is exactly the point of the tale. Guyot transformed the *Little Red Riding Hood* tale from one that preaches the control of appetites to one that questions the need to control desire, preference, and expectations. By turning the tale upside down, Guyot was one of the first writers to signal the great experimentation with *Red Riding Hood* in the 1920s and 1930s, when expressionism and surrealism were encouraging writers to be daring and innovative.

It was with humor and irony most of all that writers began tinkering with the Red Riding Hood pattern. This can be clearly seen in Milt Gross's Yiddish-American rendition of *Sturry from Rad Ridink Hoot*—part of a volume of stories entitled *Nize Baby* (1925) —in which numerous traditional stories are retold by the neighbors in a New York tenement house, especially "ferry tales" for a baby so that he will be pacified and eat or go to sleep. Thus, Gross's *Rad Ridink Hoot* was not told as a warning; rather, the seriousness of the tale is parodied, making the stringent sexual code appear ridiculous. The art of parodying *Red Riding Hood* was also being cultivated at the same time in Germany. Ringelnatz's highly irreverent tale, *Kuttel Daddeldu Tells His Children the Fairy Tale about Little Red Cap*, was written in 1923, during a period of great literary experimentation with fairy tales in the Weimar Republic. In fact, the realm of fairy tales was a virtual battleground, where educators and writers with varying pedagogical ideas and with social-democratic, liberal, communist, and fascist leanings fought over the welfare of children. Ringelnatz's own position was that of the satirist who conveyed an ironic attitude toward the traditional rearing of children and accepted notions of sexuality. Neither Little Red Cap nor the children who are implicitly integrated as audience in his tale were treated with kid gloves. The major intention of the tale was to smash the conservative expectations of the readers, to provoke, and to criticize the notion that children were soft, lovable creatures to be protected at all costs. The narrator, who identified with the grandmother, sought to fulfill his own needs and addressed his listeners bluntly and somewhat insolently. If we recall the difficult beginnings of the Weimar period—inflation, unemployment, poverty—Ringelnatz was apparently seeking to provide a sober perspective on harsh realities in Germany. The idyllic, conservative notions of the traditional *Little Red Cap* yielded to a rude awakening when the grandmother devoured everything in sight.

In contrast to the Gross and Ringelnatz parodies of *Little Red Riding Hood*, two American adaptations from the 1920s express an ambivalent attitude toward the conservative notions of the traditional tale. Both Thomason's play *Red Riding Hood* (1920) and Gruelle's story *All about Red Riding Hood* (1929) appear to have been written on behalf of "good" government in direct response to the political upheavals engendered by World War I and the continuous socio-economic crises. Thus, they refrain from parody and address children in a sober and serious vein. Thomason wrote her play in English and French, and it is eminently clear that the wolf represents Germany, the foreign enemy *par excellence*. As the play

*Grimms' Fairy Tales,* **New York: Cupples & Leon, 1914. Illustrator
Johnny Gruelle.**

unfolds, it assumes the form of a "political" liberation: all the characters sing the Marseillaise at the end. However, although the play
may say something about the defeat of a wicked marauder, it says
nothing about basic liberties and women's liberation. As usual,
Riding Hood and granny are sweet, naive, and totally dependent
on a male hero. Moreover, the dainty language and meager alterations of the plot tend to belittle the character of Riding Hood,
transforming her into a type of Kewpie doll. On the other hand,
Gruelle's story appears at first to offer a remarkably different picture
of Riding Hood. She is not given moral instructions by her mother
and shows herself to be brave and smart like her grandmother.
However, the story takes a strange twist toward the end, when the
woodcutters save the two females and pose as the strong arm of justice. Gruelle transforms the tale into a law-and-order story in the

tradition of the Grimms, asserting as a clear-cut conclusion that policemen and prisons are needed because there are evil people who cannot listen to reason or be persuaded to do right. Obviously the reigning powers are just, and anyone who questions the status quo is to be looked upon as a wolfish deviate. Considering that this tale was published during the depression, its message legitimized the selective political repression and elitism then growing stronger in the United States and assuming a still more ominous shape in Germany.

For instance there were other German writers than Ringelnatz, like Werner von Bülow, who saw in *Little Red Cap* a special type of "teutonic awakening," which could inspire a national feeling for law and order. Von Bülow did not invent a new fictional version of *Little Red Riding Hood/Little Red Cap* during the 1920s, but he did compose a highly mythopoeic interpretation linking the wolf to the early Roman Empire, Red Cap to Germania, and the hunter to the great German protector or *Führer*. Published by the Hakenkreuz or Swastika Publishing House,[55] von Bülow's essay on *Little Red Cap* drew a propagandistic parallel to the "knife-in-the-back" conspiracy theory, which was being spread at that time by reactionaries as the reason Germany lost World War I.

> So we are also justified in view of the wolf's swallowing Little Red Cap in thinking about the materialistic lust for profits which is threatening to destroy German idealism right in our own times. And we can garner hope from the outcome of the fairy tale that this idealism will be liberated from its unworthy prison by the spiritual humanity appropriately selected and represented in the fairy tale by the symbol of the hunter. . . . The genuine, childlike moral of the story as well as the thoroughly naive freshness of the narrative are very much suited to make an impression on the child's soul. However, there is such a painful experience of German history running throughout the plot that it is about time, especially in our own day after such an incredible deception of the German people by wolfish trickery, that the German people open their eyes which have been oh much too trusting.[56]

Von Bülow's racist and exaggerated nationalistic interpretation of an originally French folk tale and French literary fairy tale was no exception in the Weimar and fascist periods in Germany. Von Bülow was supported by a host of folklore specialists such as Rudolf Viergutz,[57] who sought to ground all the Grimms' tales in German blood and soil, though many actually originated in France and elsewhere in Europe. Fortunately there were various disbelievers during fascism who sought to counter Nazi propaganda as best they could. Ulrich Link, for example, wrote a version of *Little Red Cap* in 1937, which was printed in the *Münchner Neueste Nachrichten*, a daily newspaper.[58] Link's story is worth relating in full.

A long, long time ago in Germany there was a wood which the ministry of labor had not yet cleared, and in this wood lived a wolf. Now on one beautiful Sunday—it was the harvest day of thanksgiving—a little girl from the League of German Maidens[59] went through the wood. She wore a little red cap and wanted to visit her Aryan grandmother who had been living in the Mothers Home of the National Socialist Club.[60] She carried a basket with donations and a bottle of ancestral wine.

Then she met the wicked wolf who had such very brown fur that nobody would sense his racially alien intentions at the start. Nor did Little Red Cap suspect anything evil since she knew that all elements harmful to the people were sitting in concentration camps, and so she believed that she was face-to-face with a common sort of bourgeois dog.

"Heil, Little Red Cap," said the wolf. "Where are you going?" Little Red Cap answered: "I'm going to my granny in the Mothers Home." "So," the wolf said. "But then bring her some flowers planted by the office for the Beautification of Woodwork[61] to ornament the woods!" At once Little Red Cap began to pluck flowers for a harvest bouquet. However, the wolf rushed to the Mothers Home, ate the grandmother, slipped into her clothes, pinned the badge of womanhood on himself and lay down in bed.

Then Little Red Cap entered right through the door and asked: "Well, granny dear, how are you?" The wolf attempted to imitate the folkish voice of the granny and answered: "I'm fine, my dear child." Little Red Cap asked: "Why are you speaking so strangely to me?" The wolf answered: "The speech education lessons this morning have taken a lot out of me." "But, granny, what large ears you have!" "The better to hear the whispers of complainers!" "What big eyes you have!" "The better to see the agitators!" "What a big mouth you have!" "You know, don't you, that I'm on the cultural council!" And with these words he ate Little Red Cap, lay down in bed, and fell asleep snoring in his reckless way.

Outside, the district forester[62] passed by. He heard the snoring and thought: How can an Aryan grandmother snore in such a racially alien way? And when he checked it out, he found the wolf. And he shot him, even though he did not have a hunting permit for wolves, and he assumed the entire responsibility himself. Then he slit open the wolf's stomach and found the grandmother and child alive. What a joy that was! The wolf was distributed among the Reich's nutrient producers and made into meat in his own juice. The district chief hunter was permitted to wear a gold-woven wolf on his uniform, Little Red

❊ 55 ❊

The Trials
and
Tribulations
of Little Red
Riding Hood

Cap was promoted to scout leader in the League for German Maidens, and the grandmother was allowed to take a trip to Madeira to recuperate on board a brand new "Strength through Joy"[63] steamship.

The critique of Nazism and conformism needs no explanation, except to say that it reverses the cultural pattern in the traditional Red Riding Hood story. In other words, implicit in the *literary* tradition is a notion of conformism and strict obedience, which has deep roots in reactionary movements, much deeper than we suspect. But more about these roots, which are tied to the witch craze of the Reformation, later.

In England and Ireland during the 1920s and 1930s there is not much evidence of radical change or political disputation concerning fairy tales. The reigning fairy-tale writers of this period were of a conservative bent,[64] and the socio-economic situation in Great Britain at this time was so weakened by the tottering colonial empire that there was a strong tendency to dwell on the preservation of traditional moral values. Both fascism and communism appeared distasteful to the English ruling class, and it is within the British context of upholding solid Christian ethics threatened by radical political movements and moral decadence that one must regard the versions of *Little Red Riding Hood* written by Walter de la Mare in 1927 and Edith A. O. Somerville in 1934. De la Mare transforms Little Red Riding Hood into a pouting, spoiled little shrew who must be taught a lesson. Her vanity and greed lead to the swallowing scenes by the gluttonous wolf. Only the reliable woodman, full of good British common sense, is capable of rescuing granny and her granddaughter. As usual, virtue in the form of law and order triumphs over chaos in the form of the voracious wolf.

Somerville's charming Irish adaptation of *Little Red Riding Hood* elaborates on the traditional motif of taming the shrew, too, but there is a sense of admiration for the wild spirit of Moira Clocadearg. In this unusual blarney version the wolf, in the form of Curley Brech, seduces and marries Moira. The farms they will inherit are thus joined together in a good match, and their "wild" days will live on in their memory. The threat to their order will also continue to persist in the shape of treacherous fairies in the woods. The tale is essentially an extension of the traditional Red Riding Hood pattern in that on her eighteenth birthday (Valentine's Day) Moira and Curley learn to channel their sexual drives in a holy union. The *male* hero is older and typically becomes the mighty protector of the weaker female. Both their wild urges can only be brought under control through orderly behavior in societies where men rule with weapons.

However, James Thurber's short version, *The Little Girl and the Wolf*, demonstrates that this cultural pattern was on the verge of being severely questioned by 1939, at least in America. His "Red Riding Hood" does not need a name. She is a little "no-nonsense" girl who is not easily deceived—the image of a new, more independent, woman in the making. Instead of waiting to be rescued in the belly of the wolf, she takes matters into her own hands and shoots him calmly with her automatic. In apparent disdain of Perrault's *moralité*, Thurber writes a blunter, more contemporary moral: "It is not so easy to fool little girls nowadays as it used to be."[65]

This moral could have also served as the basis for a remarkable Marxist dramatization of *Little Red Riding Hood* by the renowned Russian playwright Evgenii Shvarts,[66] who wrote numerous fairy-tale plays for children and adults during the 1930s and 1940s. Many were veiled attacks on Stalinism. It is conceivable for one to regard his *Little Red Riding Hood* of 1937 as a comment on the Moscow show trials and "witch hunts" in the Soviet Union of that time. Certainly Shvarts was too aware of the purges and spying not to be unaffected by the political repression. On a more positive level, his play is about a new view of women and collectivity. Little Red Riding Hood has been teaching the animals in the woods to become more courageous and independent so that they can be self-sufficient. She herself is depicted as fearless and resourceful. In fact, it is because she sets such an example for all the other animals in the woods that the wolf and the fox want to kill her. However, the rabbit, bear, snake, and birds work together to protect her in the woods. Eventually they are separated by the wiles of the treacherous fox, and though Little Red Riding Hood is capable of fighting the wolf on her own terms, he overcomes her by using great deceit. Swallowed alive, Little Red Riding Hood and her grandmother sit in the wolf's stomach as if in a prison. In the meantime, the animals fetch the forester, who is responsible for peace and justice in the woods, and he and Riding Hood's courageous mother rescue the girl and her grandmother. The predatory beasts are thus thwarted and arrested, and harmony is restored to the woods. Though it is clear that Little Red Riding Hood as an individual provides a model for the animals and audience as a brave, democratic, and resourceful girl, the play stresses collectivity as the means to over-

❀ 57 ❀

The Trials
and
Tribulations
of Little Red
Riding Hood

*Märchen der Brüder Grimm,* Berlin: Knaur, 1937. Illustrator Ruth
Koser-Michaëls.

come potential tyrannical rulers. The *social* order of the woods is
based on principles of equality, and force is only used to quell dicta-
torships. Here, too, there is no bloodbath or killing. The wolf and
fox, are arrested and incarcerated. The Marxist implications of this
*Red Riding Hood* drama are apparent, and must be seen in the context of the 1930s. Fascism had spread throughout Europe, and in
the Soviet Union itself the communist revolution had disintegrated into a repressive political system. Thus, Shvarts's stress on
friendship, solidarity, and courage introduced qualities that all little girls and boys would need during World War II, and in the post-
war years as well.

The perspective was somewhat different in the United States, at
least in H. I. Phillips's version of *Little Red Riding Hood,* told in 1940
for adults "as a Dictator Would Tell It" (Tale 19). Here Phillips, like
Shvarts, criticizes totalitarianism and ironically portrays Little Red

Riding Hood as "a vile provocateur and an agent of capitalistic in-terests." By making her into an aggressor, the wolf/Hitler can ratio-nalize all his aggressive actions and pretend to be fighting for com-mon peace and happiness in the world. So by 1940, in Europe and the United States, Little Red Riding Hood appeared to have become the symbol for real democracy or democratic socialism. If we take into account Thurber's tale, too, there is no doubt but she seemed to be bent on more rebellious ways as World War II dawned.

After the war, Riding Hood continued to change radically throughout Europe and America. Beginning with Catherine Storr's *Little Polly Riding Hood* (1955; Tale 20), options to the traditional cultural pattern of the virtuous, helpless Riding Hood were being formed, and there was some agreement among the "rebel" fairy-tale writers that she need not curb her imagination and sensuality and wait for a strong, orderly, male hero to rescue her. This literary change can be attributed to the gradual rise of civil rights and women's movements, along with progressive developments in child rearing and sexual education. The 1960s added a strong political component to all counter-cultural tendencies, and often they were substantiated by critical psychological insights and social attacks on conformity presented in such key books as Herbert Marcuse's *Eros and Civilization* and *One-Dimensional Man*[67] and R. D. Laing's *The Politics of Experience*.[68] Marcuse and Laing became counter-cultural heroes, influencing numerous intellectuals and reformers. In addition, there was an important rediscovery of Wilhelm Reich and other radical psychologists and educators from the 1920s and 1930s, and this recall for a rebellious past stimulated contemporary critics to analyze traditional notions of sexuality and socialization in a political light.[69] The reception of these writers was only symp-tomatic of a great clamor for real democratic change. The overall result from 1945 to 1993 in the Riding Hood tradition was an in-flux of critical ideas pointing to the necessity for changing our so-cial views of sexuality and domination. In contrast to the adapta-tions of the 1920s, 1930s, and 1940s, the new versions of the fairy tale addressed both children and adults at the same time, though some were still highly sophisticated and intended solely for adults. It is also interesting to note that many of these radical versions have been translated into different languages, which suggests that there are cross-cultural patterns in Great Britain, America, France, and West Germany corresponding to the problematic tendencies and legitimation crises in corporate capitalist societies.[70]

In general it appears that there are three major currents in the radical Riding Hood tales from 1950 to 1993. First, many narratives portray Little Red Riding Hood coming into her own, developing a sense of independence without help from males. Second, certain tales and poems seek to rehabilitate the wolf. Third, there are stories which are unusual aesthetic experiments, debunking traditional narrative forms and seeking to free readers and listeners so that they can question the conventional cultural patterns. All of these radical currents overlap or merge to form critical statements about the way we view sexuality on the basis of the Riding Hood pattern. Let us consider some of the more significant examples of these different currents.

❋ 59 ❋
The Trials
and
Tribulations
of Little Red
Riding Hood

The first strong vote for independence was sounded by Storr's *Little Polly Riding Hood* of 1955. This tale belongs to a collection of *Clever Polly* stories in which Polly continually outwits a conceited foolish wolf. The girl is level-headed, fearless, and practical. She needs nobody's help to contend with the wolf, who frequently discloses his own tricky plots. Storr's delightful parody exudes a young girl's self-confidence, and clever Polly knows that she has the brains and ability to counter potential seducers. This theme is repeated more seriously in another English adaptation of *Red Riding Hood* (1972; Tale 24) by committed feminists of the Merseyside Fairy Story Collective in Liverpool (Audrey Ackroyd, Marge Ben-Tovim, Catherine Meredith, and Anne Neville). In contrast to Storr's tale there is a little humor here. The wolf is a wild inimical force and poses a real natural threat to Nadia and her great-grandmother. However, the two women combine their strength and wit to overcome the wolf, who provides a lining for Nadia's tattered winter coat. In the course of events, Nadia learns to deal with her timidity, and her red coat becomes a symbol of courage.

The symbolism of the red hood, cap, or coat has generally been ambivalent in the past 300 years. In Max von der Grün's version of *Little Red Cap* (1974; Tale 26), it reflects upon the prejudices and intolerance of people who are afraid of something different. Whether von der Grün had the anti-Semitism of Germans in mind or the fear of the communist "red peril" is difficult to say. However, it is clear that the tale totally reverses the cultural code transmitted by the stories of Perrault and the Grimms. Instead of praising conformity, von der Grün questions the dependence on uniformity that can lead to rabid terrorism on the part of conventional people. Little Red Cap's experience of arbitrary and seemingly senseless

**Beatrice Schenk de Regniers, *Red Riding Hood,* New York: Atheneum, 1972. Illustrator Edward Gorey.**

prejudice is a maturation process that she will never forget, and the ending of this "bad fairy tale" punctures the mythical happy ending of conformist Riding Hood tales.

Tony Ross punctures the conformist illusion even more irreverently in his *Little Red Hood: A Classic Story Bent Out of Shape* (1978; Tale 32) by using contemporary hip talk and commercial jargon to parody commodity fetishism. He depicts Red Riding Hood as a tough kid, who once she "hits puberty" begins fighting for her rights against her indolent father Rocky, the owner of a woodmill.

He suspects her of being a commie, but she merely wants to go her own way. The comic spoof breaks down in the end, when Little Red Hood is prevented by the wolf from going her own way, needs to be saved by Rocky, and returns to the family fold. Here the roguish clichés of the story tend to belittle the struggle for women's rights, transforming it into a fashionable television situation comedy, which everyone can watch and laugh about over pizza and wine. Such travesty is also the case in Anneliese Meinert's *Little Red Cap '65* (Tale 21), in which the heroine is a "spoiled product" of Germany's economic miracle. In contrast, O. F. Gmelin's West-German *Little Red Cap* (1978; Tale 31) is more in line with radical sexual politics, introducing us to a fearless girl who uses her wits to cut her own way out of the wolf's belly. She and her grandmother team up to uncover the wolf's true identity, and it is clear from the ending that everyone can satisfy his or her own needs. Such self-satisfaction, however, can also become dangerous if overdone, according to Margaret Kassajep's *Little Red Cap with Crash Helmet* (1980). Here Little Red Cap as representative of the "no-future" generation visits her granny in an old age home. Since she and her friend Wolfi want to have granny's money to enjoy life, they kill the poor woman (to be sure, without causing her pain) and then take off into the wide blue yonder on Wolfi's Suzuki motorcycle without leaving a trace behind them. These latest "models" of Little Red Riding Hood and the Wolf from West Germany are products of a consumer society where crime has become more or less accepted as a way of life. Unfortunately, it seems that both the girl and the wolf have adapted to the inhuman standards that the adapted story itself ironically criticizes through its blasé tone.

Despite the differences in adaptation, all the tales of this first group share one basic element in common: Little Red Riding Hood is no longer innocent, helpless, and disobedient. Rather, she is fearless, intelligent, and confident. She demonstrates a capacity to learn through experience and can stand on her own feet. Though the wolf may indeed be dangerous, Red Riding Hood is equal to the tasks he sets her. Through confrontation with him she establishes her own identity and becomes her own person.

In the second current of radical tales there are various writers who have endeavored to question the "truth" of the classical Perrault and Grimm tales by viewing the contents from the wolf's perspective. Rudolf Otto Wiemer's ironic poem "The Old Wolf" (1976; Tale 28) is a good introduction here since it sets the tone:

the surprising wolf casually threatens Red Riding Hood by remark-
ing that it is discourteous to spread "wild stories" about his reputation. But it is Tomi Ungerer who suggests more positively that the
wolf is not a male predator. His version of *Little Red Riding Hood*
(1974; Tale 27) portrays the girl as prey to the fears and needs of
her parents and grandmother. The slandered wolf seeks to overcome his bad reputation by helping the girl and offering his hand in
marriage. There need not be fear of sex or fear of one's own sexuality, according to the non-conformist Ungerer. His tale indicates
that Riding Hood does not have to combat the wolf as a carnal
symbol but rather must learn to trust her own senses. This is also
true in Hans Joachim Schädlich's comic *Criminal Fairy Tale* (1977)
in which Ulf, a petty thief, is rebuffed by Rosie and then drinks so
much whiskey that he is caught robbing grandmother's house. His
mock tale of sorrow is told from his perspective in a prison cell.
Rosie is clearly Ulf's downfall, and yet the "wolf" appears to be
more defeated by his own ineffectuality than by Rosie's courage.

If the wolf is not devious, wicked, and mean, then what is he? Iring
Fetscher supplies a tongue-in-cheek interpretation that transforms
the wolf into a scapegoat: he serves to justify socially conditioned
human aggression. Fetscher's *Little Redhead and the Wolf* (1972; Tale
23) is a pre-Red Cap story, which historically explains that the wolf
did not desire to molest the little girl sexually but wanted to avenge
himself for the brutal manner in which Little Red Cap's father had
treated the wolf's friend Little Redhead, who happened to be the
brother of Little Red Cap, in other words, the father's son, who does
not live up to the high expectations of the father. Though Fetscher
chiefly pokes fun at psychoanalytical interpretations of *Little Red
Cap,* there is more truth than he realizes to his assertion that the tale
is a neurotic male projection. This will become more apparent when
we consider how the literary tradition was founded on a male conception of women and sexuality. Here the impudent questioning of
the psychological motivations behind the tale serves to shed a different light on the wolf as symbol. Portrayed as a maltreated creature of
nature and a good-natured "underdog," the wolf strikes back against
society to teach humans a lesson: nature will rule out in the end.
That is, at least in this version.

We also have other versions where wolves have given up on
humans and society and merely seek their peace. In Philippe
Dumas's and Boris Moissard's *Little Aqua Riding Hood* (1977; Tale
29), set in contemporary Paris, the granddaughter of Little Red

Riding Hood tries to relive the old tale and gain fame by freeing a wolf from the zoo in the Jardin des Plantes. However, the wolf, a grandnephew of the wolf in Perrault's story, is unwilling to play along. He likes the zoo, where he is well fed and can sleep the entire day. Besides, he knows what happened to his granduncle. On the other hand, he would also like to be free to roam the woods. So he pretends to comply with the wishes of Little Aqua Riding Hood, but instead heads straight for Siberia to be among his brothers and friends and to warn them about little French girls and the dangers of men who threaten to exterminate wolves. The moral of this story reads: "Certain men are more dangerous than wolves."[71]

Like the radical adaptations that have transformed Little Red Riding Hood into a fearless, independent girl, the versions that rehabilitate the wolf undermine the assumptions of the traditional cultural pattern. The first obvious explanation for this is that wolves as animals are virtually extinct in Western societies and no longer represent a menace to humans (if they ever did). Second, the wolf as representative of sexuality in general is less a threat today. Fears of sex have diminished because greater scientific control over the body has been achieved. In fact, the body is no longer equated in contemporary literature with unruly nature, but more and more comparisons are drawn with machines. Thus, if the body itself is no longer "natural" but "manufacturable," then its collapse cannot be brought about by nature but by malfunctioning parts. The ideal in Western society today is not the organic natural body but the scientifically machine-like body. This leads us to a third point, which is linked to the ecological movements of the 1960s and 1970s. To rehabilitate the wolf in Red Riding Hood tales is a great reversal of *homo homini lupus*, or at least, it indicates how far we have come in destroying our inner nature. To recapture the wolf in us is part of a general counter-cultural movement against the nuclear extinction of the human species, made possible in the name of technological progress. As raw nature, the wolf is threatened by chemical pollution, scientific automation, and the general drive for scientific human perfection. This is why the wolf is no longer pictured as a real threat in radical adaptations of the traditional Red Riding Hood story.

This is also evident in the third current of radical tales. For instance, Jean Merrill and Gianni Rodari tear the traditional narrative discourse and contents asunder, and play sardonically with conservative expectations. In Merrill's *Red Riding* (1968), Katy's little brother Tony ruins the story of Red Riding Hood because he is constantly adding incredible motifs or questioning the events. Tony asks why the woods are dangerous and wants to supply more ferocious beasts. He also suggests that Red Riding share her deviled eggs with the wolf. Later, Red Riding hides from the wolf who appears on the television screen, and, when the wolf is finally killed, he is buried with flowers. By making the events of the story appear harmless and absurd through a witty dialogue of brother and sister on a rainy afternoon, the narrator frees the reader from the traditional story-line to invent his or her own alternatives. Here the very narrative technique radically conceives a discourse that opens possibilities for change. This is also true in Gianni Rodari's *Little Green Riding Hood* (1973; Tale 25), where a grandpa mixes up the story so much that he makes a mess out of it and frustrates his grandchild.

By far the two most experimental versions from a socio-aesthetic point of view are Anne Sexton's poem "Red Riding Hood" (1971; Tale 22) and Angela Carter's story *The Company of Wolves* (1979; Tale 33), both intended primarily for adults. Sexton rewrote various of the Grimms' tales in her book *Transformations*; her poems depict how women are used as sex objects and how their lives become little more than commodities or hollow existences when they follow the social paths designed for them. Her utmost concern is with the ways and means women become drained of their energy, creativity, and power. In her blunt free verse, which parodies advertisement slogans and American dreams of the wholesome life, Sexton retells the Red Riding Hood story as one of deception, and she cynically concludes the tale with the "saved" grandmother and Red Riding Hood in a state of social amnesia. By *not* remembering how empty and treacherous their lives had been, they will obviously repeat the mistakes they had made in the past. In contrast to Sexton's pessimistic poem, Carter's Gothic version of *Red Riding Hood* recalls the superstitious past to transcend it. Relying on the folk tradition of the peasant girl and the werewolf, Carter blends the past with stark notions of sexuality and social behavior from the present. She deftly illustrates how a "strong-minded child" can fend for herself in the woods and tame the wolf. The savagery of sex reveals its tender side, and the girl becomes at one with the wolf to soothe his tormented soul.

Carter's remarkable adaptation of the traditional French folk tale is significant because it reflects the changing attitudes toward women and sexuality in Western society in a more positive way than Sexton. Interestingly, in China, a recent version of *Little Red*

❋ 65 ❋

The Trials
and
Tribulations
of Little Red
Riding Hood

*Little Red Riding Hood,* New York: Harcourt Brace Jovanovich, 1968.
Illustrator Harriet Pincus.

*Riding Hood* entitled *Goldflower and the Bear* (1979; Tale 34), by
Chiang Mi, expresses the same sentiments as Carter's story.[72] Written expressly for children, this tale returns to the oral folk tale to
explore its potential for the development of children's social and
personal sensibilities in today's world. Goldflower is a self-confident girl who uses her wits to protect her younger brother and to
outsmart the predatory bear. She is entirely capable of defending
herself on an individual level, and it is apparent that she also signifies young Chinese society on a political level by overcoming a
*bear,* symbolic of gigantic Russia, instead of a wolf.

Both in the East and the West great strides have been made in
society and literature to offset male domination through the projection of images of girls and women who have diverse skills and
roles. Nevertheless, the culture industry, particularly in the West,
insists on maintaining conservative stereotypes of women in advertisements, films, television, radio, and literature to profit from traditional male expectations. If we look at three contemporary American versions of *Little Red Riding Hood,* which are slight adaptations
of the Grimms' tale and are more widely circulated among children
than the radical adaptations, then Sexton's concern about sexual

deception, exploitation, and social amnesia must be taken more seriously. Beatrice Schenk de Regnier's *Red Riding Hood* (1972), retold in verse for boys and girls to read to themselves, is interesting insofar as the moral imperatives are downplayed. Little Red Riding Hood does break her promise to her mother, but all is forgotten and forgiven. The verse simplifies the story to make it easy to read and delectable for young children. The wolf is wicked; granny and Little Red Riding Hood are gobbled up; the hunter saves them. This is also the case in two popular versions by Mabel Watts and Jane Carruth, sold throughout the United States in bookstores, drugstores, and supermarkets and attractively illustrated to stress Red Riding Hood's virtuous nature and helplessness. In Watts's adaptation—which evidently was influenced by the Walt Disney sterilization process—the wolf is prevented from touching grandma and Little Red Riding Hood; the tale is neutered, and everyone can have some good clean fun. Even the wolf retreats alive. There is no slicing his belly or death. Both the woodcutter and grandma are the rescuers and guarantee Red Riding Hood that everything is all right and that they can live in peace and quiet. Similar things occur in Carruth's more elaborate, somewhat Victorian, adaptation of 1979. A fatherly hunter saves Little Red Riding Hood and guides her safely back to her mommy. Though Riding Hood is not scolded, the tale stresses that she landed in trouble because she was disobedient and could not curb her desire to run into the woods and pick wild flowers. Furthermore, the paternal hunter, who more or less lends Red Riding Hood life and her identity, is given a major role.

All three versions, by de Regnier, Watts, and Carruth, continue the stereotyping of little girls as innocent creatures who must be protected by strong male guardians because as females they cannot control their "natural urges" and thus make themselves prey to vicious animals. Despite the contemporary Western change of attitude toward women and toward puritanical and repressive child-rearing, and despite numerous radical adaptations of Red Riding Hood's life history, the Perrault and Grimm traditional patterns remain strong, and are continually reinforced by modified versions preaching obedience and the regulation of little girls' sexuality.[73] One can talk about a "Red Riding Hood syndrome" in Western culture, and its persistence at all levels of society is remarkable. This syndrome involves a perversion of sexuality that began during the 17th century and led to an instrumentalization of the body. As

❋ 67 ❋
The Trials
and
Tribulations
of Little Red
Riding Hood

Michel Foucault and others have demonstrated,[74] sexual forces have been deployed in the development of bio-politics to bring about the supervision of the body as a machine for maximum use and profit. Concern with the body has been associated with eugenics and the advancement of the human species. However, the categorization and care of the body in the name of progress has ironically led to a perverted sense of sexuality. The question we must now ask is what is at the root of this cultural syndrome as reflected in the *Red Riding Hood* tales.

❋ *The Medieval Tale in Socio-Religious Context*

To answer this question we must return to the late Middle Ages, werewolves, witches, and the socio-religious crises which engendered a new view of nature and sexuality. We have already seen that the original folk version of *The Story of Grandmother* emanated from a general superstition in France about werewolves. However, we have not yet explored notions about werewolves, nature, sexuality, and heresy in the late Middle Ages, which will enable us to grasp the significant differences between the oral tale and the two major versions—by Perrault and the Grimm brothers, who were largely responsible for the *Red Riding Hood* literary syndrome.

To begin with the werewolf, it is interesting to note the etymology of the word, which generally means "man-wolf." It originated thousands of years ago in pagan rituals, where the wolf was actually celebrated as a protector. Witch doctors, shamans, and other spiritual leaders often wrapped themselves in a wolfskin or bearskin and were said to have been possessed by the animal, thereby acquiring magical powers. The word "berserk" is also derived from the man wearing a wolfskin or bearskin, possessor and possessed of supernatural gifts. This wolf-man was generally regarded with great awe by hunting tribes. As attitudes changed and tribes became more settled and transformed into grazing societies, wolves and werewolves gradually became associated with hostile forces, or outcasts who lived in the woods outside society and preyed upon humans. Eventually the wolf became associated with legal terminology designating a social misfit, or a deviate who was dangerous and had to be expelled from society.[75] Both werewolf and wolf were endowed with the same ferocious and aggressive qualities, with the exception that the werewolf was identified more with the gods, suspected of possessing unique powers of transformation, and considered uncontrollable, untamable, and yet necessary for the cultural process. Perhaps the best definition of a werewolf has been given by Hans Peter Duerr:

> A werewolf is a human being who can dissolve the boundary between civilization and wilderness in himself and is capable of crossing over the fence which separates his "civilized side" from his "wild side." A werewolf is a creature who looks "straight into the eyes" of his "animal nature," which is usually kept under lock and key by his culture. Consequently, this creature is the first to develop a consciousness of his "cultural nature."[76]

As Duerr demonstrates in his book Traumzeit, primitive tribes and societies looked upon the werewolf positively (even though with awe) because the werewolf pointed the way toward integration of the cultural and the wild elements of humans. Ironically, to learn to howl with the wolves (or to learn to dance with the witches) meant opening oneself up to the essence of nature, and through this experience, one could achieve greater self-awareness. In order to be able to live in a social order and in order to be tame and self-aware, archaic societies believed that one had to have spent some time in the wilderness. One could only know what one's inner nature meant by having gone outside oneself.

Up through the Middle Ages most Europeans—particularly the peasantry—believed in werewolves. The superstition was strongest in France. Gradually the reverence and awe shown toward the werewolf lost its positive ritual meaning. What is most noteworthy is that the werewolf was considered destructive, bloodthirsty, cunning, and supernatural, but he was not directly associated with the devil until the late Middle Ages. It was particularly during the time from 1400 to 1700 that the notion of the werewolf underwent a profound change. As Konrad Müller and many others have pointed out, certain awesome characteristics of the werewolf became associated with witches and the devil, especially the magical transformations, which were supposedly explained by numerous religious tracts about werewolves and lycanthropy.[77] Whereas it had previously been considered sinful or nonsensical to believe in werewolves from the official Catholic viewpoint, in an about-face toward the end of the 15th century, the Church deemed it necessary to believe in their existence—as accomplices of the devil. This was directly connected to the holy dictum to believe in witches. Along with cats, werewolves were allegedly the favorite cohorts of witches, and in many werewolf trials of the 16th and 17th centuries there was no real distinction made between werewolf and witch.

All this was initiated by Pope Innocent VIII in the *Papal Bull Summis Desiderantes Affectibus* in December 1484, and further elaborated in the *Malleus Maleficarum* (*Hammer of Witches*, 1486). Both proclaimed that the devil had spread his rule to the earth and had to be combated, and Satan's deputies such as witches and werewolves had to be annihilated. The witch craze began and spread rapidly throughout Europe, and, as H. R. Trever-Roper maintains,

> a general mandate was given, or implied. And the *Malleus*, which is inseparable from the bull, gave force to that mandate. First, by its content, by gathering together all the curiosities and credulities of Alpine peasants and their confessors, it built up a solid basis for the new mythology. Secondly, by its universal circulation, it carried this mythology, as a truth recognized by the Church, over all Christendom. Finally, the *Malleus* explicitly called on other authorities, lay and secular, not merely not to obstruct, but positively to assist the inquisitors in their task of exterminating witches. From now on, the persecution which had been sporadic, was—at least in theory—made general, and secular authorities were encouraged to use the methods and mythology of the Inquisition. Rome had spoken.[78]

Not only Rome but also Protestantism spoke, because of the general crisis of religious belief and the growth of heresies and nonconformism. This led to institutionalized social intolerance. Everyone and anyone had to come under suspicion as a heretic in order for Christianity to maintain its rule in Europe. Catholics attacked Protestants as deviates and vice versa, but their real common enemies were the non-believers in Christianity associated with Jews, witches, werewolves, and other non-Christian types who were equated with one another and were suspected of working in league with the devil. They were all named explicitly by the Church, its official inquisitors, and such venerable scholars as Pierre de l'Ancre, whose influential book *L'Incrédulité et mescréance du sortilege pleinement convaincue* (1622) argued that Jews were condemned by God because of their filthy stench and were sentenced to crawl around the world like snakes. As great magicians they allegedly could turn themselves into wolves by night and could not be converted into good Christians.[79] There was only one remedy for Jews, werewolves, and witches—extermination.

In all the religious diatribe of the 16th and 17th centuries there were constant parallels drawn between the devil and his associates, the Jews, witches, and werewolves, and this had a profound effect on the popular imagination. As Müller has documented:

One feature was continually stressed time and again in all the trial protocols and religious sermons of that time: the connection of the transformed human being to the devil; the help which the devil provides in the transformation; the arrangement of a personal relationship to him and similar things. . . . Since the connection of the devil to the werewolf was based on the impact of generally valid, spiritual Christian teachings in the mind of the people, this feature was naturally not limited to specific localities but appeared throughout France, England, the Netherlands, and Germany.[80]

It is apparent today that the *firm Christian belief* in werewolves in the 16th and 17th centuries derived from a strident campaign by the Church to exploit folk superstition in order to keep all social groups under its control. As Trevor-Roper and other historians have proven,[81] the witch hunts (including the persecution of werewolves) can be regarded as a form of institutionalized terrorism on the part of the Church, supported by Protestantism and secular authorities.[82] But there is even more here, involving structural social changes that influenced general notions of sexuality and nature.

By studying the rise of the witch cultural pattern in the early Middle Ages, its "demonization" in the 15th century, and its decline as a valid social category of heresy by the end of the 17th century, Claudia Honegger has shown that

with the social changes since the 12th century the domination of nature in regard to humans became a problem. Only at the time when woman became the representative of nature did the polemics between feminism and anti-feminism flare up in all their sharpness. The ideal of woman disintegrated first into the two contrasting images of the unnatural virgin and the naturally potent witch and ultimately found its temperate and fragile synthesis only in the 18th-century "good Mother." However, time and again the two figures of the virgin and witch emerged in the conceptual world of bourgeois society whenever the precarious balance of the mother, who was continually threatened by nervous breakdowns, appeared to be destroyed. The Maria Cult and the witch craze introduced that transformation which changed the woman as feared representative of nature into an object no longer capable of dominating her nature.[83]

In the 16th and 17th centuries women more than men were declared witches and were burned because they were associated with untamed nature and potential heresy. The actions of the Church, which lasted well over 200 years in Western Europe and spread to America, were not simply police measures that affected social structures. They also had a profound effect on social consciousness, customs, and habits in Western society. Gradually there was a shift in the socialization processes. In particular, the witch and werewolf crazes were aimed at regulating sexual practices and sex roles for the benefit of male-dominated social orders, which were depending more and more on economic rationalization in the production and reproduction spheres. Whereas people in the early Middle Ages had assumed their nature to be determined by the social order and had also accepted the unity of inner and outer nature, the emergence of bourgeois relations of production and the increasing technological capacity to control nature brought about a division between human beings as subjects and the objective outside world. Along with these socio-economic factors, the Church distinguished human beings as "electors" distinct from nature. The task of all good Christians was to subdue nature, drive out Satan and heretics from the world, restore order, and bring about God's kingdom on earth. As the Europeans of the 16th and 17th centuries sought to make progress and change nature, they supervised their own behavior in a most diligent and often self-defeating manner. The efforts made to imbue outside nature with Christian virtues and to bring about divine harmony were based on the belief that God revealed and manifested Himself in outer nature. Moreover, if outer nature displayed defects, this reflected upon the moral degeneration of humankind. In accordance with new forms of production, which depended on reason, discipline, and machine technology, people—and especially the upper classes, who were the first to operate on themselves—began to separate their sensual drives from their intellects, and to view themselves objectively as technically capable of achieving some form of moral perfection. In both Catholic and Protestant thinking of the 16th and 17th centuries the greatest fear was chaos, which was associated with sensuality and uncontrollable inner and outer nature. Thomas Hobbes summed up this fear most succinctly, using wolf imagery to express it: *Homo homini lupus*.

As Honegger has shown in her discussion of witches,

> the religious and social views of nature and sexuality which were undergoing a change at this time must be regarded in connection with socio-economic advances and shifts. With the development of capitalist conditions of production in Western Europe, the progressive domination of nature by technology and the formation of the modern state (monopoly on taxes, constant administration, standing armies and police) the gap be-

tween the individual and society, individual and nature, theoretically conveyed through religious change, was also deepened in everyday life. This restructuration of the economic and political conditions required the collapse of the organic unity of society and nature, and it was important that this gap continue to be widened and deepened. The increasing dissolution of the feudal estates, which until then had guaranteed people an ordered, fully coordinated life context in which societies had derived their laws from the laws of nature and the natural laws had been derived from the political order, led to the liberation and projection of the individual into a world which had to appear more and more senseless and corrupt. Nature, which had gradually become more the object of exploitation, could no longer provide a direct basis of legitimation for the state which, implanted by positive law, served only the subjugation, punishment, and security of individuals who stood opposed to each other in competition. Therefore, the state was just as incapable of providing the meaning of existence as fallen nature.[84]

Ironically, the conceptual depiction of utopias, which were supposed to help overcome the socio-religious crisis of the 16th and 17th centuries, generated a contradictory development: human progress through reason and Christian morality was to involve the unreasonable and immoral exploitation of women, children, and minority groups, and the irresponsible technological domination of nature for profit.[85] Cultural processes were brought into line with new visionary projections of paradise on earth, which essentially furthered bourgeois hegemony in Western Europe and America. Again, Honegger is helpful, clarifying what was necessary to realize the ideals of the time.

> The adaptation to such demands necessitated an immense increase in self-discipline and an exacting regimentation of one's life by the subjects. "The domination of nature inside and outside" became "the absolute purpose in life for them." This was valid to a large degree particularly for the rising industrial bourgeoisie, but also for the court aristocracy, the bureaucracy and the military. Whoever could not or did not want to be integrated was punished with hate and despisal. Numerous "primitive" and heretical peoples were decimated; the poor and insane were interned in their own society or annihilated through the new race laws; the peasantry was oppressed and dispossessed. In this process the sexual roles which were transmitted in tradition also experienced a legal definition of opposition: the basis of every state order was now considered the dominance of the sole reasonably gifted man over woman as so-called natural creature.

❀ 73 ❀

*The Trials
and
Tribulations
of Little Red
Riding Hood*

***Little Red Riding Hood and Other Stories,*** New York: A. L. Burt, 1907.
**Illustrator unknown.**

The claim to domination of reason over material and natural
needs, the devaluation of the unordered elementary nature and
natural human beings was additionally strengthened by abstract
and irrational religiosity which penetrated the gap between reason and nature and found its most precise expression in Calvin-
ism. Here human beings are definitely evil, and nature, depraved.

...The result for humankind was a neurotic compulsory fixation on the laws of God and the normative system which
emanated from this, and authoritarian subjugation of all deviate
ways of behavior through disciplinary measures.[86]

The appropriation of folk customs and beliefs was translated by
the Church and civil order into forms and modes of control to
legitimate the dominance of Christianity, men over women and
children, and rising industrial groups, specifically among the bourgeoisie, over all other social classes. Max Weber equated this with
the formation of the Protestant ethic,[87] but the impact of the ratio-
nalized moral code for exploitation was not limited to Protestantism. This can be documented by studying the socio-political development of werewolves and witches in the 16th and 17th centuries
as heretics and non-conformists, which gave rise to cultural patterns in oral folklore and literary fairy tales. The fact that the *Little
Red Riding Hood* syndrome as a cultural configuration of legalized
terror has endured and remained so powerful can only be attributed
to the significant role it played in the rise of a new ideology. This
can be traced to the socio-religious transition during the Renais-
sance and Reformation. That is, *Little Red Riding Hood* as part of
the literary socialization process came to reinforce socially accepted ways of viewing women, sexuality, and nature. The key tales
that gave rise to the *Little Red Riding Hood* syndrome are the oral
tale of *The Grandmother*, Perrault's adaptation of folklore, and the
Grimms' puritanical version. Let us now re-examine them in light
of the socio-historical background of werewolves, witches, and
legalized terror in the 16th and 17th centuries.

If we assume that Paul Delarue's integral text of *The Story of the
Grandmother* (quoted earlier in this Introduction; see pp. 21–22)
emanated from peasant superstition and actual case histories from
1400 to 1700, then we can interpret it as a transitional secular folk
tale, which had not yet been contaminated by Christian notions
linking the werewolf to the devil, or by ideas aimed at controlling
children. The tale, which carries a peasant viewpoint, has nothing
to do with obedience or the curbing of sexual drives, even though
it is a warning. In fact, the sexual cravings of the wolf are debunked
and treated as harmless because the little girl knows how to take
care of herself in nature. She does not have a special name, cap, or
color. She is an average little girl visiting her grandmother. She is
*not* afraid of the woods. She is *not* terrified by the wolf. She exposes
herself but takes care of herself. The oral tale does not mince

words. It frankly repeats a familiar superstition as a comical warning to children in which a little girl outwits the wolf. Clear sympathy is expressed for children, and the female figure is regarded as
naturally equal to the werewolf. As Foucault has pointed out:

❀ 75 ❀

*The Trials
and
Tribulations
of Little Red
Riding Hood*

> At the beginning of the seventeenth century a certain frankness
> was still common, it would seem. Sexual practices had little
> need of secrecy; words were said without undue reticence, and
> things were done without much concealment; one had a toler-
> ant familiarity with the illicit. Codes regulating the coarse, the
> obscene, and the indecent were quite lax compared to those of
> the nineteenth century. It was a time of direct gestures, shame-
> less discourse, and open transgressions, when anatomies were
> shown and intermingled at will, and knowing children hung
> about amid the laughter of adults: it was a period when bodies
> "made a display of themselves."[88]

Clearly the original folk tale of *The Grandmother* reflected the
sexual frankness of the peasantry during the late Middle Ages, as
well as a general tolerance of differences. As we know, all this was
on the verge of changing.

### *Regulatory Significance of Perrault's*
### *and the Brothers Grimm's Moralité*

By the time Perrault began to revise the oral folk tale of *The
Grandmother*, it was no longer necessary to believe in witches or
werewolves, especially if one were a member of the upper classes,
for the witch craze had subsided and was no longer fashionable. It
was now necessary to project an image of woman as innocent, helpless, and susceptible to the chaotic, somewhat seductive, forces of
nature, capable of making a pact with the devil or yielding to her
fancy. Delarue is quite right when he points out that Perrault decided to change the werewolf into a simple wolf because werewolves had lost their significance after the decline of the witch
hunts. Nevertheless, Perrault's audience still identified the wolf
with the bloody werewolf, the devil, insatiable lust, and chaotic
nature, *if not with a witch*. The wolf as witch may strike readers
today as far-fetched, but it was not far from the minds of 17th- and
18th-century readers. Thus, let us proceed to reinterpret Perrault's
tale according to the French ideology of his time.

As we know, numerous modern studies have focused on the red
cap in Perrault's tale as a symbol either of the sun or of puberty.
Neither viewpoint is correct. Perrault used the word *chaperon*, which
was a small stylish cap worn by women of the aristocracy and mid-

*Le Petit Chaperon Rouge,* Epinal: Imagene Pellerin, c. 1885. Illustrator
unknown.

dle classes in the 16th and 17th centuries.[89] Since clothing was
codified and strictly enforced under Louis XIV, it was customary for
middle-class women to wear cloth caps, whereas aristocratic ladies
wore velvet. Bright colors were preferred, especially red, and the
skull cap was generally ornamental. For a village girl, in Perrault's
story, to wear a red *chaperon* signified that she was individualistic

and perhaps nonconformist. Perrault probably intended that she bear the sign of the middle class, and by giving her a name he made something special out of her.[90] Again there is something definitely individualistic about Little Red Riding Hood. We already know that she is the prettiest creature around, spoiled by her mother and grandmother. Thus, the image of this young girl suggests that she contains certain potential qualities which could convert her into a witch or heretic. Her *natural* inclinations do in fact lead her into trouble. In the woods, which was a known haunting place of were-wolves, witches, outlaws, and other social deviates, Little Red Riding Hood talks naturally to the wolf because she is unaware of any danger. She trusts her instincts. If it were not for the *male* woodcut-ters (for only men can serve as protectors), the wolf would have indulged his appetite on the spot, in his natural abode. Instead he is forced to make a "pact" with her. Certainly, according to 17th-century beliefs, anyone who entered into an agreement with a dia-bolic figure was contaminated and would have to fight for his or her soul. The motif depicted here was fully and consciously developed in 18th-century France by writers of bourgeois morality plays, like Louis Sebastien Mercier and Denis Diderot, who depicted dec-adent aristocrats seducing young virtuous bourgeois ladies.[91] This dramatic genre, labeled *comédie sérieuse*, became extremely popular and lasted well through the 19th century into the 20th. Interest-ingly enough, it served as the basis for Boieldieu's 1818 opera *Le petit Chaperon rouge*. In 18th-century Germany this type of drama was cultivated by Gotthold Ephraim Lessing in *Miss Sara Sampson* and *Emilia Galotti*, and he was followed by such *Sturm und Drang* writers as J. M. R. Lenz, Henrich Leopold Wagner, Friedrich Maxi-milian Klinger, and even Friedrich Schiller in *Kabale und Liebe*. And, of course, the constellation of diabolic wolf and virtuous bour-geois damsel served as the basis for Part I of Goethe's *Faust*, where the transformed Faust (a type of werewolf) with the aid of Meph-istopheles seduces Gretchen, who must pay for *her* sin. It is impor-tant to note that Faust is a necromancer doing the devil's work, and it is apparent that Gretchen's bourgeois/village forebear was none other than Little Red Riding Hood. All French and German writ-ers of the 18th century knew that Little Red Riding Hood had been punished for her "crime" of speaking to the devil and of laying the grounds for her own seduction and rape.

The eating or swallowing of Little Red Riding Hood is an obvi-ous sexual act, symbolizing the uncontrollable appetite or chaos of nature. Moreover, Little Red Riding Hood becomes at one with the wolf. That is, her "natural" potential to become a witch is realized because she lacks self-discipline. As Honegger has made clear, the flip side of the Maria cult, the supreme virgin, is the witch. All this is summarized in the *moralité* of the fairy tale. The blame for the diabolical rape is placed squarely on the shoulders of naive young girls who are pretty and have correct manners. Ostensibly, the seduction would not have occurred had Little Red Riding Hood not stopped to listen to a stranger. Her "dallying" or her undisciplined ways lead her into the wolf's lair. Perrault obviously extends the definition of wolf to include deceptive male seducers of bourgeois women. Still, the overall notion of the fairy tale concerns the regulation of sex roles and sexuality. Where order and discipline reign —Perrault supported the absolutism of Louis XIV—young girls will be safe from both their own inner sexual drives and outer natural forces. Inner and outer nature must be brought under control, otherwise chaos and destruction will reign.

The cultural code and pattern embedded in *Little Red Riding Hood* make it obvious that this tale in particular was bound to become an immediate favorite in the 18th and 19th centuries, particularly among members of the aristocracy and bourgeoisie. However, it was not until the Grimms morally improved upon the Perrault version, showing more clemency for Little Red Riding Hood, that the tale became an explicit narrative of law and order. As we know, by the time the Grimms touched up Perrault's tale, a bourgeois Red Riding Hood syndrome had been established throughout Europe and America, and it went under the name of "virtue seduced." Obviously, the middle classes were reflecting in general upon the fact that, if they did not discipline themselves and their children and rationalize their lives, they would be "raped" by the depraved aristocracy or experience a fall due to unruly natural forces. Then they would have to succumb to the uncouth lower classes. Fear of chaos as dangerous for sound and orderly business was overwhelming among members of the third estate, and, even though the French Revolution had brought turmoil with it, this upheaval had been deemed necessary in order to clean out decadent aristocratic squalor and to bring more order, rationality, and just conditions into France. The effect that the French Revolution had on Ludwig Tieck and the Brothers Grimm has already been documented. Now it is more important to note how the Grimms doctored *Little Red Riding Hood* as *Little Red Cap* to make a comment on sexual norms and sex roles.

*Les Contes de Perrault,* **Paris: Flammarion, 1927. Illustrator Felix
Lorioux.**

The Grimms were responsible for making Little Red Riding
Hood definitively into a disobedient, helpless little girl. Before she
makes a pact with the devil, she makes one with her good mother.
Thus, they also prepared the way for clemency. Yet, with this clemency they also introduced more phrases and images suggestive of
authority and order, and they elaborated on the woods scene to
show that Little Red Riding Hood wants to break from the moral

❋ 80 ❋

JACK ZIPES

restraints of her society to enjoy her own sensuality (inner nature) and nature's pleasures (outer nature). She is much more fully to blame for her rape by the wolf because she has a nonconformist streak which must be eradicated. But times had changed since Perrault, and the 19th-century moralists no longer argued for killing or burning heretics, especially not their own children. First they displayed the power of their authority in the form of the police, in this case the hunter-gamekeeper, and then they set an example of punishment using a misfit or outsider from the lower classes—that is, the wolf. Foucault has thoroughly outlined the panopticum principle of discipline and punishment in the 19th century, where a watchful eye is constantly on the alert for social deviates.[92] Thus, in the Grimms' tale, a policeman appears out of nowhere to save Little Red Riding Hood, and, when she is granted the opportunity to punish the wolf by filling his stomach with rocks, she is actually punishing herself. The sterile rocks in his stomach will also prevent her from rising and fulfilling her potential. As she carries out this punishment, she internalizes the restraining norms of sexuality in a political manner. The actual form of the fairy-tale narrative partakes in such repressive socialization.

It is impossible to exaggerate the impact and importance of the Little Red Riding Hood syndrome as a dominant cultural pattern in Western societies. In this regard, I want to stress that in her two most popular literary forms, which have fully captured the mass-mediated common imagination in our own day, Little Red Riding Hood is a male creation and projection. Not women but men—Perrault and the Brothers Grimm—gave birth to our common image of Little Red Riding Hood. "The point is," as Andrea Dworkin rightly maintains in her book *Woman Hating*:

> We have not formed that ancient world—it has formed us. We ingested it as children whole, had its values and consciousness imprinted on our minds as cultural absolutes long before we were in fact men and women. We have taken the fairy tales of childhood with us into maturity, chewed but still lying in the stomach, as real identity. Between Snow-white and her heroic prince, our two great fictions, we never did have much of a chance. At some point, the Great Divide took place: they (the boys) dreamed of mounting the Great Steed and buying Snow-white from the dwarfs; we (the girls) aspired to become that object of every necrophiliac's lust—the innocent, victimized Sleeping Beauty, beauteous lump of ultimate, sleeping good. Despite ourselves, sometimes unknowing, sometimes knowing, unwilling, unable to do otherwise, we act out the roles we were taught.[93]

Viewed in this light, *Little Red Riding Hood* reflects men's fear of women's sexuality—and of their own as well. The curbing and regulation of sexual drives is fully portrayed in this bourgeois literary fairy tale on the basis of deprived male needs. Red Riding Hood is to blame for her own rape. The wolf is not really a male but symbolizes natural urges and social nonconformity. The real hero of the tale, the hunter-gamekeeper, is male governance. If the tale has enjoyed such a widespread friendly reception in the Perrault and Grimm forms, then this can only be attributed to a general acceptance of the cultural notions of sexuality, sex roles, and domination embedded in it.

❀ 81 ❀
*The Trials
and
Tribulations
of Little Red
Riding Hood*

All this is not to say that the tale is outmoded and totally negative, that it should be censored by the women's movement and local school boards, or that it should be replaced by non-sexist versions. The problem is not in the literature, nor can it be solved through censorship. Given the conditions in Western society where women have been prey for men, there is a positive feature to the tale: its warning about the possibility of sexual molestation continues to serve a social purpose. At present, where I teach, women are forced to carry whistles (not a red cap) in the library and classroom buildings and on campus because of rape and violence, and this institution of academic learning is not an exception. Until men learn that they need not be wolves or gamekeepers to fulfill their lives, the tale offers a valuable lesson for young girls and women—albeit a lesson based on the perversion of sexuality.

As we have seen, signs of change have already been depicted in the radical *Little Red Riding Hood* adaptations of the 20th century. However, it took 200 years of hunting witches and werewolves to give birth to the traditional helpless Red Riding Hood and restrictive notions of sex and nature, then another 200 years to establish the proper bourgeois image of the obedient Red Riding Hood learning her lessons of discipline; it may take another 200 years for us to undo all the lessons Red Riding Hood, and the wolf as well, were forced to learn.

1. For the mythological interpretations of sunrise and sunset, see Hya-cinthe Husson, *La chaîne traditionelle* (Paris: Franck, 1874), p. 7; Franz Linnig, *Deutsche Mythenmärchen* (Paderborn: Schöningh, 1883), p. 184; Andrew Lang, *Myth, Ritual and Religion* (London: Longmans, Green, 1882); idem, *Perrault's Popular Tales* (London: Longmans, Green, 1888), p. lix; Hermann Zech, *Perrault's Contes de ma mère l'oye und die Grimmischen Märchen* (Stuttgart: Schulprogramm, 1906), p. 25; p. Saintyres, *Les Contes de Perrault et les récits parallèles* (Paris: Nourry, 1923), pp. 215–229; Henry Brett, *Nursery Rhymes and Tales* (Detroit, 1924), pp. 20–22.

2. See Macleod Yearsley, *The Folklore of Fairy Tales* (London: Watts, 1924), pp. 218–221. C. G. Jung uses this notion as the basis of his psychological interpretation to explain certain neuroses involving sexual intercourse. The wolf is the father, and the fear of being swallowed concerns fear of intercourse and conception. See Jung's "Versuch einer Darstellung der psychoanalytischen Theorie" (1913), in *Gesammelte Werke*, vol. 4 (Zurich: Rasch, 1971), p. 237. For a more Freudian approach, cf. Bruno Bettelheim, *The Uses of Enchantment* (New York: Knopf, 1976), pp. 166–183.

3. The mythological interpretations have helped to stimulate this notion and have often included it. See Lee Burns, "Red Riding Hood," *Children's Literature*, 1 ( 1972), p. 31. The depiction of the wolf as the absolute category of evil led racist folklorists in Germany to equate the beast with alien or racially inimical forces.

4. See Gottfried Henssen, "Deutsche Schreckmärchen und ihre europäischen Anverwandten," *Zeitschrift für Volkskunde*, 51 ( 1953), pp. 84–97; and Marianne Rumpf, "Ursprung und Entstehung von Warn- und Schreckmärchen," *FF Communications*, 160 (1955), pp. 3–16.

5. In addition to Rumpf's significant essay "Ursprung und Entstehung von Warn- und Schreckmärchen," see her doctoral dissertation *Rotkäppchen: Eine vergleichende Märchenuntersuchung*. University of Göttingen, 1951, and "Caterinella: Ein italienisches Warnmärchen," *Fabula*, 1 (1957), pp. 76–84.

6. "Les conres merveilleux de Perrault et la tradition populaire," *Bulletin folklorique d'Ile-de-France* (1951), pp. 221–228, 251–260, 283–291; (1953), pp. 511–517; "Le Petit Chaperon Rouge," *Le Conte Populaire Français*, vol. I (Paris: Erasme, 1957), pp. 373–383.

7. "Le Petit Chaperon Rouge," *Nouvelle Revue Française*, 16 (1968), pp. 429–443; and "From Tales of Warning to Formulettes: The Oral

Tradition in French Children's Literature," *Yale French Studies*, 43 (1969), pp. 2–3.

8. See Elliott O'Donnell, *Werwolves* (London: Methuen, 1912), pp. 110–125; and Montague Summers, *The Werewolf* (New York: Dutton, 1934), pp. 217–241.

9. Cf. Leubuscher, *Ueber die Wehrwolfe und die Thierverwandlungen im Mittelalter* (Berlin: Reimer, 1850); and Wilhelm Hertz, *Der Werwolf* (Stuttgart: Kröner, 1862).

10. This case has been repeatedly documented in histories of werewolves. See Summers, *The Werewolf*, pp. 223–225.

11. Cf. Soriano, "Le petit chaperon rouge," pp. 429–43. See also Soriano's excellent critical biography, *Les Contes de Perrault: Culture savante et traditions populaires* (Paris: Gallimard, 1968).

12. Soriano, "From Tales of Warning," pp. 27–28.

13. See "Conte de la mère grande," in Delarue, *Le Conte Populaire Français*, pp. 373–74.

14. A slightly different version translated by Austin E. Fife can be found in Paul Delarue, ed., *The Borzoi Book of French Folk Tales* (New York: Knopf, 1956), pp. 230–232.

15. Henssen, "Deutsche Schreckmärchen."

16. "Grand-mères, sie vous saviez: le Petit Chaperon Rouge dans la tradition orale," *Cahiers de Littérature Orale*, 4 (1978), pp. 17–55.

17. Ibid., pp. 43–44.

18. "Le Petit Chaperon Rouge," *Le Conte Populaire Français*, p. 383.

19. *A Social History of Family Life* (New York: Knopf, 1962). See also his essay "At the Point of Origin," *Yale French Studies*, 43 (1969), pp. 15–23.

20. The use of a red sign or hat to stigmatize social nonconformists or outcasts was common throughout the Middle Ages and Reformation. For instance, Venetia Newall in her article "The Jew as a Witch Figure" reports that Jews in Central Europe were obliged to wear a Judenhut in the later Middle Ages. "This was a special hat, usually red, the brim shaped to resemble a pair of horns. The demoniacal implications of this item of headgear need not be enlarged upon, and there is additional evidence of alleged links between satanism and Jewry." See *The Witch Figure*, ed. Venetia Newall (London: Routledge & Kegan Paul, 1973), p. 104. In France and Germany Jews were supposed to appear in mystery plays wearing satanic pointed caps. Sidney Oldall Addy has also recorded that in parts of England witches were

> dressed exactly like fairies. They wear a red mantle and hood, which covers the whole body. They always wear these hoods. An old woman living at Holmesfield, in the parish of Dronfield, in Derbyshire, who wore "one of those hoods called

'little red riding hoods,' used to be called the old witch." The favourite meeting-places of witches are cross-ways, or "four lane ends," or toll-bars, where they bewitch people.

See *Folk Tales and Superstitions* (London: E.P. Publishing, 1973), pp. 70–71, a reprint of the 1895 edition. The connection between the devil, Jews, werewolves, witches, and fairies with Little Red Riding Hood will be made clearer later in this Introduction.

21. Cf. Mary Elizabeth Storer, *La Mode des contes des fées* (1685–1700) (Paris: Champion, 1928).

22. Charles Perrault, *Contes*, ed. Gilbert Rouger (Paris: Garnier, 1967), p. 89.

23. Cf. Marc Soriano, *Les Contes de Perrault, Culture savante et traditions populaires* (Paris: Gallimard, 1968), and *Le Dossier Perrault* (Paris: Hachette, 1972).

24. *The Civilizing Process: The History of Manners*, vol. 1, trans. Edmund Jephcott (New York: Urizen, 1978), p. 36.

25. Ibid., pp. 59–143.

26. Ibid., p. 108.

27. Paris: Minard, 1978, p. 40.

28. For one of the best accounts of the historical development of *Little Red Riding Hood*, see Harry B. Weiss, *Little Red Riding Hood: A Terror Tale of the Nursery* (Trenton: Privately Printed, 1939). See also "Die Verbreitung der Perraultschen Märchen," in Marianne Rumpf's dissertation *Rotkäppchen: Eine vergleichende Märchenuntersuchung*, University of Göttingen, 1951, pp. 92–94; and Paul Tesdorpf; *Beiträge zur Würdigung Charles Perraults und seiner Märchen* (Stuttgart: Kohlhammer, 1910).

29. Cf. *Die älteste Märchensammlung der Bruder Grimm* (Cologny-Genève: Fondation Martin Bodmer, 1975), pp. 390–392.

30. Ibid., p. 391.

31. "The Influence of Charles Perrault's *Contes de ma Mère L'Oie* on German Folklore," *Germanic Review*, 5 (1930), pp. 4–18. See also Lilyane Mourey, *Introduction aux contes de Grimm et de Perrault* (Paris: Minard, 1978), pp. 31–35, 52–55.

32. *The History of Sexuality* (New York: Pantheon, 1978), p. 104.

33. "Trägt Rotkäppchen eine Jakobiner-Mütze? Über mutmaßliche Konnotate bei Tieck und Grimm," in *Literatursoziologie*, ed. Joachim Bark, vol. 2 (Stuttgart: Kohlhammer, 1974), pp. 159–180.

34. Ibid., p. 175.

35. Cf. Rumpf, *Rotkäppchen*, pp. 92–105.

36. See Carole and D. T. Hanks, "Perrault's 'Little Red Riding Hood': Victim of Revision," *Children's Literature*, 7 (1978), pp. 68–77.

❦ 85 ❦

The Trials
and
Tribulations
of Little Red
Riding Hood

37. See Lutz Röhrich, "Zwolfmal Rotkäppchen," in *Gebärden—Metapher—Parodie* (Düsseldorf: Schwann, 1967), pp. 130–152.

38. Aside from Charles Marelle's *La Veritable Histoire du Petit Chaperon d'or* (1888), which I shall discuss, see Armand Legrand, Junien Champeaux, and Auguste Gombault, *Le Petit Chaperon Rouge: Conte en Action* (Paris: Duvernois, 1823); Ernest Blum and Raoul Toché, *Le Petit Chaperon Rouge: Operette en trois actes* (*Musique de Gaston Serpette*) (Paris: Choudens, 1885); and E. Baneux, *Le Petit Chaperon Rouge* (Paris: Libraire Théatrale, 1888).

39. For the French text, see *Le Petit Chaperon rouge, Opera-feerie, en Trois Actes et en Prose*, de M. T. Théaulon (Paris: C. Ballard, 1818). For the English translation, see *The Little Red Riding Hood*, trans. W. F. F. (Baltimore: E. J. Coale, 1831).

40. See E. van Heurck and G.J. Boekenoogen, *Histoire de l'Imagerie populaire flammande* (Brussels: Oest, 1910) and A. van Gennep, "Remarques sur l'Imagerie populaire," *Revue d'Ethnographie et de Sociologie*, 2 (1911), pp. 26–50.

41. *The Red Fairy Book* (London: Longmans, Green, 1890), pp. 215–219.

42. *Fairy Stories and Fables* (New York: American Book Co., 1898), pp. 38–44.

43. See the notes and afterword by Walter Scherf in Ludwig Bechstein, *Sämtliche Märchen* (Darmstadt: Wissenschaftliche Buchgesellschaft, 1970), pp. 779–871.

44. "Das Rothkäppchen" in *Märchen nach Perrault* (Stuttgart: Halberger, 1869), p. 4.

45. There is a discussion of both the anonymous Gothic version and Bayley's tale in Harry B. Weiss, *Little Red Riding Hood: A Terror Tale of the Nursery* (Trenton: Privately Printed, 1939).

46. See Harry B. Weiss, *A Forgotten Version of Little Red Riding Hood* (New York: New York Public Library, 1950).

47. Foucault, *The History of Sexuality*, pp. 120–21.

48. *Red Riding Hood*, verse adaptation, c. 1890, reprinted by Merrimack Publishing Corp., New York, 1979.

49. Ibid.

50. Baring-Gould wrote numerous books dealing with folklore. Aside from the adaptation of Perrault's tale, he wrote a more literal translation of the Grimms' *Little Red Cap* in *Fairy Tales from Grimm* (London: Wells Gardner, Darton, 1894). He also wrote one of the first sober histories of werewolves in English. See *The Book of Were-Wolves: Being an Account of a Terrible Superstition* (London: Smith, Elder, 1865).

51. *A Book of Fairy Tales*, 2d ed. (London: Methuen, 1895), p. 55.

52. See *Little Red Riding-Hood: An Operetta for Juveniles* in Harrison Millard, *Silver Threads of Song for School and Home* (New York: S. T. Gordon, 1875), pp. 125–151.

53. Ibid., p. 148.

54. *Star Nursery Rhymes* (Zanesville, Ohio: Schultz, c. 1895), p. 3.

55. *Märchendeutungen durch Runen* (Hellerau bei Dresden: Hakenkreuz Verlag, 1925), pp. 28–32.

56. Ibid., pp. 28-29.

57. Cf. *Von der Weisheit unserer Märchen* (Berlin, 1942). See also Georg Schott, *Weissagung und Erfullung im Deutschen Volksmärchen* (Munich: Hermann A. Wiechmann, 1925); and Josef Prestl, *Märchen als Lebensdichtung* (Munich: Max Hueber, 1938).

58. Fasching edition of the *Münchner Neueste Nachrichten*, entitled the *Münchner Netteste Nachrichten* (1937). Reprinted in Röhrich, *Gebärde—Metapher—Parodie*, pp. 137–38.

59. Link constantly parodied the fascist bureaucracy and official organizations which controlled the daily lives of the Germans. Here Little Red Cap is referred to as a *BDM-Mädel*. The *Bund Deutscher Mädel* was a Hitler Youth Group.

60. The *Mutterheim der National Sozialistischer Vereinigung* was a type of convalescent home where women went to rest, recuperate, and reside.

61. *Das Amt für Schönheit der Holzarbeit* was Link's designation for the ministry of forestry.

62. *Kreisjäger* was Link's designation for a forest ranger.

63. *"Kraft durch Freude"* (KdF) was a slogan invented by the Nazis to stimulate the workers so that they would work harder. This slogan became the name of a recreational organization that provided cruises in the Mediterranean, among other things. Thus, Link refers to a Kdf-Dampfer.

64. Cf. Cornelia Meigs, ed., *A Critical History of Children's Literature*, rev. ed. (New York: Macmillan, 1969), pp. 446–483.

65. *Fables for Our Time* (New York: Harper, 1939), p. 5.

66. Cf. Irina H. Cotten, "Evgenii Shvarts as an Adapter of Hans Christian Andersen and Charles Perrault," *Russian Review*, 37 (1978), pp. 51–67. Floh de Cologne, a German political rock group, has adapted the play with music and made an excellent recording of their production. See Floh de Cologne, "Rotkäppchen. Ein Märchen mit viel Rock und Pop für kleine und grosse Kinder," Pläne K20905.

67. Boston: Beacon, 1955, 1964.

68. New York: Pantheon, 1967.

69. See Wilhelm Reich, *The Sexual Revolution*, 4th ed. rev., trans. Theodore P. Wolfe (New York: Farrar, Straus & Giroux, 1970); and *Sex-Pol Essays 1919–1934*, trans. Anna Bostock, Tom Du Bose, and Lee Baxandall (New York: Vintage, 1972); and Paul A. Robinson, *The Freudian Left* (New York: Harper, 1969).

❦ 87 ❦
The Trials
and
Tribulations
of Little Red
Riding Hood

70. Cf. Jürgen Habermas, *Legitimation Crisis*, trans. Thomas McCarthy (Boston: Beacon, 1975).

71. *Contes à l'envers* (Paris: L'Ecole des loisirs, 1977), p. 26.

72. For other Chinese variations, see Isabelle C. Chang, "The Chinese Red Riding Hoods," in *Chinese Fairy Tales* (New York: Barre, 1965).

73. For example, see *Le petit chaperon rouge* (Paris: Editions R.S.T., 1973) with illustrations by Elisabeth and Gerry Embleton and printed in several different languages.

74. *The History of Sexuality*, pp. 135–139. See also Stephan Chorover, *From Genesis to Genocide: The Meaning of Human Nature and the Power of Behavior Control* (Cambridge: MIT Press, 1979).

75. See Michael Jacoby, *Wargus, vargr. 'Verbrecher' 'Wolf'* (Uppsala: Almquist & Wiksell, 1974).

76. *Traumzeit: Über die Grenze zwischen Wildnis und Zivilisation* (Frankfurt am Main: Syndikat, 1978), p. 108.

77. Cf. Müller, *Die Werwolfsage*, pp. 47–51; and Summers, *The Werewolf*, pp. 1–132.

78. "The European Witch-Craze," in *Religion, the Reformation and Social Change* (London: Macmillan, 1967), p. 102.

79. Paris, 1622, pp. 446–501.

80. *Die Werwolfsage*, pp. 47–48.

81. Cf. Jules Michelet, *La Sorcière* (Paris: Garnier-Flammarion, 1966), reprint of 1862 ed. Joseph Hansen, *Zauberwahn, Inquisition und Hexenprozess im Mittelalter* (Munich: Oldenburg, 1900); Robert Mandrou, *Magistrats et sorciers en France au XVIIe Siècle* (Paris: Plon, 1968); Alan Macfarlane, *Witchcraft in Tudor and Stuart England* (London: Routledge & Kegan Paul, 1970); Keith Thomas, *Religion and the Decline of Magic* (London: Weidenfeld & Nicolson, 1970); Jeanne Favret, "Sorcières et Lumières," *Critique*, 27 (1971), 351–376; Jeffrey Burton Russell, *Witchcraft in the Middle Ages* (Ithaca: Cornell Univ. Press, 1972); Gabriele Becker et. al. *Aus der Zeit der Verzweiflung: Zur Genese und Aktualität des Hexenbildes* (Frankfurt am Main: Suhrkamp, 1977).

82. Cf. Trever-Roper, "The European Witch-Craze," pp. 126–128.

83. *Die Hexen der Neuzeit* (Frankfurt am Main: Suhrkamp, 1978), pp. 61–62.

84. Ibid., pp. 89–90.

85. See William Leiss, *The Domination of Nature* (Boston: Beacon, 1972).

86. *Die Hexen der Neuzeit*, p. 91.

87. Max Weber, *The Protestant Ethic and the Spirit of Capitalism*, trans. Talcott Parsons (New York: Scribner, 1958). See also R.H. Tawney, *Religion and the Rise of Capitalism* (New York: Harcourt, Brace, 1926).

88. *The History of Sexuality*, p. 3.

89. Cf. James Robinson Planché, *Encyclopedia of Costume*, vol. 1 (London: Chatto & Windus, 1876), pp. 241–294; Carl Köhler, *A History of Costume* (London: Harrap, 1928), pp. 163–178; Francois Boucher, *20,000 Years of Fashion* (New York: Abrams, 1967), pp. 531–700.

90. Earlier I discussed the significance of the red hat in relation to Jews, witches, werewolves, and the devil. It is difficult to determine exactly why Perrault used the color red, but we do know that it was associated with witches and the devil in his time. In discussing the initiation ritual of witches, Andrea Dworkin points out:

> Once the neophyte made the decision for the horned god, she went through a formal initiation, often conducted at the sabbat. The ceremony was simple. The initiate declared that she was joining the coven of her own free will and swore devotion to the master of the coven who represented the horned god. She was then marked with some kind of tattoo which was called the witches' mark. The inflicting of the tattoo was painful, and the healing process was long. When healed the scar was red or blue and indelible. One method particularly favored by the witch hunters when hunting was to take a suspected woman, shave her pubic and other bodily hair (including head hair, eyebrows, etc.) and, upon finding any scar, find her guilty of witchcraft." See *Woman Hating* (New York: Dutton, 1974), pp. 142–43. Suspected women not possessing such a mark would be given one, such as the scarlet letter "A." Even redheads, natural redheads, were suspected for a long time of being in league with the devil or the offspring of the devil. The famous Austrian playwright Johann Nestroy wrote an entire play about the difficulties encountered by redheads. See *Der Talisman* (1840).

91. See W. W. Pusey, *Louis-Sebastien Mercier in Germany: His Vogue and Influence in the Eighteenth Century* (New York: Columbia Univ. Press, 1939); and Henry Majewski, *The Preromantic Imagination of L. S. Mercier* (New York: Humanities Press, 1971).

92. See *Discipline and Punish: The Birth of the Prison* (New York: Pantheon, 1978).

93. *Woman Hating*, p. 33. Cf. Kay Stone, "Things Walt Disney Never Told Us," in *Women and Folklore*, ed. Claire R. Farrer (Austin: Univ. of Texas Press, 1975), pp. 42–50; and Madonna Kolbenschlag, *Kiss Sleeping Beauty Good-Bye* (New York: Doubleday, 1979).

# ❦ *Notes on the Texts* ❦

THE VERSIONS OF *Little Red Riding Hood/Little Red Cap* presented on the following pages are intended to offer the reader a chronological and comprehensive overview of the literary tradition that has made the girl and wolf constellation famous in France, Germany, Great Britain, and the United States. Two versions, from Italy and China, have been included to show how experimentation with the content of the tale has spread. Other interesting *Red Riding Hood* versions are noted in the Introduction, but they were either unavailable, repetitious, or too lengthy to include in this anthology.

Unless otherwise indicated, all translations are my work. In my translations of the original stories by Perrault and the Brothers Grimm I have endeavored to be as literal as possible without losing the flavor of the different styles. Perrault's verse *moralité* has been set in prose to convey his message as exactly as possible. Although we know that *chaperon* does not mean "riding hood," I have followed the English custom of using "riding hood" in the translations, with the exception of the German tales. There I make a distinction by consistently translating *Käppchen* as "cap."

At the end of the collection of tales appears a Bibliography of Red Riding Hood Texts, arranged chronologically. My focus has been on France, Germany, Great Britain, and the United States because it seemed to me that the development in these countries was paradigmatic for the way people in the West have come to look at sexuality, sex roles, and socialization. Red Riding Hood is a pervasive sign. You can find the constellation of the little girl and the wolf on television, billboards, restaurant marquees and menus, postcards, posters, games, and toys, and in newspapers, magazines, cartoons, and films. The signification of the constellation always depends on the socio-historical context and the cultural struggle of the sexes over social roles. In their present context I hope that the

*Red Riding Hood* tales indicate clearly how and why the constellation originated. Perhaps readers will even be provoked to try their hands at changing fairy tales like *Little Red Riding Hood*, as such tales pass through their lives as part of the civilizing process.

# Little Red
# Riding Hood

## By Charles Perrault

## (1697)

O NCE UPON A TIME there was a little village girl, the prettiest that had ever been seen. Her mother doted on her, and her grandmother even more. This good woman made her a little red hood which suited her so well that she was called Little Red Riding Hood wherever she went.

One day, after her mother had baked some biscuits, she said to Little Red Riding Hood: "Go see how your grandmother is feeling, for I have heard that she is sick. Take her some biscuits and this small pot of butter." Little Red Riding Hood departed at once to visit her grandmother, who lived in another village. In passing through a wood she met old neighbor wolf, who had a great desire to eat her. But he did not dare because of some woodcutters who were in the forest. He asked her where she was going. The poor child, who did not know that is dangerous to stop and listen to a wolf, said to him: "I am going to see my grandmother, and I am bringing some biscuits with a small pot of butter which my mother has sent her."

"Does she live far from here?" asked the wolf.

"Oh, yes!" said Little Red Riding Hood. "You must pass the mill which you can see right over there, and hers is the first house in the village."

"Well, then," said the wolf. "I want to go and see her, too. I'll take this path here, and you take that path there, and we'll see who'll get there first."

**Jean Boullet, *La Belle et la Bête,* Paris: Le Terrain Vague, 1958. Illustration ca. 1890 taken from Collection Boullet.**

The wolf began to run as fast as he could on the path which was shorter, and the little girl took the longer path, and she enjoyed herself by gathering nuts, running after butterflies, and making bouquets of small flowers which she found. It did not take the wolf long to arrive at the grandmother's house. He knocked: Toc, toc.

"Who's there?"

"It's your granddaughter, Little Red Riding Hood," said the wolf, disguising his voice, "I've brought you some biscuits and a little pot of butter which my mother has sent you."

The good grandmother, who was in her bed because she was not feeling well, cried out to him: "Pull the bobbin, and the latch will fall."

The wolf pulled the bobbin, and the door opened. He threw himself upon the good woman and devoured her quicker than a wink, for it had been more than three days since he had last eaten. After that he closed the door and lay down in the grandmother's bed to wait for Little Red Riding Hood, who after awhile came knocking at the door. Toc, toc.

"Who's there?"

When she heard the gruff voice of the wolf, Little Red Riding Hood was scared at first, but, believing that her grandmother had a cold, she responded: "It's your granddaughter, Little Red Riding

Hood. I've brought you some biscuits and a little pot of butter which my mother has sent you.

The wolf softened his voice and cried out to her: "Pull the bobbin, and the latch will fall."

Little Red Riding Hood pulled the bobbin, and the door opened. Upon seeing her enter, the wolf hid himself under the bedcovers and said to her: "Put the biscuits and the pot of butter on the bin and come lie down beside me."

Little Red Riding Hood undressed and went to get into bed, where she was quite astonished to see the way her grandmother was dressed in her nightgown. She said to her: "What big arms you have, grandmother!"

"The better to hug you with, my child."

"What big legs you have, grandmother!"

"The better to run with, my child."

"What big ears you have, grandmother!"

"The better to hear you with, my child."

"What big eyes you have, grandmother!"

"The better to see you with, my child."

"What big teeth you have, grandmother!"

"The better to eat you."

And upon saying these words, the wicked wolf threw himself upon Little Red Riding Hood and ate her up.

### MORAL

One sees here that young children,
Especially young girls,
Pretty, well brought-up, and gentle,
Should never listen to anyone who happens by,
And if this occurs, it is not so strange
When the wolf should eat them.
I say the wolf, for all wolves
Are not of the same kind.
There are some with winning ways,
Not loud, nor bitter, or angry,
Who are tame, good-natured, and pleasant
And follow young ladies
Right into their homes, right into their alcoves.
But alas for those who do not know that of all the wolves
the docile ones are those who are most dangerous.

# ❊ 2 ❊

## *The Little Red Riding Hood*

## *By Robert Samber*

## (1729)

THERE WAS ONCE UPON A TIME a little country girl, born in a village, the prettiest little creature that ever was seen. Her mother was beyond reason excessively fond of her, and her grandmother yet much more. This good woman caused to be made for her a little red Riding-Hood; which made her look so very pretty, that every body call'd her, *The little red Riding-Hood.*

One day, her mother having made some custards, said to her, Go my little *Biddy,* for her christian name was *Biddy,* go and see how your grandmother does, for I hear she has been very ill, carry her a custard, and this little pot of butter. *The little red Riding-Hood* set out immediately to go to her grandmother, who lied in another village. As she was going through the wood, she met with *Gossop Wolfe,* who had a good mind to eat her up, but he did not dare, because of some faggot-makers that were in the forest.

He asked of her whither she was going: The poor child, who did not know how dangerous a thing it is to stay and hear a Wolfe talk, said to him, I am going to see my grandmamma, and carry her a custard pye, and a little pot of butter my mamma sends her. Does she live far off? said the Wolfe. Oh! ay, said *the little red Riding-Hood,* on the other side of the mill below yonder, at the first house in the village. Well, said the Wolfe, and I'll go and see her too; I'll go this way, and go you that, and we shall see who will be there soonest.

The Wolfe began to run as fast as he was able, the shortest way; and the little girl went the longest, diverting her self in gathering nuts, running after butterflies, and making nose-gays of all the little flowers she met with. The Wolfe was not long before he came to the grandmother's house; he knocked at the door *toc toc*. Whose there? Your granddaughter, *The little red Riding-Hood*, said the Wolfe, counterfeiting her voice, who has brought you a custard pye, and a little pot of butter mamma sends you.

The good grandmother, who was in bed, because she found herself somewhat ill, cried out, Pull the bobbin, and the latch will go up. The Wolfe pull'd the bobbin, and the door open'd; upon which he fell upon the good woman, and eat her up in the tenth part of a moment; for he had eaten nothing for above three days before. After that he shut the door, and went into the grandmother's bed, expecting *the little red Riding-Hood*, who came some time afterwards, and knock'd at the door *toc, toc, Who's there? The little red Riding-Hood*, who hearing the big voice of the Wolfe, was at first afraid; but believing her grandmother had got a cold, and was grown hoarse, said, it is your granddaughter, *The little red Riding-Hood*, who has brought you a custard pye, and a little pot of butter mamma sends you. The Wolfe cried out to her softening his voice as much as he could. Pull the bobbin, and the latch will go up. The *little red Riding-Hood* pull'd the bobbin, and the door opened.

The Wolfe seeing her come in, said to her, hiding himself under the clothes. Put the custard, and the little pot of butter upon the stool, and come into bed to me. *The little red Riding-Hood* undressed her self, and went into bed, where she was very much astonished to see how her grandmother looked in her night-cloaths: So she said to her, Grandmamma, *what great arms you have got!* It is the better to embrace thee my pretty child. Grandmamma, *what great legs you have got!* It is to run the better my child. Grandmamma, *what great ears you have got!* It is to hear the better my child. Grandmamma, *what great teeth you have got!* It is to eat thee up. And upon saying these words, this wicked Wolfe fell upon *the little red Riding-Hood*, and eat her up.

THE MORAL

*From this short story easy we discern
What conduct all young people ought to learn.
But above all, the growing ladies fair,*

ROBERT
SAMBER

*Whose orient rosy Blooms begin t'appear:*
*Who, Beauties in the fragrant spring of age!*
*With pretty airs young hearts are apt t'engage.*
*Ill do they listen to all sorts of tongues,*
*Since some enchant and lure like Syrens songs.*
*No wonder therefore 'tis if overpowr'd,*
*So many of them has the Wolfe devour'd.*
*The Wolfe, I say, for Wolves too sure there are*
*Of every sort, and every character.*
*Some of them mild and gentle-humour'd be*
*Of noise and gall, and rancour wholly free;*
*Who tame, familiar, full of complaisance;*
*Ogle and leer, languish, cajole and glance;*
*With luring tongues, and language wondrous sweet,*
*Follow young ladies as they walk the street,*
*Ev'n to their very houses and bedside,*
*And though their true designs they artful hide,*
*Yet ah! these simpring Wolves, who does not see*
*Most dang'rous of all Wolves in fact to be?*

## 3

# The Story of
# Little Red
# Riding Hood

## Anonymous

## (1796)

T HERE LIVED IN A CERTAIN VILLAGE, a little country girl, the prettiest creature that ever was seen, and so very good withal, that her mother was exceedingly fond of her; and her grandmother doated on her much more. This good woman got made for her a little red riding hood to go to school in the winter, which became the girl so extremely well that every body called her Little Red Riding Hood.

One day her mother having made some custards, said to her, "Go, my dear, and see how thy grand-mamma does, for I hear she was very ill; carry her a custard and this little pot of butter." Little Red Riding Hood being always ready to obey her mamma, set out immediately, and going thro' the woods met with Gossop Wolf, who had a very great mind to eat her up, but he durst not because of some faggot-makers who were at work hard bye in the forest, and the poor child, who did not know it was dangerous to hear a wolf talk, said to him, "I am going to see my grand-mamma, and carry her a custard and a little pot of butter, from my mamma." Does she live far off? said the Wolf. Oh, ay, answer'd little red riding hood, it is beyond that mill you see there, at the first house. Well, said the Wolf, I'll go this way, and do you go that, and we shall see who will be there soonest.

The Wolf began to run as fast as he could, taking the nearest way, and the little girl went by the farthest about, diverting herself in gathering nuts, running after butterflies, & making nose-gays of such flowers as she met with. The Wolf was not long before he had got to the old woman's house; he knocked at the door, tap, tap. Who's there? Your grand child, Little Red Riding Hood, replied the wolf, counterfeiting her voice, who has brought you a custard and a little pot of butter, sent you from mamma.

The good grandmother, who was in bed, because she found herself somewhat ill, cried out, pull the bobbin; and the latch will go up. The Wolf pulled the bobbin and the door opened, and then presently he fell upon the good woman, and eat her up in a moment, for it was above three days that he had not touched a bit. He then shut the door, and went into the grandmother's bed expecting Little Red Riding Hood, who came some time afterwards and knocked at the door, tap, tap. Who's there? Little Red Riding Hood, hearing the big voice of the Wolf, was at first afraid, but believing her grandmother had a cold, and was hoarse, answered, 'Tis your grand child, Little Red Riding Hood, who has brought you a custard and a little pot of butter mamma sends you. The Wolf cried out to her, softening his voice as much as he could. Pull the bobbin and the latch will go up. Little Red Riding Hood pulled the bobbin, and the door opened.

The wolf seeing her come in, said to her, hiding himself under the bed cloathes, put the custard and the little pot of butter upon the stool, and lie down by me. Little Red Riding Hood undressed herself, and went into bed where being amazed to see how her grandmother looked in her night cloathes, said to her, grandmamma, what great arms you have got? That is the better to hug thee my dear. Grandmamma, what great ears you have got? That is to hear better. What great eyes.you have got? It is to see the better my child. Grandmamma, what great teeth you have got? That is to eat thee up: And saying these words, the wicked wolf fell upon poor Little Red Riding Hood and eat her all up.

And was not he a very naughty wolf, to kill such a pretty little creature?

# ❋ 4 ❋

## The Life and Death
## of Little Red Riding Hood:
## A Tragedy

### By Ludwig Tieck

### (1800)

Adapted from the German
by Jane Browning Smith 1852

PROLOGUE
Spoken by Hans-Wurst*

MY DEAR LITTLE CHILDREN, instead of a story,
I am quite well aware that some people would bore ye
With knowledge of FACTS, for they think it must please
A good child to be told that the butter and cheese
Are made of cow's milk, that the table is hard,
His little hand soft, or that paper and card
Were once nothing but rags. On a higher flight yet
I have know some young imps in the nursery set,
Of steam-engines prattle, and e'en mathematics!
Or hang a thermometer out of their attics,
And tell you they're studying meteorology!
For that very long word I must make an apology.
In the world, soon or late, you will find hard reality—
But in childhood, at least, let us have ideality;
And perhaps it is true that the happiest are those
Who, in this sense, are children until their life's close.
Now should anyone ask if our play has morality,

*The German Jack-Pudding.

*The Sleeping Beauty in the Wood & Little Red Riding Hood,* London:
Dean & Munday, ca. 1830. Illustrator unknown.

I must say a few words just to prove its legality.
The Wolf is a villain—that everyone knows—
But still his soliloquy palpably shows
That the very worst mortals much better would be
If we gave, with out good advice, kind sympathy.
That the pious old Grandmother should be the prey
Of so cruel a monster afflicts me, and yet,
Being ready to go, I can only regret
That her exit is made in so shocking a way.
I grieve, too, for the grandchild, and all I can say is
That such, upon earth, very often the way is:
Death plucks the young flower—no doubt meant to show us
That there's something *above* us as well as below us—
And my last picture tells, though Red Ridinghood dies,
Like a sweet little cherub she mounts to the skies,
Borne aloft by the birds and the bright butterflies.
Thus, if upon earth you should have tribulation,
Just look up above and you'll find consolation.
But I see you're impatient the play should begin;
The curtain draws up—let the actors come in.

Persons of the Drama

❋ 101 ❋

*The Life
and Death
of
Little Red
Riding
Hood*

| Human | Brute |
|---|---|
| Little Red Ridinghood | The Wolf |
| The Grandmother | The Dog |
| The Huntsman | The Cuckoo |
| Jenny | The Nightingale |
| Peter | First Robin Redbreast |
| Peter's Bride | Second Robin Redbreast |
| A Peasant | |

## SCENE I.

*Time—Sunday Morning. Interior Of The Cottage.
The* Grandmother *Sits In Her Armchair Reading.*

#### Grandmother.

What a fine sunshiny day!
'Twould make a very heathen pray,
And fills the pious heart with love
And gratitude to God above.
The flowers seem to breathe a prayer,
And I could almost think I hear
Hymns of thanksgiving from the trees
As they bend rustling to the breeze.
The bells are ringing now—quite near
They sound at times, because the air
Is this way blowing. Were it so,
How gladly I to church would go!
But this is such a long way off—
And I so lame, besides a cough,
Which will always come when it should not—
I wish with all my heart it would not.
But though I stay at home, I read
The blessed Prayer-book and the Creed;
The good Lord takes the will for the deed.

[*She reads a little while, then grows drowsy, yawns and shuts the book.*

Alack! Alack! This is the way
With us poor sinners made of clay.
My daughter Betty baked last night;

The little lass, if I guess right,
Will soon be here. Can that be she?
Or is't the wind that stirs the tree.

[*The door opens gently, and* LITTLE RED RIDINGHOOD *comes in.*

RED RIDINGHOOD.
Good morning, Granny! How d'ye do?

GRANDMOTHER.
Thank you, my darling,—but so, so.

RED RIDINGHOOD.
I came quite softly in for fear
I should disturb you, Granny dear!
I would not even give a tap,
Lest I should wake you from your nap.

GRANDMOTHER.
I haven't been asleep, my bird,
But reading in God's Holy Word.

RED RIDINGHOOD.
You are so pious! But, see here!
What mother sends; the largest share
Of a great cake she made last night.

[*She takes the cake from her basket.*

GRANDMOTHER.
Bless me! That is a pretty sight!
And where's your mother gone to-day?
Your father, too? They would not stay
At home, I guess, this charming weather.

RED RIDINGHOOD.
O, they are gone to church together.
The organ, as I came along,
I heard—and how the chaunters sung!
The church is very full to-day;
The Curate's sick, as people say

And so the Rector preaches. He
Expounds the scriptures cleverly!
How nice your room looks—you have strew'd
Fresh sand.

❀ 103 ❀

*The Life
and Death
of
Little Red
Riding
Hood*

GRANDMOTHER.

'Tis Sunday, and one should
Be clean and neat upon that day;
How else would Christian folk, I pray,
Be known from Infidels or Jews!

RED RIDINGHOOD.

I too have got on my new shoes,
A clean frock; and I don't forget
The pretty hood you gave your pet
Last Christmas eve. They say that hood
For every day is much too good;
But I must have it on my head,
No colour looks so well as red!

GRANDMOTHER.

True, pretty one; it suits thee too.
Red Ridinghood thou'rt call'd, I hear;
So wear it while it's fresh and new,
And when it's worn out, never fear,
We'll find another far or near.

RED RIDINGHOOD.

Yes; when I go to confirmation
You'll give me one. A fine sensation
My brave red hood will cause I trow!

GRANDMOTHER.

Hush, naughty child! it is not so
That you must speak of holy things;
Such vanity no blessing brings.
A close white coif is what they wear,
Deem'd worthy in that rite to share.
And such the cap that I shall give,
If God should grant me grace to live
To see thee at his table kneeling;

But that's not likely—I've a feeling
My sand is well nigh run. . . .

                    RED RIDINGHOOD.
Nay, nay!
Such things as that you must not say.

                    GRANDMOTHER.
Time goes—Death comes. To stand or fall
We're in His hands who made us all.
I may be near my end. . . .

                    RED RIDINGHOOD.
No, no!
Dear Granny, pray don't grieve me so.
Next time I come here I will bring
My little dog—a pretty thing!
'Twill make you merry—then you'll stay
And play with us—not go away.

                    GRANDMOTHER.
My child, we're never sure a day
How near we are to death—the rather
When he seems farthest. How's your father?

                    RED RIDINGHOOD.
His legs are swell'd; one knee so bad
He scarce can walk.

                    GRANDMOTHER.
That's very sad!
He should take something for it, child.

                    RED RIDINGHOOD.
All sorts of things he tries, and grows
No whit the better. People think,
And say too, that it comes from drink.

                    GRANDMOTHER.
Hush, hush, girl! It is never well
For children of such things to tell.

RED RIDINGHOOD.
*[taking some wild-flowers from the pocket of her apron.*

Dear me! I had almost forgot
These pretty flowers; not a spot
In all the wood but there they sprung
Out peeping, and the thickets rung
With songs of birds.

GRANDMOTHER.
Poor flowers! they
Are almost wither'd. Well-a-day!
Thou wert and art a thoughtless thing.

RED RIDINGHOOD.
They would just in the footpath spring;
I couldn't choose but pluck them. Hark!

*[A dog barks.*

What makes that dog so fiercely bark?

GRANDMOTHER.
I'm told a wolf some days ago
Was lurking hereabouts; if so,
They hunt him perhaps.

RED RIDINGHOOD.
'Tis pleasant here
To have the wood so thick and near
Against the window. I can see
The little birds, from tree to tree,
Go hopping, singing, blythe and gay;
Don't you love them, Granny?—Say.

GRANDMOTHER.
I do; by dawn they're all awake,
And such a merry music make
In the green wood, one's very heart
Seems ready to one's lips to start.

RED RIDINGHOOD.
What tree is that, for ever quaking?
Its leaves, without a breath, are shaking.

GRANDMOTHER.

The aspen-tree.

RED RIDINGHOOD.

There is a word
About that tree I've often heard—
"To tremble like an aspen bough."
Why does it tremble? Tell me now.

GRANDMOTHER.

That will I, child; but thou must hearken:
Our Saviour, Christ, hath set a mark on
That very tree. When here below
He dwelt, through woods and fields, you know,
He often walk'd.

RED RIDINGHOOD.

He travell'd, too,
The dreary wilderness all through;
And there five thousand men he fed,
Though they had brought scarce any bread.
And when his cruel wrongs were ended,
Up into Heaven again ascended.

GRANDMOTHER.

Good child! I'm very glad to find
Thee, though so young, thou'rt not behind
In knowledge of God's Holy Word.
Well, as I told you, Christ the Lord
Was travelling on from place to place
To heal the sick, and give his grace
To us poor mortals. Through a wood
He pass'd, and all the trees that stood
Along his path bow'd down before him,
With humble reverence to adore him:
The oak, the beech, and every one;
All, save the aspen. That alone
Stood stiff and stately in its pride,
As if the Saviour it defied.
Then spake the Lord, "Thou wilt not bend,
Thou stiff-neck'd tree! Then, without end,

❀ 107 ❀

*The Life
and Death
of
Little Red
Riding
Hood*

**Foldout, ca. 1925. Illustrator unknown. Collection of Jack Zipes.**

I bid thee tremble on for ever!
Without a breath in stillest weather
From this day forward thou shalt quiver
In every leaf and every spray."
And so the tree began to shiver,
And will until the judgement-day.


RED RIDINGHOOD.

Who won't hear reason gets a blow!—
Good-bye; 'tis time for me to go.


GRANDMOTHER.

But sing, before you go away,
That song you learnt the other day.


RED RIDINGHOOD *sings*.

Pussy, walking above
On the roof of the house,
Thought to catch a young dove;
She was tired of mouse,
But fancied a pigeon might do.
   Mïeu, mïeu!
To the poor pigeon's hold
Quite softly she stole;

But scarce is she in
When her troubles begin;
She fell into a trap
Set the weasels to snap,
And dying cried, "Thieving won't do!"
    Mïeu, mïeu!


GRANDMOTHER.
A pretty song; I hope you'll mind it.
Who keeps the honest path will find it
A safer road than any other.
Good-bye my Precious! Give your mother
My blessing;—she is good and tender
To the old woman;—God befriend her!


RED RIDINGHOOD.
Good-bye, dear Granny; I shall come back soon,
And bring your supper in the afternoon.
[Exit LITTLE RED RIDINGHOOD.


GRANDMOTHER.
                    [looking after her from the window.
The careless gipsy! She forgets to close
The gate, and strangers may come in—no matter—
Small chance of that to-day. How fast she grows;
So wild too; but I love to hear her chatter;
A winsome thing she is, the truth to tell,
And that red hood becomes the lassie well.


SCENE II.
The Wood.


[The HUNTSMAN enters.


HUNTSMAN.
For ever and always a huntsman to be,
Is a life that won't suit a fine fellow like me!
Through the wood and the wold,
In hot weather or cold,
To ramble by night and by day—
Who would like it, I pray?

In snow, rain or sleet,
I must drag my poor feet
Through the mud and the mire,
To hunt a wild beast,
While other men feast,
Or sit by the fire
With children and wife.
Were it not for my pipe,
I'd as soon be a snipe
As lead such a life.

❀ 109 ❀

*The Life
and Death
of
Little Red
Riding
Hood*

[*He strikes fire and lights his pipe.*

'Tis a wonderful thing
That fire should spring
From the contact of steel and of stone;
How first it was known—
Who can tell? Just the same
How all other arts came.
What a creature is man!
Everything that he can
He turns to his use, and goes on
Growing wiser and wiser from father to son.
I should like to be told
How our heads are to hold
All this wisdom unless they grow larger:
A gun bursts if you overcharge her.

[*Enter* LITTLE RED RIDINGHOOD.

Ha! Little Redcap, whither stray ye?
Out as early as a May-bee!

RED RIDINGHOOD.
I come from Grandmother's;—and you
Are hunting, I suppose.

HUNTSMAN.
That's true;
Hunting a wolf, a graceless glutton,
Who gobbles up the farmer's mutton.

RED RIDINGHOOD.

'Tis true then, what the people say.
I wonder that the wolf should stray
So near the village.

HUNTSMAN.

O, the sinner
Goes anywhere to get a dinner.

RED RIDINGHOOD.

And are you not afraid to meet him?

HUNTSMAN.

Afraid! Were he the Devil's son,
I only wish that I could treat him
To a round bullet from this gun.

RED RIDINGHOOD.

O, don't talk so, but have a care
Lest he should jump out unaware.

HUNTSMAN.

A hunter must be brave and daring
With ready weapon, courage warm,
And a bold heart never caring
For the wild beast or the storm;
Else it were as well he sat
Beside the fire and nursed the cat.

RED RIDINGHOOD.

I see to-day you have put on
A smart new jerkin; in the sun
Your hunting knife shines brightly too.

HUNTSMAN.

Ay, ay—that hunting-knife shall do
For Master Wolf; his hide won't hack it.
And how d'ye like my fine new jacket?

RED RIDINGHOOD.

It's well enough for such a sort of thing.

HUNTSMAN.

What can you then against it bring?

❧ 111 ❧

*The Life
and Death
of
Little Red
Riding
Hood*

RED RIDINGHOOD.

'Twould suit you better if 'twere red,—
Like my hood. . . .

HUNTSMAN.

Bless your silly head!
D'ye think that all the world must be
Flame-color, like thy cap? Just see
How green outshines it. Look around;—
The fields, the wood, the trees, the ground!
There's something in that color green,—
Something quite living. What a sheen
Beams from it! One might almost swear
It is alive. . . .

RED RIDINGHOOD.

Yes, everywhere,
Like common people, you may find it;
But red leaves green as far behind it
As kings the crowd. That tempting hue
Will often make the longing child
Forbidden dainties dearly rue;
If but a scarlet berry wild,
Or sour hedge crab, the lip must try,
Whene'er that colour charms the eye;
And, oh, how happy any child would be
Who could put on a fine red cap, like me!

HUNTSMAN.

Give me a kiss, you silly little urchin!

RED RIDINGHOOD.

I shan't;—tobacco's my aversion!

HUNTSMAN.

If you can't bear tobacco, on my life,
No man will ever take you for his wife.

[*He goes.*

RED RIDINGHOOD *alone.*

If we don't fancy *them*, they always say
That no one will like *us*. That's just their way!
And if a man but gets a fine new coat,
He thinks the lasses all on him must doat.

[*Two* ROBIN REDBREASTS *fly from a tree and hop before her.*

THE BIRDS.

Well met in the greenwood,
Little Red Ridinghood!

RED RIDINGHOOD.

What can the pretty creatures mean?

BIRDS.

Where are you going to? Where have you been?

RED RIDINGHOOD.

I'm going home, you pretty thing!
How on their tiny legs they spring;
They wear, too, on the neck and breast,
The colour that I love the best.

BIRDS.

We are like thee drest,—
Thou like the Redbreast;
Thou art our friend.
We will attend
Little Red Ridinghood
All through the greenwood.

RED RIDINGHOOD.

Merry playmates are we,
For plainly I see,
He who made you and me
Meant all things to be
Gay and happy. He spread
The blue sky overhead,
And that beautiful red
On you neck and your breast;
I can never believe

He likes gloomy things best;
We will not fret and grieve,
Pretty birds, but be merry.
You shall wear your red vest,
And I will be drest
In a cap like a cherry!

[She goes.

BIRDS.

Our friend Red Ridinghood is right—
The sky is blue, the sun is bright.

[The BIRDS fly after her.


SCENE III
A Thicket in the Wood.
The WOLF alone.


WOLF.

Here, in the thickest covert, I must hid,
Or, like an outcast, wander up and down.
No living creature is there can abide
My presence; none will trust me; any clown
May take my life. Both man and beast they shun me.
And what the crime, I ask, which hath undone me?
Because I am no hypocrite, nor can
Bow down to fawn and flatter a mean man.
For this they speak ill of me, and I'm driven
From land to land; worried and slander'd; none
Take pity on me;—blows enough are given,
But, as for sympathy, that piece of stone
Might show as much. They shoot at me; they set
All sorts of traps; the pitfall and the net
Are laid to catch me. If I show my nose
By daylight, then they cry "Ha! ha! there goes
The Wolf!" and all the while they dare to gabble
Of tolerance! I hate such idle babble!
But worse than man is that slavehearted hound,
My sister's son; and yet he's always found
Leagued with the tyrants of or common race.
Ha! here comes Pincher; how I hate his face!

LUDWIG
TIECK

WOLF *sarcastically.*
Pincher! my noble fellow, how d'ye do?
When Fortune frowns I have a friend in you?

DOG.
This is your summer villa, is it?
I have been walking around to visit
The hares and rabbits: a strong inclination
For game impell'd me, but the recreation
Was spoilt by terror of the keeper's gun.
Poaching will never pass with him for fun.

WOLF.
Art still in service with young Red Cap's father?

DOG.
Why, yes; I'm there, for it suits me rather.
Good housekeeping, and I get what remains.
The child, too, likes me, and from her my gains
Are dainty morsels. In return, I bring
A stick thrown in the water,—anything;
Sometimes, for her amusement, chase the cat;
Or on the ground stretch myself out quite flat,
Not yet to die, thank Heaven! but shamming dead.

WOLF.
Such are the tricks by which you gain your bread!

DOG.
This fortnight past we're trotting through the wood
Continually, with messages and food
To the sick Grandmother, who must be tended.
More bones meanwhile for me; and when all's ended,
If she should die, the son-in-law inherits
Her little property. Not much he merits,
But greatly needs it; for, with cards and drink,
He's over head and ears, and soon must sink.
But what care I for that? One thing alone
Disturbs my comfort; if that child a stone,

However weighty throws, it seems that I
Must go and fetch it. Fain I'd let it lie;
I growl and snarl, but take it up at last.
Now here, now there I'm sent, until I'm past
All patience; and my teeth they suffer for it!

WOLF.

A hateful life, good friend! I should abhor it.
You've no will of your own; you are not free,
But do another's bidding. Pardon me,
If all your boasted pleasures and proud station,
Instead of envy, rouse my indignation.

DOG.

Speak your mind freely, we are friends of old;
But surely one so wise need not be told
In practice it will very rarely do
To act on what, in theory, is true.

WOLF.

Your bread is butter'd on both sides, I see,
And when it suits your turn you'll give up me.

DOG.

No, no! I am an honourable hound
And to my old companion closely bound.
I only say 'twere wiser if you could
A little soften down that savage mood—
Become more human; then, in time, we might
Make something of you yet, and set all right.

WOLF.

No, friend! no more of that. There was a time
In earlier years, alas! ere grief and crime
Had turn'd my blood to gall, when ardent longing
For glorious deeds possess'd my youthful soul.
High aspirations, lofty thoughts were thronging
Before my fancy, and—a worthy goal!—
I thought to dedicate myself to man,
To learn his arts, and wonders work. This plan
Was blasted, as I told thee. . . .

❈ 115 ❈

*The Life
and Death
of
Little Red
Riding
Hood*

DOG.

I would fain,
If not too painful, hear the tale again.

WOLF.

Our first acquaintance, you may recollect,
Began when you by Farmer Hodge were kept.
I then had left the woods, my kith and kind
Abandon'd, and resolved myself to bind
Unto the body politic. I grew
More docile than a dog; all arts I knew
My master's property to watch and guard;
I chased away the thieves, I kept the yard
From beggars free. Oft in the rain I lay;
Often from hunger suffer'd; many a day
was cudgell'd, too, severely; yet no king
Happier than I. It was a glorious thing
To be *of use*, I thought, and well contented;
My chosen lot I never once repented.

DOG.

Hist! Was that not a hare I heard?

WOLF.

Be silent, fool! nor thus disturb
The story of my tragic woes.
Stop, if thou canst, that glutton's nose,
And listen while I tell the fate,
The cruel injuries, that turn'd to hate
My friendship for the human brood,
Once loved like brothers. O, I would
These teeth could crunch them all at once,
Nor leave of man a single ounce
To cumber earth! Well, at that time,
My fancy in its youthful prime
Was budding, and it chanced one day,
While taking in the wood a stroll,
I met a young she-wolf at play;
Her form so fair, her yet more lovely soul,
How shall I, friend, describe? Her winning look,
Modest, yet dazzling;—you might write a book

On her perfections. Words are weak to tell
The charms I loved, "not wisely, but too well!"

DOG.

I'm not in love, my friend, and you may spare
Raptures in which I really cannot share.

WOLF.

Let it suffice—we married very soon,
And enter'd on the blissful honeymoon.
I met her in the wood, in secret she
Return'd my visits; none more blest than we,
Until one luckless morn, our tête-à-tête
Beguiled the hours, and in the barn too late
She linger'd. Led by some malignant fate,
The peasants came, and at the very door
They slew my hapless wife! That thrashing-floor
Was ruddy with her blood! What could avail
My helpless rage against their cruel flail?

DOG.

Your budding herbs of grace must have been well
Trod down, I fancy. The conclusion tell.

WOLF.

"Monsters!—I mutter'd—is it thus ye sever
The bonds of faithful love? Accursed for ever
Be all your progeny!" The cruel wound
Rankled within; revenge and hate profound
Were there. But though no outward sign betrayed
The thoughts I harbour'd, it is truly said,
"The injured are suspected." Tyrants must
Trample their victims in the very dust.
My faithful services were all forgotten;
They called me "Wolf," and said I long'd for mutton.
They chain me next, and after that declare
That they must draw my teeth; and at the fair
Sell me to him who leads about the bear;
Show me from town to town, and, when I'm past
All farther service, kill me at the last.
O, Pincher! Pincher! was it not enough
To break my heart if made of common stuff!

❋ 117 ❋

*The Life
and Death
of
Little Red
Riding
Hood*

DOG.

A curiosity they meant to make you;—
A sort of raree-show. Don't let it shake you.


WOLF.

I rent my chain with one strong bound,
And in the nearest forest found
A present shelter. But since then,
The wrongs I have endured from men!
The daily snares, the nightly fears;
The bullets whistling round my ears;
The insults heap'd upon my head;
Hunted by dogs till nearly dead;
Up hills, down precipices hurried;—
No creature ever was so worried!
And now my sole delight shall be
To treat mankind as they treat me;
To ruin all, and nothing spare;
The bridegroom from the bride to tear.
The child upon its mother's knee
Shall tremble when they speak of me.
Havoc and horror I will spread,
And eat up men as they eat bread!
Nor men alone, but all the slaves
Who fawn upon those wretched knaves.
I had already made an end
Of *thee*, wert not my trusted friend.


DOG.

I thank you for the kind exception;
But have you not, in moments of reflection,
Some feelings of remorse? Have you no faith
In immortality? no fear of death,
And future judgement on each guilty deed?


WOLF.

No! Pincher. 'Tis a superstitious creed.
The grapes of Paradise hang all too high
For us to reach. What in my stomach I
Have got is really mine; and this I hold
To be a doctrine doctors can't deny.

DOG.

I grieve, indeed, to find you are so bold
An infidel. A dog of my gentility
In future must avoid you. Such freethinking
Alarms me for my own respectability.
Your crimes I could excuse; but there's no winking
Your heterodoxy, so I say Good-bye!

[*Exit the* DOG.

❀ 119 ❀

*The Life
and Death
of
Little Red
Riding
Hood*

WOLF *alone.*

A shallow-pated fool, who can't rely
Upon himself, but always takes his note
From others! If I seized his throat
And strangled him, it were no crime.
His dear Red Ridinghood long time
I've meant to eat—and will; that blow
Will reach her father, whom I owe
Full many a grudge. Revenge is sweet!
This very night I'll have the treat.

[*Exit* WOLF.

SCENE IV.

*A Footpath through the Wood.*
RED RIDINGHOOD *and* JENNY

JENNY.

'Tis almost night—I can no farther go.

RED RIDINGHOOD.

The sun has not yet sunk below
The mountain.

JENNY.

Ere I can get back,
It will be night quite dark and black.

[*Enter* PETER *and his* BRIDE.

BRIDE.

Red Ridinghood! Are you out walking?

PETER.

I love to tease that child with talking
A little nonsense. 'Tis a pretty pet!
Red Ridinghood, have you determined yet
To be my little wife?

RED RIDINGHOOD.

No, no.
You have a wife already.

PETER.

Oh!
Then you will be my second—hey?

BRIDE.

Don't mind him, child. Peter, don't say
Such foolish things;—it may do harm.

RED RIDINGHOOD.

O, let him talk! He cannot charm
Me, even as he is to take him,
And by that time old age will shake him.
I need not wait for him to find
A bridegroom much more to my mind.

BRIDE *to* PETER.

See what you get! That baby knows
As much as we. What wit she shows.

[*Exit* BRIDE, *followed by* PETER.

[*Enter a* PEASANT.

PEASANT.

They should not let the children roam
About this wood. Hark, little ones, go home;
It's getting late, and perhaps the Wolf may come.

RED RIDINGHOOD.

I go to Grandmother's to take
Her supper; all your wolves won't make
Me to turn back.

❀ 121 ❀

*The Life
and Death
of
Little Red
Riding
Hood*

PEASANT.

That's very well
For talk; but if he comes, you'll tell
A different story. So fool-hardy
You children are. Come, don't be tardy.

[*Exit* PEASANT.

JENNY, *plucking a dandelion.*

See, here's a dandelion; it will show
How long we have to live. Just blow
The flower thus.

CUCKOO, *behind the scene.*

Cuckoo! Cuckoo!

JENNY *blows the flower.*

Ah, I shall live a little less
Than fivescore years.

RED RIDINGHOOD.

I must confess
That seems too long.

JENNY.

I'm safe, you see;
It shows the Wolf will not take me.

RED RIDINGHOOD.

Ah! So it does. Now let me try.

[*She blows the flower, and all the seeds fly away.*

JENNY.

All gone, you see—so soon to die!

RED RIDINGHOOD.

I leave my pretty hood to you.—
But, never mind, it is not true,
And I the longest of the two
Shall live; I am so strong, you see.
The seeds may fly, it can't hurt me.

Besides, I have been taught too well
To think that silly flower can tell
Such things. 'Tis yellow first, then grey,
Like an old man; beside the way
It grows; and if the wind comes nigh,
Its downy seeds away they fly.

CUCKOO, *behind the scene.*

Cuckoo! Cuckoo! Cuckoo!

JENNY.

Don't you believe it? I can tell
Another way which does as well.
The Cuckoo will an answer give
If ask'd how long one has to live.

RED RIDINGHOOD.

Cuckoo, Cuckoo, say how long
I have to live.

JENNY.

He stops his song!
Poor child! If I should never see
Thee more, in death remember me,
And I in life will think of thee.

[*Exit* JENNY.

RED RIDINGHOOD *alone.*

A simple child! but old enough
Not to believe such foolish stuff.

[*The* CUCKOO *flies in and hops before her.*

Red Ridinghood.
What has this bird with me to do?

CUCKOO.

Cuckoo! Be wary—Cuck—Cuck—koo!
I can't speak as I wish to you.
Cuckoo! Take care. The Wolf! Beware!
Cuckoo! Cuckoo!

[*He flies away.*

RED RIDINGHOOD.

He can't say much, indeed; that's true.

❈ 123 ❈

*The Life
and Death
of
Little Red
Riding
Hood*

[*Enter the* DOG.

Ha! Pincher, how came you down this way?
D'ye smell the meat? Down, down, I say.

DOG.

Bow, wow! There's danger near, beware!

RED RIDINGHOOD.

Down, Pincher! You shall have your share
When I get home. What would he way?

DOG.

Bow, wow! Upon my knees I pray—
Don't be too bold. The Wolf! This way,
Come back. Bow, wow!

RED RIDINGHOOD.

No, Pincher, no!
You've lost your wits, I think. Go, go.

[*Exit* RED RIDINGHOOD.

DOG.

Bow, wow! Bow, wow! Don't be too bold.

CUCKOO.

Cuckoo! Cuckoo! In vain she's told.

NIGHTINGALE, *behind the scene.*

Tira, lira, li! from all!
In a thousand tongues they call.
Notes high and low,
In ceaseless flow.
All are singing,
None so ringing
Clear and fine,
As the note
From my throat:
Hark to mine!
Swelling, falling,
Never palling,

Gentle hearts it pleases ever!
Hark! the sound
Echoes round!
Gentle ear it wearies never!

CUCKOO.

Cuckoo! Cuckoo! Warning from all!
Cuckoo! Cuckoo! Pride has a fall!

SCENE V.

*Interior of the cottage—time, evening.*
*The* WOLF *in bed.*

WOLF.

By good luck I got in
Without rousing a mouse.
The gate was left open,
The door of the house
Was also ajar.
A fortunate star
Has brought me thus far.
The old woman I seized;
She was not at all pleased,
And tried to defend;
But I soon made an end
Of her. Under the bed
She now lies quite dead;
And I am expecting
Red Ridinghood's tap.
But nothing neglecting
To forward my plan,
The Grandmother's cap
I will wear if I can;

                                       [*He puts on the cap.*

Her old dressing-gown, too:—

                              [*He puts on the dressing-gown.*

Now I think I shall do,
If I seem to be dozing;
The evening is closing—
The evening is closing—
It soon will be dark.

                              [*A tap at the door.*

*Les Contes de Perrault,* Paris: J. Hetzel, 1862. Illustrator Gustave Doré.

There's Red Ridinghood! Hark!

[RED RIDINGHOOD *comes in.*

RED RIDINGHOOD.

Why, Granny, are you gone to bed?

WOLF.

Yes, little one! I found my head
So very bad.

RED RIDINGHOOD.

I've brought a chicken,
With Mother's love; a little picking
Will do you good. But, goodness me!
Your feet are where your head should be:
And what strange hands! all over hair!

WOLF.

They hold fast, child; you needn't care.

RED RIDINGHOOD.

My Mother bid me stay with you
To-night; she said it would not do
To come home in the dark. O, dear!
Grandmother, what a monstrous ear
You have! I thought your ears were flatter,
And not so long. . . .

WOLF.

Child, child no matter—
I hear the better. Come to bed;
You quite distract my poor old head.

RED RIDINGHOOD.

It must be cold—my teeth so chatter—
I'll shut the window. . . .

WOLF.

No, child, no—
Just come to bed, and leave it so.

RED RIDINGHOOD.

I don't know what it is I fear,
But it all seems so strange and queer.
Why, Grandmother, your eyes have grown
Immense. . . .

WOLF.

Pray let my eyes alone;
They serve to see with.

RED RIDINGHOOD.

But your nose! . . .

WOLF.

My child, it is the twilight throws
Uncertain light on all around.

RED RIDINGHOOD.

But what a mouth! 'tis like a hound!

WOLF.

'Twill serve to eat you, I'll be bound!
  [*The* WOLF *seizes her, and the curtain of the bed falls down before*
                                                                    *them.*

RED RIDINGHOOD, *behind the curtain.*

Help, help! O, save me! I shall die!

WOLF.

You're dead already, and can cry
No longer, little fool! Good bye!
  [*The two* ROBIN REDBREASTS *fly in through the open window.*

FIRST BIRD.

Come, follow me, and let us fly
Into the room. . . .
                      SECOND BIRD.

Ay, that will I;
Our friend Red Ridinghood is there.

❀ 127 ❀

*The Life
and Death
of
Little Red
Riding
Hood*

FIRST BIRD.

She's gone to bed—she is not here.

[*He hops behind the curtain.*

SECOND BIRD.

Through door and window gently blow
The evening breezes. . . .

FIRST BIRD, *coming back.*

Grief and woe!

SECOND BIRD.

What hast thou seen?

FIRST BIRD.

The Wolf in bed;
And poor Red Ridinghood quite dead!

BOTH BIRDS.

O, grief and woe! O, lamentable fate!

HUNTSMAN, *looking in through the window.*

Why, what's the matter? Passing by the gate,
I heard a cry.

BIRDS.

Alas! You come too late;
Red Ridinghood is dead! That savage beast,
The Wolf, is eating her!

HUNTSMAN

His cruel feast
This gun shall end, unless I miss my aim.

[*The* WOLF *puts his head outside the curtain; the* HUNTSMAN *fires
and shoots him dead.*

HUNTSMAN.

The Wolf is dead! He'll never stir again.
Let other wolves take warning by his fate:
Vengeance o'ertakes the wicked soon or late.

[*The Curtain falls*

## ❋ 5 ❋

### *The Wolf-King;*[1]
### *or, Little Red-Riding-Hood:*
### *An Old Woman's Tale*

### *Anonymous*

### (1801)

Veteres avias tibi
de pulmone revello.
Persius

Translated from the Danish of the author of the Water-King, etc.,
and respectfully inscribed to M. G. Lewis, Esq., M.P., as an humble attempt
to imitate his excellent version of that celebrated ballad.

T HE BIRDS THEY SUNG, the morning smiled,
The mother kiss'd her darling child,
And said—"My dear, take custards three,
"And carry to your grand-mummie."—

The pretty maid had on her head
A little riding-hood of red,
And as she pass'd the lonely wood
They call'd her small Red-riding-hood.

Her basket on her arm she hung,
And as she went thus artless sung,
—"A lady lived beneath a hill,
"Who, if not gone, resides there still."—

The Wolf-King saw her pass along,
He eyed her custards, mark'd her song,
And cried—"That child and custards three,
"This evening shall my supper be!"—

Now swift the maid pursued her way,
And heedless trill'd her plaintive lay,
Nor had she pass'd the murky wood,
When lo! the Wolf-King near her stood!

—"Oh! stop, my pretty child so gay!
"Oh! whither do you bend your way?"—
—"My little self and custards three,
"Are going to my grand-mummie;"—

—"While you by yonder mountain go,
"On which the azure blue-bells grow;
"I'll take this road; then haste thee, dear,
"Or I before you will be there.

"And when our racing shall be done,
"A kiss you forfeit, if I've won;
"Your prize shall be, if first you come,
"Some barley-sugar and a plumb!"—

—"Oh! thank you, good Sir Wolf," said she,
And dropp'd a pretty courtesie;
The little maid then onward hied,
And sought the blue-bell'd mountain's side.

The Wolf sped on o'er marsh and moor,
And faintly tapp'd at granny's door;
—"Oh! let me in, grand-mummy good,
"For I am small Red-riding-hood."—

—"The bobbin pull," the grandam cried,
"The door will then fly open wide."—
The crafty Wolf the bobbin drew,
And straight the door wide open flew!

He pac'd the bed-room eight times four,
And utter'd thrice an hideous roar;
He pac'd the bed-room nine times three,
And then devour'd poor grand-mummie!

He dash'd her brains out on the stones,
He gnaw'd her sinews, crack'd her bones;
He munch'd her heart, he quaff'd her gore,
And up her lights and liver tore!!!²

Grand-mummy's bed he straight got in,
Her night-cap tied beneath his chin;
And waiting for his destin'd prey,
All snug between the sheets he lay.

Now at the door a voice heard he,
Which cried—"I've brought you custards three;
"Oh! let me in, grand-mummy good,
"For I am small Red-riding-hood."—

—"The bobbin pull," the Wolf-King cried,
"The door will then fly open wide!"—
The little dear the bobbin drew,
And straight the door wide open flew.³

She placed the custards on the floor,
And sigh'd—"I wish I'd brought you *four*.⁴
"I'm very tired, dear grand-mummie,
"Oh! may I come to bed to thee?"—

—"Oh! come," the Wolf-King softly cried,
"And lie, my sweet one, by my side;"—
Ah little thought the child so gay,
The cruel Wolf-King near her lay!

—"Oh! tell me, tell me, granny dear,
"Why does your *voice* so gruff appear?"—
—"Oh! hush sweet-heart," the Wolf-King said,
"I've got a small cold in my head!"—

❧ 131 ❧

*The Wolf-
King; or,
Little Red
Riding
Hood*

—"Oh! tell me, grand-mummie so kind,
"Why you've a *tail* grows out behind?"—
—"Oh! hush thee, hush thee, pretty dear,
"My pin-cushion I hang on here!"—

—"Why do your *eyes* so glare on me?"—
—"They are your pretty face to see."—
—"Why do your *ears* so long appear?"—
—"They are your pretty voice to hear."—

—"Oh! tell me, grammy, why, to-night,
Your *teeth* appear so long and white?"—
Then growling, cried the Wolf so grim,
—"They are to tear you limb from limb!"—

His hungry teeth the Wolf-King gnash'd,
His sparkling eyes with fury flash'd,
He oped his jaws all sprent with blood,
And fell on small Red-riding-hood.

He tore out bowels one and two,
—"Little maid, I will eat you!"—
But when he tore out three and four,
The little maid she was no more!

Take warning hence, ye children fair;
Of wolves' insidious arts beware;
And as you pass each lonely wood,
Ah! think of small Red-riding-hood.

With custards sent nor loiter slow,
Nor gather blue-bells as ye go;
Get not to bed with grand-mummie,
Lest she a ravenous wolf should be!

※ 133 ※

*The Wolf-
King; or,
Little Red
Riding
Hood*

## ※ *Notes* ※

1. Though the northern states of Europe are not conceived, even by the most violent alarmists, to be much infected by the principles of jacobinism, yet in their *disloyal* languages "King" is often used as a term for a *fiend*, whose business is to destroy the happiness of mankind, and whose delight is in human misery.

2. This stanza is borrowed from an affecting and sanguinary description in a German ballad by Professor Von Splüttbach, called "Skulth den Belch, or Sour Mthltz." In English (as far as translation can convey an idea of the horror of the original), "The Bloody Banquet, or the Gulf of Ghosts!!!" a very terrible and meritorious production!

3. Repetition is the soul of ballad-writing.

4. The reader will do my heroine the justice to remember, that she set out with only *three*, consequently her wish that another had been added, arose from a motive purely affectionate and characteristic. This benevolent trait, thus ingeniously insinuated, excites the interest of the reader for her, and adds horror to the catastrophe.

5. Our heroine is here lost in *double* astonishment; not only the *length*, but the *whiteness* of her grand-mother's teeth excites her wonder and suspicion!

*Le Petit Chaperon Rouge,* Chatellerault: René Touret, c. 1950. Illustrator Thomen.

## ❉ 6 ❉

## *Little Red Cap*

## *By Jacob & Wilhelm Grimm*

## (1812)

ONCE UPON A TIME there was a sweet little maiden. Whoever laid eyes upon her could not help but love her. But it was her grandmother who loved her most. She could never give the child enough. One time she made her a present, a small, red velvet cap, and, since it was so becoming, the girl always wanted to wear only this. So she was simply called Little Red Cap.

One day her mother said to her: "Come, Little Red Cap, take this piece of cake and bottle of wine and bring them to your grandmother. She is sick and weak. This will strengthen her. Be nice and good, and give her my regards. Don't tarry on your way, and don't stray from the path, otherwise you'll fall and break the glass. Then your sick grandmother will get nothing."

Little Red Cap promised her mother to be very obedient. Well, the grandmother lived out in the woods, half an hour from the village. And, as soon as Little Red Cap entered the woods, she encountered the wolf. However, Little Red Cap did not know what a wicked sort of an animal he was and was not afraid of him.

"Good day, Little Red Cap."

"Thank you kindly, wolf."

"Where are you going so early, Little Red Cap?"

"To Grandmother's."

"What are you carrying under your apron?"

"My grandmother is sick and weak, so I'm bringing her cake and wine. We baked yesterday, and this will strengthen her."

"Where does your grandmother live, Little Red Cap?"

"Another quarter of an hour from here in the woods. Her house is under the three big oak trees. You can tell it by the hazel bushes," said Little Red Cap.

The wolf thought to himself, this is a good juicy morsel for me. How are you going to manage to get her?

"Listen, Little Red Cap," he said, "have you seen the pretty flowers which are in the woods? Why don't you look around you? I believe that you haven't even noticed how lovely the birds are singing. You march along as if you were going straight to school in the village, and it is so delightful out here in the woods."

Little Red Cap looked around and saw how the sun had broken through the trees and everything around her was filled with beautiful flowers. So she thought to herself: Well, if I were to bring grandmother a bunch of flowers, she would like that. It's still early, and I'll arrive on time. So she plunged into the woods and looked for flowers. And each time she plucked one, she believed she saw another one even prettier and ran after it further and further into the woods. But the wolf went straight to the grandmother's house and knocked at the door.

"Who's there outside?"

"Little Red Cap. I'm bringing you cake and wine. Open up."

"Just lift the latch," the grandmother called. "I'm too weak and can't get up."

The wolf lifted the latch, and the door sprung open. Then he went straight inside to the grandmother's bed and swallowed her. Next he took her clothes, put them on with her nightcap, lay down in her bed, and drew the curtains.

Little Red Cap had been running around after flowers, and, only when she had as many as she could carry, did she continue on her way to her grandmother. Upon arriving there she found the door open. This puzzled her, and, as she entered the room, it seemed so strange inside that she thought: Oh, oh, my God, how frightened I feel today, and usually I like to be at grandmother's. Whereupon she went to the bed and drew back the curtains. Her grandmother lay there with her cap pulled down over her face so that it gave her a strange appearance.

"Oh, grandmother, what big ears you have!"

"The better to hear you with."

"Oh, grandmother, what big eyes you have!"

"The better to see you with."

"Oh, grandmother, what big hands you have!"

"The better to grab you with."

"Oh, grandmother, what a terrible big mouth you have!"

"The better to eat you with."

With that the wolf jumped out of bed, leapt on Little Red Cap and swallowed her. After the wolf had digested the juicy morsel, he lay down in bed again, fell asleep, and began to snore very loudly. The hunter happened to be passing by and wondered to himself about the old lady's snoring: You had better take a look. Then he went inside, and, when he came to the bed, he found the wolf whom he had been hunting for a long time. He had certainly eaten the grandmother. Perhaps she can still be saved. I won't shoot, thought the hunter. Then he took a shearing knife and slit the wolf's belly open, and, after he had made a couple of cuts, he saw the glowing red cap, and, after he made a few more cuts, the girl jumped out and cried: "Oh, how frightened I was! It was so dark in the wolf's body." And then the grandmother came out alive. So now Little Red Cap fetched large heavy stones with which they filled the wolf's body, and, when he awoke, he wanted to jump up, but the stones were so heavy that he fell down dead.

So all three were pleased. The hunter skinned the fur from the wolf. The grandmother ate the cake and drank the wine that Little Red Cap had brought, and Little Red Cap thought to herself: Never again in your life will you stray by yourself into the woods when your mother has forbidden it.

§§§

It is also said that once when Little Red Cap went to her grandmother again to bring some baked goods, another wolf spoke to her and sought to entice her to leave the path. But this time Little Red Cap was on her guard, went straight ahead, and told her grandmother that she had seen the wolf, that he had wished her good day, but that he had such a mean look in his eyes "as if he would have eaten me were it not for the fact that we were on the open road."

"Come," said grandmother, "we'll shut the door so he can't come in."

Soon thereafter the wolf knocked and cried out: "Open up, grandmother. It's Little Red Cap. I've brought you some baked goods." But they kept silent and did not open the door. So the wicked one went around the house several times and finally jumped on the roof. He wanted to wait until evening when Little Red Cap was to go home. Then he wanted to sneak after her and eat her up in the darkness. But the grandmother realized what he had in mind. In front of the house was a big stone trough. "Fetch the bucket, Lit-

*Little Red Riding Hood,* Chicago: Reilly & Lee, 1908. Illustrator John R. Neil.

tle Red Cap, I cooked sausages yesterday. Take the water they were boiled in and pour it into the trough." Little Red Cap kept carrying the water until she had filled the big, big trough. Then the smell of the sausages reached the nose of the wolf. He sniffed and looked down. Finally, he stretched his neck so far that he could no longer keep his balance on the roof. He began to slip and fell right into the big trough and drowned. Then Little Red Cap went merrily on her way home.

# *Little Red Riding Hood*

## *By F. W. N. Bayley*

## (1846)

### INTRODUCTION OF THE HEROINE
### TO THE READER

I
N A SWEET LITTLE VILLAGE,
Surrounded by tillage,
Too retired for rows and too peaceful for pillage,
Fit alike for fair youth, in rude health, or for ill age,
    Stood a sweet little cot,
    Quite the gem of the spot;
No peasant near hand had a prettier got;
A nicer was never to Sir nor to Ma'am let;
    In fact you might call,—
    With its chimney so tall,
And its bed-room, and kitchen, and parlour, and all,—
  It nearly the neatest concern in the hamlet;
Which hamlet was neither, we whisper you plain,
Hamlet the jeweller, nor Hamlet the Dane!
    Not Prince of the Danes,
    Who sold gold-headed canes;
Nor Princes' Street Hamlet, who spent his rhet-*oric*
In the flower of youth on the scull of poor Yorick!
But a hamlet, the sweetest that ever was seen;
    So soft, so serene,
    And so simple I ween,

That it wore not the guise
Of a knowing one's eyes.
For about it you always *could* see *something green!*

In this hamlet of houses, of grass and of glade,
    Dwelt a rare little,
    Fair little,
    Care-little
        Maid:
    A beautiful relic
        Of British rusticity,
    Of very angelic,
        Pure, tender simplicity,
    With a sweet pair of eyes,
    That were blue as the skies;
    A nose and a chin,
    That knew nothing of sin;
    A pearl-row of teeth;
    And a heart far beneath,
So entirely void of all guile, and untainted,
That no heart could be better, unless it were sainted.
Had you seen her you then would have loved her by half, O,
   And admired her far
More than the serene self-possessed little Sappho,
   Who sang day and night at the Lowther Bazaar;
    A smart little creature,
    In form and in feature,
With notes of an actress and not of a child.
Now, *my* beauty's carols—were wood-notes, and wild—
She ne'er thought of gain at their end or beginning,
But Sappho "keeps varbling bekase she is *Vinning.*"

All the love that this little girl's ma' could afford her,
Just amounted to this,—that she fairly adored her;
While her grandmamma deemed it a pride and an honour,
To be everlastingly *doating* upon her.
    Two shades of affection,
    Without an objection,
For which we this plausible reason have got,
That grandma' *was* in *doat*-age—but mother was not.

There's another

Grandmother,

Whose dotage is silly,—and not quite so good,

As that of the Grandam of Red Riding Hood;

But as her fame's spread from the south to the north,

There's now no occasion to *Herald* it forth!

Oh, how shall my heroine's virtues be told?

They deserve to be written in letters of gold;

But as a poor author, when verses inditing,

Has seldom much gold to bestow upon writing,—

My very dear reader, pray what will you think,

If I try the achievement in letters of ink?

She was, then, most prime,

For a child of her time;

You'd have spared her a tanner,

For mildness of manner;

Then, her sweet thankful smile would have finished your job,

And, no doubt, in your joy, you'd have spared her a *bob*!

Her mother such hold

Had obtained of her heart,

That she never made bold,

Without leave, to depart

From home,—so when absent—this proves beyond doubt—

That her mother must always have—*known she was out.*

She did *not* suck her thumbs

Till she whitened their dibs;

She *was* fond of plums,

But she didn't tell fibs.

And when off she went,

To her grandmother sent,

She trudged to her hut, on her dear little legs,

With many a purpose of kindness, i'fegs,

But never to teach her *the way to suck eggs!*

The child was so good

That she'd plenty of food;

With cakes and with virtues, endowed and endued,

And sweetmeats, you might measure out by the rood—

(Now, reader, we both should put on a night-*cap* here,

And indulge in a vision while taking a *Nap here*;
For my muse has just hinted, or else I mistake her,
That *Roods* make us dream of the glories of *Acre*;
Which glories, however, I honestly yield,
Were won on the ocean, and not on the *field*;
By *fleet* ships of war, that were manned by our brave,
And, instead of the meadows, kept *ploughing* the wave:)
Yes, sweetmeats that out by the rood you might measure,
Which she used to suck with a vast deal of pleasure.
   At such childish delight,
  In these days, we are railers.
    But she held it tight,
    Did that dear little lass,
    And would not let it pass
Away from her then, for the best glass of grog,
The raciest morsel of maritime prog,
  Or the finest tobacco that's chewed by the sailors!

Well, all through this little girl's being so good,
    Her neighbours,
    (Were *they* boors?)
Subscribed to procure her a little red hood;
A hood, that when going out *walking* she'd wear,
   (And not in doors abiding)
To shelter her shoulders, and bind down her hair,
By land or by meadow, in hay or in clover,
Which accounts for their calling her Little Red *Riding*
   Hood—all the world over!

   She was a lively little pet,
    So full of playfulness and honour,
   That though she couldn't earn one yet,
    They put a lively-hood upon her!
Her sweet eyes had a very *good* wink,
'Tis clear she never meant to hood-wink;
Knowing she couldn't mean to smother good,
You felt for her a kind of brother-hood;
And, at this pause,—the only other Hood
That I remember, 's he who found,
Britain sold butter by the *pound*,
   And Erin by the *Pat*;

He wasn't born on Irish ground,
  He didn't come from Munster;
    But, reader, you may tell by *that*,
*Riding* nor *walking* Hood is he,
Nor Hood, that sailed upon the sea,
But a (quill)-*driving* Hood, by me
  Called, Thomas Hood the punster!
Resistless at a jest or gibe,
And quite the king of all his tribe

THE MOTHER OF THE HEROINE—
DOUGH V. ROE
AND THE PEELER

Little Red Riding Hood sat in a chair,
  All in her mother's cot,
And she saw the little red fire, that there
  Was making the oven hot;
And it rose in flame, and burned in flakes,
While Little Red Riding Hood's mother made cakes!

This gentle lady's brows we'll here environ,
With a few bays plucked by the muse of Byron.

Her mother was a homely woman, famed
  For every branch of pastry-making known,
By every Christian baker ever named;—
  Her pies were equalled by her tarts alone; She made the clev-
    erest *restaurant* ashamed;
  And even the cooks with inward envy groan,—
Finding themselves so very much exceeded
In making crust, by all the cakes that she did.

Her memory was a mine: she knew by heart
  All Glass and Ude, and Kitchener (that sweet book!—
So that if any cook had missed his part,
  She might have served him as a new receipt-book;
For her confections were a kindling art,
  And she herself a sort of living treat-book.
Sweets could so well be blended by no other—
That is, in cakes,—as by our heroine's mother.

Her favourite place of pleasure was her oven,—
　　Her noblest virtue was her way of heating it;—
The sphere—for she, too, had her sphere—she'd move in,
　　She quite made flagrant with her way of sweeting it:—
Her paste had all the elements of love in,—
　　Pure cupboard love,—in fact, there was no beating it:—
She was a sort of priestess—though a sloven—
At pastry's burning shrine,—to wit—the oven!

　　　　"The Queen of Hearts,
　　　　She made some tarts,"
　　　On which Canning's muse,
　　　Did one day choose
　　　To have some critical fun done;
But Little Red Riding Hood's dear mamma,
Was working up different things by far,
　　　And as yet her cakes were undone.
She ducked and she dabbled her hands in *dough*,
Though she didn't care two-pence for Richard *Roe*,
　　　As some *bucks* do in London!

When the bailiff touches his shoulder and jeers,
It's the only tap that the drunkard fears;
　　　　And when John Doe comes,
　　　　In the manner of bums,
　　　　For the various sums
　　　That he owe for liquor so free did,
There's a very natural shout of, "Oh!
Upon my soul you're the only Doe
　　　That I never could have *needed*!"

　　Little Red Riding Hood's ma' in a trice,
　　　　Though we've called her a sloven,
　　Made up a bundle of cakes very nice,
　　　　And crammed them into the oven—
　　Till they should be done as brown, you know,
　　As any *cake* that is done by Doe!

"What are these cakes for," Riding Hood said,
　　　　"Mother dear,
　　　That you have been making,
　　　And oven is baking,

Here?"
Riding Hood's mother smiled with glee:—
"Ask your grandmother, child," said she;
But as her grandmother was not there,
She thought such an answer was hardly fair;
So she laughingly tossed up her dear little head,
And went to look into the oven instead!
       "Oh! what fun,
       The cakes are done—
   Mother dear, won't you give me one?"
"If you're good, miss, perhaps I may;
Meanwhile, you'll do me the favour to stay,
As they're burning, *in*—till I get them *out*;
And then, 'We'll *see* what it's *all* about.'"

Riding Hood's mother a peeler got,
And crammed it in where the cakes were hot;
Which she ladled out so remarkably soon,
You soon discovered that *she* was no spoon;
No spoon—but only a woman of mettle,
Spreading out cakes, to cool and settle.

      But what *is* a Peeler?
      By way of a feeler
      For mundane knowledge
      Not got at college,
      The reader cries:—
      So I'll open his eyes,—
Unless to the phrase a lady demurs,
And then, by the powers, I'll open hers!

A Peeler is one whose political mission
   S to vote for Peel,—
A startling fact, which the opposition
   Can't chose but feel;
Peeler, I think, to call the "gemman"
   'T were no misnomer,
Who is making punch, and peels the lemon
   To get the aroma
(Perhaps in parliamentary feeling
This is more *paring off* than Peeling);
   A Peeler's one who's, I may say,

Mixed up with *punch* another way;
 For, or my brains I bother,
  When two men fight,
  By day or night,
  Upon the floor
  They *peel*, before
 They punch each other!
(What Punch I pray *may you* best take?
*Mark! Lemon* punch, and no mistake)
Peelers—our thieves and rogues who fleece men,
Are wont to dub our new policemen;
O'Connell, too, or I'm a dunce,
Has proved a peeler more than once;
  For Dan
  'S the man,
 Who shouted in the heart of strife,
 "I'm a *re*-pealer all my life!"

But neither Dan, who will not cease
Repealing,—nor the New Police,—
Nor they who punch each other's eyes,—
Nor lemon-peeler, punch-bowl wise,—
Nor Peeler, who for Peel is voting,—
Nor Peel himself will bear the quoting;
Like that same peeler, made of oak;
 Which Little Riding Hood's old mother
Did into the hot oven poke,
 To draw her cakes, one after t' other:
That was, a peeler that was *dead*—
A peeler, which they use for bread.
Had she a *living* Peeler put
In any oven in her hut:
Granted, he could be got into it;
And more,—supposing she could do it;
 It's clearly my opinion *that*, O,
 She'd ne'er have baked another *gateau*;
  (The French for cake
  And no mistake),
 But rather *have* been tried, condemned, and hung;
Called by the people's most inspired tongue,
The blackest Jezabel that ever swung!

The Dismissal.—The Journey, and Adventures
on the Road

❀ 147 ❀

*Little Red
Riding
Hood*

   The cakes are cold,
   Ere the hour grows old, .
And Little Red Riding Hood's mother makes bold
    To say,—"Here, child, take
    This one little cake,
And eat it yourself for your grandmother's sake."

    And then mamma,
    With a look "*comme ça,*"
Says,—"Little Red Riding Hood rise, my dear,
I have something for your good grandmother here;
It's a pot of fresh butter," her mother said,
"Which you will carry a-top of your head;
And a cake the sweetest that ever she got,
And *that* you'll put neath the fresh butter-pot;
And last of all, because you are good,
You shall cover your head with your little red hood.

    You'll go,
    I know,
   And not very slow,
By the dingy wood where the tall trees grow,
And the dark-green water whose rivulets flow
Where no pretty sunbeams glisten or glow;
    But you'll not be afraid,
    For an innocent maid
Has little to tremble at, whether or no;
  And when you get to your grandmother's door,—
    Who is easily found,
    For she lives on the ground-
    Floor,—
You'll go quietly in; for no noise you must make,
But put down your butter, and put down your cake,
And say,—"Grandmother, mother sent these for your sake.
   Then curtseying sweetly,
    And neatly,
    And featly,
As you would to a beau whom you wanted to marry you
    You'll take a new tack,

**F. W. N. Bayley,** *Little Red Riding Hood,* **London: Orr, 1846. Illustrator Alfred Croquill.**

And come suddenly back,
As fast as your dear little legs, love, will carry you.

The pretty child,
With her ringlets wild;—
And her eyes of blue, that beamed so mild;—
Mouth the sweetest that ever smiled;—
And a heart more free,
In its mirthful glee,
Than man's happiest moment of revelry;—
Trod lightly along
With her natural song,
That was sung to the woodbirds, and not to the throng,
In a voice that seemed like a voice of love,
Which the wings of the angels were wafting above.

It was no disaster
To hear Madame Pasta;
It is n't so easy
To outvie the Grisi;
Rubini charms men, or
I do n't know his tenor;
And mighty Lablache
Does n't sing *"Comme une vache,"*

Which means, in plain English, he does n't know how
To astonish the natives, and chant like a cow!

   Even Adalaide Kemble,
    Now Madame Sartoris,
   Will voice not dissemble,
    Unless her throat sore is;
   But singing her best
   To the ears of the blest,
I doubt whether she, in the height of her glory,
 Or any of those who before her I've named,
Could sing like the beauty of my pleasant story,
 Or be half so gentle, or half so far-famed;—
   In a sentence I could,
   Must, might, can, will, and would,
Declare that none of them were ever so good
    As my fair little,
    Rare little,
Red Riding Hood!

   She  skipped along, naught fearing,
    With blithsome heels and hips,
   All down wood-paths careering,
    With music on her lips.
   She  tripped among the flowers,—
    She skimmed along the grass,—
   And laughed at the young hours,
    As lightly they did pass.

Her heart was glad within her,
 As childhood's heart is glad:—
If too young to be a sinner,
 *Then* too sinless to be sad!—
Still fate would not exempt her
 From his unhappy list;
For there came to her a tempter,
 Whom she could not resist!

A grisly Wolf, whose jump
 Cleared the forest thistles,
Came before her plump,

With all his hairs and bristles!
Who taught wolves to speak?—
   Æsop, in his fable,—
With voice of roar and squeak,
  As if escaped from Babel!

   This he mouthed and minced,
While his eyes shone brightness,
   Under which she winced,—
     That is, our pet
  Not being quite convinced
     As yet
That Wolf intended nothing but politeness!

"Where are you going, my dear?" said he.
"Going to grandmother, sir," said she.
"And pray where may your grandmother live?"—
"Why, the best direction that I can give,"—
Said this merry little young lady of *nous*,
"Is, that my grandmother lives in her house!"
With which the wolf gave a sniff with his nose,
And said—"So it's there, dear, you're going, I s'pose!

"I am," said she. Says the Wolf—"Adieu."
    And then he did mutter,—
    "With that cake and butter,
  Unless uncommonly fast you run,
   The odds are more than fifty to one
That I see your grandmother sooner than you!"

He runs,—he flies,—he leaps,—he bolts,—
Not the frisky limbs of a thousand colts
  Over the ground could more rapidly whiz,
  He's an animal steam-engine, that he is,
  With all the steam in the boiler riz!
Oh! that tap at the door of the child's grandmother,
And that husky voice that he tries to smother,
I know are no other—
     Than his!

WOLF'S COTTAGE ECONOMY—
HIS ARRANGEMENT OF FURNITURE
HIS DISPOSAL OF INMATES.—REMORSE AND MORAL.

❋ 151 ❋

*Little Red
Riding
Hood*

Tap, tap,
  Went the knowing old chap!
Tap, tap, and he put on the good,
Soft little voice of the sweet Riding Hood.
And when Granny coughed out, "Who's there?"—Said he,
"Why, if you please, Grandmother, it's me;
I've brought you butter,—I've brought you cake,
The best that ever my mother could make,—
And I've also brought it uncommonly quick,
Because my mother observed you were sick.
      I know by the smell
      It'll make you well;
  Now how shall I open the door, pray tell?"

      Loud Grandmother cries,
      With joy in her eyes,—
      "The string just catch,
      And you'll lift up the latch,
Then you've only to pull the old door a bit back,
And, child, you'll be into my room in a crack!"

The Wolf, with his eyes of appetite full,
Has given the bobbin a jolly good pull;
And the string, in the words of a find old catch,
Has given a jolly good pull to the latch;
And the latch is up, in a crack, from the door,
With such leap as never made latch before;
And Wolf, who's alert as a shark for his pottage,
Gets fairly inside of Old Grandmother's cottage!

      *She* is not asleep,
        But he *is* wide awake;
      So he gives her no butter,
        He gives her no cake;
But allows her at once to find out her mistake,
By seizing her quick, as she coughs with surprise,
And rapidly eating her, just as she lies;

Or, rather, by stopping her bronchial fits,
And supping upon her, then, just as she sits!
     Said poor Grandmother, crying,
      While tortured and dying,
  And pouring out groans that she couldn't well smother,—
"Oh! this is too hard,—much too hard!"—"Yes," and "So,"
Growled the cannibal Wolf in the midst of her woe,
  "I think ma'am are you!" as he eat the Grandmother!

     Ah! he finished her quite,
     With his sharp appetite;
     But, alas! there his spite
Didn't end where it could have done;
     For there's nobody knows,
     When he'd settled her woes,
     How he put on her clothes,
And look just the reverse of the chap that he should have done;
     When he turned into bed,
     In poor Grandmother's stead,
With her old-fashioned night-cap surrounding his head,
And the bed-gown, et cetera, of she who was dead;
Encasing his body beneath the patch quilt,
As he lay there brimful of Grandmother and guilt.

     But now his sin
     Soon worked within,
Remorse did make him weep:
  With sorrow and with supper crammed,
  His head between the sheets he rammed,
And then he fell asleep.

  He fell asleep, but soon did dream;
  His tears they poured out in a stream,—
His groans out in a snore,—
  And, as digestion grew more hard,
  A thousand fiends did gallopade
Before his sight galore.

  Greatly his vision did extend,—
  He saw grandmothers without end,
Whose moans did daunt and din him;

Until repenting of his sup,
  He almost wished he could bring up
The one he had within him!
    And as he dreamt,—oh, well-a-day!
    One supper on his conscience lay,
More heavy than ten dinners.
    He leaped and kicked, but couldn't wake,—
    He suffered pangs, and no mistake;
    So ever may grandmothers rake
The wolf-insides of sinners!

I leave Wolf's spirits down at zero,
      Reader mine;
May you or I have nought to fear O,
      Sup we heartily or dine.
Meanwhile, let's see where is our hero-
      ine!

Pretty maid! she idly lingers,
  As young thoughtless children will,
By the wood-wild path of flowers,
  Through the valley, o'er the hill;
Now a little playful triller
  Of some carol, music-fraught,—
Now a light and laughing lisper
  Of some glad and happy thought.

Careless of her very errand,
  From all fear of chiding far,
With the dauntless heart of childhood,
  Playing with her cake and jar.
Look! they are in air above her,—
  She upthrows them one and all!
They are falling,—no, Lord love her!
  She will never let them fall!

Her blythe spirit,—who'd control it?—
  Who would dim its joy with wrath?
Ha!—the cake is round,—she'll roll it
  Like a hoop upon her path!

There!—the changeful creature tires;—
    Cake and jar are both laid by,
And a whirring-top is spinning
    Underneath her merry eye.

Chasing every sportive vision
    That before her fancy stirs,
What world-heart is so Elysian
    In its happiness as hers!

Stay!—a cloud comes o'er her spirit,—
    One grey little tiny cloud
That, with just a feather's ruffle,
    Not more roughly, nor more loud,
Moves her into staid reflection—
    Of her gladness dims the sky;
Hinting,—"Why this gamesome loitering?—
    What a careless child am I!"

Soon no more of playful frolic—
    Childhood's honey—does she sip,
But with sweet demureness wending,
    And a gravely pouted lip,
She re-finds the path she quitted;
    Pauses there,—to ponder fain,
Like a butterfly back-flitted,
    Resting on its rose again!

Thought and breath they came together:—
    She hath scattered all her woes
In one moment, and now briskly
    Smiling on her way she goes.—
Her young steps have made the journey,
    Skipping on more fast than far,
And she gains her Granny's cottage
    Safely with her cake and jar.

Little Red Riding Hood, there you are
    At your Grandmother's old abode;
But the Wolf has travelled too fast by far,
    For you who stopped on the road.
He has eaten your Grandmother, bone and shin,—

He has eaten your Grandmother, nose and chin,—
He has eaten your Grandmother, hair and skin!
You're of your Grandmother quite bereft,
 And, terrible woe betide!
For there isn't a bit of your Grandmother left,
 Except in the Wolf's inside!

And there, as before her door you tread,
Without the slightest idea that she's dead,
She,—why, yes,—she certainly is in her bed,—
But then it is also sure—no doubt of it—
That she won't be there when the Wolf jumps out of it!
Depend upon it I can't be in fun,
When I say she's entirely swallowed and done!

Wolf—Wolf—is awaked from his dream
 (For he sleeps no more):—
 By Riding Hood's tap at her Grandmother's door
 Molested;
But he doesn't start with a groan or scream,
Like a sinner that fears he'll be kicking the beam,—
By conscience stricken he doth not seem,
 For Grandmother's all digested!

 He sits up in bed
 With the knowingest head,
That listens so sharp to Red Riding Hood's tread;
 And, for fear of mishap,
 The knowing old chap
Puts the Grandmother's voice on at Riding Hood's tap;
Just as—hasty rogue!—on occasion, the other
He used Riding Hood's voice to get at her Grandmother!

"Who's there?"—the voice seemed gruff and old.
 "I see;
Poor Grandmamma has got a cold,"
Said Riding Hood, as she made bold
 To mildly answer—"Me!"
"Who's me?"—"Your little grandchild good,
Whom people call Red Riding Hood;
 My mother sent me here."
 "Come in."—"But how come in, I pray?

I wish you'd tell me first the way,
    My kindly Granny, dear."

"Oh! pull the string,—bless your sweet eyes!
Yes! pull the string," the Wolf replies,—
    "The string will lift the latch;"
And then the monster turned his head,
And unto his own heart he said,
    "You'll find it is no catch!"

The string is pulled—the maid is in,
The Wolf sits there in all his sin,
    And fain would still dissemble.
The little maid, who not a whit
Suspects, goes by his side to sit,
    And doesn't even tremble.

She did n't sit upon a chair,
Because she did n't see one there;
   She did n't sit upon a table,
   There being none, she was n't able;
   She did n't—but we may as well
   The truth, and no mistake, here tell.
   There was one circumstance befel [sic],
   When first our Wolf began to dwell
Within the cot,—and now if you discern it, you're
   A clever person;—'tis this much:—
   That, Wolf's great appetite was such,
   Not only Grandmother and crutch
He ate—but ALL THE FURNITURE!

So this is the upshot—when all's done and said,
That Little Red Riding Hood sat on the bed;
And was very soon puzzled to know, I declare,
What kind of a Grandmother she had got there.
The Wolf, who surveyed her, began with a kiss,
And the short conversation that followed, was this:—

   "Oh! come to bed Red Riding Hood,-
   Oh! come to bed with me! For I am here,
      Your Granny, dear,
   As deftly you may see."

           The little maid
           Ne'er disobeyed
An order that she was told;
           So away she fakes,
           And off she takes
Her little red hood in a brace of shakes;
And sporting her night-gown then, I ween,
In a bed-post twinkle she slides between
Two sheets that are not especially clean,
     As she thinks with her Granny old.

Now little Riding Hood, though beyond doubt
She hadn't yet found her predicament out,
Yet twigging the Wolf, who was really a rum 'un,
Thought her Granny a very astonishing woman;
Most ugly, ungainly, uncombed, and uncommon!
What marvel, then, that at first glimpse of her charms,
She cried—"Granny, you've got most remarkable arms!"
To which Wolf responded, with *his* ugly mug,—
"The better, my darling, to give you a hug."
"But, Granny, your ears are so hairy and wild!"
"The better it strikes me to hear you, my child."
"But then, Granny, your eyes!—Oh, what terrible eyes!"
"If I don't see you with them 't will give me surprise."
"And your teeth!"—Here the Wolf, who saw Riding Hood
           shrink,
Cried—"The sooner I eat you the better I think!"
Whereon he laid hold of the poor little soul,
And his ravenous spirit, too mad to control,
He gave her a bite, and a crunch and a roll,
And the gulping old vagabond swallowed her whole!
Then when he was sure she was thoroughly dead,
           He leaped out of bed,
           And the neighbourhood fled,
Taking with him the curses of bad and of good,
And, also, his poor little victim's red hood;
Furthermore, it is said, that he died in a wood,—
           A sort of wolf sage,
           At a much-advanced age,
With no one in Wolfendom knowing the name of him,—
No young posterity full of the fame of him,—
And nobody caring a dump what became of him!

F. W. N.
BAYLEY

With our amusement we would blend some good,
    And having in a new fashion told,
      The story old
Of Little Red Riding Hood,
  We by no means wish to have it said,
For want of a moral the *Riding Hood* we
Had written and published, deserved to be
    In reality *Little Read.*

    First, to little girls with grandmothers,
        And others,
      We would seriously say,
      Do n't loiter on the way
      To trifle or to play,
      But always answer nay
      To any one, by night or day,
      Who would your footsteps stay.
Ne'er talk to strangers that you meet,
In field, in forest, or in street;
      For, by the young,
      A flattering tongue
Is thought of a good heart the token,
And even wolves are sometimes civil spoken.
Secondly:—'T would be quite as well,
    As a general rule to lay it down,
    To idle inquirers, in country or town,
Your plans and intentions never to tell;
    Lest, ere your business is completed,
    Your object be defeated.
If Little Red Riding Hood only had thought
Of these little matters as much as she ought,
In the trap of the Wolf she would ne'er have been caught,
Nor her Grandmother killed in so cruel a sort,
      Nor Riding Hood's tale
      Should we have to bewail;
And that of our moral's the long and the short.

# ❀ **8** ❀

## *The Romance of*
## *Little Red*
## *Riding Hood*

### *By Alphonse Daudet*

### (1862)

 CROSSROADS IN THE WOODS. *Flowers, birds, butterflies. Red Riding Hood is wearing the traditional dress of her family—without forgetting the cake or the pot of butter.*

### SCENE ONE

RED RIDING HOOD: For my cake's sake! There are those days when one is just happy to be on this earth, when it seems that your boots are like wings, that your eyes launch rockets, that your veins are crammed with saltpetre—yes, there are those days when one feels a raging desire to prance upon the grass, to jump on some person's back, and to tug the tips of the poplars. Today I'm completely in this kind of mood and, between you and me, I have many days like this one. (*She skips.*) Tra, la, la. Giddy-up! Tra, la, la!

POLONIUS (*enters*): What a strange girl! She seems madly in love. I've seen this pretty face somewhere before.

RED RIDING HOOD: What can this old man want of me?

POLONIUS: Hey! You there, young girl! Come here so I can say a few words to you.

RED RIDING HOOD: Please, let's hurry. I'm in a rush,

POLONIUS: Just wait a second. My God! I'm convinced that I know

159

you. That short skirt, those embroidered knickers, that scarlet head dress, that basket, that cake . . . Where the devil have you come from, my little Red Riding Hood?

RED RIDING HOOD: I'm coming from our house, and I'm going to my grandmother's to bring her this pot of butter,

POLONIUS: My word of honor! Are you little Red Riding Hood? The true Red Riding Hood?

RED RIDING HOOD: Of course! My God, yes! What's so astonishing about that?

POLONIUS: Nothing in the world, my dear child. I don't want to reawaken cruel memories in you, but . . . I believe . . . I've heard said that you were devoured on a certain day. . . .

RED RIDING HOOD: Alas!

POLONIUS: By an evil wolf who was disguised . . .

RED RIDING HOOD: That's right.

POLONIUS: And all of this would not have happened if you had not been so thoughtless. . . .

RED RIDING HOOD: That's all very true!

POLONIUS: But, then, since you've compensated for having been devoured. . . .

RED RIDING HOOD: I want you to know, monsieur, that I've been devoured an infinite number of times, and each time it is my fault. There you have it! Four thousand years that I've had the same accident, four thousand years that I am revived, four thousand years, by an incredible fatality, I'm going to put myself inevitably in the paws of the wolf. What do you want? I always die very young, and when I return to the world, I only have a vague memory of my previous existences, very vague. . . . Oh, how interesting it would be to write and peruse that *Story of Red Riding Hood in all the centuries!* Monsieur Perrault has sketched but only one chapter. How fortunate is he who will write the others.

POLONIUS: I've never seen such a unique creature in my life.

RED RIDING HOOD: And now, doctor, if you have nothing more to say to me, I'll kiss your hands.

POLONIUS: But, no! Not at all! On the contrary, I have a great deal to say to you. . . . Is it possible that you know me since you call me doctor?

RED RIDING HOOD: Doctor Polonius, your little name is world renowned.

POLONIUS: That's it, that's it! How kind you are! Tell me, my girl, since you are going to your grandmother's, and since I, too, am going in the same direction, we could go together. Would you like to?

❀ 161 ❀

*The
Romance
of Little Red
Riding
Hood*

RED RIDING HOOD: Oh! What luck! We'll have a good time. You'll see! Let's be off right now, doctor. But you'd better roll up your coat so you'll be able to run and skip more easily. . . . Full steam ahead! Follow me! . . .

POLONIUS: Hold on! Hold on! Where are you going, my young wisp of air? That's not the way to your grandmother's house. The main road will take us there in a direct line.

RED RIDING HOOD: Bah! Are you going to take the main road? What about the dust? The sun? And the carriages? Ah! You're going to take the main road! . . . Thanks but no thanks!

POLONIUS: Don't be such a little fool! Think about it for once in your life. The main road is a bit boring, I agree, but you're certain to arrive on time and without a great deal of trouble.

RED RIDING HOOD: Oh! Doctor, look at how lovely this path is. The birds, the daisies, the mulberries, the tender grass, the streams. If you take this path, you'll see how we'll laugh. I'll make you bouquets, bouquets as large as my head. We'll search for all sorts of blue and red beasts at the base of the flowers, and we'll make a garland out of them with a piece of thread. You'll see, you'll see. Let's go! Let's prance on the grass! Let's go! A handful of mulberries. Do you like mulberries, big belly?

POLONIUS: And the wolf, my little unfortunate one!

RED RIDING HOOD: Ah! Yes, it's true, the wolf! . . . Bah! There aren't wolves every day, and anyway, if one of them comes, well then, we'll eat him.

POLONIUS (*feeling her forehead*): This child is totally lacking in foresight, and it's frightening to see.

RED RIDING HOOD: You absolutely won't come with me? No! Well then, good evening. Why the devil did you waste my time?

POLONIUS: Ah! How unfortunate she is!

RED RIDING HOOD: Good by, doctor. Watch out for the rays of the sun, my dear!

*They exit.*

## SCENE TWO

*A little later in the forest. Always the same setting.*

RED RIDING HOOD (*alone, then a boy joins her*): Bah! It's time to get rid of those sad ideas! Besides, a wolf is not as evil as one says he is. Perhaps he'll take pity on me, this one time. I'm very pretty today.

I've just caught a glimpse of myself in a drop of water on a leaf. . . .
Besides, I'm much stronger than most people. I'll take my wolf by
the neck, and crack! All the same, it would have amused me to
have coaxed that old windbag into the woods and to have made
him join the grand family of riding hoods. But no! A narrow mind,
drawers in order, always locked by a key. It would have been impossible to pull anything out. I'll find something better than that,
*The boy enters.*

BOY (*crying*): Oh, my God! I'm really to be pitied!

RED RIDING HOOD: Why are you so desolate, my pet?

BOY: I'm crying, my pretty mademoiselle, because I must go to
school and it's very boring in weather like this.

RED RIDING HOOD: First of all, you're silly to cry. The good God did
not give you eyes to make reservoirs. Besides, if you use up all your
tears today, what will you do when you're grown up? You've got to
put something by for a rainy day, by dickens! Come sit down next
to me at the foot of that tree over there! Now, tell me your name.

BOY: I'm called little Picou, the son of big Picou who squints.

RED RIDING HOOD: Very good! Picou, if you trust me, everything
will turn out all right. First we're going to eat something. Then . . .
we'll see. What do you have in the basket?

BOY: Oh! You musn't touch anything there, mademoiselle. That's for
my snack, and mother Picou would get mad and grumble a great deal.

RED RIDING HOOD: Aren't you hungry?

BOY: Don't know! I ate a large bowl of cabbage soup just a quarter
of an hour ago, but I'd have a nibble of something any way.

RED RIDING HOOD: What are you waiting for then, you little fool?
Open your basket. Good! Jam and fresh nuts. As for me, I've got a
cake and pot of butter. They're for my grandmother. But she won't
eat any of this, the poor dear woman! (*They eat.*) Hey, how do you
like it?

BOY (*with a full mouth*): Tastes great. . . . Yes, but what will my
mother Picou say?

RED RIDING HOOD: Why should you care? She could scold you to
kingdom come, but that won't stop you from eating more of the jam.

BOY: That's true, quite true! But then I'll have nothing left for my
snack.

RED RIDING HOOD: You really are stupid! You won't be hungry at
snack time. Are you hungry now?

BOY: No . . . hardly. (*He stands up.*)

RED RIDING HOOD: You see! Where are you rushing off to?

BOY: To school, of course!

RED RIDING HOOD: Bah! But you're about to cry.

BOY (*hesitating*): It's because . . . I'm afraid of the whip . . . for tomorrow.

RED RIDING HOOD: If you go now, you'll get a whipping for taking your time on the way to school. So, you might as well enjoy yourself today since you're here. The spanking of tomorrow won't be any more terrible than that of today. Besides, who knows? From one day to the next, the teacher could break a leg. A thunderbolt could strike the school. It's right next to the church, and thunderbolts only strike churches.

BOY: Mademoiselle! There's some truth to what you say.

RED RIDING HOOD: Let's go. Don't think about school anymore. . . . Do you hear the blackbirds singing up there? Get me a couple of their nests. Do the birds go to school? Pick some strawberries, a basket full of forest strawberries. By heaven! That's what I call a wonderful snack! It's too warm at school. Here you can take off your clothes and stretch yourself, completely naked, your whole body on the sand of the brook. The trees will bow to fan you and chase away the mosquitos. With your knife you will carve boats from the bark of trees. Tear up your handkerchief and make wings out of them, and entrust me with all of the blue ants and beasts, for heaven's sake. . . . You'll see how much you'll enjoy yourself.

BOY: Oh Jesus! Mary! Your words are like true music! Do you want to take me away with you? I already love you with all my heart.

RED RIDING HOOD (*shaking her head*): No, Picou. You see, it's better if you stay here. If something bad should happen to you while you're with me, I'd feel terrible. Come and give me a hug and a kiss. . . .

BOY: Gladly. You smell so nice! That's really something, to place my lips on yours.

RED RIDING HOOD (*with emotion*): Good bye. Enjoy yourself.

BOY: Oh! Yes, I certainly will! . . . All the same, I'd willingly eat the crusts of bread.

## SCENE THREE

*A clearing in the woods. The writer is stretched out on his back, a notebook on his stomach, a pencil between his teeth.*

WRITER: It's all for nought! I've tortured my brain and buried my eyes in books in vain. Nothing! . . . Not even the beginning of a sentence, nor the end of an idea. Yet, I promised my novel for

tomorrow, without fail. . . Ah! Such laziness! And to think I went
to the meadows in order to work with better taste. . . .
*Red Riding Hood appears.*
RED RIDING HOOD (*singing*):

> I'm a bastard of a butterfly,
> the grasshopper's own godchild.
> People say I've got a fine eye
> And a figure like a cricket's thigh.
> Come rain, come snow or hail,
> I run through meadow and field
> without umbrella or parasol.

(*Spoken*): Oh, oh! A man who's working. What an unusual idea!
(*She approaches the writer.*) I can tell that you're an artist, monsieur.
Am I right?
WRITER (*raising himself on his elbows*): Where do you see that, my
charming child?
RED RIDING HOOD: Who else would ever think of making the forest
into a study?
WRITER: My faith! Yes, I'm an artist, a novelist, and I've come here
to write from nature. . . . But . . . if I'm not mistaken . . . I've seen
you somewhere before. . . . Ah! I know you. You're Red Riding Hood.
RED RIDING HOOD: Why, yes. That's what they say.
WRITER: No! It's impossible. I'm dreaming with my eyes open.
Quick, some holy water. Quick, a sign of the cross so that I can
chase away this vision of the devil.
RED RIDING HOOD: There's really some other one at work right now.
WRITER: *Vado retro, Satanas.* You're the demon of laziness, the demon of carelessness, the demon of the unexpected. *Vado retro,* do
you hear me? Oh, I know you quite well. You are our most terrible
enemy. Get out of here, purveyor of ruin! Get out of here, succubus
of Hell! What evil have you done? What have you done to Hé-
giésippe and Gustave Planche and to poor Gérard? What would
you have done to Lamartine? What did you do to Abadie? What
did you do to Traviès?
RED RIDING HOOD: When will you be finished, my dear?
WRITER: I'll finish by wiping you out if you don't get out of here
soon, you cursed snake.
RED RIDING HOOD: You're not very gentle, you know? Oh, I'm
going. I'm going! However, let me tell you that those people to

whom I brought evil never complained. They thoroughly enjoyed those delectable hours that I enabled them to spend, and they were grateful to me for all their happiness. Yes, I am Red Riding Hood, the queen of the *far niente*, the fantastic goddess of the lazzarones and the poets. I am your mistress for all, and you all have built a temple for me at the bottom of your hearts. Go, I am going to pardon you for your insults because I love you and you love me. . . Again you now owe me a day of happiness, you ungrateful villain. Look, the weather is superb. The woods are filled with a silent lustre. Above your head, the song of birds. At your feet, the song of rivers. Close your eyes, my sweet poet. Lay your head on this lawn of grass. Let yourself go. Let yourself go. Twelve hours of dreams lie ahead of you. Twelve beautiful hours in white garbs and crowned with flowers. Good by, my poet. The woods are woods, a dreamer is a dreamer. . . . Good night. (*She throws his notebook above the trees.*)
WRITER (*docile*): Kiss me, Red Riding Hood. God! . . . I . . . feel . . . so . . . well!

SCENE FOUR

*At the edge of a wood full of thickets. Two lovers enter. Red Riding Hood is hidden behind a bush, and she watches them as they approach.*
HE: You're tired, Marie. Take my arm for support.
SHE: No, I'd prefer to sit down. Look, a clearing. The sun's dried the grass. Let's stop here a moment.
RED RIDING HOOD (*hidden*): It's funny. Women always take the initiative in love.
HE: Do you want me to open your umbrella and hold it above your head?
RED RIDING HOOD (*hidden*): What a bumbling fool! As if his hands were stopping him.
SHE: No, thanks. The branches of this larch are enough to cover me.
HE: It's nice here, isn't it, Marie? Far from the noise, far from people. There's shade here, silence, and our love.
RED RIDING HOOD (*hidden*): Bravo! I saw it coming.
SHE (*leaning her head on his shoulder*): Yes! But I'm afraid. See! I'm trembling in spite of myself. I don't know what I'm feeling. The slightest breeze stirs me. The slightest noise makes me shudder. Oh! I'm afraid!
HE: Get a grip on yourself, my dear treasure. What are you scared of

and why tremble? Do you want to move closer to the farm or return home to your mother?

RED RIDING HOOD (*hidden*): Imbecile! Go! His eighteen years are showing.

SHE: Oh! No, I'm very happy just to be with you. (*A moment of silence.*)

RED RIDING HOOD (*irritated*): You see they're not saying anything to each other.

SHE: Ah! My poor dear, why did I ever make your acquaintance? (*Noise of kisses.*)

RED RIDING HOOD: Well, they finally made up their minds. (*She comes out of her hiding place.*) It doesn't matter. I'm going to show myself and give them some advice.

THE TWO LOVERS (*at the same time*): Heavens! Oh, great God!

RED RIDING HOOD: Now, now! Don't get frightened. I'm Red Riding Hood, young like you at heart, and moreover, the patron of lovers. Go ahead and embrace. It makes my heart rejoice, and each one of your kisses titillates my lips with pleasure. Do it once more! Once more!

HE (*does not want to continue kissing*): Ah! My poor Red Riding Hood, we are very much to be pitied.

SHE (*wants to continue kissing*): Oh! Yes, we're to be pitied very much!

RED RIDING HOOD: And why is that, my good sir?

HE: Well, you understand, we love each other with all our heart and soul, and they won't let us marry.

RED RIDING HOOD: And so?

HE: And so . . . That's all. Isn't that enough?

RED RIDING HOOD: Could you tell me, my children, what are roses good for, and why has God placed them on our path if not to be gathered and to smell sweetly? Could you also tell me why one finds nice and thick bushes like that at the corner of the paths in the forest? Why do they grow there if not for lovers? Ah! They don't want to let you marry, poor children. I pity you with all my heart. Good by, my little ones. Don't forget that tomorrow is only a great liar . . . . Even more important, don't forget how to put the roses and bushes to use. (*She makes off.*)

SHE: Have you understood?

HE: No. And you?

SHE: I think I do.

SCENE FIVE

❀ 167 ❀

*The
Romance
of Little Red
Riding
Hood*

*In the dense forest.*

RED RIDING HOOD: Seeing those two young ones troubled me. What a beautiful thing love is! As for myself, nobody loves me. Some people pity me, others regard me as an object of hate. Those who adore me never tell me so. Nevertheless, I remember a red throat that was passionately in love with me. . . . I believe he died because of it. . . . What do you know! It must be raining. I've got a drop of water on my hand. Sometimes I happen to cry, but never for a long time. (*She sings.*)

> I'm a bastard of a butterfly,
> the grasshopper's own godchild. . . .

Good God! What a strange person I see there! Look at his skips and jumps! Now he's walking on his head! He's really funny! Really amusing! Ahhh! I must ask him to play with me. Hey! Young man! Young man!

MADMAN (*enters*): Who's calling me? Is it you, young girl? Were you the one calling me?

RED RIDING HOOD: Yes, it's me, Red Riding Hood, and I'd like to ask you if you wouldn't mind having fun with me. You appear to have a cheerful air about you.

MADMAN: To be cheerful I'm very cheering. Ah! You. You're Red Riding Hood. What's that? Yes, I remember, a young girl who loves flowers very much and who always takes the path that leads to the crossroad. Me, too, I love flowers. Do you want me to make you a crown with the branches of this willow? It is very pretty like that. A propos, you've already told me your name, but I've forgotten it.

RED RIDING HOOD: Red Riding Hood.

MADMAN: I always forget. Tell me. You won't take me back there, will you! (*Crying.*) I'm so happy to be free. I won't harm a soul. Little girl, please, don't take me back there.

RED RIDING HOOD: Where's there?

MADMAN: To the doctor. He's a large man with glasses, and he pours cold water on me every day like a vegetable garden.

RED RIDING HOOD: So, that's it! A madman. I would never have guessed it.

MADMAN: My mind is a bit sick, but that's no reason to bruise my skull and to hurt my ears.

RED RIDING HOOD: Don't be afraid. I won't take you back there. Has it been a long time since you escaped?

MADMAN: I don't know. When one is happy, one never knows since when. Do you want me to tell you a story about the hummingbird and the princess? But, before I do, you must tell me your name. I always forget.

RED RIDING HOOD: You really are amusing! It must be ten times that I've repeated it to him. My name's Red Riding Hood.

MADMAN: Well, my Hood, sit down on my knees and listen to my story.

RED RIDING HOOD: No! No siree! It's getting late. Almost nightfall. I must run quickly to my grandmother's house.

MADMAN: Here we go. I'm beginning. . . .

RED RIDING HOOD: No. Be quiet. I'm going. . . (*Without moving from her place.*) Good bye!

MADMAN: Go.

RED RIDING HOOD: Well then, no! I'm going to stay. . . Tell me your story.

(*They hear the howl of a wolf.*)

MADMAN: Come and sit on my knees. What's the matter? You're trembling.

RED RIDING HOOD: Didn't you hear that bad beast? Owww! Owww!

MADMAN: Don't be scared. I'm here.

RED RIDING HOOD: How nice you are, my madman! Let's go. I'm listening. (*She places her arms around the neck of her friend.*)

MADMAN: Once upon a time there was a hummingbird and a prince who were madly in love with one another. . . . Are you sleeping?

RED RIDING HOOD: No, my friend, a hummingbird and a princess.

MADMAN: But, the king and queen were against their marriage because the hummingbird was too. . . . Are you listening?

RED RIDING HOOD: Yes, but don't speak so loudly.

MADMAN: One night, the hummingbird said to the princess. . .

RED RIDING HOOD (*half asleep*): It's . . . nice . . . very nice . . . your story.

MADMAN: She's sleeping. Her sweet breath slides down my neck. She's breathing slowly. Her earrings are touching my skin. I'm very happy.

(*He falls asleep. The wolf runs by them.*)

❦ 169 ❦

The
Romance
of Little Red
Riding
Hood

*Little Red Riding Hood,* London: Routledge, 1866. Illustrator Walter Crane.

## SCENE SIX

*The next day. It is a beautiful day. The birds sing upon waking. In the center is the grandmother's house. The shutters are closed. At the side of the house, a well.*

BOY: (*enters with red eyes and a stick in his hand*): I'm going to sit down here and wait until she arrives. Then I'm going to give her a drubbing and finished it off with some whacks from this stick. (*He sits down in a corner.*)

WRITER (*enters and appears totally broken down*): Where is that wretched adviser? I'll strangle her a little, and then I'll spread her body over the face of the earth!

BOY: If it's Red Riding Hood you're looking for, sit down like me. She'll be coming from over there.

LOVER (*enters sobbing*): Oh! That miserable creature! I'll hide somewhere and make her pay for all the trouble that she's caused.

## SCENE SEVEN

*The Madman and Red Riding Hood arrive arm in arm in a gay mood.*

RED RIDING HOOD: You see, my friend. I was speaking frankly. You're the only person in the world who's been able to understand me, and I swear that I'll never forget you as long as I live. Promise me that you'll think about me from time to time.

MADMAN: I want to very much. I want to. But you must tell me your name. Have you already told it to me?

RED RIDING HOOD (*wiping a tear*): Alas! The only man that I've ever loved! My friend, lend me your back so that I can climb the cherry tree. I want to make some earrings for myself with the cherries.

BOY, WRITER, AND LOVER (*show themselves all at once*): Finally! There she is!

RED RIDING HOOD (*a little frightened*): What do you want of me, my good people? What's the matter with you? You all have such furious faces.

ALL THREE (*at the same time*): It's you, you alone that we want. . . . It's your blood we want.

RED RIDING HOOD (*to the Madman*): Hey! My friend, help me! Help me!

MADMAN: They're very good, the cherries!

RED RIDING HOOD: Gentlemen, gentlemen, first explain. You can have my blood afterwards. (*To the boy.*) You. Begin. What do you want of me?

CHILD: To tell you how wretched you are! You're the cause of all my troubles. Thanks to you, they've kicked me out of school. Father Picou gave me a thrashing with a stick, and mother Picou (*with a sob*) no longer wants to feed me.

RED RIDING HOOD: One down. Now to the next.

WRITER: I was right not to trust you. You encouraged me to be lazy and to succumb to my foolish dreams. I put my work aside, and now I won't have any money for a month.

RED RIDING HOOD: Sinned, and you?

LOVER: I want to ask you the reason why you gave me such bad advice and placed such wicked ideas in my head. My poor Marie got some spots of green on her white dress. Her mother guessed everything and has put her in a convent.

RED RIDING HOOD: And is that all? You have nothing more to say?

ALL: What more do you want?

RED RIDING HOOD: Listen to me, my children. Listen to me for a few minutes. I'm not the pernicious and wretched devil that you think I am, and I feel deeply sorry for all the terrible things that have happened to you. But, after all is said and done, are you really to be pitied? Thanks to me, each of you has had a lovely day. It's true, of course, this day has only lasted twenty-four hours, but that's not my fault. Wouldn't it be more worthwhile to accept your bad present situation as a memory of a happy past, to be a little resigned, and to thank me a great deal? Right now you see me as I am, my poor friends, but I'm going to pay for my pleasures of yesterday and last night in a few moments. A wolf is there, and he is impatiently waiting for me, and, alas, there's nothing I can do to avoid his cruel teeth! It is part of my destiny as Red Riding Hood to accept this death without complaining. Follow my example, my dear children, and never regret a pleasure no matter how much you must pay for it. Happiness does not have a price. Only fools haggle over its price. And now I'll abandon myself to your vengeance. You may do with me as you wish.

ALL: So pretty and so wicked! How could we possibly want to do anything to her?

RED RIDING HOOD: There! I was quite sure that you would not harm me. You're children, good children, and I'm going to leave you with something to remember me by. (*Taking off her earrings.*) A cherry for each one of you. Take them, and keep them until tomorrow. . . . That's a long time, isn't it? . . . It's time to go. Good bye, my friends, and think of Red Riding Hood from time to time. (*Addressing the madman.*) And you! Do you want to come and give me a kiss, one final kiss?

MADMAN (*skipping about without understanding*): So then, the hummingbird said to the princess: the moment has come for us to part. . . . Tra la la, deri deri, la la.

RED RIDING HOOD: My lover doesn't have much of a memory. . . . (*The clock strikes eight.*) The time has come. All romances have an end, mine like all the others. It is shorter, and that's all. Good night, gentlemen. (*She enters the house.*)

ALL: Good by, Riding Hood. (*A loud noise can be heard inside.*)

SCENE EIGHT

*The same characters. Polonius comes running at full speed.*
POLONIUS: Stop! Stop! . . . Alas! Always too late! Oh, how lame experience and wisdom are whenever they run after insanity and heedlessness! I rushed in vain. I can never extricate Red Riding Hood from the jaws of the wolf. (*Addressing the others around him.*) Well, you others, I suppose that you're the victims of this wicked little girl. Follow me. I'll repair the damage and set you on the good path once again. (*To the madman who does not hear.*) Come, monsieur!

MADMAN: No, thank you, thank you. I've finished my story, and the hummingbird is dead. You would only take me back to the hospital. I prefer to drown myself. I love those romances that end badly. (*He jumps down the well.*)

POLONIUS (*gravely*): There you have it—the fate of madmen and people who throw caution to the winds. The fate of Red Riding Hood and her kind. Warning to the public.

*They exit.*

## ❀ 9 ❀

## *The Story of Little Red Riding Hood*

## *By Richard Henry Stoddard*

## (1864)

"Red Riding-Hood, the darling,
The flower of fairy lore,"
—L. E. L.

I.

SOMEWHERE IN MERRY ENGLAND
(The time was long ago),
There lived a little maiden,
Whose story you shall know.
She came of simple people,
Whose homely cottage stood,
With a slip of garden near it,
Against an ancient wood.
Her father,—he made fagots,
The firewood of the poor,
While her mother sat a-spinning
Beside the cottage door.
*There she lived, and there she grew,*
*As the country children do;*
*Eight years old, and fair as good,*
*The little maid, Red Riding-Hood.*

## II

RICHARD
HENRY
STODDARD

They rose while she was sleeping,
    And her father trudged away,
With his axe upon his shoulder,
    Before the break of day;
Her mother scoured three platters,
    And set beside her bed
A cup of sweetest honey,
    And the freshest crust of bread;
Then went about her spinning
    As softly as she could,
But the old wheel's endless humming
    Woke little Riding-Hood,
Who rubbed her rosy eyelids,
    And started up in glee:
"What, is it you, dear mother?
    I thought it was a bee!"
    *"They should be bees, and busy, too,*
    *Who have a many drones like you."*
    *She shook her head: "It isn't good*
    *To say such things of Riding-Hood."*

III.

She had an aged grandmother
    This pretty little may,
Dwelling within the forest,
    A league or more away;
Who, on her eighth sweet birthday,
    When leaves began to fall,
Gave her a riding-habit,
    With a ruffled hood and all.
And O, but it was bonny
    To see it on her head;
Why, when she walked i' th' garden,
    The rose was not so red!
And when the neighbors spied it,
    Like morning through the wood,
They said to one another,
    "Here comes Red Riding-Hood"

*Such the name the darling bore,*
*From the scarlet hood she wore;*
*For her christened name it stood—*
*She was known as Riding-Hood.*

IV.

"Rise up, rise up, my daughter,"
   One morn her mother said,
"For you must go to Granny's,
   I hear she's sick abed;
A pat of nice fresh butter
   Will do the poor soul good."
"And let me send my honey,"
   Said litle Riding-Hood.
The churn goes fast, and faster,
   The pat of butter's made,
And with a pot of honey
   Is in a basket laid.
The loving child is ready,
   Behold her where she stands,
In her pretty riding-habit,
   The basket in her hands;
Beneath the morning-glories
   That drape the cottage door,
She lingers for a moment,
   To con her message o'er.
"We heard that she was ailing,
   And I have brought her this;
And father's very sorry,
   And mother sends a kiss."
*Here she hears her mother say,*
*   "Daughter must n't stop to play."*
*And she answers, "I'll be good,*
*   Or my name's not Riding-Hood.*

V.

Along the winding pathway
   The merry maiden went,
So light her tripping footsteps

RICHARD
HENRY
STODDARD

The grass was hardly bent!
'Twas strung with silver dew-drops,
  With spider webs o'erspread,
Like sheets of linen, bleaching
  For Mab, the fairy's, bed.
At length she reached the forest,
  A still and dreamy place,
Whose brooding shadows darkened
  The beauty of her face;
Save where the morning struggled
  In long and golden lines.
The narrow path was slippery
  With needles of the pines;
Ferns grew along its borders,
  And vines were stretched across,
And here were spotted toadstools,
  And there were beds of moss:
By bush, and brier, and bramble,
  She glided like a shade,
Nor made the dry leaves rustle,
  Nor any thing afraid.
The robins fed their young ones
  The rabbits never knew
The tripping of her footsteps
  From the dripping of the dew!!
But where the wood grew darker,
  So dense the roof o'erhead,
Besides her pattering footfall
  There was a heavy tread,
That made the dead leaves rattle,
  That crushed the tender flowers,
That brushed the low-hung branches,
  And shook the dew in showers!
Who was it stole behind her?
  What tracked her through the wood?
It was a wolf that followed
  The helpless Riding-Hood!
She turned her head and saw him,
  And stood stock still with fear,
So fierce his eyes and cruel,
  And his sharp teeth so near!

"I wonder will he kill me?
    "Thought little Riding-Hood;
"He knows I never harmed him,
    And would not if I could."
"She'll make a dainty morsel,"
    He muttered in reply;
"Shall I eat her where she's standing?
    Or wait till by and by?"
While this he was debating
    But certain of his prey,
She snatched her fallen basket,
    And hurried on her way.
*Where the tangled pathway wound;*
*Past the trees that shut around;*
*Through the thick and gloomy wood*
*Went the wolf and Riding-Hood.*

VI.

At last the sound of voices
    Was indistinctly heard;
Or was it but the halloo
    Of some half-human bird?
It was the fagot-makers,
    At work within the wood,
About the path where wandered
    The wolf and Riding-Hood.
The creature heard them talking,
    And slacked at once his pace;
It would not do to chase her
    In such an open place:
You would have thought to see him—
    "How could she be afraid?
It is a good old house-dog
    That loves the little maid."
They met a fagot-maker,
    Who chopped a fallen bough:
"Red Riding-Hood, good morning,
    Where are you going now?"
She stopped, and swung her basket
    With pretty shame, and said:

RICHARD
HENRY
STODDARD

"I'm going, sir, to Granny's,
  For she is sick abed."
Meantime the wolf comes closer,
  To see how matters stand:
He rubs his head against her,
  He tries to lick her hand!
"Why, here's a wolf," they shouted,
  And hastened at the sight:
"I think it is the villain
  That stole my sheep last night."
"Upon my honor, gentleman,
  I never in my life"—
One raised his axe, with "Kill him!"
  Another drew his knife:
"Pray don't! he mayn't be guilty,"
  Cried tender Riding-Hood;
"I'm sure he didn't harm me,
  When I was in the wood."
"For your sake then we spare him,
  He owes his life to you;
But if more sheep are missing,
  We'll all know what to do."
Back to their work they plodded,
  With many a look behind.
"A thousand thanks, my lady,"
  The cunning creature whined:
"I'll not forget your kindness,
  Indeed, you are too good;
But now I must be going,
  Adieu, sweet Riding-Hood."
He trotted toward the forest,
  But soon came back and said:
"The Grandmamma you spoke of,
  I think, she is sick abed.
Poor soul!"—he sighed for pity,
  "Where lives the good old dame?"
"You see that little cottage,
  Whose windows are aflame?
With jessamines and woodbines
  The porch is covered o'er"—
"And, pray, how do you enter?"

"By tapping at the door,
And Granny then will tell you
   (But you must hark to hear),
That you must pull the latch-string;
   She'll say, 'Come in, my dear.'
   *"Pull the string, and then you're in;*
   *Wordly wits are sure to win."*
   *He took a short cut through the wood,*
   *Laughing at Red Riding-Hood.*

VII.

Red Riding-Hood was troubled,
   Not knowing what he meant;
And, glad that he had vanished,
   She wondered where he went.
But brief the stay of sorrow
   In such a childish mind;
A cloud the wind is chasing,
   That leaves no trace behind!
The path led through a meadow,
   Where flowers so thickly grew
You knew not which were the thickest,
   The flowers or the dew!
They flaunted in the sunshine,
   They hid in shady nooks,
They clambered through the grasses,
   They dipped along the brooks.
"I'll gather some for Granny,"
   Said Red Riding-Hood anon,
Stopping to save a blossom
   She nearly trod upon:
She picked a lady-slipper,
   Was larger than her own;
She stripped a royal rose-tree
   Of all the buds were blown:
Handfuls of yellow cowslips,
   Whose cups are full of spots;
And knots of frail sweet-purples,
   And dear forget-me-nots:
The daisy, and the primrose,

RICHARD
HENRY
STODDARD

The rustic marigold—
She heaped her little apron
   As full as it would hold!
Then, tired with her sweet labor,
   She sat beneath a tree,
To sort her dewy treasures,
   As busy as a bee.
She made a pretty nosegay,
   Of posies white and red,
To fill the earthen pitcher
   That stood by Granny's bed:
She bound a bunch of violets,
   And lilies of the vale.
With a rose that was the sweetheart
   Of the noble nightingale:
She wove a wreath of purples
   In many a curious twine,
With glossy leaves of ivy,
   And tendrils of the vine:
And while her twinkling fingers
   Were braiding bud and flower,
The lark, the morning's watchman,
   Was singing in his tower;
High up above the meadow
   Where lay his grassy nest,
Where slept the glassy river,
   No ripples on its breast:
Where slid the snake, where burrowed
   The rabbit and the mole,
And where the tiny field-mouse
   Was peeping from his hole!
As she was idly watching
   Their labor and their play,
A wasp, abroad for honey,
   Came buzzing on his way.
He struck the trail of odor
   That floated in the air,
And followed it as surely
   As does the hound the hare;
Across the dewy meadow,
   And through a belt of wood,

Until he reached the apron
   Of dear Red Riding-Hood,
In which he darted so sharply,
   So many and so fine
The flowers whose cups he plundered,
   So sweet their honey-wine.
Right well she knew the difference
   Between a wasp and bee;
The humming-bee how thrifty—
   And what an idler, he!
Yet, seeing God had made him
   She killed him not, but said:
"The thoughtless drone is hungry,
   And God would have him fed."
The wasp buzzed loud, and louder,
   As if he understood
Her pity, and was thankful
   To good Red Riding-Hood!
She rose that morn so early,
   Before the east was red,
She quite forgot her breakfast
   Of honey and of bread:
But just as she was starting,
   She heard her mother say:
"Here's something for my darling
   To eat along the way."
She drew it from her pocket,
   And found it was a cake,
Such as on merry Saints' Days
   Her mother used to bake.
There came a hungry robin
   As she began to eat,
The sugared crumbs to gather
   That fell about her feet.
At first he pecked the furthest
   And often stopped in fear,
With many a trembling twitter;
   But soon he ventured near;
For wherefore fear a Creature
   So gentle to the rest,
Whose dress was like the morning

RICHARD
HENRY
STODDARD

That burned upon his breast?
And Riding-Hood, who eyed him,
   As nigh her hand he stood—
She loved him that he buried
   The Children in the Wood!
And as he pecked and twittered,
   "Eat, pretty bird," said she;
"There still will be a plenty
   For Granny and for me."
   *"Thanks," the grateful robin cried;*
   *"Many thanks," the wasp replied:*
   *Both together: "She is good,*
   *And we love Red Riding-Hood."*

VIII.

By this the child was rested,
   And her sweet task was done;
So she arose light-hearted,
   And faced once more the sun,
Which now had scaled the forest,
   Above the topmost trees:
The birds were singing round her,
   And merrily hummed the bees.
It was an ancient woman,
   Who stooped beside a brook,
As if she searched for something:
   She had a weary look;
Her hair with white was sprinkled,
   And her palsied hands she wrung:
She seemed as old as Nature,
   That is so old—and young!
"What do you look for, Goody?"
   Asked little Riding-Hood,
Who stopped to watch the woman,
   And help her, if she could.
"I gather water-cresses,
   "The feeble creature said;
"A sorry trade to live
   It does not give me bread."
"'Tis hard the wasp and robin
   Should have their fill of food,

And she be pinched with hunger,"
  Thought tender Riding-Hood,
Who drew from out her pocket
  The fragment of her cake,
Rejoicing she had saved it,
  For that poor woman's sake!
"Here's something for you, Goody,"
  And she led her to a seat;
"I'll pick your water-cresses,
  While you sit down and eat."
Along the glassy water
  She went a little space,
Until she found a cluster
  That hid her happy face;
The greenest, crispest, coolest,
  That drank the sun and rain:
From this she heaped her apron,
  And hurried back again.
The old dame smoothed her ringlets,
  "I thank you, Riding-Hood."
Stronger she looked, and younger,
  and more erect she stood.
Then, "Meeting the green huntsman,
  Bear this," she charged, "in mind:
Give him my love, and tell him
  That game is in the wind."
"I'll take your message Madam,"
  Red Riding-Hood replied,
Whose little heart with wonder
  Was thumping at her side:
Nor was her wonder lessened,
  When turning back she found
No sign of that old woman
  In all the meadow round!
The woman was a fairy,
  Forever young and fair;
Her rags were robes of crystal,
  And like the light her hair!
She waved her wand a moment,
  And crooned some magic words,
The charm by which she governed

RICHARD
HENRY
STODDARD

The insects and the birds:
The wasp and the robin knew it,
    And flew obedient there;
She whispered each his errand,
    And vanished in the air!
Red Riding-Hood saw nothing,
    For all her looking back,
Except the wasp and robin
    That followed on her track;
Until, within a hollow,
    She found a stagnant lake,
So stiff with scum no ripple
    Could o'er its surface break;
And there was seen the huntsman,
    In green from top to toe;
About his waist a bugle,
    And in his hand a bow!
He stood so tall and stately,
    And not a word he said,
But watched the birds in circles
    That wheeled above his head!
"Good morning, Master Huntsman,"
    Said Little Riding-Hood;
"I met a strange old woman
    When I was through the wood,
Who promised I should meet you,
    And said that I must mind
And give her love, and tell you,
    'The game is in the wind.'"
As when the wind is blowing,
    And trees are bowing round,—
He nodded so, and stooping
    He listened at the ground:
(What heard he?—distant voices,
    Or but the waters flow?)
He rose, and took an arrow,
    And bent his mighty bow!
    *What did his strange silence mean?*
    *Who the huntsman clad in green?*
    *Lord of water, or of wood?*
    *It sorely puzzled Riding-Hood.*

## IX

Her thoughts outran her footsteps,
  And wandered far and near,
Till what at first was wonder,
  Was fast becoming fear.
At last she saw the cottage,
  Whose windows shone afar,
And flying to its garden,
  She found the gate ajar;
She did not stop to close it,
  Her heart so gladly beat,
Nor note along the gravel
  The marks of stealthy feet!
(By son of man or woman
  Such prints were never made:
Red Riding-Hood, my darling,
  I fear you are betrayed!)
She crossed the patch of garden,
  She reached the rustic porch,
Where many a scarlet creeper
  Did lift its fiery torch;
Beneath the wedded woodbines
  And jessamines she stood,
And spots of sun and shadow
  Were falling on her hood.
"Rap! rap!"—her little knuckles
  Are tapping at the door;
She hearkens, but for answer
  She hears her heart, no more!
"Rap! tap! rap! tap!" still louder,
  She bends again her ear:
"Who's there?" And she, "Red Riding—"
  A gruff "Come in, my dear."
She twitched the clocking latch-string,
  And pushing back the door,
A streak of moted sunshine
  Was shivered on the floor;
Then, heavily and harshly,
  The door swung to again,
And the creaking of its hinges

Was like a shriek of pain!
Across the darkened chamber
    She stole in growing dread,
Until she gained the bedside
    Where, breathlessly, she said:
"We heard that you were ailing,
    And I have brought you this:
And father says he's sorry,
    And mother sends a kiss."
A voice beneath the bed-clothes,
    As gruff as gruff could be,
Growled out, "Put down the basket,
    And come to bed to me."
She pulled aside the curtain,
    And buried in the bed
There was a rumpled night-cap—
    But was it Granny's head?
"How large your ears are, Granny."
    "The more, my love, I hear."
"How large your eyes are, Granny."
    "The more I see, my dear."
"How large your teeth are, Granny."
    "So much the more I eat;
And you, you silly chitling,
    Will make a morsel sweet!
*Prepare!*" It was not Granny
    That sprang at Riding-Hood;
It was the wolf that chased her
    When she was in the wood!
Nor had he missed the darling
    Who knelt to him in vain,
But for the wasp that stung him,
    Until he howled with pain!
And the robin at the window,
    Another watchman near,
He flew to the green huntsman,
    and twittered in his ear,
"Red Riding-Hood's in danger,"
    And by his magic art
He shot a mighty arrow,
    That cleft the monster's heart!

Red Riding-Hood, the darling
    So strangely snatched from death,
She laughed and cried together—
    Was all things in a breath!
But who came now? 'Twas Granny,
    Whose turn of illness past,
Had been to see a neighbor,
    And had returned at last!
"No need to tell the story,
    I know it all by *this*."
Twas "Granny" then, and "Sweetest,"
    And many a hug and kiss!
    *They kissed and smiled, but tears would rise*
    *In sudden drops to Granny's eyes:*
    *"Such peril, and to one so good.!"*
    *"The wolf is dead!" said Riding-Hood.*

# ❋ 10 ❋

## Ye True Hystorie of
## Little Red Riding Hood
### or
## The Lamb in Wolf's Clothing

### By Alfred Mills

### (1872)

ONCE UPON A TIME there lived a little girl who had such a sweet temper that she seemed to be made of sugar and spice, like the little girl in the nursery rhyme. Her mother was very fond of her, and, in order to set off her beauty, made her a hood out of an old red flannel petticoat, in which she looked very pretty, and all the neighbors, in admiration, called her Little Red-Riding-Hood. Now, although she was a very good girl, her school-fellows said that Little Red-Riding-Hood had one very naughty little fault, which no girl, little or big, ever had before in any age of the world: she was vain—just a little vain. They even whispered that she had been known to tie two old brass ear-rings to her ears with bits of cotton, pretending that her ears had been *really* pierced; and that more than once she had made up her dress into an unseemly bunch behind, pretending to have a Grecian bend! One day her mother called to her as she came home from school, and said, "I've been making some cheese-cakes and dough-nuts to-day, and, as I'm afraid your grandmother is ill, you shall take her some of those very digestible articles." She then stuck the bright red hood upon the back of her little girl's head, giving her a big basket full of cakes, and a lecture on the vanity of wearing gaudy colors. Now Little Red-Riding-Hood had a wonderful little lamb. He did not know how to spell as well as his young mistress, but that he was a clever critic any one could see, for whenever she read the intellectual stories out of her spelling-book, he showed his discernment by crying "Bah! bah!" He imitated his mistress, and was a vain little lamb. So, when Little Red-Riding-Hood had set out with her cakes, he looked about for some finery for himself, and finding a wolf's skin hanging up in the wardrobe (where, of course, such things always are), he put it on, and concluded that he looked best of all the lambs—ba-ing none! On the way to her grandmother's, as Little Red-Riding-Hood was trudging along, thinking how nice it must be to be an old lady and ill, with such a big basket of cakes as medicine, the little lamb overtook her, looking for all the world like a great ugly wolf. When she saw this horrible sight, thinking it was a real wolf come to gobble up herself and the cakes, she tried to hide her face in the soft part of the stem of a tree, concluding very logically that, if she couldn't see the wolf, he couldn't see her. Having waited in this position for two seconds, expecting every moment to hear the wolf give his well known and terrible roar, her patience was naturally exhausted, and she turned round fully prepared to scream to any extent. The lamb, upon this, overjoyed at what he thought a recognition, for he thought she had "cut him dead," was so agitated that he could not open his mouth, and so, instead of expressing his feeling vocally, he kicked up his heels, and away he went—a merry somersault before the astonished eyes of the little maid. When Little Red-Riding-Hood saw this strange freak of the terrible beast, she was terribly frightened, and, seeing a street-car passing, she concluded it would be better and cheaper to ride, and certainly more pleasant to run the chance of being "taken in" at the hands of a conductor than to be taken in by the jaws of a wolf.

The lamb, however, knowing the geographical fact that two miles by car take just as long as four by foot, resolved to take a nearer way, and get to the old lady's house before Red-Riding-Hood. He set off at full speed, the wolf's head hanging over his shoulder, never heeding whom he might run over in his flight, for he was as careless of other people's comfort and lives as any New York driver. Unfortunately, the ass of the neighborhood had convened a meeting of the beasts for the purpose of discussing their common rights, and to it he had specially invited the goose, the pig, and other intellectual animals. They had met in a nice little spot in the middle of a wood, near a pool of water, which they thought very convenient, as it would serve to liquefy the eloquence of the speaker who was longest on his legs (probably the giraffe, should he be present), and it might also be an inducement to the duck, who they feared would make some excuse for not attending, and whose presence they particularly wanted, as she was the editor of a weekly paper which in the most delightful way propounded wild theories—(for the duck was a "wild" one)—about female suffrage, and, at the same time, preached in the most agreeable way the stupidest blasphemy. The goose, who contributed to the "Daily Cackler," brought his wife, whose delightful little book, entitled "The Way to *shell-out,*" is universally used as a class-book in all schools of chickens, goslings, and young oysters. Mr. Bull had come all the way from Oxford on purpose to attend the meeting; and the hare, the frog, and many other animals, were also present, as well as a very fair gathering of birds. The most extraordinary animal who was there was a rough, wicked-looking school-boy, and no one suspected his presence, for he was hidden behind a tree. This unfortunate youth had a strong and uncommon propensity for applying his tongue to candy and other sweet-stuffs, and his schoolmaster, a most generous and sweet-tempered man, finding him that morning in the very act of committing this dreadful offense, had promised him a "licking" of another sort. The boy, whose parents were very proud of his high spirit—which spirit he showed chiefly by pinching his little sister, running pins through the tails of cockroaches, and annoying every other human being—knowing how vast a difference there is between licking and being licked, resolved, like the highly respectable cashier of the Diddleyou Bank, to abscond before accounts were balanced. Accordingly, considering justly that it was more pleasant to be hiding of his own will among the trees than to receive a hiding at the master's will in school, he went on a botanizing expedition into the very wood where the congress of beasts was assembled in earnest discussion; the ass, who was chairman, was braying loudly; the pig grunted acquiescence; the goose was applauding; and the ox, on the opposition side, was humming a low tune in defiance, while the boy behind the tree, with a pebble-stone in his hand, prepared to let fly among them. The debate increased in interest, and the noise caused by a discussion between the ass and the owl (who acted as reporter), concerning a *hare*-brained remark from one of the smaller beasts, was almost as great as that caused sometimes by human congresses, while their language was certainly of a higher and more intelligible order. How it all might have ended no one could tell, for at this unfortunate moment the lamb in wolf's clothing came tumbling in, and dissolved the beastly congress before they had passed a single act. Not

"Ye True Hystorie of Little Red Riding Hood; or, The Lamb in Wolf's Clothing," in *Nast's Illustrated Almanac,* New York: Harper, 1872. Illustrator Thomas Nast.

knowing that it was the "season for lamb," the members, of course, were unprepared to offer any resistance. With unblushing haste the disturber of the peace pursued his way and arrived at the old lady's cottage. Too much agitated by his feelings, he did not wait to knock, but turned his heels to the door and began to kick in style. The old lady was lying in bed, surrounded by bottles and dishes containing physic and other delicacies, and attended by her favorite cat. She (I mean the old lady, not the cat) had once been a beauty, but, of course, as she told little girls, she was never vain; and now in her old age she innocently spent her time in considering by-gone fashions, and sorrowing that she could not use them still. Just as the lamb arrived she had taken up an old volume of the Anglo-Saxon period, called *Harper's Bazar* [sic], to which St. Dunstan used to contribute fancy patterns; and was piously thinking of the mutability of all earthly things—especially fashions! Upon hearing the horrible noise outside, the paper dropped from her hands, and her companion arched his back as if expecting a *catastrophe*. Meanwhile the lamb, whose garment did not fit well, and who looked in the midst of his exertions like a twofold and many-legged monster, finding kicking of no avail, determined to try the soft-soap dodge, and began gently to pat at the door. Reassured by this Christian-like sound, the dame instructed her attendant to open the door, and Tom, who, with the exception of a white tie, looked as solemn as any flunky, immediately raised the latch with the greatest gravity. In rushed the disguised lamb, with a most awful countenance. The old lady looked at him through her goggles for a moment, and then fled with a terrific yell, her cat following suit. The lamb, innocently thinking to salute her, had leaped to the bed, upsetting in his haste the physic bottles, dishes, and all; but, seeing the door shut behind the old lady, he thought to wind up his day's fun by playing a trick upon his mistress. He first arrayed himself in the old lady's cap and goggles, glancing in the glass with great satisfaction; and then, having fortified himself with a draught from the only unbroken medicine bottle, which was very properly labeled "Bourbon—*Poison*," he laid down in the bed, hiding all but the cap beneath the clothes. Soon after this Little Red-Riding-Hood knocked at the door. "Come in," said the lamb, but in such a tone that the little girl thought her grandmother must have made herself ill with too much "physic!" She entered, however, and went up to the bed as usual to kiss the old lady. The lamb pulled down the clothes, disclosing a wolf's head surrounded by a night-cap. Little Red-Riding-Hood screamed, and would have gone into hysterics, only she was too young to know that that was the proper thing to do. As it was, she ran away, uttering the most piteous screams. At the door, however, she tumbled over her grandmother, who had now mustered up her courage, and was returning, armed with her best silver goggles, and protected by Little-toes, her grandchild, and Tom—her only gentleman friend. The three returned to the scene of the tragedy, and there found the terrible wolf transformed into the meekest of lambs, his wolf's skin (to which an extraordinary *tail* was attached) remaining in the bed. Little Red-Riding-Hood, in imitation of her grandmother, began to lecture the lamb on his absurd vanity, which had been the cause of so much trouble and loss, for she had left her cakes in the car; but the old lady, whose spirits had now returned, embraced them all, whereupon the four-footed author of all this confusion repented of his evil deeds, became quite a reformed character, and, in proof thereof and of his patriotism, he shed his blood a few months after, if not for the good of his country, at least for the good of his friends.

# ❋ 11 ❋

## The True History
## of Little Golden Hood

### By Charles Marelle

### (1888)

Y OU KNOW THE TALE of poor Little Red Riding-hood, that
the Wolf deceived and devoured, with her cake, her little
butter can, and her Grandmother; well, the true story happened quite differently, as we know now. And first of all the little
girl was called and is still called Little Golden-hood; secondly, it
was not she, nor the good grand-dame, but the wicked Wolf who
was, in the end, caught and devoured.

Only listen.

The story begins something like the tale.

There was once a little peasant girl, pretty and nice as a star in its
season. Her real name was Blanchette, but she was more often
called Little Golden-hood, on account of a wonderful little cloak
with a hood, gold- and fire-coloured, which she always had on.
This little hood was given her by her Grandmother, who was so old
that she did not know her age; it ought to bring her luck, for it was
made of a ray of sunshine, she said. And as the good old woman was
considered something of a witch, everyone thought the little hood
rather bewitched too.

And so it was, as you will see.

One day the mother said to the child: "Let us see, my little Golden-hood, if you know how to find your way by yourself. You shall
take this good piece of cake to your Grandmother for a Sunday treat

to-morrow. You will ask her how she is, and come back at once, without stopping to chatter on the way with people you don't know. Do you quite understand?"

"I quite understand," replied Blanchette gaily. And off she went with the cake, quite proud of her errand.

But the Grandmother lived in another village, and there was a big wood to cross before getting there. At a turn of the road under the trees, suddenly "Who goes there?"

"Friend Wolf."

He had seen the child start alone, and the villain was waiting to devour her; when at the same moment he perceived some woodcutters who might observe him, and he changed his mind. Instead of falling upon Blanchette he came frisking up to her like a good dog.

"'Tis you! my nice Little Golden-hood," said he. So the little girl stops to talk with the Wolf, whom, for all that, she did not know in the least.

"You know me, then!" said she; "what is your name?"

"My name is friend Wolf. And where are you going thus, my pretty one, with your little basket on your arm?"

"I am going to my Grandmother, to take her a good piece of cake for her Sunday treat to-morrow."

"And where does she live, your Grandmother?"

"She lives at the other side of the wood, in the first house in the village, near the windmill, you know."

"Ah! yes! I know now," said the Wolf. "Well, that's just where I'm going; I shall get there before you, no doubt, with your little bits of legs, and I'll tell her you're coming to see her; then she'll wait for you."

Thereupon the Wolf cuts across the wood, and in five minutes arrives at the Grandmother's house.

He knocks at the door: toc, toc.

No answer.

He knocks louder.

Nobody.

Then he stands up on end, puts his two fore-paws on the latch and the door opens.

Not a soul in the house.

The old woman had risen early to sell herbs in the town, and she had gone off in such haste that she had left her bed unmade, with her great night-cap on the pillow.

"Good!" said the Wolf to himself, "I know what I'll do."

He shuts the door, pulls on the Grandmother's night-cap down to his eyes, then he lies down all this length in the bed and draws the curtains.

❀ 195 ❀
The True
History of
Little
Golden
Hood

In the meantime the good Blanchette went quietly on her way, as little girls do, amusing herself here and there by picking Easter daisies, watching the little birds making their nests, and running after the butterflies which fluttered in the sunshine.

At last she arrives at the door.

Knock, knock.

"Who is there?" says the Wolf, softening his rough voice as best he can.

"It's me, Granny, your little Golden-hood. I'm bringing you a big piece of cake for your Sunday treat to-morrow."

"Press your finger on the latch, then push and the door opens."

"Why, you've got a cold, Granny," said she, coming in.

"Ahem! a little, a little . . . " replies the Wolf, pretending to cough. "Shut the door well, my little lamb. Put your basket on the table, and then take off your flock and come and lie down by me: you shall rest a little."

The good child undresses, but observe this! She kept her little hood upon her head. When she saw what a figure her Granny cut in bed, the poor little thing was much surprised.

"Oh!" cries she, "how like you are to friend Wolf, Grandmother!"

"That's on account of my night-cap, child," replies the Wolf.

"Oh! what hairy arms you've got, Grandmother!"

"All the better to hug you, my child."

"Oh! what a big tongue you've got, Grandmother!"

"All the better for answering, child."

"Oh! what a mouthful of great white teeth you have, Grandmother!"

"That's for crunching little children with!" And the Wolf opened his jaws wide to swallow Blanchette.

But she put down her head crying:

"Mamma! Mamma!" and the Wolf only caught her little hood.

Thereupon, oh dear! oh dear! he draws back, crying and shaking his jaw as if he had swallowed red-hot coals.

It was the little fire-coloured hood that had burnt his tongue right down his throat.

The little hood, you see, was one of those magic caps that they used to have in former times, in the stories, for making oneself invisible or invulnerable.

So there was the Wolf with his throat burnt, jumping off the bed and trying to find the door, howling and howling as if all the dogs in the country were at his heels.

Just at this moment the Grandmother arrives, returning from the town with her long sack empty on her shoulder.

"Ah, brigand!" she cries, "wait a bit!" Quickly she opens her sack wide across the door, and the maddened Wolf springs in head downwards.

It is he now that is caught, swallowed like a letter in the post.

For the brave old dame shuts her sack, so; and she runs and empties it in the well where the vagabond, still howling, tumbles in and is drowned.

"Ah, scoundrel! You thought you would crunch my little grandchild! Well, to-morrow we will make her a muff of your skin, and you yourself shall be crunched, for we will give your carcass to the dogs."

Thereupon the Grandmother hastened to dress poor Blanchette, who was still trembling with fear in the bed.

"Well," she said to her, "without my little hood where would you be now, darling?" And, to restore heart and legs to the child, she made her eat a good piece of her cake, and drink a good draught of wine, after which she took her by the hand and led her back to the house.

And then, who was it who scolded her when she knew all that had happened?

It was the mother.

But Blanchette promised over and over again that she would never more stop to listen to a Wolf, so that at last the mother forgave her.

And Blanchette, the little Golden-hood, kept her word. And in fine weather she may still be seen in the fields with her pretty little hood, the colour of the sun.

But to see her you must rise early.

## ❊ 12 ❊

## *Little Red*
## *Riding Hood*

### *By Sabine Baring-Gould*

### (1895)

A

LL IN A LITTLE COTTAGE
There lived a little maid,
The sweetest little maiden that ever was seen,
And her mother loves her well
But her granny loves her better,
   And she had a little red hood, just like a little queen.

Now, because this little girl wore a red cloak with a red hood,
everybody called her Little Red Riding-Hood. It chanced one day
her mother had made some custards and a little plum-pudding.
And she said:

   "Now take the little basket,
   And the little custard too,
And the little pudding boiled for your granny dear.
   But don't you stop or stay,
   Do not idle on the way,
On the highroad little Riding-Hood will nothing
   have to fear.

   "Go," said her mother, "straight along to your grandmother, give
her the nice things in your basket, and then come straight home
again and tell me how the old lady is. Mind, talk to no one on the
way."

   So little Red Riding-Hood set off immediately to go to her grandmother, who lived in a cottage beyond the wood.

197

Instead of taking the highway, she went through the wood, and there she met the old grey wolf, who wanted to eat her, but he durst not, for there were men in the wood, making faggots. But he stopped her and said: "What have you got in your basket, my dear?"

"Only some custard and plum-pudding and a little pat of butter."

"And where are you going, my dear?"

"I am going to see granny."

"Where does granny live, my dear?"

"In the cottage beyond the wood," answered Red Riding-Hood.

"And when you get to the cottage, what do you do?"

"I knock at the door."

"And what does your grandmother say?" asked the wolf.

"She says, 'Who is there?'" answered the little girl.

"And what do you do next?"

"I answer and say, 'I am little Red Riding-Hood, and I have brought you a custard and plum-pudding and a little pat of butter.'"

"What does grandmother then say?" inquired the wolf.

"She says, 'Pull the bobbin, and the latch will go up.'"

Well, when the wolf heard this, off he ran as fast as he could, taking the nearest way; and the little girl, forgetting again her mother's commands, idled on the way, picking hazel-nuts, running after butterflies, making posies of the wild-flowers.

The wolf was not long before he got to the old woman's door. He knocked—tap, tap.

"Who is there?" called a voice from within.

"Your grandchild, little Red Riding-Hood," replied the wolf, imitating the child's voice as nearly as possible. "I have brought you a custard and a little plum-pudding and a little pat of butter."

The old grandmother, who was infirm and in bed, cried out:

"Pull the bobbin, and the latch will go up."

The wolf pulled the bobbin, and the door opened, and then he fell on the poor old woman, and gobbled her up in a moment, for he had eaten nothing for many days. He then shut the door, and jumped into the grandmother's bed, and pulled on the grandmother's nightcap, which he had not eaten, but had reserved, lest it should spoil his appetite for what was coming. Presently he heard little Red Riding-Hood's tap, tap, at the door. So he called out: "Who is there?"

"It is your grandchild, little Red Riding-Hood, who has brought you a custard and a little plum-pudding and a little pat of butter."

The wolf cried out to her, softening his voice as much as he could:

***Leſ Conteſ de Perrault,*** **Paris, 1927. Illustrator Felix Lorioux.**

"Pull the bobbin, and the latch will go up."

Little Red Riding-Hood pulled the bobbin, and the door opened.

The wolf, seeing her come in, drew the bedclothes up about his shoulders and said:

"Put the custard and the plum-pudding and the pat of butter on the table, and come and sit on the stool beside the bed and tell me how your mother is."

"She is very well, thank you, granny," answered the girl, as she put the articles she had brought on the table.

"Mother said I was to bring back the basket," she said, "so that she may be able to send you something nice in it again, another day."

"That is very good of your mammy. Come and sit on the stool, my dear."

So little Red Riding-Hood came over and sat close by the bed, and she was much amazed to see how her grandmother looked. So she said:

"Grandmamma, what great arms you have got!"

"The better to hug you, my dear."

"Grandmamma, what a long nose you have got!"

"The better to smell you, my dear."

"Grandmamma, what great eyes you have got!"

"The better to see you, my dear."

"Grandmamma, what great teeth you have got!"

"The better to eat you, my dear."

Saying these words, the wicked wolf threw off the bed-clothes, jumped out of bed, and fell on little Red Riding-Hood to eat her up.

But at that very moment—Bang! through the door a gun was fired, and the grey old wolf rolled over, shot through the head. Then in came the forester, and this was little Red Riding-Hood's father. He had seen the wolf hasting off in the same direction in which he saw afterwards his little daughter had gone, so thought the cunning and cruel beast was after mischief, and he hastened in the same direction with his gun. Poor little Red Riding-Hood was so frightened that she could not walk home, and could only sob and cling to her father, and so he carried her, and as he carried her, he said: "A little maid

Must be afraid

To do other than her mother told her.

Of idling must be wary,

Of gossiping must be chary,

She'll learn prudence by the time that she is older."

# ❦ 13 ❦

## *Little Green Riding Hood: A Drama for Little People*

## *By Pierre Cami*

## (1914)

### ACT ONE
### Tragic Coincidences
*Inside a house.*

FATHER OF LITTLE GREEN RIDING HOOD: We are living in the house where the celebrated Little Red Riding Hood who was eaten by the wolf used to live.

MOTHER OF LITTLE GREEN RIDING HOOD: A strange coincidence. Our ravishing little girl wears a little green riding hood with such grace that people call her Little Green Riding Hood wherever she goes.

FATHER: Another extraordinary coincidence. The grandmother of our little daughter lives in the very next village just like Little Red Riding Hood's grandmother did, and to go there, you must cross the nearby forest.

MOTHER: Isn't it also said that the famous wolf who devoured Little Red Riding Hood and her grandmother still roams the forest?

FATHER: Yes. All these coincidences are particularly troubling.

MOTHER: Even more troubling is that I've baked some cake this very day and . . .

FATHER (*turning pale*): Cakes! That's awful! Ah! I can guess what will happen next! You're going to send our Little Green Riding

Hood to carry some cake to her grandmother, aren't you?

MOTHER: Yes, a cake and little pot of butter.

FATHER: A little pot of butter! That's horrible! Those are extraordinary and tragic coincidences! But, be quiet! I hear Little Green Riding Hood returning from school.

MOTHER (to Little Green Riding Hood): Go and see how your grandmother is feeling. Take her this cake and this little pot of butter.

LITTLE GREEN RIDING HOOD (joyously): Well now, just like Little Red Riding Hood!

MOTHER (with anxiety): Like Little Red Riding Hood! Oh! My heart is filled with somber presentiments. Should I let her depart?

LITTLE GREEN RIDING HOOD: Have no fear, my dear parents. Little Green Riding Hood is much more clever than Little Red Riding Hood. If by chance I find the wolf in grandmother's bed, he won't be able to devour me. I have an idea. (She departs.)

## ACT TWO
### Little Green Riding Hood's Ruse
*Inside the grandmother's house.*

THE WOLF WHO PREVIOUSLY ATE LITTLE RED RIDING HOOD (lying in bed): Ever since I caught sight of Little Green Riding Hood heading to her grandmother's house, I've done the exact same things that I did with Little Red Riding Hood. I arrived first at her grandmother's house. I quickly ate the old woman and took her place in bed. And now I'm waiting for Little Green Riding Hood who will soon be knocking at the door.

LITTLE GREEN RIDING HOOD (knocking at the door): It's your granddaughter, Little Green Riding Hood, who's brought you some cake and a little pot of butter.

WOLF (sweetening his voice): Pull the bobbin and the latch will fall. (Little Green Riding Hood enters.) Put the cake and the little pot of butter in the bin, and come lay down beside me.

LITTLE GREEN RIDING HOOD (aside): Heavens! It's the wolf! I recognize the same words that he used to get Little Red Riding Hood into his bed. The miserable cur is in the process of digesting my grandmother, but thanks to my idea, he won't be able to devour me.

WOLF: Well, aren't you coming to lie down, my child?

LITTLE GREEN RIDING HOOD (lying down next to the wolf): Here I am. Oh, grandmother, what big arms you have!

WOLF: The better to hug you with, my child.

LITTLE GREEN RIDING HOOD: Grandmother, what big legs you have!

WOLF: The better to run with, my child.

LITTLE GREEN RIDING HOOD: Grandmother, what big ears you have!

WOLF: The better to hear you with, my child.

LITTLE GREEN RIDING HOOD: Grandmother, what big eyes you have!

WOLF: The better to see you with, my child! (*Aside.*) Get ready now!

LITTLE GREEN RIDING HOOD: Grandmother, what big arms you have!

WOLF (*disconcerted*): But you've already said that, my child.

LITTLE GREEN RIDING HOOD (*continuing*): Grandmother, what big legs you have!

WOLF: But you're repeating the same thing! Let's see, there are some other things you could ask. For example (*hinting*): Grandmother, what big teeth . . .

LITTLE GREEN RIDING HOOD: . . . big ears!

WOLF: Not at all, big . . . big . . . (*hinting a great deal*) It begins with a "T".

LITTLE GREEN RIDING HOOD: Big legs!

WOLF (*jumping out of bed*): Hell and damnation!!! This Green Riding Hood is playing with me! This cunning little girl refuses to say: "Grandmother, what big teeth!" So, naturally, I can't pounce on her and respond: "The better to eat you with!" (*With a sigh of regret.*) Ah! Where are those naive children who were easy to eat in the good old days? (*He exits furiously.*)

# ❄ 14 ❄

## *Kuttel Daddeldu*
## *Tells His Children the Fairy Tale*
## *about Little Red Cap*

### By Joachim Ringelnatz

### (1924)

S O KIDS, IF YOU CAN keep your mouths shut for just five minutes, then I'll tell you the story about Little Red Cap when I can still make sense out of it. Old Captain Muckelmann told it to me long ago when I was still little and dumb like you are now. And Captain Muckelmann never lied.

So perk your ears. There was once a little girl. She was dubbed Little Red Cap—that means, she was given the name because she wore a red cap on her head day and night. She was a beautiful girl, red as blood and white as snow, and black as ebony with large round eyes. From behind her legs were very thick and in front—well, to be brief, she was a hell of a beautiful, wonderful, fine lass.

And one day her mother sent her through the woods to grandmother who was naturally sick. And the mother gave Little Red Cap a basket with three bottles of Spanish wine and two bottles of Scotch and a bottle of Rostocker rye and a bottle of Swedish punch and a bottle of schnapps and some more bottles of beer and cake and all kinds of junk that was supposed to help the grandmother strengthen herself.

"Little Red Cap," the mother said extra. "Don't stray off the path, for there are wild wolves in the woods? (The entire story must have taken place in Nikolayev or somewhere in Siberia). Little

Red Cap promised everything and took off. And the wolf met her in the woods. "Little Red Cap," he asked, "where are you going?" And she told him everything you already know. And he asked: "Where does your grandmother live?"

And she told him the exact address: "Schwieger Strasse thirteen, ground floor."

And then the wolf showed the child where there were juicy raspberries and strawberries and enticed her from the path deep into the woods.

And while she busily picked berries, the wolf ran full sail ahead to Schwieger Strasse number thirteen and knocked on the door of the ground floor at Grandmother's place.

The grandmother was a suspicious old woman with many holes in her teeth. That's why she asked rudely: "'Who's knocking there at my door?"

And then the wolf answered outside with a disguised voice: "It's me, sleeping beauty."

And then the old woman called out: "Come in!" And the wolf swept into the room. And then the old woman put on her nightgown and bonnet and ate the wolf all up.

In the meantime Little Red Cap had lost her way in the woods. And she was just like most dumb-ass girls are so she began to bawl. And the hunter heard her deep in the woods and rushed to her side. Well—and what matter is it to us what the two of them wanted to do there deep in the woods since it had become very dark in the meantime. At any rate he did bring her to the right path.

So she ran now to Schwieger Strasse. And there she saw that her grandmother had become fat and bloated.

And Little Red Cap asked: "Grandmother, why do you have such big eyes?" And the grandmother answered: "That's so I can see you better!"

And then Little Red Cap asked again: "Grandmother, why do you have such big ears?"

And the grandmother answered: "That's so I can hear you better!"

And then Little Red Cap asked again: "Grandmother, why do you have such a big mouth?"

Now is that the right thing for children to say to a grown-up grandmother?

So the old woman became stark raving mad and couldn't utter one more word. Instead she ate Little Red Cap all up. And then she moved like a whale. And just then the hunter passed by outside.

JOACHIM
RINGELNATZ

And he wondered how a whale could have landed in the Schwieger Strasse. And so he loaded his rifle and drew his long knife out of its sheath and entered the room without knocking. And there to his horror he saw the bloated grandmother in bed instead of the whale.

And—diavolo caracho!—You'll be wiped off your feet!—It's hard to believe!—But the gluttonous old woman ate up the hunter too.

Yeah, you brats are gaping with wide-open mouths, waiting for something more to come.—But clear out of here now quick as the wind, otherwise I'll tan your hides.

My throat's become completely dry from these dumb, stinken stories which are only all lies anyway.

March yourselves out of here! Let your father drink one down now, you leftover small fry!

## ❦ 15 ❦

### *Sturry from*
### *Raд Riдink Hoot*

### *By Milt Gross*

### (1926)

WHOO! NIZE BABY!!! Itt opp all de wheatinna—so momma'll gonna tell from "Leedle Rad Ridink Hoot!" Leedle Rad Ridink Hoot was going wid a weesit to de grenmodder wot she leeved in de woots! So it came along a beeg beeg wolf und he sad "Goot-monnink, Leedle Rad Ridink Hoot—to where do you going??" So she sad, "I'm going to mine grenmodder wid a beeg beeg Strubbery-Shut Cake!!" So de doidy wolf he snicked in de houze und he ate opp de grenmodder—(Nize baby, take annoder spoon wheatinna). So in de min time dot doidy wolf he put in on de grenmodder's nightgown und he laid down in de bad. So Leedle Rad Ridink Hoot reng de bell, so de wolf sad, "Come in dollink." So Leedle Rad Ridink Hoot sad, "Grenmodder, wot a horse woice you got!!" So de wolf sad—"Hm—don't esk! A whole night long I was cuffing und snizzing—I tink wott I'm getting de greep!!!" So Leedle Rad Ridink Hoot sad, "But Grenmodder—Sotch a beeg harms wot you gott!" "Hm—de better I should hog you weet dollink." "Bot, Grenmodder—Sotch a beeg mout wot you gott!!"— "De batter I should eat you opp."—So he jomped out from de bad dot doidy wolf—he should itt opp Leedle Rad Ridink Hoot. So it came in a honter wid a bow und harrow und he keeled de wolf. (Hm! sotch a dollink baby—ate opp all de wheatinna!!).

207

# ❊ 16 ❊

## *Little Red*
## *Riding Hood*

### By *Walter de la Mare*

### (1927)

I<small>N THE OLD DAYS</small> when countrywomen wore riding-hoods to keep themselves warm and dry as they rode to market, there was a child living in a little village near the Low Forest who was very vain. She was so vain she couldn't even pass a puddle without peeping down into it at her apple cheeks and yellow hair. She could be happy for hours together with nothing but a comb and a glass; and then would sit at the window for people to see her. Nothing pleased her better than fine clothes, and when she was seven, having seen a strange woman riding by on horseback, she suddenly had a violent longing for such a riding-hood as hers, and that was of a scarlet cloth with strings.

After this, she gave her mother no peace, but begged and pestered her continually, and flew into a passion or sulked when she said no. When, then, one day a pedlar came to the village, and among the rest of his wares showed her mother a strip of scarlet cloth which he could sell cheap, partly to please the child and partly to get a little quiet, she bought a few yards of this cloth and herself cut out and stitched up a hood of the usual shape and fashion, but of midget size and with ribbons for strings.

When the child saw it she almost choked with delight and peacocked about in it whenever she had the chance. So she grew vainer than ever, and the neighbours became so used to seeing her wearing it in all weathers, her yellow curls dangling on her cheeks and her bright blue eyes looking out from under its hood, that they called her Little Red Riding-Hood.

Now, one fine sunny morning her mother called Little Red Riding-Hood in from her playing and said to her: "Now listen. I've just had news that your poor old Grannie is lying ill in bed and can't stir hand or foot; so as I can't go to see her myself, I want *you* to go instead, and to take her a little present. It's a good long step to Grannie's, mind; but if you don't loiter on the way there'll be plenty of time to be there and back before dark, and to stay a bit with Grannie, too. But *mind*, go straight there and come straight back, and be sure not to speak to anybody whatsoever you meet in the forest. It doesn't look to me like rain, so you can wear your new hood. Poor Grannie will hardly know you!"

Nothing in this long speech pleased Red Riding-Hood so much as the end of it. She ran off at once, and as she combed her hair and put on her hood, she talked to herself in the glass. There was one thing: Red Riding-Hood liked her Grannie pretty well, but she liked the goodies her Grannie gave her even better. So she thought to herself: "If the basket is heavy, I shall take a little rest on the way; and as Grannie's in bed, I shall have plenty to eat when I get there because I can help myself, and I can bring something home in the empty basket. Grannie would like that. Then I can skip along as I please."

Meanwhile, her mother was packing up the basket—a dozen brown hen's eggs, a jar of honey, a pound of butter, a bottle of elderberry wine, and a screw of snuff. After a last look at herself in a polished stew-pan, Red Riding-Hood took the basket on her arm and kissed her mother goodbye.

"Now, mind," said her mother yet again, "be sure not to lag or loiter in the Low Forest, picking flowers or chasing the butterflies, and don't speak to any stranger there, not even though he looks as if butter wouldn't melt in his mouth. Do all you can for Grannie, and come straight home."

Red Riding-Hood started off, so pleased with herself and with her head so packed up with greedy thoughts of what she would have to eat at the end of her journey that she forgot to wave back a last goodbye before the path across the buttercup meadow dipped down towards the woods and her mother was out of sight.

On through the sunny lanes among the butterflies she went. The hawthorns, snow-white and crimson, were in fullest flower, and the

Julius Hoffmann, *Märchenwelt*. Stuttgart: Thienemann, ca. 1890.
Illustrators C. Offterdinger and R. Kepler.

air was laden with their smell. All the trees of the wood, indeed,
were rejoicing in their new green coats, and there was such a medley and concourse of birds singing that their notes sounded like
drops of water falling into a fountain.

When Red Riding-Hood heard this shrill sweet warbling she
thought to herself: "They are looking at *me* as I go along all by
myself with my basket in my bright red hood." And she skipped on
more gaily than ever.

But the basket grew heavier and heavier the further she jour-
neyed, and when at last she came to the Low Forest the shade there
was so cool and so many strange flowers were blooming in its glens
and dingles, that she forgot everything her mother had told her and
sat down to rest. Moss, wild thyme and violets grew on that bank,
and presently she fell asleep.

In her sleep she dreamed a voice was calling to her from very far
away. It was a queer husky voice, and seemed to be coming from
some dark dismal place where the speaker was hiding.

At sound of this voice calling and calling her ever more faintly,
she suddenly awoke, and there, no more than a few yards away,
stood a Wolf, and he was steadily looking at her. At first she was so
frightened she could hardly breathe, and could only stare back at
him.

But the moment the Wolf saw that she was awake he smiled at
her, or rather his jaws opened and he grinned; and then in tones as
wheedling and butter-smooth as his tongue could manage he said:
"Good-afternoon, my dear. I hope you are refreshed after your little
nap. But what, may I ask, are *you* doing here, all alone in the forest,
and in that beautiful bright red hood, too?" As he uttered these
words he went on grinning at her in so friendly a fashion that little
Red Riding-Hood could not but smile at him in return.

She told him she was on her way to her Grannie's.

"I see," said the Wolf, not knowing that through his very wiliness
he would be stretched out that evening as cold as mutton! "And
what might you have in that heavy basket, my dear?"

Little Red Riding-Hood tossed her head so that her curls glinted
in a sunbeam that was twinkling through the leaves of the tree
beneath which she was sitting, and she said, "My Grannie is very
very ill in bed. Perhaps she'll die. So that's why I'm carrying this
heavy basket. It's got eggs and butter, honey and wine, and snuff
inside it. And I'm all by myself!"

"My!" said the Wolf. "All by yourself; and a packet of snuff, too!

But how, my little dear, will you be able to get in at the door if your Grannie is ill in bed? How will you manage that?"

"Oh," said Red Riding-Hood, "that will be quite easy. I shall just tap seven times and say, 'It's me, Grannie'; then Grannie will know who it is and tell me how to get in."

"But how clever!" said the Wolf. "And where does your poor dear Grannie live? And which way are *you* going?"

Little Red Riding-Hood told him: then he stopped grinning and looked away. "I was just thinking, my dear," he went on softly, "how lucky it was we met! I know your Grannie's cottage well. Many's the time I've seen her sitting there at her window. But I can tell you a much, *much* shorter way to it. If you go *your* way, I'm afraid you won't be home till long after dark, and that would never do. For sometimes one meets queer people in the Low Forest, not at all what you would care for."

But what this crafty wretch told her was a way which was at least half a mile further round. Red Riding-Hood thanked him, seeing no harm in his sly grinning, and started off by the way he had said. But he himself went louping off by a much shorter cut, and came to her grandmother's cottage long before she did. And there was not a living thing in sight.

Having entered the porch, the Wolf lifted his paw and, keeping his claws well in, rapped seven times on the door.

An old quavering voice called, "Who's there?"

And the Wolf, muffling his tones, said, "It's me, Grannie!"

"Stand on the stone, pull the string, and the door will come open," said the old woman.

So the Wolf got up on his hind legs and with his teeth tugged at the string. The door came open, and in he went; and that (for a while) was the end of Grannie.

But what Master Wolf had planned for his supper that evening was not just Grannie, but Grannie *first* and then—for a tidbit— Red Riding-Hood afterwards.

And he knew well there were woodmen in the forest, and that it would be far safer to wait in hiding for her in the cottage than to carry her off openly.

So, having drawn close the curtains at the window, he put on the old woman's clean nightgown which was lying upon a chair, tied her nightcap over his ears, scrambled into her bed, drew up the clothes over him, and laid himself down at all his long length with his head on the pillow. There then he lay, waiting for Red Riding-Hood and thinking he was safe as safe; and an ugly heap he looked.

All this time Red Riding-Hood had been still loitering, picking wild flowers and chasing the bright-winged butterflies, and once she had sat down and helped herself to a taste or two of her Grannie's honey.

But at last her footsteps sounded on the cobbles; and there came seven taps at the door.

Then the Wolf, smiling to himself and mimicking the old woman, and trying to say the words as she had said them, called "Who's there?" Red Riding-Hood said, "It's me, Grannie!"

And the Wolf said, "Stand on the stone, pull the string, and the door will come open.

Red Riding-Hood stood on her tiptoes, pulled the string, and went in; and one narrow beam of sunshine strayed in after her, for she left the door a little ajar. And there was her Grannie, as she supposed, lying ill in bed. The Wolf peered out at her from under the old woman's nightcap, but the light was so dim in the cottage that at first Red Riding-Hood could not see him at all clearly, only the frilled nightcap and the long, bony hump of him sticking up under the bedclothes.

"Look what *I've* brought you, Grannie," she said. "Some butter, a jar of honey, some eggs, a bottle of wine, and a packet of snuff. And I've come all the way by myself in my new red riding-hood!"

The Wolf said, "Umph!"

Red Riding-Hood peeped about her. "I *expect* Grannie," she said, "if I was to look in that cupboard over there, there'd be some of those jam-tarts you made for me last time I came, and some cake too, I *expect*, to take home, Grannie; and please may I have a drink of milk *now?*" The Wolf said, "Umph!"

Then Red Riding-Hood went a little nearer to look at her Grannie in bed. She looked a long, long time, and at last she said, "Oh, Grannie, what very bright eyes you have!"

And the Wolf said, "All the better to *see* with, my dear."

Then Red Riding-Hood said, "And oh, Grannie, what long pointed nails you have!"

And the Wolf said, "All the better to *scratch* with, my dear."

Then Red Riding-Hood said, "And what high hairy sticking-up ears you have, Grannie!"

"All the better to *hear* with, my dear," said the Wolf.

"And, oh, Grannie," cried Red Riding-Hood, "what great huge big teeth you have!"

"All the better to *eat* with!" yelled the Wolf, and with that he leapt out of bed in his long nightgown, and before she could say

"Oh!" Little Red Riding-Hood was gobbled up, nose, toes, hood, snuff, butter, honey and all.

Nevertheless, that cunning greedy crafty old Wolf had not been cunning enough. He had bolted down such a meal that the old glutton at once went off to sleep on the bed, with his ears sticking out of his nightcap, and his tail lolling out under the quilt. And he had forgotten to shut the door.

Early that evening a woodman, coming home with his axe and a faggot when the first stars were beginning to shine, looked in at the open cottage door and instead of the old woman saw the Wolf lying there on the bed. He knew the villain at sight.

"Oho! you old ruffian," he cried softly, "is it *you?*"

At this far-away strange sound in his dreams, the Wolf opened— though by scarcely more than a hair's breadth—his dull, drowsy eyes. But at a glimpse of the woodman, his wits came instantly back to him, and he knew his danger. Too late! Before even, clogged up in Grannie's nightgown, he could gather his legs together to spring out of bed, the woodman with one mighty stroke of his axe had finished him off.

And as the woodman stooped over him to make sure, he fancied he heard muffled voices squeaking in the wolf's inside as if calling for help.

He listened, then at once cut him open, and out came Red Riding-Hood, and out at last crept the poor old Grannie. And though the first thing Red Riding-Hood did, when she could get her breath again, was to run off to the looking-glass and comb out her yellow curls and uncrumple her hood, she never afterwards forgot what a wolf looked like, and never afterwards loitered in the Low Forest,

As for poor old Grannie, though that one hour's warmth and squeezing had worked wonders with her rheumatism, she lived only for twenty years after. But then it was on the old woman's seventieth birthday that Red Riding-Hood had set out with her basket.

It was a piece of rare good fortune for them both, at any rate, first, that the woodman had looked in at the cottage door in the very nick of time; next, that he had his axe; and last, that this Wolf was such a senseless old glutton that he never really enjoyed a meal, but swallowed everything whole. Else, Red Riding-Hood and her Grannie would certainly not have come out of him alive, and the people in the village would have had to bury the wicked old rascal in the churchyard—where he would have been far from welcome.

# ❊ 17 ❊

## Little Red
## Riding Hood

### By Edith Anna Œnone Somerville

### (1934)

MOIRA CLOCA-DEARG (and that means, in Irish, Mary of the Red Cloak, and the way you'd say it in English is "Cloka-dharrig") was a nice young girl of about seventeen years. She lived with her mother, a decent widow woman by the name of Margaret Sheehan, who had a small handy little farm that wasn't maybe more than a couple o' miles out from the town of Caher-civeen in the County Kerry.

The neighbours put the name of Cloca-dearg on Moira for she having a tasty red coat, and a hood on it, that the Mother made for her to wear when she'd be riding after the hounds.

It might be thought a strange thing and against nature that a small farmer's daughter would have the way and the fancy to follow hounds. But sure these weren't grand English quality hounds at all. They were no more than only them big black dogs, Kerry Baygles they calls them, that the farmers' sons keeps to be hunting the foxes, that wouldn't leave a hen nor a goose in the country if they'd be let alone. And it was the way Moira seen pictures in the town of hunters in red coats, and after she getting the pony, the world wouldn't content her without she'd get a red coat the same as she seen in the pictures.

But wait till I tell you how she got the pony that was as near and dear to her as the blood of her arm.

215

She had the fancy always to be going away by herself in lonely places. She would be by the way of going to school—that was a good two miles back in the town—and the Mother would give her a bit of soda-bread and one o' them hot-bottles with milk, for her lunch. But maybe in place of going to school at all, she would stray away in the hills, and queer stories she would bring back with her to the Mother.

One day it was a little old manneen that was no higher than her knee that met her, and requested her in Irish would she come with him to the Fort above on Slieve Liath, and see the neat pair of shoes he was making for one of the High Quality there, and he said he might make as good a pair for herself, once he had the length of her foot. She hadn't but ten years then, but young as she was, she had sense. She thanked him kindly, but she told him she had all the shoes she wanted. Sure she knew well enough it was a Cluricaune he was, and if she put a foot into a shoe he made, if it was into the lake he went itself, she should follow him. She told the Mother how she had met the Cluricaune, and that he had a neat red cap on him, and deeshy-daushy little apron, and a nice civil little old lad he was too, and good company. The Mother cautioned her she had no business keeping such company. But sure the world wouldn't stop her roaming that way. Every once in a while she'd come home and say to the Mother she seen this and that—a child, maybe, that she'd think was going astray, and she'd hear it crying, and would run after it different ways, and when it had her tired out, it'd soak away into the hill from her. Or she'd hear like laughing in the air, or horns blowing. There are plenty would friken at the like o' that, but sure that was all like nothing to Moira Cloca-dearg, for her being so used to it. And another day it might be the little Manneen that she might see, from her, like, and he'd be gone again in the minute, but he might wave the red cap to her, like he was friendly to her.

There was a day when the Widow Sheehan had a couple o' hundred cabbage plants to set for her cows, and she says to Moira:

"Ye're so great with the fairies, it's a pity ye wouldn't ask them would they give me a hand to set the cabbages."

Well, that I may never sin, if the next morning she didn't find the cabbage plants all set, but where were they growing only in the path down from the hill to the cottage! The poor woman had to give the day digging them out, and setting them where they should be in the potato-garden. And wasn't that like a lesson to Moira she should keep out from the like o' them? But divil a hair did she care.

Moira was about thirteen years when her Mother sent her back in the hills to look for a milking-goat that had gone astray on her. The little girl was searching the hill, hither and over, till she was beat out entirely, and in the finish, when she could get no trace of the goat at all, she sat down to rest herself by one of them old forts that was back on the hill, Dun-na-shee it was called for being a place that the old people said was greatly resorted to by the fairies. Moira sat down on a big stone that was beside the ope in the wall of the fort. It was very early of a summer morning and the grass was grey with the dew. She heard a sound of music inside in the fort. Very light and sweet it was, and it came out to her through the ope in the wall. It went past her then where she was sitting. As the music went past her she saw the dew brushing away off the grass, like that people were passing, but not a sign of e'er a one could the little girl see.

Well, as tired as she was, she rose up and she followed the music. She told the Mother, after, she'd nearly have to dance it was that jolly. She hadn't gone above twenty perches when she came to a level place, with good grass and ferns, and a stream running through it, and a great growth of fox-gloves, that the people say is a great fairy plant—"Fairy Fingers" they calls it, but Lusmore is the name in Irish for it—growing thick by the stream, as gay as a garden. The stream was running out from under a big rock the size of a house, and beyond the stream, lying down under the rock in the grass, so cozy, what was there but me goat! And standing beside her, taking a sup of water for itself, there was a pure white yearling pony! As white as the drivelling snow it was. You'd hardly see the like in a circus.

The music went winding on always. Round the far end of the big rock it went, but sure Moira Cloca-dearg forgot it entirely when she seen the pony.

"O my darling little pony-een!" says she, and she crossed the stream to the pony, and the creature stood, like as if it knew her, and looked at her as wise as a man. It was about the size of a good ass.

"O if I could carry you home with me!" says Moira petting it.

"Ho, Ho, Ho!" says it, like it was agreeable to go with her.

She turned about then and roused up the old goat, and she said goodbye like to the pony—for how could she drive the two of them?—and she started to drive the goat down the hill. She was hardly past the level ground and going on down the glen, when she heard a sound behind her, and what was it but the white pony following after her!

When Moira saw the pony coming on this way, she was greatly delighted.

"Come along my little jewel," she says, "we'll live and die together!" In the minute she heard a screech of laughter from back up the hill, and a horn blew a salute, like what a huntsman would blow when he seen the fox starting to run away. But Moira didn't mind at all.

"Blow away!" says she, "I have her now and I'll keep her!" says she, "and Lusmore is the name I'll put on her, for finding her where she was, with the Fairy Fingers around her!"

But look, from that day out the fairies had a spit agin her.

That now was how she got the pony. Every step of the way home it followed her, and when the Mother seen it she was delighted altogether. "For," says she, "in two years' time it'll be grown, and many a good basket o' turf it'll carry for us!"

Moira made her no answer, but says she to herself, "It's me it'll be carrying, and not turf at all!"

The Widow Sheehan had a near neighbour by the name of John Wolfe. His farm was next to hers, and the name of it was Caher-brech, which means the Fort of the Wolves, and not long ago they say there was wolves there in plenty. I believe there was one of them patriots one time by the name of Wolfe Tone, but John Wolfe had no call or claim to him; he was no patriot at all, but a quiet, respectable man, with no wish for fighting, and having a nice stall of cows, and a good share of money put away in the bank.

But the son he had was a wild lad. Cornelius was his name, and Curley Brech was the name the people had for him, and there was no mischief and tricks done in the country but what he was at the back of them. His near way to school was through the Widow Sheehan's ground, and it was hardly he'd pass her house without he'd do some mischeevious thing to her property or herself. He was older than Moira by three years, and he was the divil's own play-boy, and never tired with tormenting her and her Mother.

And as he got older it was only worse and more tormenting he grew. He was for ever running after Moira, and bringing by the way of presents for her Mother, pounds of butter, or a leg of pork when his father'd have a pig killed; but if he did, he'd hide them in some wrong place, like one time when he had a comb of honey for her, and where did he leave it only in her bed, and didn't the poor woman throw herself down on it, and the curses she put out of her'd fill a house, and her own child only to laugh at her! And

there wouldn't be a day hardly that he'd not be teazing Moira. He
was a great play-actor, and as full of tricks as a fairy. He'd be waiting
in an amberbush, maybe, to lep out at her, with an old hat on him,
the way he'd be a tramp, and then letting on to console her, and
trying to kiss her when she'd be crying with the fright—the raging
scamp! And another day he might steal his Mother's old clothes
and dress himself up like an old woman, and come begging to the
Widow for a sup o' tay for God's sake. And when the creature'd
have it made—for mind ye she was charitable that way—nothing
would content the old *calliach* that he let on to be. It'd be too wake,
or too strong, or he didn't want but the colour of milk and she had
it drowned with cream, or it was rotten with sugar, and the like o'
that. The Widow would get mad entirely, and would bid him walk
out of her house, and then the lad would begin to strip the old
clothes off of him and throw them on the floor, and herself'd think
it was a madwoman he was, and would roar for the Polis, God help
her, with the Barracks two miles away!

Didn't he go one winter night with a pot of that red raddle that
they mixes in whitewash, and he painted Lusmore, the white pony,
with big patches of red, the same as a cow. When Moira went in the
dark morning to feed her she thought it was a cow was in it.

"O Mother, Mother!" says she, giving the big mouth, "The
Fairies have me pony stole away, and a little rackling of a heifer left
in place of her!"

It wasn't till the pony roared to her for her feed that she knew
her. The Mother and Moira gave the day washing her, and in spite
of them she was as red as a new-born child for a week after.

The Pony was up to three years when Cutler Brech done this to
her, and a fine stout puck of a pony she was too. Moira would ride
her far and near in a grand saddle that had two crooked horns on it,
the same as a Kerry cow. The Mother got it one time at an Oxtion.

"Here!" says the Oxtioneer, "The man that brings this home'll
get a kiss that'd wather a horse!"

"I want no kisses," says the Widow Sheehan. "I'll bid ye two
pound for the saddle, and divil blow the ha'penny more I'll give!"
And faith, she got it.

It was then Moira started to follow the hounds, and the Mother
made her the tasty red riding-coat, and she put a hood on it, the
way the girl'd cover her head if the weather'd be bad, and it was
then the people put the name of Cloca-dearg on her.

Every Sunday and every Holy-day the boys would be out with

the hounds. Eighteen dogs o' them there were of the black Baygles, and they'd mostly have a couple of bracket hounds—that's the way you'd say "spotted" in English—white they'd be and black and brown spots on them, like them English hounds. They has the like o' them the way you'd see them away from you when the black dogs would hardly be seen at all, for the hills being so dark like. They were strewed out through the country. One lad'd have two, and maybe another three, and another might have but the one. Each hound would follow his own till they'd all be met together, and then they should be answerable to the horn. And who was the lad that had the horn only me bold Curley Brech! He was the leader for them, and an arch boy he was, that could run like a hound himself, and was as cute as a pet fox, let alone a mountainy one! All the lads followed after the dogs on their own legs, but if Moira got the chance when the Mother wouldn't know, she'd pounce up on the pony, and away with her after the hunt!

The way the huntsmen had, they'd drive the dogs before them till they'd find a fox, or maybe start a hare, and if it was a hare, that'd run back and forth round a valley, the boys would wait on a hill above and see the hunt, and run down and take the hare from the hounds if they cot her. But if it was a fox they had, it might be dark night before the lads'd see them again, and it'd be no better for Moira, and she on a mountainy pony that could run on the rocks like a bird. But sure the fox'd take the hounds away entirely, where horse nor man couldn't follow them.

As sure as Moira would be in the hunt it'd always be a fox they'd find, and back in the mountains he'd carry the dogs, and as sure as there's a harp on a ha'penny that'd be the fox they'd never ketch! "And why not?" says you.

Because it'd be a fairy fox sure! It was the spite the fairies had agin Moira, for carrying away the white pony, that they'd keep a fox handy, and the dogs never be let ketch him, and them and Moira'd be put astray, and it might be dark night before she'd get home or the dogs either. Half dead they'd all be, and the pony the worst of all.

Well, there was a fine day came in Febbiverry, it was Valentine's day (and by the same token, that year it was the last day of Shraft) and Moira was eighteen years the same day. Her Mother says to her,

"Ketch the pony," says she, "and throw the saddle on her, and you'll go see your Grannema, and bring her the nice present that I have for her, and maybe yourself'd get a present from her, for this being your birthday. And," says the .Mother, says she, looking at Moira very sevare, "Let you go straight there, and no idling and gosthering with any that'd be in your road, and if you meet that limb o' the divil, Curley Brech, mootching and purshawling," says she, "give him the go-by, cool and nice," says she, "Leave him go his way and you go yours."

"Faith and I will too!" says Moira, "I've no wish for him, or the likes of him!" says she, as proud as the Queen of Spain.

The Mother then puts a nice pat o' fresh butter, and a nice comb o' honey, and a lovely soda-loaf, and a dozen fresh eggs in a basket, and Moira puts on her new red riding-coat, and away with her to ride across the hill to the Grandmother. (The Grandmother was old Mrs. Dan Sheehan, that was Moira's grandmother by the father. She had a power o' money, and the Widow Sheehan, that was her daughter-in-law, was for ever sending Moira to see her, and paying her little compliments of eggs and butter, and the like o' that.)

Moira wasn't gone farther than John Wolfe's farm when who should she see before her only Curley Brech, and two hounds with him, and one of them was a big black baygle, by the name of Bugler, and the other was a little young bracket bitch, whose name was Comfort; and them was the two best hounds in the country.

Curley Brech ketches the pony by the head, and puts his arm over her neck. The pony wasn't but fourteen hands, and Curley was a tall straight boy.

"Where are ye goin'?" says he to Moira, grinning at her, and shaking her by the hand, and not letting it go. "So smart ye look in your red ridin' coat, Darlin'!" says he.

"*I'm* not your darlin'!" says Moira, pulling the hand from him (but sure she couldn't keep from laughing at the impidence he had).

"For two pins I'd give ye a good box on the ear!" says she.

"Ah, ye would not!" says Curley Brech, coaxing her, and looking at her the way you'd say he'd like to eat her. "And listen," says he, "I'm waiting now for the hounds, and let you wait too and have a hunt." "And what'll I do with me present for Grannema?" says Moira.

"I'll run back with it to me Mother," says Curley, "and can't ye get it from her when the hunt's over—"

Well now, that was where the mistake was for Moira. But to think of the hunt enticed her, and she was said by Curley Brech.

It was shortly then all the lads come along with the hounds, and me bold Curley outs with the horn, and off with them all up into the hill of Slieve Liath—that means the Grey Hill, but green and sunny it was that fine Valentine's Day, and sure a person's heart'd rise on a day like it, and the hounds playing around, and hunting through the rocks, and putting yowls out o' themselves if they seen as much as a rabbit or a weasel in the heather before them.

Curley Brech, with the horn, went on before the other lads, giving a shout now and again to hearten the hounds, and walking beside the pony, and looking at Moira, and saying to her to tell him when she seen a fox, "for none of us," says he, looking up at her so tender, "has the sight to see a fox the way your blue eyes can!"

Moira wouldn't let on she heard him, but Curley seen the blush on her cheek, and he knew by her she was pleased.

They weren't gone deep into the hill at all when what'd Moira see close beside them, only the little Cluricaune, and he sitting on a flat rock and the tools of his trade beside him. He took the red cap off his head and he wove it to her. Moira returned him a salute.

"Who are ye saluting at all?" says Curley, looking around, but shure he hadn't *the Sighth*, the way Moira had. But old Bugler, that was the oldest of the hounds, saw the manneen, and the hair stood up on the poor dog's back, and he growled furious; and Comfort, the little bracket bitch, seen the manneen too, and she made a drive to bite him, but in the minute he was gone, and no trace of him on the rock!

"Ax no questions," says Moira to Curley, teasing him, "and ye'll be told no lies!" but she had it hardly said when she seen the manneen again, standing up on the rock, and waving his red cap up to the hill, saying "Tally-Ho!" and giving little small screeches, that not a one heard only Moira, and old Bugler, and Comfort, the little bracket bitch. Moira looks up at the hill, and what was there but a big grey fox on a stretch of rock and he looking down at them as cool as ·Christian!

"Look at him above! Look at him! Look at him!" screeches Moira, "Tally Ho forrad!" says she, and she comminces to gallop at the hill, with Lusmore, the white pony, pulling mad, and old Bugler and Comfort out ahead of her!

Well, then was the ecstases! Curley, and all the crowd of lads, shouting and legging it up the hill after Moira, and the hounds coming from all parts and sweeping through the crowd! Believe me, the fox didn't wait long! What a fool he'd be, with them black Baygles, like Black Death itself, yowling after him! They gethered like bees on the rock he was on, and then old Bugler thew up his head, and

"Yow! Yow! Yow!" says he, "Here's the way he went!" says he. And Comfort, the little bracket bitch, give a squeal like ye'd say it was a pig and it having the throat cut, and away on the line goes the two o' them, and all the rest o' the dogs roaring after them!

By the mercy o' God there was a good cattle-track going up the glen. Up it goes Moira, with the pony pulling like she wanted to ketch the fox herself, and all the lads coming on after her, and Curley Brech blowing his horn for fear would any hounds be behind them (but faith, it wasn't long before the breath failed him!) When they got to the top of the glen, there was a level place that wasn't level entirely, for it slanted up to another rise of hill. The hounds had it nearly crossed when Moira got up to it. Boggy it was, but not too deep; she faced the pony at it, and sure the pony went away over it easy and independent as a snipe, and Curley and the boys following on always.

On the hill beyond the bog they could see the hounds, but hardly. Them black hounds when they gets away in the heather, melts like into it. You'd nearly say it was a shadow only you say, if it wasn't for Comfort, the bracket bitch, that shewed where they were. White she was, and spotted, and a yellow head on her, like her dam, that was an English hound John Wolfe had one time. Great hounds to hunt they are, and the cry they had was like a band o' music, and the sound went beating from one hill to another, most lovely.

As tired as the boys were, they couldn't stop running with that in their ears, and with the sight always of the white pony, galloping away before them up the next hill beyond, and as steep as it was, she facing up to it as hardy as a goat.

And as for Moira Cloca-dearg, she was in glory!

Not a thought in the world in her only to keep up with the hounds. Faith, she was as proud as that wouldn't call the King her cousin! And no blame to her! Sure she had the boys all left behind, and the white pony under her ready to run to Cork.

Well, above that hill was another one, and it steeper again! I declare when a person'd be climbing mountains, the nearer he'd get to the top, the further off he'd find it! And that was the way for Moira. When she got above that hill, she seen before her a big stretch of wet watery bog, and a kind of an island in the middle of it, and a wide sort of a fence that divided the bog in two halves, and crossed out to the island, and follied on from it to the far side of the bog. And there were all the hounds, and they not running at all, but going this way and that, and the smell of the fox lost to them.

Faith the pony wasn't sorry at all to stand still, and Moira seen that out beyond the bog was hills, going away away, up into the sky, to further orders, as they say! Moira looks around for the boys, but deuce a one could she see.

"O what'll I do now at all?" says she, and she mad with the hurry that was in her. "It must be that blagyard Fairy Fox we're hunting agin!" says she.

The hounds came up round her and stood there, and they waving their tails, and looking up at her, and blaming her for themselves losing the smell.

"Sure I can't help ye, my darlings," says she to them, "I d'no no more than yoursels what way is he gone at all!"

With that some o' them lies down and comminces to roll, and more comminces to scratch, and old Bugler comes up to the pony's shoulder, and sits down, and looks at Moira, with his long ears hanging down beside his nose, and his eyes drooping in his head, like his heart was broke. And Comfort, the little bracket bitch, strays away for herself, and goes wandering around, nosing every place, and getting no satisfaction. Moira was fit to cry; and not for herself alone, but for the dogs that were waiting on her, and she not able to do a thing for them.

And that now was the minute she heard the horn! Not Curley Brech's horn at all, but a little fairy horn, no louder than a blackbird's pipe, and it going on strong, blowing "Gone away!" And then what did she see but two crowds of fairies, and they galloping along out of the little island, on the top of the fence across the bog! Some o' them was on little weeshy horses, and some only floating in the air, and all colours on them like butterflies! And then old Bugler rose up and begins to growl, and what was it but the manneen with the red cap beside her! "Let you not go that way at all!" says he in Irish. Moira lepped in her saddle.

"And why not?" says she, jumping mad to start after the fairies; "isn't that the way the fox went?" says she. "Surely I will go!" says she.

"It's no good for ye!" says the manneen.

But there was no holding Moira. She ketches the pony by the head and away with her down to the fence that crossed the bog, and she screeching to the hounds:

"Forrad! Forrad! Forrad! Tally-Ho forrad!"

Well! The hounds that were so idle and dull, come sweeping on after her like a flood of black water, and the young ones throwing

their tongues, and not knowing the reason why at all—the creatures! Old Bugler and Comfort, the little bracket bitch, weren't
running with the rest at all, but going either side of the pony, and
not a word out of them. When Moira comes down to where the
fence started to cross the bog, all the pack mounts up on the fence
before her, only Bugler and Comfort never stirs, and they stands
still before Moira like they wanted to stop her going on the fence.

"What ails ye?" says Moira, scolding them; "Get forrad there!"
says she, "Ware horse!" says she, very angry, riding at them.

They let her pass then, and up on the fence she goes after the
hounds that was racing out along it with their heads down, and the
cry that they rose then'd put the heart across in your body! Away
they streams along the top o' the fence, the way the fairies went,
and Moira and the white pony after them as clever as one o' them
Frenchmen that can walk a rope!

But will ye believe me, half-way across the bog, when Moira got
to the little island that was in it, she saw the hounds check, and
then, one after the other, she seen them lep out of her sight!

Lusmore, the white pony, stops short.

"What's the matter with ye?" says Moira, mad angry, hitting her
a slap with the little *kippen* she had for a whip.

The pony walks on a few steps, and what was there before them
but a gap between the island and where the fence continued on,
twenty feet and more wide, of deep dark water! When Moira got to
it, the most of the hounds was in it, swimming across, and the leaders climbing up on to the fence beyond, and follying on the way the
fairies went.

Moira looks at the black water, and she knew then it was the
divilment of the fairies that had led her that way, and if it wasn't
for the pony being a match for their tricks, she might have gal-
loped into it and never come out of it at all. (Sure bog-holes the
like o' that goes down into the next world altogether!)

"It's as good for us to go home," says she to Lusmore the white
pony, and she like to cry, seeing the hounds going from her. She
turns around and back with her along the crown o' the fence, and
there was old Bugler, and Comfort, the little bracket bitch, sitting
waiting for her.

"Shew me the way home, good hounds!" says she. Bugler looks
up at her, and he growls.

And there was the Cluricaune sitting on the rise o' ground beside her, and he laughing at her!

"Bad luck to them fairies!" says Moira to him, "putting me astray this way."

"Why wouldn't ye be said by me?" says the manneen in Irish. "Go home now," he says, "and do as your Mother bid ye."

He commences to hammer at the little brogue he was making, and while Moira was looking at him, he soaked away into the hill.

It was only then that Moira thought of the basket she was to take to the Grandmother.

"O murder!" says she, "Mamma'll kill me!"

It was well for her Bugler and Comfort was Curley Brech's, and it was for Caherbrech farm they made, and Moira after them, to fetch the basket. Five long Irish miles back in the hills she was; the rain had begun; she put the hood of the Cloca-dearg over her head, and followed on after the two hounds.

The day was closing in when she comes to Caherbrech. Mrs. Wolfe, that was Curley's mother, comes to the door, and Moira asks her for the basket.

"Sure Curley came back from hunting two hours ago," says Mrs. Wolfe, "and he said himself'd run over with the basket to your Grandmother. Come in, girl, out o' the rain, and have a cup o' tea, you're in the want of it, my dear," says she.

"Thank you, Ma-am," says Moira, "I'd be thankful for it, but I must go see my Grandmother, and bring home the basket, or my Mother'll kill me."

Mrs. Wolfe let Moira go then. Herself and the grandmother, that was old Mrs. Dan Sheehan, were for making a match with Moira and Curley, for the farms being convenient that way; they didn't say a word yet to the girl or the Mother, but Mrs. Wolfe knew well that the boy would be willing, and there was time enough, with them both being as young as they were. But sure women must always be matchmaking.

When Moira Cloca-dearg got to old Mrs. Dan's house, the half-door was shut.

"I wonder," says she to herself, "is she home at all?—But hardly she'd be out in the rain and it so late—"

She gets down off the pony and ties her to the gate of the garden, and knocks at the door of the house.

"The door's not locked at all," says a wake kind of a voice inside, like a hen that'd have the croup. "Come in, Asthore, come in why."

Moira opens the door and goes in.

The kitchen was very dark, but she sees the Grandmother sitting

back in a big hurlo-thrumbo of a chair that she had, down by the
fire. She had a big white cap on her, and a grey shawl over it, and an
old quilt over her knees.

"Did ye get the eggs and the butter me Mother sent ye, Grannema?" says Moira.

"I did, I did, Asthore," says the quare voice out o' the chair.
"Come here till I thank ye for them!"

Moira goes nearer, but she felt frightened like. She looks down
into the chair. She sees nothing only the old woman's spectacles
shining with the fire in them.

"Why have ye the specs on in the dark like this, Grannema?"
says she.

"The way I can see you better, Asthore!" says the old woman.
"Come here to me, me eyes is dark, I can't see ye at all—"

Moira goes closer. She looks under the big cap and the shawl,
and she sees a big mouth, laughing, and it full of white teeth! "O
Grannema!" says she, hardly knowing at all what was she saying for
getting worse frightened every minute. ("It's a wicked fairy that's in
it, and not Grannema at all!" says she to herself.)

"Those are me own teeth, child, sure I have them always!" says
the wicked fairy. "Come here to me and I'll show ye what I have
the big mouth for!"

And with that, Curley the Wolf—for who was it but himself, the
blagyard!—leps up out o' the old chair, with the cap and shawl and
all falling from him, and he ketches the little girl and kisses her till
ye'd think he'd ate the face off her!

"Let me go!" says Moira, trying to loose his arms that were round
her.

"What have ye done with me Grandmother?" Curley Brech
holds her tight.

"She's gone to settle with the Priest," says he. "There's time yet!
This is the last day of Shraft, and I'll wait no longer," says he;
"We'll be married to-night!" says he.

And so they were too, and if ye'll believe me, the little Cluricaune
was before them, and they coming out of the Chapel, and he threw
a little shoe after them that ye wouldn't get the like of in the whole
world, no, nor in the globe of Ireland neither.

James Thurber, "The Girl and the Wolf," in *Fables for Our Time and Famous Poems*, New York: Harper, 1939. Illustrator James Thurber.

# ❧ 18 ❧

## *The Girl
and the Wolf*

### *By James Thurber*

### (1939)

O NE AFTERNOON A BIG WOLF waited in a dark forest for a little girl to come along carrying a basket of food to her grandmother. Finally a little girl did come along and she was carrying a basket of food. "Are you carrying that basket to your grandmother?" asked the wolf. The little girl said yes, she was. So the wolf asked her where her grandmother lived and the little girl told him and he disappeared into the wood.

When the little girl opened the door of her grandmother's house she saw that there was somebody in bed with a nightcap on. She had approached no nearer than twenty-five feet from the bed when she saw that it was not her grandmother but the wolf, for even in a nightcap a wolf does not look any more like your grandmother than the Metro-Goldwyn lion looks like Calvin Coolidge. So the little girl took an automatic out of her basket and shot the wolf dead.

*Moral: It is not so easy to fool little girls nowadays as it used to be.*

## Little Red Riding Hood as a Dictator Would Tell It

### By H. I. Phillips

### (1940)

O NCE UPON A TIME there was a poor, weak wolf. It was gentle and kindly and had a heart of gold. It loved everybody and felt very sad when it looked around and saw so much deceit, selfishness, strife, treachery and cunning on the loose. All it wanted was to be let alone.

Now in a cottage near the edge of the forest there lived a little girl who went by the name of Little Red Riding Hood. (It was obviously an alias.) She was a spy, a vile provocateur and an agent of capitalistic interests. Anybody could tell by one look at Little Red Riding Hood that she was full of intrigue. Her golden curls reeked with base designs. Her pink skin showed tyranny in every pigment.

To the casual spectator, perhaps, Little Red Riding Hood might seem just a pretty little ten-year-old child, but this was a superficial piece of character analysis. The kid was not to be trusted an inch. She was a rattlesnake, a viper and an imperialist. And on top of all that she was not interested in peace or a better world order.

Little Red Riding Hood had a grandmother who lived about two miles away. Grandma was a louse too!

No wolves liked her. They never invited her anywhere.

It came to pass that one day the poor, weak, helpless wolf took an aspirin and some spring tonic, to brace himself up, and then went for a little walk.

When the wolf walked he liked to think things over. He liked to dwell on the unhappiness in the world and to think up ways for ending it and making everybody happy and self-sustaining. This took a lot of concentrating and when he was concentrating the wolf sometimes got lost in thought and didn't know what he was doing. Suddenly, and before he knew what was what, he found himself not only in Grandma's cottage but in her bedroom!

He had kicked down the door.

Grandma was pretty startled and demanded, "What is the meaning of this?"

"I am repulsing an invasion," the wolf explained, scorning all subterfuge.

Grandma was an aggressor. That was clear.

So the wolf ate her up.

It was a counterattack with pursuit.

Then the wolf heard footsteps in the hall. He was terribly frightened by this time. It had been such a harrowing morning.

Suddenly there came a faint knock on the door. The wolf realized at once that he was in for more persecution.

"Who's there?" he asked.

"Little Red Riding Hood," came the reply in a child's voice.

The wolf saw it all now. He was surrounded!

So he put on Grandma's nightgown and nightcap and jumped into bed to do some more thinking. He liked to think in bed. It was next best to thinking when out walking in the woods.

"Come up, my child!" the wolf cried to Little Red Riding Hood, his teeth chattering with fear and apprehension.

Little Red Riding Hood started upstairs, and oh, what an ordeal that was to the poor little wolf! It seemed that she would never make the top landing, "Clumph, clumph, clumph!" came her footsteps, stair by stair. "Clumph, clumph, clumph!"

The wolf was in terror, but he summoned all his courage and waited.

At last Little Red Riding Hood came striding into the bedroom. She was very overbearing, the big bully!

The wolf watched while she put down her huge basketful of groceries. "Poisoned food," he thought. The wolf was no fool. The wolf had been around.

"I've brought you some nice goodies, Grannie," said Little Red Riding Hood with a smile that might have fooled the democratic states, but that made no impression on the wolf. He knew that kind of smile. He had seen it on all photographs of international bankers in the newsreels. He saw that he was now in greater danger than ever.

"I don't feel like eating now," he said. "We'll come to that later." He was just stalling for time, of course, as his eyes ran over Little Red Riding Hood from her ankles to her head. "Come, sit over here on the bed!"

Little Red Riding Hood jumped at the invitation. The wolf was now in a panic. Never had he been in such danger.

"Why Grandma, what big eyes you have!" exclaimed Little Red Riding Hood, after a moment.

"The better to see you with, my dear."

"And Grandma, what a big mouth you have!"

The wolf didn't like that crack. "The better to kiss you with, my sweet," he stalled.

"And Grandma, what big teeth you have!" said Little Red Riding Hood.

This was too much. She was getting too personal. In fact, she was exhausting the patience of the wolf. And if there was one thing the wolf couldn't stand it was having his patience exhausted.

"Ah, let's quit stalling!" the wolf cried, rebelling against deceit and trickery in any form. "I'm not your grandma. I'm a wolf. I'm a good wolf, a nice friendly wolf. I don't want any trouble with anybody. And what happens? First your grandmother ambushes me . . . and now you try to cut off my retreat!"

"What became of Grandma?" asked Little Red Riding Hood, always looking for trouble.

"I question the propriety of your asking me that question," said the wolf, who was a stickler for international law. "But if you insist, put it in writing and address it to me via the proper diplomatic channels."

"I want to know what happened to Grannie," repeated Little Red Riding Hood, pulling a knife on him.

Well no self-respecting wolf could stand for a brazen attitude like that. And besides there was the matter of candor and honesty.

"Oh well, since you want to know, I ate her up," the wolf announced. "I ate her in self-defense."

Little Red Riding Hood got off the bed and stood looking at the wolf now. The wolf watched her weep and wring her hands. She gave way to all these emotions of ferocity, barbarism and hatred.

"Ah," said the wolf, "so now you are going to attack me, too!"

Little Red Riding Hood now got onto the floor on her hands and

❧ 233 ❧

*Little Red
Riding
Hood as a
Dictator
Would
Tell It*

*Les Contes de Perrault,* **Paris, 1928. Illustrator Lucien Boucher.**

knees and showed her teeth. She crouched for a spring. She began growling.

There was not a minute to lose. The wolf was in deadly peril. He was encircled. This was a fight for his existence. Leaping from the bed, he struggled with Little Red Riding Hood, using nothing but his superior strength, his long claws, his enormous teeth and his jaws of steel, while the kid used brass knuckles, knockoutdrops, poison gas, a magnetic bomb, a sledge hammer and a hatchet.

Little Red Riding Hood fought savagely and barbarously, violating all the rules, ignoring all treaties and showing contempt for ethics. It was a terrific struggle. But the wolf won by sheer courage. He tore Little Red Riding Hood to pieces to preserve his dignity and ate her as a matter of principle.

"I'll teach 'em not to terrorize me," said the wolf, resuming his walk through the woods, thinking and thinking.

He was getting his patience back now.

# ❄ 20 ❄

## *Little Polly Riding Hood*

## By Catherine Storr

## (1955)

ONCE EVERY TWO WEEKS Polly went over to the other side of the town to see her grandmother. Sometimes she took a small present, and sometimes she came back with a small present for herself. Sometimes all the rest of the family went too, and sometimes Polly went alone.

One day, when she was going by herself, she had hardly got down the front door steps when she saw the wolf.

"Good afternoon, Polly," said the wolf. "Where are you going, may I ask?"

"Certainly," said Polly. "I'm going to see my grandma."

"I thought so!" said the wolf, looking very much pleased. "I've been reading about a girl who went to visit her grandmother and it's a very good story."

"Little Red Riding Hood?" suggested Polly.

"That's it!" cried the wolf. "I read it out loud to myself as a bedtime story. I did enjoy it. The wolf eats up the grandmother, *and* Little Red Riding Hood. It's almost the only story where a wolf really gets anything to eat," he added sadly.

"But in my book he doesn't get Red Riding Hood," said Polly. "Her father comes in just in time to save her."

"Oh, he doesn't in *my* book!" said the wolf. "I expect mine is the true story, and yours is just invented. Anyway, it seems a good idea."

234

"What is a good idea?"

"To catch little girls on their way to their grandmothers' cottages," said the wolf. "Now where had I got to?"

"I don't know what you mean," said Polly.

"Well, I'd said, 'Where are you going to?'" said the wolf. "Oh yes. Now I must say 'Where does she live?' Where does your grandmother live, Polly Riding Hood?"

"Over the other side of town," answered Polly.

The wolf frowned.

"It ought to be 'Through the Wood,'" he said. "But perhaps town will do. How do you get there, Polly Riding Hood?"

"First I take a train and then I take a bus," said Polly.

The wolf stamped his foot.

"No, no, no, no!" he shouted. "That's all wrong. You can't say that. You've got to say, 'By the path winding through the trees,' or something like that. You can't go by trains and buses and things. It isn't fair."

"Well, I could say that," said Polly, "but it wouldn't be true. I do have to go by bus and train to see my grandma, so what's the good of saying I don't?"

"But then it won't work," said the wolf impatiently. "How can I get there first and gobble her up and get all dressed up to trick you into believing I am her, if we've got a great train journey to do? And anyhow I haven't any money on me, so I can't even take a ticket. You just can't say that!"

"All right, I won't say it," said Polly agreeably. "But it's true all the same. Now just excuse me, Wolf, I've got to get down to the station because I am going to visit my grandma even if you aren't."

The wolf slunk along behind Polly, growling to himself. He stood just behind her at the booking-office and heard her ask for her ticket, but he could not go any further. Polly got into a train and was carried away, and the wolf went sadly home.

But just two weeks later the wolf was waiting outside Polly's house again. This time he had plenty of change in his pocket. He even had a book tucked under his front leg to read in the train.

He partly hid himself behind a corner of brick wall and watched to see Polly come out on her way to her grandmother's house.

But Polly did not come out alone, as she had before. This time the whole family appeared, Polly's father and mother too. They got into the car which was waiting in the road, and Polly's father started the engine.

*French broadsheet, Epinal,* ca. 1880. Illustrator unknown. Collection
Pierre Ullman.

The wolf ran behind his brick wall as fast as he could, and was
just in time to get out into the road ahead of the car, and to stand
waving his paws as if he wanted a lift as the car came up.

Polly's father slowed down, and Polly's mother put her head out
of the window.

"Where do you want to go?" she asked.

"I want to go to Polly's grandmother's house," the wolf answered.
His eyes glistened as he looked at the family of plump little girls in
the back of the car.

"That's where we are going," said her mother, surprised. "Do you
know her then?"

"Oh no," said the wolf. "But you see, I want to get there very
quickly and eat her up and then I can put on her clothes and wait
for Polly, and eat her up too."

"Good heavens!" said Polly's father. "What a horrible idea! We
certainly shan't give you a lift if that is what you are planning to do."

Polly's mother screwed up the window again and Polly's father
drove quickly on. The wolf was left standing miserably in the road.

"Bother!" he said to himself angrily. "It's gone wrong again. I
can't think why it can't be the same again as the Little Red Riding

Hood story. It's all these buses and cars and trains that make it go wrong."

But the wolf was determined to get Polly, and when she was due to visit her grandmother again, a fortnight later, he went down and took a ticket for the station he had heard Polly ask for. When he got out of the train, he climbed on a bus, and soon he was walking down the road where Polly's grandmother lived.

"Aha!" he said to himself, "this time I shall get them both. First the grandma, then Polly."

He unlatched the gate into the garden, and strolled up the path to Polly's grandmother's front door. He rapped sharply with the knocker.

"Who's there?" called a voice from inside the house.

The wolf was very much pleased. This was going just as it had in the story. This time there would be no mistakes.

"Little Polly Riding Hood," he said in a squeaky voice. "Come to see her dear grandmother, with a little present of butter and eggs and—er—cake!"

There was a long pause. Then the voice said doubtfully, "*Who* did you say it was?"

"Little Polly Riding Hood," said the wolf in a great hurry, quite forgetting to disguise his voice this time. "Come to eat up her dear grandmother with butter and eggs!"

There was an even longer pause. Then Polly's grandmother put her head out of a window and looked down at the wolf.

"I beg your pardon?" she said.

"I am Polly," said the wolf firmly.

"Oh," said Polly's grandmother. She appeared to be thinking hard. "Good afternoon, Polly. Do you know if anyone else happens to be coming to see me today? A wolf, for instance?"

"No. Yes," said the wolf in great confusion. "I met a Polly as I was coming here—I mean, I, Polly, met a wolf on my way here, but she can't have got here yet because I started specially early."

"That's very queer," said the grandma. "Are you quite sure you are Polly?"

"Quite sure," said the wolf.

"Well, then, I don't know who it is who is here already," said Polly's grandma. "She said she was Polly. But if you are Polly then I think this other person must be a wolf."

"No, no, I am Polly," said the wolf. "And, anyhow, you ought not to say all that. You ought to say 'Lift the latch and come in.'"

"I don't think I'll do that," said Polly's grandma. "Because I don't want my nice little Polly eaten up by a wolf, and if you come in now the wolf who is here already might eat you up."

Another head looked out of another window. It was Polly's.

"Bad luck, Wolf," she said. "You didn't know that I was coming to lunch and tea today instead of just tea as I generally do—so I got here first. And as you are Polly, as you've just said, I must be the wolf, and you'd better run away quickly before I gobble you up, hadn't you?"

"Bother, bother, bother and *bother!*" said the wolf. "It hasn't worked out right this time either. And I did just what it said in the book. Why can't I ever get you, Polly, when that other wolf managed to get his little girl?"

"Because this isn't a fairy story," said Polly, "and I'm not Little Red Riding Hood, I am Polly and I can always escape from you, Wolf, however much you try to catch me."

"Clever Polly," said Polly's grandma. And the wolf went growling away.

## ❧ 21 ❧

### *Little Red Cap*
### *'65*

### *By Anneliese Meinert*

### (1965)

L ITTLE RED CAP," the mother said, "I've prepared a basket for granny. Cake and whisky. I've got to rush to an appointment, so be nice and bring it to her."

Little Red Cap was not too happy about this. She had a date. But since she was a friendly person, she growled, "Give it to me." Little Red Cap jumped into her sportscar. She zoomed through the woods. Though the road was not a highway, there was so little traffic that one could speed. Past the trees. Past the warning signs with silhouettes of animals marked on them. A gray shadow stood on the side of the road and signaled to hitch a ride. Nothing doing!

Granny didn't seem to be particularly pleased by the visit. "You've come at a bad time, my child. I have a bridge party. And what's gotten into your mother's head anyway? Cake and whisky! I'm on a diet. I've got to take off a few pounds. Get that stuff out of here before I'm tempted."

"Yes, Granny." Little Red Cap grabbed the little basket which she had put on the table. Then she asked: "Granny, how come you have such sparkling eyes?"

"So that I can see you better," Granny laughed. "Contact lenses. They're much better than glasses."

"How come you wear such big ear-rings?"

"So that I can hear better. This is the latest invention. The hearing aids are built into the ear-clips."

Now Little Red Cap laughed, too. "Granny, your mouth is un-usual." "That's so I can eat you better! No, that's not it. I've got new dentures. The dentist made them so that the corner of my mouth won't hang. But I don't want to detain you any longer, my child. . . . "

Little Red Cap hopped into her car and drove off. Her young friend Hunter waited at the usual time. "Late," he muttered as he climbed in. "Where were you fooling around so long?"

"I wasn't. I was at Granny's. And, if you don't believe me—there's the little basket she gave me."

Hans Hunter opened the bottle of whisky. "You didn't meet a soul?" he asked as he took a hefty swig.

"Oh, just old Mr. Wolf. He wanted to hitch a ride, and I almost ran him over."

"Mmmmm good," mumbled Hans, for he had his mouth full of cake. They drove over the highway and through the woods. They didn't notice the flowers growing along side the road or the ones which were prettier and further in under the trees. Nor had Little Red Cap noticed them before when she had been alone in the car. How could she, especially when one is going a hundred miles an hour!

## 22

## *Red Riding Hood*

## *By Anne Sexton*

## (1971)

MANY ARE THE DECEIVERS:

The suburban matron,
proper in the supermarket,
list in hand so she won't suddenly fly,
buying her Duz and Chuck Wagon dog food,
meanwhile ascending from earth,
letting her stomach fill up with helium,
letting her arms go loose as kite tails,
getting ready to meet her lover
a mile down Apple Creast Road
in the Congregational Church parking lot.

Two seemingly respectable women
come up to an old Jenny
and show her an envelope
full of money
and promise to share the booty
if she'll give them ten thou
as an act of faith.
Her life savings are under the mattress
covered with rust stains

and counting.
They are as wrinkled as prunes
but negotiable.
The two women take the money and disappear.
Where is the moral?
Not all knives are for
stabbing the exposed belly.
Rock climbs on rock
and it only makes a seashore.
Old Jenny has lost her belief in mattresses
and now she has no wastebasket in which
to keep her youth.

The standup comic
on the "Tonight" show
who imitates the Vice President
and cracks up Johnny Carson
and delays sleep for millions
of bedfellows watching between their feet,
slits his wrist the next morning
in the Algonquin's old-fashioned bathroom,
the razor in his hand like a toothbrush,
wall as anonymous as a urinal,
the shower curtain his slack rubberman audience,
and then the slash
as simple as opening a letter
and the warm blood breaking out like a rose
upon the bathtub with its claw and ball feet.

And I. I too.
Quite collected at cocktail parties,
meanwhile in my head
I'm undergoing open-heart surgery.
The heart, poor fellow,
pounding on his little tin drum
with a faint death beat.
The heart, that eyeless beetle,
enormous that Kafka beetle,
running panicked through his maze,
never stopping one foot after the other
one hour after the other

until he gags on an apple
and it's all over.

And I. I too again.
I built a summer house on Cape Ann.
A simple A-frame and this too was
a deception—nothing haunts a new house.
When I moved in with a bathing suit and tea bags
the ocean rumbled like a train backing up
and at each window secrets came in
like gas. My mother, that departed soul,
sat in my Eames chair and reproached me
for losing her keys to the old cottage.
Even in the electric kitchen there was
the smell of a journey. The ocean
was seeping through its frontiers
and laying me out on its wet rails.
The bed was stale with my childhood
and I could not move to another city
where the worthy make a new life.

Long ago
there was a strange deception:
a wolf dressed in frills,
a kind of transvestite.
But I get ahead of my story.
In the beginning
there was just Red Riding Hood,
so called because her grandmother
made her a red cape and she was never without it.
It was her Linus blanket, besides
it was red, as red as the Swiss flag,
yes it was red, as red as chicken blood.
But more than she loved her riding hood
she loved her grandmother who lived
far from the city in the big wood.

This one day her mother gave her
a basket of wine and cake
to take to her grandmother
because she was ill.

Wine and cake?
Where's the aspirin? The penicillin?
Where's the fruit juice?
Peter Rabbit got camomile tea
But wine and cake it was.

On her way in the big wood
Red Riding Hood met the wolf.
Good day, Mr. Wolf, she said,
thinking him no more dangerous
than a streetcar or a panhandler.
He asked her where she was going
and she obligingly told him.
There among the roots and trunks
with the mushrooms pulsing inside the moss
he planned to eat them both,
the grandmother an old carrot
and the child a shy budkin
in a red red hood.
He bade her to look at the bloodroot,
the small bunchberry and the dogtooth
and pick some for her grandmother.
And this she did.
Meanwhile he scampered off
to Grandmother's house and ate her up
as quick as a slap.
Then he put on her nightdress and cap
and snuggled down into the bed.
A deceptive fellow.

Red Riding Hood
knocked on the door and entered
with her flowers, her cake, her wine.
Grandmother looked strange,
a dark and hairy disease it seemed.
Oh Grandmother, what big ears you have,
ears, eyes, hands and then the teeth.
The better to eat you with, my dear.
So the wolf gobbled Red Riding Hood down
like a gumdrop. Now he was fat.
He appeared to be in his ninth month

and Red Riding Hood and her grandmother
rode like two Jonahs up and down with
his every breath. One pigeon. One Partridge.

He was fast asleep,
dreaming in his cap and gown,
wolfless.
Along came a huntsman who heard
the loud contented snores
and knew that was no grandmother.
He opened the door and said,
So it's you, old sinner.
He raised his gun to shoot him
when it occurred to him that maybe
the wolf had eaten up the old lady.
So he took a knife and began cutting open
the sleeping wolf, a kind of caesarian section.

It was a carnal knife that let
Red Riding Hood out like a poppy,
quite alive from the kingdom of the belly.
And grandmother too
still waiting for cakes and wine.
The wolf, they decided, was too mean
to be simply shot so they filled his belly
with large stones and sewed him up.
He was as heavy as a cemetery
and when he woke up and tried to run off
he fell over dead. Killed by his own weight.
Many a deception ends on such a note.
The huntsman and the grandmother and Red Riding
    Hood
sat down by his corpse and had a meal of wine and cake
Those two remembering
nothing naked and brutal
from that little death,
that little birth,
from their going down
and their lifting up.

## 23

## Little Redhead
## and the Wolf

### By Iring Fetscher

### (1972)

A S IN THE FAIRY TALE ABOUT *The Wolf and the Seven Kids*, the wolf also appears in *Little Red Cap* as devious, wicked and mean. His crime—the swallowing of grandmother and grandchild—is not motivated by a voracious appetite, nor is it explained sufficiently in any other way. The narrator assumes that the wolf is "radically evil by nature," and here, too, one greatly suspects that the assertion of general animal aggression involves an early justification of socially conditioned human aggression. Yet, once again, progressive folklorists have been successful in their research about this case. They recently uncovered a fairy-tale fragment which had been believed to have been forgotten, and now this fragment can shed light on the true motives of the wolf.

Once upon a time there was a little red-headed boy who was named Little Redhead by everyone—at home, in the village, and at school. However, since redheads in his village were not common, and since people often reject and condemn the uncommon without any reason, he had no friends and felt himself to be an outcast.

His father, who was dissatisfied with the son's efforts in school, had only hard words for him and had already beaten him many times. Though the mother had made a red hat for Little Redhead's younger sister and named her "Little Red Cap" so that Little Redhead would not always be the object of special attention, this only helped a little.

Whenever he could, Little Redhead ran alone into the woods to play with the animals and dream. This is also what happened when he arose late one day and was afraid to go to school. As soon as he was far enough from his home and could not be seen by his parents, he stole into the woods. He moved deeper and deeper into the thickets until he came to a spot so unfamiliar that he no longer knew how to proceed. There he met a wolf who spoke to him in a friendly way, proposed that they pick beautiful wild strawberries together, and then he would show Little Redhead the way home.

And this is also the way it happened, and towards noon they had filled three large thatched baskets with fresh, red wild strawberries. "You know what," said the wolf, "tie two of the baskets together with a branch from the field and hang them over my back, then you'll only have to carry one basket, and we'll get home faster."

Filled with joy, Little Redhead set upon the way with the wolf. In the meantime he had long since forgotten the school, village and teasing of his classmates, and in his thoughts he pictured how jubilantly he would be welcomed at home because he was bringing such beautiful berries. The wolf, too, could not imagine it any other way: he would be praised and received with gratitude.

However, everything turned out much differently. In the meantime Little Redhead's father had learned that his son had not been in school, and, when he saw him coming so contently with the wolf by his side, he became enraged, and he hit the wolf with a large club on the animal's sensitive beak so that the wolf—with the familiar howling—bit the dust in a hurry.

Little Redhead was punished with a beating, locked in his room, and was not allowed to visit his grandmother with Little Red Cap the next day to bring her presents for her birthday. This is where the fairy tale of Little Red Cap begins as it is generally known and has been transmitted by the Brothers Grimm.

The wolf's deceiving of Little Red Cap can now be easily explained by the animal's need to gain revenge for the treatment of his friend Little Redhead, who had to remain in the dim dark room on the sunny Saturday, and by the wolf's need to get even with the wicked father. The wolf sensed or at least suspected that the wicked father of Little Red Cap and Little Redhead had never broken the ties of a strong mother fixation which had made him into a difficult husband and hard father. Therefore, the wolf wanted to touch him to the quick by swallowing his mother.

To be sure, swallowing is often erroneously confused with gobbling while it is, however, very clear that the wolf made every concerted effort to swallow the grandmother and later the grandchild, too—without even harming the two in the least. The meaning of this effort can only be deduced from the fact that the wolf wanted to scare the father and bring him to his senses without seriously hurting anyone in the process. So the revenge of the wolf was indeed more humane and reasonable than the undeserved beating which the father had doled out to the wolf (and his son).

Admittedly, the ending of the fairy tale reveals some problems. There, as is well known, the *hunter* happens by the house of the grandmother, hears the loud snoring of the wolf, slices open his stomach, and thus liberates the two people. After this he fills the wolf's body with stones, and this was the way the animal met with his death.

It will have become almost immediately clear to the psychoanalytically trained reader that this tale here involves a dream story, and, to be sure, *a dream which the father had of Little Redhead*. The hunter is no one else but the father himself who appears here in typical dream symbolism by assuming the shape of a uniformed bearer of authority. The wolf stands for the grandmother.

The slicing open of the grandmother's—or rather the mother's—body leads directly to the association of cutting the umbilical cord which would symbolize here the liberation from a psychological mother fixation. The dream of Little Redhead's father would therefore be a cathartic dream which could lead to a psychological curing of the mother fixation. This aspect would explain the cheerful and relieved tone of the fairy tale's ending.

Yet, there is still another point to consider: the filling of the mother's body with heavy stones reminds us of the Latin word for heavy "gravis" and the designation derived from this word for pregnancy (*Gravidität*). As a result, the ending of the fairy tale contains the typical *ambivalence*, which is characteristic of all intensive libidinal relationships. In the dream the father would not only be cured by completing the final break from the mother, but this would also happen, of course, in a macabre, distorted form—to satisfy the oedipal wish.

Incidentally, radical disciples of Wilhelm Reich could also interpret the slicing open of the body as a symbol of *defloration*. Such an

*Les Contes de Perrault,* **Paris: J. Hetzel, 1862. Illustrator Gustave Doré.**

interpretation would reveal the son's hope to be the first and only one to sleep with one's mother and the son's wish for the virginal purity of the mother which is biologically absurd even though documented in mythology.

One sees that the fairy tale of Little Red Cap—when appropriately interpreted—proves the opposite of what it superficially seems to be saying. As children we misunderstood it as a statement about the danger of wolves, and we let ourselves be intimidated. This was the ostensible repressive function attributed to the folk tale by conservative German scholars in the later phase of its transmission. However, when analyzed, the signs indicate that it is a superficially concealed dream story of a neurotic father about Little Red Cap and Little Redhead.

One can assume that even the first half of the tale—the story about the deception of the unsuspecting little Red Cap and the swallowing of the grandmother and grandchild—is part of the paternal dream. Here the dream motif would have been the wish to justify the beating of the wolf because of a guilty conscience. If the wolf had really committed those acts—now interpreted as unmotivated, pure aggression—then the beating with the club would have only been a legitimate means of defense.

Here, too, it is important to recall the ambiguity: the wish to kill or see the beloved person killed co-exists constantly with a close libidinal tie. Both emotional ties would have found their clear expression in the dream about Little Red Cap—if one sub-scribes to the Reich school of thought, even in a double way: the aggressive side (*destruo*) in swallowing, and the libidinal side in the slicing open of the stomach. Then again, we can see it in the slicing open of the stomach (now understood as *defloration*) and in the filling of the stomach with stones (impregnation, gravidity). The fact that swallowing also has an ambivalent meaning is gener-ally known from the common expression "I love you so much I could swallow you."

This fairy tale fragment of Little Redhead and the wolf which was thought to have been forgotten along with the psychoanalyti-cal interpretation of the fairy tale allows us finally to include even this piece of German folk tradition in our educational work for progress and enlightenment.

## ❋ 24 ❋

### *Red Riding Hood*

*By the Merseyside Fairy Story Collective*

*Audrey Ackroyd*
*Marge Ben-Tovim*
*Catherine Meredith*
*Anne Neville*

(1972)

IN THE FAR NORTH, beside a river which froze hard as rock in the dark days of winter, there stood a great timber mill and a town built out of wood. The wood came from the trees of the deep forest which surrounded the town and stretched into the far distance.

In this town lived a quiet and shy little girl, called Red Riding Hood. Her real name was Nadia but everyone called her Red Riding Hood because when the cold came she always wore a thick red cloak with a hood. It had been given to her by her great-grandmother who had worn it herself, long ago, when she was a child.

Her great-grandmother still lived in a cottage in the forest and Red Riding Hood loved to visit her more than anything in the world; but she would never go alone because she was frightened to walk through the forest.

Red Riding Hood was frightened of many things. She was frightened of going up to bed by herself, she was frightened of dogs and of thunder and of people she did not know. But she was most frightened of the forest. The forest seemed strange to her for she had been born far away in a city in the south, where her mother and father had gone to be trained for their work in the great timber mill.

"Why do you never play in the forest like we did when we were children?" they asked her.

"It is dark under the trees," said Red Riding Hood, "and in winter the wolves howl in the distance."

"There have been no wolves in the forest since anyone can remember," said her parents, laughing.

But her great-grandmother took the child to one side and said to her quietly, "Not everyone can hear that howling; they think it is only the wind in the trees. One winter day when I was a girl, out alone chopping wood for the stove, I was attacked by one of the grey wolves which speak."

"Oh, great-grandmother!" whispered Red Riding Hood. "What did you do?"

"I fought the wolf with my hatchet and killed it," replied the old woman, "for I was strong and agile when I was young."

But now the great-grandmother was very old and frail, and almost every day when school and work were over, Red Riding Hood went with her mother and father, or with some of the other children, to cook supper for her and to sit and talk.

Winter was coming. Snow fell. It was dark before the children came out of school and the wind grew icy cold.

In the school the children were hard at work finishing the fur jackets which they had been making to wear during the bitter weather. They were very proud of these jackets, for all of them had cut out their own with great sharp knives and were sewing the pieces together with special, strong needles and thread. Only Red Riding Hood was not making a jacket. She wanted to wear her red cloak and hood and besides she was frightened that she might cut herself on one of the sharp knives.

Her mother and father worried that she would be cold without a jacket, for the red cloak was growing worn.

"We can see to that," said the great-grandmother, as they all sat round her stove one evening. Bring the special sewing things with you after school tomorrow and I will help you make a sheepskin lining for your cloak."

"What a good idea," said Red Riding Hood's parents and Red Riding Hood thought happily about tomorrow as she walked home between them through the forest.

"Why don't you take some presents to great-grandmother?" said the father the next morning. "Here are some brown eggs and some chocolate and a pot of the blackberry jam you helped us make." "We shall be busy this evening," said her mother, "but you can easily walk to great-grandmother's on your own. The path through the forest is cleared of snow every day and there will be a full moon tonight."

Red Riding Hood said nothing. She took a basket and carefully put into it the eggs, the chocolate and the jam. She did not feel happy any more. The other children were going to stay late at school to finish their jackets. She would have to walk through the forest to her great-grandmother's cottage all alone.

Red Riding Hood was frightened. All day at school she could think about nothing but whether she dared to walk through the forest alone. At dinnertime she did not want to eat because she felt sick. She borrowed a special needle and thread and a sharp knife and put them in the basket with the presents, but when school was over she did not set out for her great-grandmother's, although she was longing to see her. She turned her back on the forest and started to walk into the town towards home.

It was dark and quiet outside the school. The other children were still inside sewing their jackets. In the distance Red Riding Hood could hear the noise of sawing from the timber mill. Then she heard another sound, from quite close, somewhere near the edge of the forest. It was the howling of a wolf.

Red Riding Hood stood listening. She knew it was one of the grey wolves. But who would believe her? They would laugh and say she had imagined it. She thought of her great-grandmother, all alone.

What if a wolf had come again for her now that she was no longer young and agile? Red Riding Hood turned around and ran into the forest and along the path to the old woman's cottage.

She ran and ran until her side hurt and her heart thumped so fast she had to stop to get some breath.

The moon shone through the bare branches of the trees onto the snow and the frozen earth. It was very still. Then a gust of wind blew snow into the air and through the wind Red Riding Hood thought she heard a cold voice calling: "Run home, little girl, run home. This is the night of the wolf."

Then she heard a low growl, and staring through the flurry of snow she saw a streak of grey moving toward great-grandmother's cottage.

Her mouth went dry and her legs felt as if she could not move them, but she made them walk on until at last she reached the cottage.

"Great-grandmother, great-grandmother!" she cried, rattling the door latch. "I'm here!"

"Lift up the latch and walk in," called a thin and quavering voice.

"Great-grandmother, are you ill?" cried little Red Riding Hood, and she opened the door and ran into the bedroom.

In the high, wooden bed there was a shape huddled down under the bedclothes. It was hard to see with only the moonlight coming through the window. Red Riding Hood peered at the shape and moved closer to the bed.

"What big eyes you have, great-grandmother," she said.

"All the better to see you with, my dear," said the thin, quavering voice.

"And what big ears you have, great-grandmother."

"All the better to hear you with, my dear," said the voice.

"And what a strange nose you have, great-grandmother," said Red Riding Hood, moving a little closer.

"All the better to smell you with, my dear," said the voice, and Red Riding Hood could see a mouth full of yellow pointed teeth. "And what big teeth you have!" she cried, backing away.

"All the better to eat you with!" snarled the shape, leaping from the bed. It was a grey wolf.

Red Riding Hood screamed and as she screamed she heard her great-grandmother calling. "Quick, child, quick! Let me in!"

Red Riding Hood flung open the door into the kitchen and there was her great-grandmother pulling a blazing branch from the stove. With this branch she advanced on the growling wolf, old and bent though she was.

The wolf was frightened of the flame. It circled fiercely around the old woman, trying to get behind her and spring on her. Red Riding Hood shrank back against the wall. She could see that soon the branch would be burnt out and then the wolf would spring on her great-grandmother. Suddenly she remembered how easily the other children had cut through skins to make their jackets. She reached into her basket and pulled out the great sharp knife. Just as the branch burnt out and the wolf gathered itself for the kill, Red Riding Hood leapt forward and plunged the knife deep into its heart. The wolf gave one terrifying snarl and fell dead on the ground in a pool of blood.

With the help of her great-grandmother Red Riding Hood skinned the wolf and together they made a lining of its fur. "Listen, great-granddaughter," said the old woman, as they worked together

**Merseyside Fairy Story Collective,** *Little Red Riding Hood,*
**Liverpool, 1972. Illustrator Trevor Skempton.**

stitching the lining into the red cloak, "this cloak now has special
powers. Whenever you meet another child who is shy and timid,
lend that child the cloak to wear as you play together in the forest,
and then, like you, they will grow brave."

So, whenever she met such a child, Red Riding Hood did as her
great-grandmother had said, but the rest of the time she wore the
cloak herself and for many years it kept her warm as she explored
deeper and deeper into the great forest.

## ❈ 25 ❈

### *Little Green Riding Hood*

### *By Gianni Rodari*

### (1974)

NCE UPON A TIME there was a little girl called Little Yellow Riding Hood.

"No! *Red* Riding Hood!"

"Oh yes, of course, Red Riding Hood. Well, one day her mother called and said: 'Little Green Riding Hood—'"

"Red!"

"Sorry! Red. 'Now, my child, go to Aunt Mary and take her these potatoes.'"

"No! It doesn't go like that! 'Go to Grandma and take her these cakes.'"

"All right. So the little girl went off and in the wood she met a giraffe."

"What a mess you're making of it! It was a wolf!"

"And the wolf said: 'What's six times eight?'"

"No! No! The wolf asked her where she was going."

"So he did. And little Black Riding Hood replied—"

"Red! Red! Red!!!"

"She replied: 'I'm going to the market to buy some tomatoes.'"

"No, she didn't. She said: 'I'm going to my grandma who is sick, but I've lost my way.'"

"Of course! And the horse said—"

"What horse? It was a wolf."

**Little Red Riding Hood, New York: Harcourt Brace Jovanovich, 1968.
Illustrator Harriet Pincus.**

"So it was. And this is what it said: 'Take the 75 bus, get out at
the main square, turn right, and at the first doorway you'll find
three steps. Leave the steps where they are, but pick up the dime
you'll find lying on them, and buy yourself a packet of chewing
gum.'"

"Grandpa, you're terribly bad at telling stories. You get them all
wrong. But all the same, I wouldn't mind some chewing gum."

"All right. Here's your dime." And the old man turned back to
his newspaper.

# Little Red Cap

## By Max von der Grün

## (1974)

O NCE UPON A TIME there was a girl from a well-to-do family. She had everything she needed and even more than enough. All her wishes were filled by her parents and grandparents, for she was very charming, an ideal child, liked by everyone in the neighborhood and at school. She was pretty and had such natural grace that there was hardly a person who was not attracted to her. Nor were her girl friends jealous in any way.

Suddenly this changed.

On her seventh birthday the girl received a red cap from her grandparents as a present. There was a small white star on the left side of the cap which was very expensive. The grandparents had bought it in an exclusive shop which carried only exquisite things. The red cap was very becoming to the girl. Now she looked even more beautiful, even more lovely than before. In fact, the girl was so much in love with the red color that she would have liked to have kept on the cap with her in bed.

But when the girl went to school the next day anticipating the admiration of all the other children, she was disappointed to find that some children laughed about the red cap. Most of them were horrified by it. Yes, she caught anxious looks following her around. During recess the girl was suddenly excluded from the usual games in the schoolyard, and during class her schoolmates were suddenly envious about her accomplishments which at one time had made them just as proud as if they themselves had done them. After school none of the girls walked Little Red Cap home as they usually did. None of them went to her home in order to copy homework. Even the children in the neighborhood suddenly turned away from her when they saw her coming on her bike. If the women in the neighborhood noticed that Little Red Cap wanted to speak with their children, they fetched them off the street. When she went shopping, the girl was treated properly, to be sure, but in contrast to former times, she was looked after in an unfriendly way. Neither sellers nor customers exchanged an unnecessary word with the girl.

Everything continued like this for days and weeks, and Little Red Cap's mother, who could not help but notice the change, asked herself what all this meant and searched for the reasons, for it never occurred to the mother or her daughter that the unfriendly attitudes around them could be connected to the red cap. The mother asked her neighbors, too, why they were being so hostile toward her over the past weeks, but they did not respond. The mother tried to be more friendly, more helpful, more agreeable than she already was, but even this did not bring about a change. The girl had become more industrious in school than she already was, the father even more inventive in the construction business than he already was. But even the father could not fail in the long run to notice the hostile looks of his associates, the jealous talk of those who were less successful. Soon the father began to worry about his job.

One day the mother sent her daughter to get something from her grandparents who lived in another part of the city. Little Red Cap rode on her bike. She carried a carton tied to the rack which contained a cake that her mother herself had just baked. As the girl rode away from her house, she already noticed that some children were following her, also on bikes and always at the same distance. When she came to a narrow curve, one of the boys from the neighborhood passed her and forced Little Red Cap to stop her bike so that she wouldn't fall. She was afraid of the boy and asked him:

"Jimmy, how come you have such big eyes?"

"So that I can see you better," Jimmy said.

"But, Jimmy, how come you suddenly have such big ears?"

"So that I can hear where you are."

"Yes, but Jimmy, how come you have such big hands?"

"So that I can grab hold of you better," Jimmy answered, and he dragged the girl from her bike, threw her into a ditch along the side of the road and began beating her. The other children stood around and laughed and clapped their hands, amused by the scene. Only when a car stopped and a man jumped out to help Little Red Cap did Jimmy stop beating her. The boy and all the other children jumped on their bikes and fled through an alley which was too narrow for the car to follow them.

The man picked up the girl. Her nose and mouth were bleeding, but she did not cry. She thanked the man for his help, then continued on her way as if nothing had happened.

The grandmother asked: "What happened to you, child?"

"I fell from my bike, grandmother."

"But child, . . . where's your red cap?"

"Cap . . . Oh, I must have lost it."

"Lost it? But child, you just don't lose such an expensive and beautiful cap. . . . What will your mother say?

It was only much later that Little Red Cap went home, and she took the roundabout way. She told her mother that she had had an accident with her bike and had fallen to the ground. "I lost my beautiful, expensive red cap."

The mother said nothing.

But on the next day as the girl went to school without the red cap, she noticed that everyone was friendly to her again, schoolmates and teachers alike, in a way they hadn't been for weeks, and, as she went shopping for her mother in the afternoon, the sellers and customers were friendly again and spoke to her. Suddenly her father's accomplishments were recognized again in the business. The neighbors spoke with her mother again and showed how appreciative they were of her helpfulness. The three of them were happy again, and, one day when the father returned home from work, the mother said: "The past few weeks were like a bad fairy tale. If I hadn't experienced it myself, I wouldn't believe it had happened, even if someone else told it to me. Do you think we caused everything? Did we behave differently? What could have been the reason?"

"I don't know," the father said, "but you're right, the past few weeks were like a bad fairy tale."

# ❊ 27 ❊

## *Little Red*
## *Riding Hood*

*Reruminated*
*by Tomi Ungerer*

(1974)

ONCE UPON MANY TIMES, in the middle of a godforsaken forest there stood a castle. In that castle lived a wolf. The woods were dark and pathless, the castle was sumptuous, and the wolf, like all wolves, was mean, broody, and ferociously ferocious. His reputation was even worse than his deeds. He lived there all alone—for he was feared by everyone—but for a rookery of ravens employed in his service. Wifeless, heirless, with whiskers turning to silver, he spent his days scanning the woods for some juicy fare.

One day, as he was gazing over a multitude of treetops from one of his many ramparts, there flew to him one of his watchcrows.

"Master venerable, lordly Duke and beloved ruler," he cawed, "in a thicket, three miles due northeast, beyond the moor, below the barrens, I sighted a little girl, morsel of a maiden, picking berries off your domain. She is dressed in reds all over like a stop sign.

"Well done, trusted lackey," growled the wolf, smacking his flapping chops. "We shall settle the matter anon." Anon was right away and off went the wolf.

The little girl in red, her name was—yes, you guessed it—Little Red Riding Hood. Not the one you might already have read about. No. This Little Red Riding Hood was the real, no-nonsense one, and this story is one-hundred-to-a-nickel genuine.

261

**Tomi Ungerer, *A Storybook*. New York: Franklin Watts, 1974, Illustrator Tomi Ungerer.**

She was as pretty as anything, pink and soft. Her braided blond hair shone like fresh bread, and birds could have flown off into the blue of her eyes. Besides, she had wit and sense. She was dressed in red because it was one of her mother's outlandish notions that her daughter might always easily be spotted that way. Little Red Riding Hood didn't mind. She thought it made her special.

Little Red Riding Hood was on her way to deliver a weekly supply of food to her mean and cranky grandmama, who lived in a rundown shack overlooking a greenish pond. The baskets she was carrying were heavy with three hogs' heads, two pints of rendered lard, two quarts of applejack, and two loaves of wrinkled bread. The old woman was a retired diva whose voice had gone sour. She was filled with superstitions and believed staunchly that she would restore her smithereened voice by eating pigs' heads—eyes, brains, and all. Her place was buzzing with flies who liked pigs' heads, too, in summer especially.

Little Red Riding Hood hated to go there. It was a hot and clammy day and her red Cheviot cape was itching and sticking to her back. The baskets were getting heavier and heavier, her arms longer and longer. Exhausted, she stopped in the cooling shade of the forest and started picking fragrant berries.

"I might just as well stop and be late and rest," she reflected. "These baskets are so heavy they feel as if something is growing inside them. All I get for my trouble is blows and insults, anyway. Each time I get there she accuses me of things I haven't done yet— that I guzzled off some of the applejack and nibbled at some pig's snout, and so on and so forth, and so beside the point, the comma, and the asterisk. I still carry on my tender skin the bluish marks of the old woman's beatings. And, here, look at the marks where she bit me in the shoulder last week. Vicious to the core, that's what she is."

"Hullo, there," growled a deep and raucous voice from behind a tree. It was the wolf, who had silently sneaked up on the trespassing child. "Hullo, cute damsel dear, what brings you browsing in my very own berry bushes?"

"Well, ho, you startled me. But yes, good day, Your Excellency," replied the damsel dear. "You find me here picking berries for my impatient little belly, and I was on my way to deliver these baskets here, full of food, to my mean old grandmother who lives by the green fly pond, and besides I have noticed no trespassing signs ever, so how could I know whose bushes I am molesting, noble Prince?"

"Coriander and marjoram, lady young, lady bright. Maybe you are sassy, maybe you are clever, but I fancy your bearings. These baskets seem heavy indeed. Ha! Do you know what? I shall help you carry them. I am strong and efficient and it's a bleeding shame, if you ask me, to burden such a sweet little red maiden with loads like that. I know of your grandmother and all I can say is that her reputation is worse than mine."

"What is a reputation, noble Prince?" queried our heroine.

"Call me Duke," replied the wolf. "A reputation is what people think you are. Reputations come in all sizes. Some are good, some are bad or very bad, like mine. Anyway, here is my plan, and it comes from somebody who has far more experience of life than you. With my strong arms, I shall carry the baskets, not to your granny's bungalow, but to my very own castle. Come along, I live lonely and bored. Come with me and I shall share with you my secrets and more of my secrets. My vaults are plastered with treasures. You will sleep in satins and live in silks. My closets sag with brocade dresses on hangers of solid gold. Your winters will be wrapped in sable furs. My servants shall kiss the very ground you walk upon. I'll make you happy, you'll make me happy, as in a fairy tale."

There was a pensive silence and Little Red Riding Hood took three steps back in distrust.

"I was told wolves feed on little children. I don't quite trust you, Mister Duke. You wouldn't eat me, would you? With a big mouth like that, you could gobble me up in a jiffy and a spiffy, bones, cape, and all."

"Nonsense, child, mere slander, that is. Wolves feed only upon ugly children, and then only on special request," replied the beast with a sugar smile. "Never, ever would I do such a thing. Upon my mother's truffle, never."

"But your jowls are enormous, they look scary, and those huge fangs, why do they twinkle like that?" asked the girl unabashedly.

"Because I brush them every morning with powdered tripoli."

"And your tongue? Why is it so pink?"

"From chewing on rosebuds. Pink and red are my favorite colors," said the wolf.

"And why do—"

"Stop asking foolish questions," interrupted the wolf. "We must get started if we want to reach my palatial abode before dark. Besides, questions are bad for your happiness. Come along," said the wolf as he lifted the baskets. "Come along, there is an exotic library in my castle, and a splash of a swimming pool in my tropical greenhouse."

"But I cannot swim," said Little Red Riding Hood. "And what happens to my parents and my mean grandmother?"

"Read the end of this story, and you'll find out," said the wolf. "We shall send your parents post cards and invite them to the wedding. Your grandmother is old enough to take care of herself, and if you cannot swim all we have to do is empty the swimming pool."

Off they went to live happily ever after. They did get married and they had all sorts of children who lived happily, too.

And the grandmother? Left without food, she shrank and shrank, until she was just six inches high. When last seen, she was scavenging someone's larder in the company of a Norway rat. And, tiny and hungry, she was just as mean as ever.

## ❊ 28 ❊

## *The Old Wolf*

## *By Rudolf Otto Wiemer*

## (1976)

T HE WOLF, now piously old and good,
When again he met Red Riding Hood
Spoke: "Incredible, my child,
What kinds of stories are spread. They're wild.

As though there were, so the lie is told,
A dark murder affair of old.
The Brothers Grimm are the ones to blame.
Confess! It wasn't half as bad as they claim."

Little Red Riding Hood saw the wolf's bite
And stammered: "You're right, quite right."
Whereupon the wolf, heaving many a sigh,
Gave kind regards to Granny and waved good-bye.

# ❊ 29 ❊

## *Little Aqua Riding Hood*

### *By Philippe Dumas*
### *&*
### *Boris Moissard*

### (1977)

CERTAINLY, EVERYONE IS FAMILIAR with the story of *Little Red Riding Hood*. But does everyone know the one about *Little Aqua Riding Hood*? We tend to forget that the famous Red Riding Hood did not remain eternally "little." In fact, after her skirmishes with the Wicked Wolf, this charming girl grew nicely and became a beautiful woman who married and had a child (a girl named Francoise). Then she also became a grandmother when Francoise, in her turn, married (such is life). Now she lives in the 13th district of Paris on the ground floor of an apartment building located on a dingy street. She's a nice old woman, who lives alone and is not talked about much, yet, has many long years ahead of her because of her good health. And, she's very happy. Her time is divided between knitting in front of the window, reading magazines, and chatting with the other old ladies in the neighborhood to whom she tells details about her famous adventure from the old days which can't be found in books.

But here is another adventure which happened to her recently through the fault of her granddaughter Lorette, who is called "Little Aqua Riding Hood," both in honor of her grandmother and because of a duffle coat in that color bought on sale in the department store Galeries Lafayette and which her mother makes her wear each time she goes outside so she won't catch a cold.

Well, a few months ago, Lorette's mother asked her to carry some balls of yarn to her grandmother (the ex-Red Riding Hood) in the 13th district at the other end of Paris. She showed her a city map and the best way to get there, and she took the precaution of repeating the number of the bus to her daughter and the name of her stop. So Lorette set out on her way not without giving her mother a kiss and, of course, not without putting on her famous duffle coat with its turned-down hood. She turned right on the Boulevard Boris-Vian, then she crossed it and went down Suzanne-Lalou Street. Finally, she turned left on the Avenue of General Batavia following the directions which her mother had given her. And, after another five minutes of walking, she came to the bus stop, took her place in line, and waited wisely on the curb of the sidewalk. When the bus arrived, she got on and handed her ticket to the driver who stamped it himself, for bus drivers are polite and helpful. They especially assist those children who are not used to travelling alone. "Where do you want to get off, my little miss?"

"At the railroad station Austerlitz," Lorette responded.

But since the driver had to shift and steer so much through heavy traffic, he soon forgot her. And Lorette got out at the stop of the Botanical Garden.

I forgot to mention that ever since she had been young, Lorette had always been jealous of her grandmother's reputation. The entire world knows about the exploits of Little Red Riding Hood which have been told to children throughout the world for over two generations. "Why shouldn't I become someone famous, too?" she always asked herself.

Having succeeded in gaining free admission to the zoo of the Botanical Garden by slipping by the ticket-taker who was dreaming about her romances, Lorette went in search of the wolf cage. And after she had found it, she leaned against the fence and called the wolf, who was about to take a nap in a corner before his five o'clock meal.

"Pssst! . . . Good afternoon, wolf. It's me, Little Aqua Riding Hood. Guess where I'm heading?"

The wolf raised an ear, quite surprised that someone was speaking to him.

"I'm going to my grandmother's house, and I'm bringing her this package which you see in my basket. And what do you think's in this package. Not balls of yarn, as my mother said, but a dozen small pots of butter. Imagine that!"

"Very nice. So now what?" answered the wolf, who was the great grand-nephew of the wolf who ate the grandmother in Perrault's story and took her place in bed, and he was also a distant relative of the wolf in La Fontaine's fable, who had made life miserable for the lamb. (So he wasn't just an ordinary wolf!) "What do you want me to do? The only thing I want is my sleep and for five o'clock to come soon so that they'll refill my bowl."

This wolf, who had read many books in his cage to kill time, and, who was sensible, had no desire to end up like his great grand-uncle, whose story he knew by heart. He avoided anything that resembled a riding hood like the plague, no matter what color it was, even if it came from Galeries Lafayette, and especially if it was worn by a young girl. But Lorette did not allow herself to be daunted by this harsh reception.

"Listen, old wolf," she said, "This is not your real place, this cage, but it should be over there with the bears because you're one of them! But that doesn't matter. Here's what I have to propose. I'm sure you must want to revive and give those paws of yours some exercise, huh? So let's have a race to my grandmother's, you and me. Let's see who'll be first."

Lorette gave the wolf her grandmother's address, and the wolf, who for a long time had been bored as a dead rat with the five square meters of his cage, and, who had been burning with desire to see the countryside, weighed the pros and cons and finally responded: "It's a deal!" Then Lorette opened the cage, and both departed, each going at a different pace and in a different direction.

After having counted to *three*, Lorette headed calmly on her way allowing the wolf to gallop away and lose himself in the horizon. She was very happy. The plan which she had concocted was working beautifully. Obviously she was a little worried about her grandmother, who was going to be eaten. But, "so what!" she said to herself. You don't make omelettes without cracking the eggs.

Upon arriving, she rang, and she was told to enter, the door wasn't locked. She pushed it open and saw someone in bed who resembled her grandmother very much: the same white hair tied in a small chignon, the same glasses, the same nightgown, and the same cashmere sweater. The disguise was perfect and could fool anyone. But Lorette recognized the wolf instantly while pretending as though she hadn't noticed anything.

*Little Red Riding Hood,* **New York: Platt & Munk, ca. 1925. Illustrator Eulalie.**

"Good afternoon, Granny. I hope you're feeling well. Mother asked me to bring you these small pots of butter which are at the bottom of my basket. She said that you'd probably be pleased by this, and that it would save you a trip to the grocer's."

"You're a real darling, little one. Thanks a lot. Please give a kiss to your mother for me. I was about to make a cup of hot chocolate for myself before taking a nap. Do you want to watch TV before returning home?"

The wolf was turning out to be a remarkable imitator. Lorette couldn't get over it. The voice of the grandmother was perfectly feigned. But this was not the moment to applaud. It was necessary to continue playing the game.

"Oh, yes! Great! Thanks, Granny. . . . I'd like to watch it from your bed. Would you mind if I stretched out by your side?" "If you want, but take off your shoes."

Lorette turned on the television after which she removed her

shoes and then slipped into her grandmother's bed, that is, the bed
of the wolf. But right when the alleged grandmother leaned over to
give the girl a kiss, she jumped up and pulled out a big kitchen
knife from under the balls of yarn which she had taken care to carry
with her. Then she said in a dry tone: "That's enough, wolf! I know
it's you all right. Stop the comedy. I'm not as dumb and naive as
Little Red Riding Hood. Let's go! Get up! Faster, we're returning to
the Botanical Garden, our point of departure."

So, Lorette, menacing her grandmother with the big kitchen
knife, conducted her to the Botanical Garden, ignoring the protests
of the old woman, who was even more disturbed because they had
forgotten to turn off the television set.

At the Botanical Garden Lorette locked her grandmother in the
wolf's cage which had remained open. Then she ran all around and
made a racket to alert the guards that the wolf had just eaten her
granny.

The guards immediately ran to the cage. They were very upset
not only for the sake of the victim (who was undoubtedly torn to
pieces in an irremediable fashion already) but also for the sake of
the beast who had a delicate liver and would feel the effects of such
a break in his diet.

However, necessity compelled them to realize that there was no
sign of the wolf in the cage, but, in his place, there was an old woman dressed in a nightgown and cashmere sweater, visibly annoyed
by what had happened to her and impatiently waiting to be set free.

As for the wolf, he was already many kilometers away from there.
Instead of going to the grandmother's house in the 13th district
which he was supposed to do, he left Paris by way of Port Charen-
ton, and, as you can imagine, he took off at full speed, crossed the
Vincennes Woods, and kept on going until nightfall. The joy of
being free gave him wings.

After a rest he continued to run, and he ran the entire night in the
country without taking a breather, through fields and woods, toward
the vast wild regions of the East which had been the cradle of his
breed. And since he was very careful in crossing the roads, particularly the highways, he succeeded in arriving safe and sound. And, in
the country of his origin he was honored with a great celebration.

This was not the case with Lorette. On the contrary, all of Paris
showed her consternation and even anger. Nobody could understand how a young girl, so intelligent and obedient, awarded first
prize in good conduct at school, could have let herself go in such a

manner. The Director of the Botanical Garden and the Under Secretary of State for Old People called her into their offices to reprimand her, one after the other. The first complained about the loss of the wolf who was the offspring of a rare species, and the second, sermonizing angrily, told her and even shouted that one shouldn't do such things like that to one's grandmother, no matter what!

The press got wind of the incident, and because of television and her photos in the newspapers all of France came to know the little Parisian who did this stupid thing. Yet, Lorette was secretly happy about this since it was exactly what she had wanted (to become famous). After that people began to worry because nobody knew the whereabouts of the wild animal, and even today people are afraid that he will suddenly appear one of these nights in the garage, in the elevator, or under the bed. The general fear and trembling have not yet reached their end, and Lorette's parents still have to contend with all sorts of false stories concerning their child.

In contrast, the wolf, to end the story with him, has enjoyed great success among his relatives on the Steppes of Siberia, as I have already told you, and feels very well there. He leads a grand life, leaving it to others to chase after sheep (he has totally lost the knack). Instead, he has dedicated himself to activities more peaceful such as chronicling the events of the world, and he performs wonders with his talent as storyteller. He struts about in salons and fashionable places and circulates spicy anecdotes about his life in Paris, never failing to embroider a little in the pinch and always giving himself the best role. Everyone listens with gaping mouths. Everyone regards him with admiration. The pretty she-wolves fight among each other to be seen by his side.

He tells the story of Little Red Riding Hood, then that of Little Aqua Riding Hood, and all his brothers are now forewarned of the danger posed by little French girls. This is why our children no longer encounter wolves and can take walks in the woods in complete safety, that is, with one reservation. It goes without saying that they must watch out for men on the prowl, but certain men are more dangerous than wolves.

# ❋ 30 ❋

## *Little Red Riding Hood*

### *By Olga Broumas*

### (1977)

I GROW OLD, OLD
without you, Mother, landscape
of my heart. No child, no daughter between my bones
has moved, and passed
out screaming, dressed in her mantle of blood

as I did
once through your pelvic scaffold, stretching it
like a wishbone, your tenderest skin
strung on its bow and tightened
against the pain. I slipped out like an arrow, but not before

the midwife
plunged to her wrist and guided
my baffled head to its first mark. High forceps
might, in that one instant, have accomplished
what you and that good woman failed
in all these years to do: cramp
me between the temples, hobble
my baby feet. Dressed in my red hood, howling, I went—

evading
the white-clad doctor and his fancy claims: microscope,
stethoscope, scalpel, all

the better to see with, to hear,
and to eat—straight from your hollowed basket
into the midwife's skirts. I grew up
good at evading, and when you said,
'Stick to the road and forget the flowers, there's
wolves in those bushes, mind
where you got to go, mind
you get there.' I
minded. I kept

to the road, kept
the hood secret, kept what it sheathed more
secret still. I opened
it only at night, and with other women
who might be walking the same road to their own
grandma's house, each with her basket of gifts, her small hood
safe in the same part. I minded well. I have no daughter

to trace that road, back to your lap with my laden
basket of love. I'm growing
old, old
without you, Mother, landscape
of my heart, architect of my body, what other gesture
can I conceive

to make with it
that would reach you, alone
in your house and waiting, across this improbable forest
peopled with wolves and our lost, flower-gathering
sisters they feed on.

# Little Red Cap

## By O. F. Gmelin

## (1978)

O NCE UPON A TIME there was a fearless girl, who was loved by all who laid eyes upon her, but most of all by her grandmother, who could never give enough things to the child. One time she brought the girl a cap made out of red velvet. And since the girl found it very becoming, she wore nothing else and was soon called Little Red Cap.

One beautiful fall day her mother placed a basket under her arm and said: "Here's a piece of cake and a bottle of wine. Take this to grandmother. She's sick and weak, and this will strengthen her.— You'd better leave now before it gets too hot. And when you're under way, go straight ahead and keep on the path, otherwise you'll fall and break the bottle. Then grandmother will have nothing.— And when you get to her house, be courteous and behave yourself and don't snoop around so much!"

"Yeah, don't worry, mom. I'll do as you say."

And Little Red Cap hurriedly gave her mother a kiss and went out the door. There she saw her brother's jackknife lying on the ground. She picked it up and stuck it in her belt quickly so that her mother wouldn't see. Then she slammed the door behind her and went on her way.

However, the grandmother lived in the woods, about half an hour from the village. And when Little Red Cap entered the woods, she met the wolf. She wasn't afraid of him and remained calm. Even

**Otto Gmelin and Doris Lerche, *Märchen für tapfere Mädchen*, Giessen: Schlot, 1978. Illustrator Doris Lerche.**

though she knew that the wolf was a dangerous animal, she said to herself: "C'mon now, the wolf is just a big mouse."

"Good morning, Little Red Cap," said the wolf. "Where are you going so early in the day?"

"To my grandmother's."

"What are you carrying in the basket?"

"Cake and wine. We baked some things for grandmother yesterday so that she can get well and strong."

"And where does your grandmother live?"

"You mice know where she lives—what are you asking for?"

"It's the house under the three oak trees, isn't it?" the wolf declared. "I've got to get a move on," said Little Red Cap.

However, the wolf thought to himself. 'This tender young thing, she's a juicy morsel. She'll taste even better than the old woman. You've got to be sly to catch both of them." He went along with Little Red Cap for awhile, and then he said: "Look at the beautiful flowers all around you. Why don't you look at them? I don't even think that you're even listening to the charming songs of the birds. You zoom straight ahead as if you were making a beeline for school, and it's really delightful here in the woods."

Little Red Cap stood still, opened her eyes and looked around. She saw the sunbeams dance here and there on the ground of the woods.

"You're right, my little mouse. It is beautiful here—and those flowers! If I were to take a bunch of flowers to grandmother, that would make her happy, and she'll give me something for it. It's still early in the day, and I have plenty of time to get to her house."

And Little Red Cap forgot the wolf and went from the path into the woods. She looked for the largest and prettiest flowers. And as soon as she picked one, she would see a prettier one further off and run after it deeper into the woods. However, the wolf went straight to grandmother's house and knocked on the door. "Who's there?"

"Little Red Cap, I've brought you cake and wine. Open up!"

"Lift the latch," cried the grandmother.

The wolf entered the house. Without saying one word, he went straight to the grandmother's bed and devoured her. Then he put on her clothes, lay down in her bed, and drew the curtains.

Meanwhile Little Red Cap had been running after the flowers. And after she had gathered more than her basket could carry, she continued on her way to her grandmother's house. She was surprised to find the door standing open. Wasn't someone snoring? And she called into the silent room: "Good morning! Hello there!" But nobody answered her.

Finally, she went to the bed and pulled back the curtains and saw somebody on her grandmother's bed covered in a shawl who didn't look like her grandmother.

"Grandmother, what large ears you have!"

"The better to hear you with."

"Grandmother, what large eyes you have!"

"The better to see you with."

"Grandmother, what large hands you have!"

"The better to grab you with."

"But, grandmother, what a large mouth you have!"

"The better to eat you with," said the wolf who sprung out of the bed and swallowed the girl.

When the wolf had satisfied his hunger, he lay down in bed, fell asleep, and began to snore very loudly. While he lay there, Little Red Cap took the knife and began to slice open the wolf's stomach from inside. After she had made the slit wide enough, she hopped out. Then out jumped her grandmother after her, alive and well. Little Red Cap quickly fetched some large stones in front of the house and filled the wolf's stomach with them. When he woke up, he saw Little Red Cap with the jackknife in her hand and became frightened.

"Why am I so terribly thirsty?" he bellowed grimly.

"Because you stuffed yourself," said Little Red Cap.

"And why can't I lift myself up?"

"Because there are stones in your belly."

"And what do I have to do to get them out?"

"You've got to stay with us and guard the house."

He tried to jump up and run away. But the stones were too heavy so that he sunk to the ground and lay there lifeless. So Little Red Cap went over to him, and in the wink of an eyelash, she had skinned the fur from the wolf. And underneath the fur was a boy with black eyebrows and blond hair. Little Red Cap went over to him and embraced him tenderly. He smiled back at her and stood there motionless. But the grandmother dragged a sack of nuts from the kitchen. And Little Red Cap and the boy went on cracking nuts until the dawn of the day.

# ❋ 32 ❋

## Little Red Hood:
## A Classic Story
## Bent Out of Shape

### By Tony Ross

### (1978)

O NCE UPON A TIME, there was a little kid without a name. Her father was into lumber, but he was a small-timer. Even though he sometimes sat it out with a cool one while the kid did the heavy hitting, Rocky was okay. She loved him and so what if he and her mother had been too busy to give her a name?

Still, she used to whack away at the wood, wondering whatever happened to the child-labor laws and thinking that she might get a couple of organizers and start a union.

Once in a while, she got time off to visit her grandmother, who lived in a forest—or at least someplace in Jersey.

The grandmother, Crazy Carmela, was a batty old biddy who loved to make clothes. She once worked in the garment industry and she still sewed up a storm like the old days in the rag trade, sitting in front of a big blown-up Polaroid of her father, Abe, when he was doorman at the Hilton and controlled the cabs, the numbers, and kept out the riffraff.

"Run me up a pair of jeans," said the little girl one day. But the old lady, who wasn't much in the head, made her a red cape instead.

Okay, so it wasn't Sasson, but the kid dug the cape anyhow and wore it around the neighborhood, showing a lot of leg. Her O.M. chased her, warning about muggers and telling her to get home and slice up some more trees.

"I'm bored with boards," the kid said, and the father knew his daughter had hit puberty and was almost out of sight. She yelled back that she was striking for better working conditions and fringes, one of which was the right to trade in the bike for a Yamaha. He called her a commie and soon the other kids had laid Little Red Hood on her as a name.

That was cool with her, better than no name, and after that Little Red Hood had more time on her hands. One day, the mother, Linda, who had just been to the deli, said: "Take some of these meatballs and pizza and a six-pack over to my mother's. It'll keep her off the streets."

"You been *cooking?*" said Red.

"Nah," said the mother. "Frozen. Linda's liberated."

Then Red and the folks did a big farewell number, just in case there was a photographer around from *People* magazine, and she schlepped along, wondering when she would take delivery of her Honda. (The big Yamaha bikes were back-ordered for five months.) Suddenly, she saw this dog, a great deal of dog, *humongous*, a real Mama Mutt.

She pulled a weed and tickled him, figuring that if this hunk sneezed, he'd clear enough trees to keep her father's lumberyard swinging for a year.

But the big thing was that the big thing was no dog. And no dummy either. The wolf figured fast that if he was going to get some local action, he'd better make nice.

He was just in from Detroit and he was, you know, meaner than a junkyard dog, but he took the tickling, smiled, showing his new caps, and said: "Listen, Farrah, there's lotsa fine stuff growing around here. Why don't you gather some, we'll sniff a little, and maybe go nuts in May?"

"Hey, animal," the kid said, "nobody uses that stuff anymore. But there are some nice organic greens here." Fine and funky, they agreed. While the kid picked, the wolf dropped the smile—Redford was never in any danger—and his eyes went to slits until he could have doubled for Dustin Hoffman. Now this wolf had a bigger nose for news than your average neighborhood wiretap. He knew the scene because he'd planted a bug in the old lady's Luxo lamp. So he figured: first blow away the bag of bones and then the kid.

Using his beak, he hit the buzzer.

"Yeah?" said Grandma Moses. She wasn't too happy about leaving the good-looking dude who was doing the six-o'clock news. Hair spray and all, he could really read a Teleprompter.

The wolf shriveled his sound and said, "It's little Red Hood, Grannie."

"Whatt'ya want?" said the crone.

"I'm your granddaughter, you turkey. You're supposed to love me. Besides, I brought you some diet Bud."

"Fan*tas*tic!" said Grams. "Come on in and pull off a couple of caps."

So the stud from Detroit busts in, puts the hit on Miss America 1918, and a minute later is licking his lips. The old bag wasn't all bones at that.

He walked up three steps in the split-level, put on the night-gown he found in the bedroom, and slipped into the sack. Until he caught a profile shot of himself in the mirror. "*Yucch*," he said, got up and flicked off the light. Saves energy, he thought—and maybe this whole bit.

The shades of night were falling fast and so were the wolf's spirits, when he finally heard the kid bop on the door downstairs.

"Come in, dearie," he squeaked, trying to make his voice sound as old as the gag was getting. "I'm topside, flaked out."

"Okay," the kid said. "See you tomorrow."

"NO!" the wolf shouted, losing his cool and what was left of his falsetto.

The kid went in cautiously. "You sure you're okay?" Then she looked closely. "Hey, Gran—you better get your ears cleaned. Or your hair done."

"I heard okay."

"And those *eyes*! You been to the optometrist or you just giving blood?"

"Contacts," said the wolf and, scrambling to remember his lines, added: "All the better to watch TV with."

The kid touched a paw. "Wow, it's dark as a disco in here," she said, "but I *mean*. You got the only hands I ever felt that need a pedicure *and* a skin graft."

The wolf opened his mouth and she reeled back. "And those teeth! That breath! Try a lung transplant. . . . "

"All the better to eat you with, my dear," he rasped in his own voice, finally trying to get the script straight, and then he zapped her.

"Man, I'm full," said the wolf three minutes later, already desperate for a Fresca.

Meanwhile, the father, pushed by Linda, who was a *noodge* anyhow, was out cruising. Even if the kid had trouble getting a bus, she was overdue. Rocky swore that if she kept on staying out late, he would lock her out of the house.

While he was mentally denying her entree, he didn't know that she had *become* the entree. And his mother-in-law the hors d'oeuvres.

Before long, with the other cats in the region sweating it out—for they liked Little Red, she was a *mensch*, real people—the father found Carmela's house. He broke open the door (which was a little unnecessary since it was unlocked) and saw the wolf with the fat gut. He fetched him a clout on the snout, followed with a right cross to the basket, and shook him until he gave up his ill-gotten goodies. It was a little overdone, like the front door, but what did Rocky know? He was just muscle.

The wolf split, but not before old Grannie Goose and Little Red had hit him with everything that wasn't nailed down—and a few things that were. He soon had more stuff coming at him than a garage sale.

That night Rocky, Linda, Carmela, Little Red Hood, and some of the crowd went off to the local *cantina* to celebrate, and there wasn't a loose clam or bowl of linguini or jug of Chianti that stood a chance.

Meanwhile, the wolf moved on to other turf, reached an agreement with the regional capo that he'd stay out of the way, went straight, and settled down.

It used to mean when somebody "Bought the farm" that he was dead—but do you want a happy ending or don't you?

# ❉ 33 ❉

## *The Company of Wolves*

## *By Angela Carter*

## (1979)

O NE BEAST AND ONLY ONE howls in the woods by night.

The wolf is carnivore incarnate and he's as cunning as he is ferocious; once he's had a taste of flesh, then nothing else will do.

At night, the eyes of wolves shine like candle flames, yellowish, reddish, but that is because the pupils of their eyes fatten on darkness and catch the light from your lantern to flash it back to you—red for danger; if a wolf's eyes reflect only moonlight, then they gleam a cold and unnatural green, a mineral, a piercing color. If the benighted traveler spies those luminous, terrible sequins stitched suddenly on the black thickets, then he knows he must run, if fear has not struck him stock-still.

But those eyes are all you will be able to glimpse of the forest assassins as they cluster invisibly round your smell of meat as you go through the wood unwisely late. They will be like shadows, they will be like wraiths, gray members of a congregation of nightmare. Hark! his long, wavering howl . . . an aria of fear made audible.

The wolfsong is the sound of the rending you will suffer, in itself a murdering.

It is winter and cold weather. In this region of mountain and forest, there is now nothing for the wolves to eat. Goats and sheep are locked up in the byre, the deer departed for the remaining pasturage on the southern slopes—wolves grow lean and famished.

There is so little flesh on them that you could count the starveling ribs through their pelts, if they gave you time before they pounced. Those slavering jaws; the lolling tongue; the rime of saliva on the grizzled chops—-of all the teeming perils of the night and the forest, ghosts, hobgoblins, ogres that grill babies upon gridirons, witches that fatten their captives in cages for cannibal tables, the wolf is worst, for he cannot listen to reason.

You are always in danger in the forest, where no people are. Step between the portals of the great pines where the shaggy branches tangle about you, trapping the unwary traveler in nets as if the vegetation itself were in a plot with the wolves who live there, as though the wicked trees go fishing on behalf of their friends—step between the gateposts of the forest with the greatest trepidation and infinite precautions, for if you stray from the path for one instant, the wolves will eat you. They are gray as famine, they are as unkind as plague.

The grave-eyed children of the sparse villages always carry knives with them when they go out to tend the little flocks of goats that provide the homesteads with acrid milk and rank, maggoty cheeses. Their knives are half as big as they are; the blades are sharpened daily.

But the wolves have ways of arriving at your own hearthside. We try and try but sometimes we cannot keep them out. There is no winter's night the cottager does not fear to see a lean, gray, famished snout questing under the door, and there was a woman once bitten in her own kitchen as she was straining the macaroni.

Fear and flee the wolf; for worst of all, the wolf may be more than he seems.

There was a hunter once, near here, that trapped a wolf in a pit. This wolf had massacred the sheep and goats; eaten up a mad old man who used to live by himself in a hut halfway up the mountain and sing to Jesus all day; pounced on a girl looking after the sheep, but she made such a commotion that men came with rifles and scared him away and tried to track him into the forest but he was cunning and easily gave them the slip. So this hunter dug a pit and put a duck in it, for bait, all alive-oh; and he covered the pit with straw smeared with wolf dung. Quack, quack! went the duck, and a wolf came slinking out of the forest, a big one, a heavy one, he weighed as much as a grown man and the straw gave way beneath him—into the pit he tumbled. The hunter jumped down after him, slit his throat, cut off all his paws for a trophy.

And then no wolf at all lay in front of the hunter but the bloody trunk of a man, headless, footless, dying, dead.

A witch from up the valley once turned an entire wedding party into wolves because the groom had settled on another girl. She used to order them to visit her, at night, from spite, and they would sit and howl around her cottage for her, serenading her with their misery.

Not so very long ago, a young woman in our village married a man who vanished clean away on her wedding night. The bed was made with new sheets and the bride lay down in it; the groom said he was going out to relieve himself, insisted on it, for the sake of decency, and she drew the coverlet up to her chin and she lay there. And she waited and she waited and then she waited again—surely he's been gone a long time? Until she jumps up in bed and shrieks to hear a howling, coming on the wind from the forest.

That long-drawn, wavering howl has, for all its fearful resonance, some inherent sadness in it, as if the beasts would love to be less beastly if only they knew how and never cease to mourn their own condition. There is a vast melancholy in the canticles of the wolves, melancholy infinite as the forest, endless as these long nights of winter, and yet that ghastly sadness, that mourning for their own, irremediable appetites, can never move the heart, for not one phrase in it hints at the possibility of redemption; grace could not come to the wolf from its own despair, only through some external mediator, so that, sometimes, the beast will look as if he half welcomes the knife that dispatches him.

The young woman's brothers searched the outhouses and the haystacks but never found any remains, so the sensible girl dried her eyes and found herself another husband, not too shy to piss into a pot, who spent the nights indoors. She gave him a pair of bonny babies and all went right as a trivet until, one freezing night, the night of the solstice, the hinge of the year when things do not fit together as well as they should, the longest night, her first good man came home again.

A great thump on the door announced him as she was stirring the soup for the father of her children and she knew him the moment she lifted the latch to him although it was years since she'd worn black for him and now he was in rags and his hair hung down his back and never saw a comb, alive with lice.

"Here I am again, missis," he said. "Get me my bowl of cabbage and be quick about it."

Then her second husband came in with wood for the fire and when the first one saw she'd slept with another man and, worse, clapped his red eyes on her little children, who'd crept into the kitchen to see what all the din was about, he shouted: "I wish I were a wolf again, to teach this whore a lesson!" So a wolf he instantly became and tore off the eldest boy's left foot before he was chopped up with the hatchet they used for chopping logs. But when the wolf lay bleeding and gasping its last, the pelt peeled off again and he was just as he had been, years ago, when he ran away from his marriage bed, so that she wept and her second husband beat her.

They say there's an ointment the Devil gives you that turns you into a wolf the minute you rub it on. Or that he was born feet first and had a wolf for his father and his torso is a man's but his legs and genitals are a wolf's. And he has a wolf's heart.

Seven years is a werewolf's natural span, but if you burn his human clothing you condemn him to wolfishness for the rest of his life, so old wives hereabouts think it some protection to throw a hat or an apron at the werewolf, as if clothes made the man. Yet by the eyes, those phosphorescent eyes, you know him in all his shapes; the eyes alone unchanged by metamorphosis.

Before he can become a wolf, the lycanthrope strips stark naked. If you spy a naked man among the pines, you must run as if the Devil were after you.

It is midwinter and the robin, the friend of man, sits on the handle of the gardener's spade and sings. It is the worst time in all the year for wolves, but this strong-minded child insists she will go off through the wood. She is quite sure the wild beasts cannot harm her although, well-warned, she lays a carving knife in the basket her mother has packed with cheeses. There is a bottle of harsh liquor distilled from brambles; a batch of flat oat cakes baked on the hearthstone; a pot or two of jam. The flaxen-haired girl will take these delicious gifts to a reclusive grandmother so old the burden of her years is crushing her to death. Granny lives two hours' trudge through the winter woods; the child wraps herself up in her thick shawl, draws it over her head. She steps into her stout wooden shoes; she is dressed and ready and it is Christmas Eve. The malign door of the solstice still swings upon its hinges, but she has been too much loved ever to feel scared.

Children do not stay young for long in this savage country. There are no toys for them to play with, so they work hard and

*Les Contes de Perrault,* **Paris: Paul Ducrocq, 1927. Illustrator Paul Cozé.**

grow wise, but this one, so pretty and the youngest of her family, a little latecomer, had been indulged by her mother and the grandmother who'd knitted her the red shawl that, today, has the ominous if brilliant look of blood on snow. Her breasts have just begun to swell; her hair is lint, so fair it hardly makes a shadow on her pale forehead; her cheeks are an emblematic scarlet and white and she has just started her woman's bleeding, the clock inside her that will strike, henceforward, once a month.

She stands and moves within the invisible pentacle of her own virginity. She is an unbroken egg; she is a sealed vessel; she has inside her a magic space the entrance to which is shut tight with a plug of membrane; she is a closed system; she does not know how to shiver. She has her knife and she is afraid of nothing.

Her father might forbid her, if he were home, but he is away in the forest, gathering wood, and her mother cannot deny her. The forest closed upon her like a pair of jaws.

There is always something to look at in the forest, even in the middle of winter—the huddled mounds of birds, succumbed to the lethargy of the season, heaped on the creaking boughs and too forlorn to sing; the bright frills of the winter fungi on the blotched trunks of the trees; the cuneiform slots of rabbits and deer, the herringbone tracks of the birds, a hare as lean as a rasher of bacon streaking across the path where the thin sunlight dapples the russet brakes of last year's bracken.

When she heard the freezing howl of a distant wolf, her practiced hand sprang to the handle of her knife, but she saw no sign of a wolf at all, nor of a naked man, neither, but then she heard a clattering among the brushwood and there sprang onto the path a fully clothed one, a very handsome young one, in the green coat and wide-awake hat of a hunter, laden with carcasses of game birds. She had her hand on her knife at the first rustle of twigs, but he laughed with a flash of white teeth when he saw her and made her a comic yet flattering little bow; she'd never seen such a fine fellow before, not among the rustic clowns of her native village. So on they went together, through the thickening light of the afternoon.

Soon they were laughing and joking like old friends. When he offered to carry her basket, she gave it to him although her knife was in it because he told her his rifle would protect them. As the day darkened, it began to snow again; she felt the first flakes settle on her eyelashes, but now there was only half a mile to go and there would be a fire, and hot tea, and a welcome, a warm one, surely, for the dashing huntsman as well as for herself.

This young man had a remarkable object in his pocket. It was a compass. She looked at the little round glass face in the palm of his hand and watched the wavering needle with a vague wonder. He assured her this compass had taken him safely through the wood on his hunting trip because the needle always told him with perfect accuracy where the north was. She did not believe it; she knew she should never leave the path on the way through the wood or else she would be lost instantly. He laughed at her again; gleaming trails of spittle clung to his teeth. He said if he plunged off the path into the forest that surrounded them, he could guarantee to arrive at her grandmother's house a good quarter of an hour before she did, plotting his way through the undergrowth with his compass, while she trudged the long way, along the winding path.

I don't believe you. Besides, aren't you afraid of the wolves? He only tapped the gleaming butt of his rifle and grinned.

Is it a bet? he asked. Shall we make a game of it? What will you give me if I get to your grandmother's house before you? What would you like? she asked disingenuously. A kiss.

Commonplaces of a rustic seduction; she lowered her eyes and blushed. He went through the undergrowth and took her basket with him, but she forgot to be afraid of the beasts, although now the moon was rising, for she wanted to dawdle on her way to make sure the handsome gentleman would win his wager.

Grandmother's house stood by itself a little way out of the village. The freshly falling snow blew in eddies about the kitchen garden and the young man stepped delicately up the snowy path to the door as if he were reluctant to get his feet wet, swinging his bundle of game and the girl's basket and humming a little tune to himself.

There is a faint trace of blood on his chin; he has been snacking on his catch.

He rapped upon the panels with his knuckles.

Aged and frail, granny is three-quarters succumbed to the mortality the ache in her bones promises her and almost ready to give in entirely. A boy came out from the village to build up her hearth for the night an hour ago and the kitchen crackles with busy firelight. She has her Bible for company; she is a pious old woman. She is propped up on several pillows in the bed set into the wall peasant fashion, wrapped up in the patchwork quilt she made before she was married, more years ago than she cares to remember. Two china spaniels with liver-colored blotches on their coats and black noses sit on either side of the fireplace. There is a bright rug of woven rags on the pantiles. The grandfather clock ticks away her eroding time.

We keep the wolves outside by living well.

He rapped upon the panels with his hairy knuckles.

It is your granddaughter, he mimicked in a high soprano. Lift up the latch and walk in, my darling.

You can tell them by their eyes, eyes of a beast of prey, nocturnal, devastating eyes as red as a wound; you can hurl your Bible at him and your apron after, granny; you thought that was a sure prophylactic against these infernal vermin. . . . Now call on Christ and his mother and all the angels in heaven to protect you, but it won't do you any good.

His feral muzzle is sharp as a knife; he drops his golden burden of gnawed pheasant on the table and puts down your dear girl's basket, too. Oh, my God, what have you done with her?

Off with his disguise, that coat of forest-colored cloth, the hat

with the feather tucked into the ribbon; his matted hair streams
down his white shirt and she can see the lice moving in it. The
sticks in the hearth shift and hiss; night and the forest has come
into the kitchen with darkness tangled in its hair.

He strips off his shirt. His skin is the color and texture of vellum. A crisp stripe of hair runs down his belly, his nipples are ripe and dark as poison fruit, but he's so thin you could count the ribs under his skin if only he gave you the time. He strips off his trousers and she can see how hairy his legs are. His genitals, huge. Ah! huge.

The last thing the old lady saw in all this world was a young man, eyes like cinders, naked as a stone, approaching her bed. The wolf is carnivore incarnate.

When he had finished with her, he licked his chops and quickly dressed himself again, until he was just as he had been when he came through her door. He burned the inedible hair in the fireplace and wrapped the bones up in a napkin that he hid away under the bed in the wooden chest in which he found a clean pair of sheets. These he carefully put on the bed instead of the telltale stained ones he stowed away in the laundry basket. He plumped up the pillows and shook out the patchwork quilt, he picked up the Bible from the floor, closed it and laid it on the table. All was as it had been before except that grandmother was gone. The sticks twitched in the grate, the clock ticked and the young man sat patiently, deceitfully beside the bed in granny's nightcap. Rat-a-tap-tap.

Who's there, he quavers in granny's antique falsetto. Only your granddaughter.

So she came in, bringing with her a flurry of snow that melted in tears on the tiles, and perhaps she was a little disappointed to see only her grandmother sitting beside the fire. But then he flung off the blanket and sprang to the door, pressing his back against it so that she could not get out again.

The girl looked round the room and saw there was not even the indentation of a head on the smooth cheek of the pillow and how, for the first time she'd seen it so, the Bible lay closed on the table. The tick of the clock cracked like a whip. She wanted her knife from her basket but she did not dare reach for it because his eyes were fixed upon her—huge eyes that now seemed to shine with a unique, interior light, eyes the size of saucers, saucers full of Greek fire, diabolic phosphorescence. What big eyes you have.

All the better to see you with.

No trace at all of the old woman except for a tuft of white hair that had caught in the bark of an unburned log. When the girl saw that, she knew she was in danger of death.

Where is my grandmother?

There's nobody here but we two, my darling.

Now a great howling rose up all around them, near, very near, as close as the kitchen garden, the howling of a multitude of wolves, she knew the worst wolves are hairy on the inside and she shivered, in spite of the scarlet shawl she pulled more closely round herself as if it could protect her, although it was as red as the blood she must spill. Who has come to sing us carols? she said.

Those are the voices of my brothers, darling; I love the company of wolves. Look out of the window and you'll see them.

Snow half-caked the lattice and she opened it to look into the garden. It was a white night of moon and snow; the blizzard whirled round the gaunt, gray beasts who squatted on their haunches among the rows of winter cabbage, pointing their sharp snouts to the moon and howling as if their hearts would break. Ten wolves; twenty wolves—so many wolves she could not count them, howling in concert as if demented or deranged. Their eyes reflected the light from the kitchen and shone like a hundred candles.

It is very cold, poor things, she said; no wonder they howl so.

She closed the window on the wolves' threnody and took off her scarlet shawl, the color of poppies, the color of sacrifices, the color of her menses, and since her fear did her no good, she ceased to be afraid. What shall I do with my shawl?

Throw it on the fire, dear one. You won't need it again.

She bundled up her shawl and threw it on the blaze, which instantly consumed it. Then she drew her blouse over her head; her small breasts gleamed as if the snow had invaded the room. What shall I do with my blouse? Into the fire with it, too, my pet.

The thin muslin went flaring up the chimney like a magic bird and now off came her skirt, her woolen stockings, her shoes, and onto the fire they went, too, and were gone for good. The firelight shone through the edges of her skin; now she was clothed only in her untouched integument of flesh. Thus dazzling, naked, she combed out her hair with her fingers; her hair looked white as the snow outside. Then went directly to the man with red eyes in whose unkempt mane the lice moved; she stood up on tiptoe and unbuttoned the collar of his shirt. What big arms you have.

All the better to hug you with.

Every wolf in the world now howled a prothalamion outside the window as she freely gave the kiss she owed him.

What big teeth you have!

She saw how his jaws began to slaver and the room was full of the clamor of the forest's *Liebestod,* but the wise child never flinched, even when he answered:

All the better to eat you with.

The girl burst out laughing; she knew she was nobody's meat. She laughed at him full in the face, she ripped off his shirt for him and flung it into the fire, in the fiery wake of her own discarded clothing. The flames danced like dead souls on Walpurgisnacht and the old bones under the bed set up a terrible clattering, but she did not pay them any heed. Carnivore incarnate, only immaculate flesh appeases him.

She will lay his fearful head on her lap and she will pick out the lice from his pelt and perhaps she will put the lice into her mouth and eat them, as he will bid her, as she would do in a savage marriage ceremony. The blizzard will die down.

The blizzard dies down, leaving the mountains as randomly covered with snow as if a blind woman had thrown a sheet over them, the upper branches of the forest pines limed, creaking, swollen with the fall. Snowlight, moonlight, a confusion of pawprints. All silent, all still.

Midnight; and the clock strikes. It is Christmas Day, the werewolves' birthday; the door of the solstice stands wide open; let them all slink through.

See! Sweet and sound she sleeps in granny's bed, between the paws of the tender wolf.

# ✬ 34 ✬

## *Goldflower*
## *and the Bear*

### *By Chiang Mi*

### (1979)

LONG, LONG AGO, THERE WAS a clever and brave girl called Goldflower who lived with her mother and brother. They were very happy.

One day, her mother said: "Your Aunty is ill. I'm going to see her and won't be back tonight. Look after your brother and ask your Granny to stay with you tonight!" Then she left with a basket of eggs and a hen.

At sunset, Goldflower herded the sheep home. After penning up the sheep, she shooed all the chickens into the coop. Then, she and her brother climbed a small hill to call Granny. Usually, after one shout, there would be an answer, but today there was no reply after several shouts. Goldflower thought: "It doesn't matter. I'm not afraid." They went home and she bolted the door.

Lighting a wick, they sat by the fire-pan and she began to tell her brother a story. Suddenly they heard a knock at the door. Brother hugged her and cried: "I'm afraid!"

They heard a strange but kindly voice saying: "I'm Granny." Brother was very happy and shouted: "Sister, open the door! Granny has come!"

Goldflower leaned against the door and asked: "Is that you, Granny? What's wrong with your voice?"

"I've a cold." Came the reply followed by coughs.

292

The boy urged his sister to open the door. Meanwhile, the voice continued: "My dear, there is something wrong with my eyes and I'm afraid of light. Please blow out the wick before letting me in."

It was so dark in the room that they couldn't see who was coming in. Goldflower invited "Granny" to a stool, but it cried out when sitting down. The children jumped in fright. The "Granny" said: "Dear, I've a boil so I can't sit on hard wood. Please give me a wicker basket."

The swishing of the Bear's-tail in the dark caused Goldflower to ask: "What's making that noise?"

"Oh! It's the fly-swatter your grandpa bought for me," replied "Granny."

The clever girl stoked the fire brighter and, wow, there was a pair of hairy feet! Now she realized this isn't Granny. It's the Bear which likes to eat children. Goldflower calmed and pretended to have seen nothing. But how to deal with this wicked Bear? Her mother had told her that bears were afraid of lice. She grabbed a handful of seeds and took off her brother's hat, pretending to be catching lice in his hair. She threw the seeds into the fire. They crackled. The Bear growled: "Don't let him sleep with me with his lice. Let him sleep outside!"

Brother was so afraid that he began to sob. Goldflower coaxed him to go to the other room to sleep. She locked the door on her way back. When she got back, the Bear asked her to go to bed. The Bear was very happy because it could have a hearty meal at midnight. But the clever Goldflower was also thinking of a way out. After sleeping for a while, she cried: "My tummy hurts! I want to go on the pot."

The Bear thought: She would not be good to eat like this. So, it tied one end of a belt to Goldflower's hand and let her go outside. After a while, the Bear pulled and then pulled again. It seemed that the girl was still on the other end. A long time passed. The Bear called several times but there was no answer. It got worried and pulled hard. Clunk. Something tumbled. The Bear was puzzled and felt its way along the belt. There was nothing at the end but a pot. The Bear was very angry. It was already midnight and the Bear started bellowing for food like any beast. Failing to find Goldflower, it stopped to drink some water from a pond before continuing the search. It saw Goldflower in the water and was overjoyed. When the Bear reached into the water to grasp Goldflower, she disappeared. The Bear angrily watched. When the water became still, Goldflower reappeared. The Bear reached out but Goldflower again vanished. The Bear did not know what to do. A laugh came from above. The Bear quickly looked up and saw Goldflower in a tree. The image in the water was her reflection. The Bear wanted to climb the tree, but Goldflower had covered it with grease. The Bear slipped again and again. The Bear could only wait under the tree hapless while Goldflower laughed up on the tree. "Granny, do you want to eat some pears? Please get me the spear in the house."

The Bear was really happy to hear this and went to fetch the spear. The Bear handed her the spear and, pointing to a few big pears, it said: "Give me those."

"Granny, open your mouth. Here comes the pear!" Goldflower threw one at the Bear's mouth.

The Bear ate it in two bites and asked her to spear some more. "Granny, this time open your mouth wide. It is a real big one."

The Bear opened its mouth as wide as it could. And with all her might, Goldflower threw the spear into its mouth. With a groan, the Bear fell flat. Goldflower slid down the tree and kicked the dead Bear. "Do you still want to eat children?"

Roosters crowed. Goldflower opened the door to her brother's room. He was sleeping soundly. She woke him and took him to the dead body. Now he knew that it was the wicked old Bear. The sun was rising red in the east. Mother came back. She was very pleased to hear what had happened and praised the brave little girl. The story of Goldflower and the Bear spread far and wide.

# ❦ 35 ❦

## *Wolfland*

## *By Tanith Lee*

## (1983)

WHEN THE SUMMONS ARRIVED from Anna the Matriarch, Lisel did not wish to obey. The twilit winter had already come, and the great snows were down, spreading their aprons of shining ice, turning the trees to crystal candelabra. Lisel wanted to stay in the city, skating fur-clad on the frozen river beneath the torches, dancing till four in the morning, a vivid blonde in the flame-bright ballrooms, breaking hearts and not minding, lying late next day like a cat in her warm, soft bed. She did not want to go traveling several hours into the north to visit Anna the Matriarch.

Lisel's mother had been dead sixteen years, all Lisel's life. Her father had let her have her own way, in almost everything, for about the same length of time. But Anna the Matriarch, Lisel's maternal grandmother, was exceedingly rich. She lived thirty miles from the city, in a great wild château in the great wild forest.

A portrait of Anna as a young widow hung in the gallery of Lisel's father's house, a wicked-looking, bone-pale person in a black dress, with rubies and diamonds at her throat, and in her ivory yellow hair. Even in her absence, Anna had always had a say in things. A recluse, she had still manipulated like a puppet-master from behind the curtain of the forest. Periodic instructions had been sent, pertaining to Lisel. The girl must be educated by this or that method. She must gain this or that accomplishment, read this or that book, favor this or that cologne or color or jewel. The latter orders were always uncannily apposite and were often complemented by applicable—and sumptuous—gifts. The summons came in company with such. A swirling cloak of scarlet velvet leapt like a fire from its box to Lisel's hands. It was lined with albino fur, all but the hood, which was lined with the finest and heaviest red brocade. A clasp of gold joined the garment at the throat, the two portions, when closed, forming Anna's personal device, a many-petaled flower. Lisel had exclaimed with pleasure, embracing the cloak, picturing herself flying in it across the solid white river like a dangerous blood-red rose. Then the letter fell from its folds.

Lisel had never seen her grandmother, at least, not intelligently, for Anna had been in her proximity on one occasion only: the hour of her birth. Then, one glimpse had apparently sufficed. Anna had snatched it, and sped away from her son-in-law's house and the salubrious city in a demented black carriage. Now, as peremptory as then, she demanded that Lisel come to visit her before the week was out. Over thirty miles, into the uncivilized northern forest, to the strange mansion in the snow.

"Preposterous," said Lisel's father. "The woman is mad, as I've always suspected."

"I shan't go," said Lisel.

They both knew quite well that she would.

One day, every considerable thing her grandmother possessed would pass to Lisel, providing Lisel did not incur Anna's displeasure.

Half a week later, Lisel was on the northern road.

She sat amid cushions and rugs, in a high sled strung with silver bells, and drawn by a single black-satin horse. Before Lisel perched her driver, the whip in his hand, and a pistol at his belt, for the way north was not without its risks. There were, besides, three outriders, also equipped with whips, pistols and knives, and muffled to the brows in fur. No female companion was in evidence. Anna had stipulated that it would be unnecessary and superfluous for her grandchild to burden herself with a maid.

But the whips had cracked, the horses had started off. The runners of the sled had smoothly hissed, sending up lace-like sprays of ice. Once clear of the city, the north road opened like a perfect skating floor of milky glass, dim-lit by the fragile winter sun smoking low on the horizon. The silver bells sang, and the fierce still air through which the horses dashed broke on Lisel's cheeks like the coldest champagne. Ablaze in her scarlet cloak, she was exhilarated and began to forget she had not wanted to come.

After about an hour, the forest marched up out of the ground and
swiftly enveloped the road on all sides.

There was presently an insidious, but generally perceptible change. Between the walls of the forest there gathered a new silence, a silence which was, if anything, *alive*, a personality which attended any humanly noisy passage with a cruel and resentful interest. Lisel stared up into the narrow lane of sky above. They might have been moving along the channel of a deep and partly-frozen stream. When the drowned sun flashed through, splinters of light scattered and went out as if in water.

The tall pines in their pelts of snow seemed poised to lurch across the road.

The sled had been driving through the forest for perhaps another hour, when a wolf wailed somewhere amid the trees. Rather than break the silence of the place, the cry seemed born of the silence, a natural expression of the landscape's cold solitude and immensity.

The outriders touched the pistols in their belts, almost religiously, and the nearest of the three leaned to Lisel.

"Madam Anna's house isn't far from here. In any case we have our guns, and these horses could race the wind."

"I'm not afraid," Lisel said haughtily. She glanced at the trees, "I've never seen a wolf. I should be interested to see one."

Made sullen by Lisel's pert reply, the outrider switched tactics. From trying to reassure her, he now ominously said: "Pray you don't, m'mselle. One wolf generally means a pack, and once the snow comes, they're hungry."

"As my father's servant, I would expect you to sacrifice yourself for me, of course," said Lisel. "A fine strong man like you should keep a pack of wolves busy long enough for the rest of us to escape."

The man scowled and spurred away from her.

Lisel smiled to herself. She was not at all afraid, not of the problematical wolves, not even of the eccentric grandmother she had never before seen. In a way, Lisel was looking forward to the meeting, now her annoyance at vacating the city had left her. There had been so many bizarre tales, so much hearsay. Lisel had even caught gossip concerning Anna's husband. He had been a handsome princely man, whose inclinations had not matched his appearance. Lisel's mother had been sent to the city to live with relations to avoid this monster's outbursts of perverse lust and savagery. He had allegedly died one night, mysteriously and luridly murdered on one of the forest tracks. This was not the history Lisel had got from her father, to be sure, but she had always partly credited the more extravagant version. After all, Anna the Matriarch was scarcely commonplace in her mode of life or her attitude to her granddaughter.

Yes, indeed, rather than apprehension, Lisel was beginning to entertain a faintly unholy glee in respect of the visit and the insights it might afford her.

A few minutes after the wolf had howled, the road took a sharp bend, and emerging around it, the party beheld an unexpected obstacle in the way. The driver of the sled cursed softly and drew hard on the reins, bringing the horse to a standstill. The outriders similarly halted. Each peered ahead to where, about twenty yards along the road, a great black carriage blotted the white snow.

A coachman sat immobile on the box of the black carriage, muffled in coal-black furs and almost indistinguishable from them. In forceful contrast, the carriage horses were blonds, and restless, tossing their necks, lifting their feet. A single creature stood on the track between the carriage and the sled. It was too small to be a man, too curiously proportioned to be simply a child.

"What's this?" demanded the third of Lisel's outriders, he who had spoken earlier of the wolves. It was an empty question, but had been a long time in finding a voice for all that.

"I think it is my grandmother's carriage come to meet me," declared Lisel brightly, though,  for the first, she had felt a pang of apprehension.

This was not lessened, when the dwarf came loping toward them, like a small, misshapen, furry dog and, reaching the sled, spoke to her, ignoring the others.

"You may leave your escort here and come with us."

Lisel was struck at once by the musical quality of his voice, while out of the shadow of his hood emerged the face of a fair and melancholy angel. As she stared at him, the men about her raised their objections.

"We're to go with m'mselle to her grandmother's house."

"You are not necessary," announced the beautiful dwarf, glancing at them with uninterest. "You are already on the Lady Anna's lands. The coachman and I are all the protection your mistress needs. The Lady Anna does not wish to receive you on her estate."

"What proof," snarled the third outrider, "that you're from Madame's château? Or that she told you to say such a thing. You could have come from anyplace, from Hell itself most likely, and they crushed you in the door as you were coming out."

The riders and the driver laughed brutishly. The dwarf paid no
attention to the insult. He drew from his glove one delicate, per-
fectly formed hand, and in it a folded letter. It was easy to recognize
the Matriarch's sanguine wax and the imprint of the petaled flower.
The riders brooded, and the dwarf held the letter toward Lisel. She
accepted it with an uncanny but pronounced reluctance.

"*Chère*," it said in its familiar, indeed its unmistakable, characters, "*Why are you delaying the moment when I may look at you? Beautiful has already told you, I think, that your escort may go home. Anna
is giving you her own escort, to guide you on the last laps of the journey.
Come! Send the men away and step into the carriage.*"

Lisel, reaching the word, or rather the name, Beautiful, had
glanced involuntarily at the dwarf, oddly frightened at its horrid
contrariness and its peculiar truth. A foreboding had clenched
around her young heart, and, for a second, inexplicable terror. It
was certainly a dreadful dilemma. She could refuse, and refuse thereby the goodwill, the gifts, the ultimate fortune her grandmother
could bestow. Or she could brush aside her silly childish fears and
walk boldly from the sled to the carriage. Surely, she had always
known Madame Anna was an eccentric. Had it not been a source
of intrigued curiosity but a few moments ago?

Lisel made her decision.

"Go home," she said regally to her father's servants. "My grandmother is wise and would hardly put me in danger."

The men grumbled, glaring at her, and as they did so, she got out
of the sled and moved along the road toward the stationary and
funereal carriage. As she came closer, she made out the flower device stamped in gilt on the door. Then the dwarf had darted ahead
of her, seized the door, and was holding it wide, bowing to his
knees, thus almost into the snow. A lock of pure golden hair spilled
across his forehead.

Lisel entered the carriage and sat on tile somber cushions.
Courageous prudence (or greed) had triumphed.

The door was shut. She felt the slight tremor as Beautiful leapt
on the box beside the driver.

Morose and indecisive, the men her father had sent with her
were still lingering on the ice between the trees, as she was driven
away.

She must have slept, dazed by the continuous rocking of the carriage, but all at once she was wide awake, clutching in alarm at the

upholstery. What had roused her was a unique and awful choir. The cries of wolves.

Quite irresistibly she pressed against the window and stared out, impelled to look for what she did not, after all, wish to see. And what she saw was unreassuring.

A horde of wolves was running, not merely in pursuit, but actually alongside the carriage. Pale they were, a pale almost luminous brownish shade, which made them seem phantasmal against the snow. Their small but jewel-like eyes glinted, glowed and burned. As they ran, their tongues lolling sideways from their mouths like those of huge hunting dogs, they seemed to smile up at her, and her heart turned over.

Why was it, she wondered, with panic-stricken anger, that the coach did not go faster and so outrun the pack? Why was it the brutes had been permitted to gain as much distance as they had? Could it be they had already plucked the coachman and the dwarf from the box and devoured them—she tried to recollect if, in her dozing, she had registered masculine shrieks of fear and agony— and that the horses plunged on. Imagination, grown detailed and pessimistic, soon dispensed with these images, replacing them with that of great pepper-colored paws scratching on the frame of the coach, the grisly talons ripping at the door, at last a wolf's savage mask thrust through it, and her own frantic and pointless screaming, in the instants before her throat was silenced by the meeting or narrow yellow fangs.

Having run the gamut of her own premonition, Lisel sank back on the seat and yearned for a pistol, or at least a knife. A malicious streak in her lent her the extraordinary bravery of desiring to inflict as many hurts on her killers as she was able before they finished her. She also took space to curse Anna the Matriarch. How the wretched old woman would grieve and complain when the story reached her. The clean-picked bones of her granddaughter had been found a mere mile or so from her château, in the rags of a blood-red cloak; by the body a golden clasp, rejected as inedible. . . .

A heavy thud caused Lisel to leap to her feet, even in the galloping, bouncing carriage. There at the door, grinning in on her, the huge face of a wolf, which did not fall away. Dimly she realized it must impossibly be balancing itself on the running board of the carriage, its front paws raised and somehow keeping purchase on the door. With one sharp determined effort of its head, it might conceivably smash in the pane of the window. The glass would lacerate, and the scent of its own blood further inflame its starvation. The eyes of it, doused by the carriage's gloom, flared up in two sudden pupilless ovals of fire, like two little portholes into hell.

With a shrill howl, scarcely knowing what she did, Lisel flung herself at the closed door and the wolf the far side of it. Her eyes also blazed, her teeth also were bared, and her nails raised as if to claw. Her horror was such that she appeared ready to attack the wolf in its own primeval mode, and as her hands struck the glass against its face, the wolf shied and dropped away.

In that moment, Lisel heard the musical voice of the dwarf call out from the box, some wordless whoop, and a tall gatepost sprang by.

Lisel understood they had entered the grounds of the Matriarch's château. And, a moment later, learned, though did not understand, that the wolves had not followed them beyond the gateway.

❀ *2*

The Matriarch sat at the head of the long table. Her chair, like the table, was slender, carved and intensely polished. The rest of the chairs, though similarly high-backed and angular, were plain and dull, including the chair to which Lisel had been conducted. Which increased Lisel's annoyance, the petty annoyance to which her more eloquent emotions of fright and rage had given way, on entering the domestic, if curious, atmosphere of the house. And Lisel must strive to conceal her ill-temper. It was difficult.

The château, ornate and swarthy under its pointings of snow, retained an air of decadent magnificence, which was increased within. Twin stairs flared from an immense great hall. A hearth, large as a room, and crow-hooded by its enormous mantel, roared with muffled firelight. There was scarcely a furnishing that was not at least two hundred years old, and many were much older. The very air seemed tinged by the somber wood, the treacle darkness of the draperies, the old gold gleams of picture frames, gilding and tableware.

At the center of it all sat Madame Anna, in her eighty-first year, a weird apparition of improbable glamour. She appeared, from no more than a yard or so away, to be little over fifty. Her skin, though very dry, had scarcely any lines in it, and none of the pleatings and collapses Lisel generally associated with the elderly. Anna's hair had remained blonde, a fact Lisel was inclined to attribute to some preparation out of a bottle, yet she was not sure. The lady wore black as she had done in the portrait of her youth, a black starred

over with astonishing jewels. But her nails were very long and discolored, as were her teeth. These two incontrovertible proofs of old
age gave Lisel a perverse satisfaction. Grandmother's eyes, on the
other hand, were not so reassuring. Brilliant eyes, clear and very
likely sharp-sighted, of a pallid silvery brown. Unnerving eyes, but
Lisel did her best to stare them out, though when Anna spoke to
her, Lisel now answered softly, ingratiatingly.

There had not, however, been much conversation, after the first
clamor at the doorway:

"We were chased by wolves!" Lisel had cried "Scores of them!
Your coachman is a dolt who doesn't know enough to carry a pistol.
I might have been killed."

"You were not," said Anna, imperiously standing in silhouette
against the giant window of the hall, a stained glass of what appeared
to be a hunting scene, done in murky reds and staring white.

"No thanks to your servants. You promised me an escort—the
only reason I sent my father's men away."

"You had your escort."

Lisel had choked back another flood of sentences: she did not
want to get on the wrong side of this strange relative. Nor had she
liked the slight emphasis on the word "escort."

The handsome ghastly dwarf had gone forward into the hall,
lifted the hem of Anna's long mantle, and kissed it. Anna had
smoothed off his hood and caressed the bright hair beneath.

"Beautiful wasn't afraid," said Anna decidedly. "But, then, my
people know the wolves will not harm them."

An ancient tale came back to Lisel in that moment. It concerned certain human denizens of the forests, who had power over
wild beasts. It occurred to Lisel that mad old Anna liked to fancy
herself a sorceress, and Lisel said fawningly: "I should have known
I'd be safe. I'm sorry for my outburst, but I don't know the forest as
you do. I was afraid."

In her allotted bedroom, a silver ewer and basin stood on a table.
The embroideries on the canopied bed were faded but priceless.
Antique books stood in a case, catching the firelight, a vast yet ran-
dom selection of the poetry and prose of many lands. From the bedchamber window, Lisel could look out across the clearing of the
park, the white sweep of it occasionally broken by trees in their
winter foliage of snow, or by the slash of the track which broke
through the high wall. Beyond the wall, the forest pressed close
under the heavy twilight of the sky. Lisel pondered with a grim irri-

tation the open gateway. Wolves running, and the way to the château left wide at all times. She visualized mad Anna throwing chunks of raw meat to the wolves as another woman would toss bread to swans.

This unprepossessing notion returned to Lisel during the unusually early dinner, when she realized that Anna was receiving from her silent gliding servants various dishes of raw meats.

"I hope," said Anna, catching Lisel's eye, "my repast won't offend a delicate stomach. I have learned that the best way to keep my health is to eat the fruits of the earth in their intended state—so much goodness is wasted in cooking and garnishing."

Despite the reference to fruit, Anna touched none of the fruit or vegetables on the table. Nor did she drink any wine.

Lisel began again to be amused, if rather dubiously. Her own fare was excellent, and she ate it hungrily, admiring as she did so the crystal goblets and gold-handled knives which one day would be hers.

Presently a celebrated liqueur was served—to Lisel alone—and Anna rose on the black wings of her dress, waving her granddaughter to the fire. Beautiful, meanwhile, had crawled onto the stool of the tall piano and begun to play wildly despairing romances there, his elegant fingers darting over discolored keys so like Anna's strong yet senile teeth.

"Well," said Anna, reseating herself in another carven throne before the cave of the hearth. "What do you think of us?"

"Think, Grandmère? Should I presume?"

"No. But you do."

"I think," said Lisel cautiously, "everything is very fine."

"And you are keenly aware, of course, the finery will eventually belong to you."

"Oh, Grandmère!" exclaimed Lisel, quite genuinely shocked by such frankness.

"Don't trouble yourself," said Anna. Her eyes caught the fire and became like the eyes of the wolf at the carriage window. "You expect to be my heiress. It's quite normal you should be making an inventory. I shan't last forever. Once I'm gone, presumably everything will be yours."

Despite herself, Lisel gave an involuntary shiver. A sudden plan of selling the château to be rid of it flitted through her thoughts, but she quickly put it aside, in case the Matriarch somehow read her mind.

"Don't speak like that, Grandmère. This is the first time I've met you, and you talk of dying."

"Did I? No. I did not. I spoke of *departure*. Nothing dies, it simply transmogrifies." Lisel watched politely this display of apparent piety. "As for my mansion," Anna went on, "you mustn't consider sale, you know." Lisel blanched—as she had feared her mind had been read, or could it merely be that Anna found her predictable? "The château has stood on this land for many centuries. The old name for the spot, do you known that?"

"No, Grandmère."

"This, like the whole of the forest, was called the Wolfland. Because it was the wolves' country before ever men set foot on it with their piffling little roads and tracks, their carriages and foolish frightened walls. Wolfland. Their country then, and when the winter comes, their country once more."

"As I saw, Grandmère," said Lisel tartly.

"As you saw. You'll see and hear more of them while you're in my house. Their voices come and go like the wind, as they do. When that little idiot of a sun slips away and the night rises, you may hear scratching on the lower floor windows. I needn't tell you to stay indoors, need I?"

"Why do you let animals run in your park?" demanded Lisel.

"Because," said Anna, "the land is theirs by right."

The dwarf began to strike a polonaise from the piano. Anna clapped her hands, and the music ended. Anna beckoned, and Beautiful slid off the stool like a precocious child caught stickying the keys. He came to Anna, and she played with his hair. His face remained unreadable, yet his pellucid eyes swam dreamily to Lisel's face. She felt embarrassed by the scene, and at his glance was angered to find herself blushing.

"There was a time," said Anna, "when I did not rule this house. When a man ruled here."

"Grandpère," said Lisel, looking resolutely at the fire.

"*Grandpère*, yes, *Grandpère*." Her voice held the most awful scorn. "Grandpère believed it was a man's pleasure to beat his wife. You're young, but you should know, should be told. Every night, if I was not already sick from a beating, and sometimes when I was, I would hear his heavy drunken feet come stumbling to my door. At first I locked it, but I learned not to. What stood in his way he could always break. He was a strong man. A great legend of strength. I carry scars on my shoulders to this hour. One day I may show you."

Lisel gazed at Anna, caught between fascination and revulsion.
"Why do I tell you?" Anna smiled. She had twisted Beautiful's gor-
geous hair into a painful knot. Clearly it hurt him, but he made no
sound, staring blindly at the ceiling. "I tell you, Lisel, because very
soon your father will suggest to you that it is time you were wed.
And however handsome or gracious the young man may seem to
you that you choose, or that is chosen for you, however noble or
marvelous or even docile he may seem, you have no way of being
certain he will not turn out to be like your beloved grandpère. Do
you know, he brought me peaches on our wedding night, all the
way from the hothouses of the city. Then he showed me the whip
he had been hiding under the fruit. You see what it is to be a
woman, Lisel. Is that what you want? The irrevocable marriage
vow that binds you forever to a monster? And even if he is a good
man, which is a rare beast indeed, you may die an agonizing death
in childbed, just as your mother did."

Lisel swallowed. A number of things went through her head
now. A vague acknowledgment that, though she envisaged admiration, she had never wished to marry and therefore never considered
it, and a starker awareness that she was being told improper things.
She desired to learn more and dreaded to learn it. As she was struggling to find a rejoinder, Anna seemed to notice her own grip on
the hair of the dwarf.

"Ah," she said, "forgive me. I did not mean to hurt you."

The words had an oddly sinister ring to them. Lisel suddenly
guessed their origin, the brutish man rising from his act of depravity, of necessity still merely sketched by Lisel's innocence, whisper-
ing, gloatingly muttering: Forgive me. I did not mean to hurt.

"Beautiful," said Anna, "is the only man of any worth I've ever
met. And my servants, of course, but I don't count them as men.
Drink your liqueur."

"Yes, Grandmère," said Lisel, as she sipped, and slightly choked.

"Tomorrow," said Anna, "we must serve you something better. A
vintage indigenous to the château, made from a flower which grows
here in the spring. For now," again she rose on her raven's wings; a
hundred gems caught the light and went out, "for now, we keep
early hours here, in the country."

"But, Grandmère," said Lisel, astounded, "it's scarcely sunset."

"In my house," said Anna, gently, "you will do as you are told,
m'mselle."

And for once, Lisel did as she was told.

At first, of course, Lisel did not entertain a dream of sleep. She was used to staying awake till the early hours of the morning, rising at noon. She entered her bedroom, cast one scathing glance at the bed, and settled herself to read in a chair beside the bedroom fire. Luckily she had found a lurid novel amid the choice of books. By skimming over all passages of meditation, description or philosophy, confining her attention to those portions which contained duels, rapes, black magic and the firing squad, she had soon made great inroads on the work. Occasionally, she would pause, and add another piece of wood to the fire. At such times she knew a medley of doubts concerning her grandmother. That the Matriarch could leave such a novel lying about openly where Lisel could get at it outraged the girl's propriety.

Eventually, two or three hours after the sun had gone and the windows blackened entirely behind the drapes, Lisel did fall asleep. The excitements of the journey and her medley of reactions to Madame Anna had worn her out.

She woke, as she had in the carriage, with a start of alarm. Her reason was the same one. Out in the winter forest of night sounded the awesome choir of the wolves. Their voices rose and fell, swelling, diminishing, resurging, like great icy waves of wind or water, breaking on the silence of the château.

Partly nude, a lovely maiden had been bound to a stake and the first torch applied, but Lisel no longer cared very much for her fate. Setting the book aside, she rose from the chair. The flames were low on the candles and the fire almost out. There was no clock, but it had the feel of midnight. Lisel went to the window and opened the drapes. Stepping through and pulling them fast closed again behind her, she gazed out into the glowing darkness of snow and night.

The wolf cries went on and on, thrilling her with a horrible disquiet, so she wondered how even mad Anna could ever have grown accustomed to them? Was this what had driven her grandfather to brutishness and beatings? And, colder thought, the mysterious violent death he was supposed to have suffered—what more violent than to be torn apart under the pine trees by long pointed teeth?

Lisel quartered the night scene with her eyes, looking for shapes to fit the noises, and, as before, hoping not to find them.

There was decidedly something about wolves. Something beyond their reputation and the stories of the half-eaten bodies of little chil-

dren with which nurses regularly scared their charges. Something to
do with actual appearance, movement; the lean shadow manifesting
from between the trunks of trees—the stuff of nightmare. And their
howlings! Yet, as it went on and on, Lisel became aware of a bizarre
exhilaration, an almost-pleasure in the awful sounds which made the
hair lift on her scalp and gooseflesh creep along her arms—the same
sort of sensation as biting into a slice of lemon—

And then she saw it, a great pale wolf. It loped by directly beneath the window, and suddenly, to Lisel's horror, it raised its long
head, and two fireworks flashed, which were its eyes meeting with
hers. A primordial fear, worse even than in the carriage, turned
Lisel's bones to liquid. She sank on her knees, and as she knelt there
foolishly, as if in prayer, her chin on the sill, she beheld the wolf
moving away across the park, seeming to dissolve into the gloom.

Gradually, then, the voices of the other wolves began to dull,
eventually falling quiet.

Lisel got up, came back into the room, threw more wood on the
fire and crouched there. It seemed odd to her that the wolf had run
away from the château, but she was not sure why. Presumably it had
ventured near in hopes of food, then, disappointed, withdrew.
That it had come from the spot directly by the hall's doors did not,
could not, mean anything in particular. Then Lisel realized what
had been so strange. She had seen the wolf in a faint radiance of
light—but from where? The moon was almost full, but obscured
behind the house. The drapes had been drawn across behind her,
the light could not have fallen down from her own window. She
was turning back unhappily to the window to investigate when she
heard the unmistakable soft thud of a large door being carefully
shut below her, in the château.

*The wolf had been in the house.* Anna's guest.

Lisel was petrified for a few moments, then a sort of fury came to
her rescue. How dared the old woman be so mad as all this and expect her civilized granddaughter to endure it? Brought to the wilds,
told improper tales, left improper literature to read, made unwilling
party to the entertainment of savage beasts. Perhaps as a result of
the reading matter, Lisel saw her only course abruptly, and it was
escape. (She had already assumed Anna would not allow her
grandchild to depart until whatever lunatic game the old beldame
was playing was completed.) But if escape, then how? Though
there were carriage, horses, even coachman, all were Anna's. Lisel
did not have to ponder long, however. Her father's cynicism on the

lower classes had convinced her that anyone had his price. She would bribe the coachman—her gold bracelets and her ruby eardrops—both previous gifts of Anna's, in fact. She could assure the man of her father's protection and further valuables when they reached the city. A vile thought came to her at that, that her father might, after all, prove unsympathetic. Was she being stupid? Should she turn a blind eye to Anna's wolfish foibles? If Anna should disinherit her, as surely she would on Lisel's flight—

Assailed by doubts, Lisel paced the room. Soon she had added to them. The coachman might snatch her bribe and still refuse to help her. Or worse, drive her into the forest and violate her. Or—

The night slowed and flowed into the black valleys of early morning. The moon crested the château and sank into the forest. Lisel sat on the edge of the canopied bed, pleating and repleating the folds of the scarlet cloak between her fingers. Her face was pale, her blonde hair untidy and her eyes enlarged. She looked every bit as crazy as her grandmother.

Her decision was sudden, made with an awareness that she had wasted much time. She flung the cloak around herself and started up. She hurried to the bedroom door and softly, softly, opened it a tiny crack.

All was black in the house, neither lamp nor candle visible anywhere. The sight, or rather lack of it, caused Lisel's heart to sink. At the same instant, it indicated that the whole house was abed. Lisel's plan was a simple one. A passage led away from the great hall to the kitchens and servants' quarters and ultimately to a courtyard containing coachhouse and stables. Here the grooms and the coachman would sleep, and here too another gateway opened on the park. These details she had either seen for herself as the carriage was driven off on her arrival or deduced from the apparent structure of the château. Unsure of the hour, yet she felt dawn was approaching. If she could but reach the servants' quarters, she should be able to locate the courtyard. If the coachman proved a villain, she would have to use her wits. Threaten him or cajole him. Knowing very little of physical communion, it seemed better to Lisel in those moments, to lie down with a hairy peasant than to remain the Matriarch's captive. It was that time of night when humans are often prey to ominous or extravagant ideas of all sorts. She took up one of the low-burning candles. Closing the bedroom door behind her, Lisel stole forward into the black nothingness of unfamiliarity.

Even with the feeble light, she could barely see ten inches before her, and felt cautiously about with her free hand, dreading to collide with ornament or furniture and thereby rouse her enemies. The stray gleams, shot back at her from a mirror or a picture frame, misled rather than aided her. At first her total concentration was taken up with her safe progress and her quest to find the head of the double stair. Presently, however, as she pressed on without mishap, secondary considerations began to steal in on her.

If it was difficult to proceed, how much more difficult it might be should she desire to retreat. Hopefully, there would be nothing to retreat from. But the ambiance of the château, inspired by night and the limited candle, was growing more sinister by the second. Arches opened on drapes of black from which anything might spring. All about, the shadow furled, and she was one small target moving in it, lit as if on a stage.

She turned the passage and perceived the curve of the stair ahead and the dim hall below. The great stained window provided a grey illumination which elsewhere was absent. The stars bled on the snow outside and pierced the white panes. Or could it be the initial tinge of dawn?

Lisel paused, confronting once again the silliness of her simple plan of escape. Instinctively, she turned to look the way she had come, and the swiftness of the motion, or some complementary draught, quenched her candle. She stood marooned by this cliché, the phosphorescently discernible space before her, pitch-dark behind, and chose the path into the half-light as preferable.

She went down the stair delicately, as if descending into a ballroom. When she was some twenty steps from the bottom, something moved in the thick drapes beside the outer doors. Lisel froze, feeling a shock like an electric volt passing through her vitals. In another second she knew from the uncanny littleness of the shape that it was Anna's dwarf who scuttled there. But before she divined what it was at, one leaf of the door began to swing heavily inward.

Lisel felt no second shock of fear. She felt instead as if her soul drifted upward from her flesh.

Through the open door soaked the pale ghost-light that heralded sunrise, and with that, a scattering of fresh white snow. Lastly through the door, its long feet crushing both light and snow, glided the wolf she had seen beneath her window. It did not look real, it seemed to waver and to shine, yet, for any who had ever heard the

Dinah Maria Craik, *The Fairy Book*. London: Macmillan, 1863. Illustrator Warwick Goble.

name of wolf, or a single story of them, or the song of their voices, here stood that word, that story, that voice, personified.

The wolf raised its supernatural head and once more it looked at the young girl.

The moment held no reason, no pity, and certainly no longer any hope of escape.

As the wolf began to pad noiselessly up the stair toward Lisel, she fled by the only route now possible to her. Into unconsciousness.

❄ *3*

She came to herself to find the face of a prince from a romance poised over hers. He was handsome enough to have kissed her awake, except that she knew immediately it was the dwarf.

"Get away from me!" she shrieked, and he moved aside.

She was in the bedchamber, lying on the canopied bed. She was not dead, she had not been eaten or had her throat torn out.

As if in response to her thoughts, the dwarf said musically to her: "You have had a nightmare, m'mselle." But she could tell from a faint expression somewhere between his eyes, that he did not truly expect her to believe such a feeble equivocation.

"There was a wolf," said Lisel, pulling herself into a sitting position, noting that she was still gowned and wearing the scarlet cloak. "A wolf which you let into the house."

"I?" The dwarf elegantly raised an eyebrow.

"You, you frog. Where is my grandmother? I demand to see her at once. "

"The Lady Anna is resting. She sleeps late in the mornings."

"Wake her."

"Your pardon, m'mselle, but I take my orders from Madame." The dwarf bowed. "If you are recovered and hungry, a maid will bring *petit déjeuner* at once to your room, and hot water for bathing, when you are ready."

Lisel frowned. Her ordeal past, her anger paramount, she was still very hungry. An absurd notion came to her—*had* it all been a dream? No, she would not so doubt herself. Even though the wolf had not harmed her, it had been real. A household pet, then? She had heard of deranged monarchs who kept lions or tigers like cats. Why not a wolf kept like a dog?

"Bring me my breakfast," she snapped, and the dwarf bowed himself goldenly out.

All avenues of escape seemed closed, yet by day (for it was day, the tawny gloaming of winter) the phenomena of the darkness seemed far removed. Most of their terror had gone with them. With instinctive immature good sense, Lisel acknowledged that no hurt had come to her, that she was indeed being cherished.

She wished she had thought to reprimand the dwarf for his mention of intimate hot water and his presence in her bedroom. Recollections of unseemly novelettes led her to a swift examination of her apparel—unscathed. She rose and stood morosely by the fire, waiting for her breakfast, tapping her foot.

By the hour of noon, Lisel's impatience had reached its zenith with the sun. Of the two, only the sun's zenith was insignificant.

Lisel left the bedroom, flounced along the corridor and came to the stairhead. Eerie memories of the previous night had trouble in remaining with her. Everything seemed to have become rather absurd, but this served only to increase her annoyance. Lisel went down the stair boldly. The fire was lit in the enormous hearth and was blazing cheerfully. Lisel prowled about, gazing at the dubious stained glass, which she now saw did not portray a hunting scene at all, but some pagan subject of men metamorphosing into wolves.

At length a maid appeared. Lisel marched up to her.

"Kindly inform my grandmother that I am awaiting her in the hall." The maid seemed struggling to repress a laugh, but she bobbed a curtsey and darted off. She did not come back, and neither did grandmother.

When a man entered bearing logs for the fire, Lisel said to him, "Put those down and take me at once to the coachman."

The man nodded and gestured her to follow him without a word of acquiescence or disagreement. Lisel, as she let herself be led through the back corridors and by the hub-bub of the huge stone kitchen, was struck by the incongruousness of her actions. No longer afraid, she felt foolish. She was carrying out her "plan" of the night before from sheer pique, nor did she have any greater hope of success. It was more as if some deeply hidden part of herself prompted her to flight, in spite of all resolution, rationality and desire. But it was rather like trying to walk on a numbed foot. She could manage to do it, but without feeling.

The coachhouse and stables bulked gloomily about the courtyard, where the snow had renewed itself in dazzling white drifts. The coachman stood in his black furs beside an iron brazier. One of the blond horses was being shod in an old-fashioned manner, the coachman overseeing the exercise. Seeking to ingratiate herself, Lisel spoke to the coachman in a silky voice.

"I remarked yesterday, how well you controlled the horses when the wolves came after the carriage."

The coachman did not answer, but hearing her voice, the horse sidled a little, rolling its eye at her.

"Suppose," said Lisel to the coachman, "I were to ask you if you would take me back to the city. What would you say?"

Nothing, apparently.

The brazier sizzled and the hammer of the blacksmithing groom smacked the nails home into the horse's hoof. Lisel found the process disconcerting.

"You must understand," she said to the coachman, "my father would give you a great deal of money. He's unwell and wishes me to return. I received word this morning."

The coachman hulked there like a big black bear, and Lisel had the urge to bite him viciously.

"My grandmother," she announced, "would order you to obey me, but she is in bed."

"No, she is not," said the Matriarch at Lisel's back, and Lisel almost screamed. She shot around, and stared at the old woman, who stood about a foot away, imperious in her furs, jewels frostily blistering on her wrists.

"I wish," said Lisel, taking umbrage as her shield, "to go home at once."

"So I gather. But you can't, I regret."

"You mean to keep me prisoner?" blurted Lisel.

Grandmother laughed. The laugh was like fresh ice crackling under a steel skate. "Not at all. The road is snowed under and won't be clear for several days. I'm afraid you'll have to put up with us a while longer."

Lisel, in a turmoil she could not herself altogether fathom, had her attention diverted by the behavior of the horse. It was bristling like a cat, tossing its head, dancing against the rope by which the second groom was holding it.

Anna walked at once out into the yard and began to approach the horse from the front. The horse instantly grew more agitated, kicking up its heels, and neighing croupily. Lisel almost cried an automatic warning, but restrained herself. Let the beldame get a kicking, she deserved it. Rather to Lisel's chagrin, Anna reached the horse without actually having her brains dashed out. She showed not a moment's hesitation or doubt, placing her hand on its long nose, eyeing it with an amused tenderness. She looked very cruel and very indomitable.

"There now," said Anna to the horse, which, fallen quiet and still, yet trembled feverishly. "You know you are used to me. You know you were trained to endure me since you were a foal, as your brothers are sometimes trained to endure fire."

The horse hung its head and shivered, cowed but noble.

Anna left it and strolled back through the snow. She came to Lisel and took her arm.

"I'm afraid," said Anna, guiding them toward the château door, "that they're never entirely at peace when I'm in the vicinity, though they are good horses, and well trained. They have borne me long distances in the carriage."

"Do they fear you because you ill-treat them?" Lisel asked impetuously.

"Oh, not at all. They fear me because to them I smell of wolf."

Lisel bridled.

"Then do you think it wise to keep such a pet in the house?" she flared.

Anna chuckled. It was not necessarily a merry sound.

"That's what you think, is it? What a little dunce you are, Lisel. I am the beast you saw last night, and you had better get accustomed to it. Grandmère is a werewolf."

The return walk through the domestic corridors into the hall was notable for its silence. The dreadful Anna, her grip on the girl's arm unabated, smiled thoughtfully to herself. Lisel was obviously also deliberating inwardly. Her conclusions, however, continued to lean to the deranged rather than the occult. Propitiation suggested itself, as formerly, to be the answer. So, as they entered the hall, casting their cloaks to a servant, Lisel brightly exclaimed:

"A werewolf, Grandmère. How interesting!"

"Dear me," said Anna, "what a child." She seated herself by the fire in one of her tall thrones. Beautiful had appeared. "Bring the liqueur and some biscuits," said Anna. "It's past the hour, but why should we be the slaves of custom?"

Lisel perched on a chair across the hearth, watching Anna guardedly.

"You are the interesting one," Anna now declared. "You look sulky rather than intimidated at being mured up here with one whom you wrongly suppose is dangerously insane. No, *ma chère*, verily I'm not mad, but a transmogrifite. Every evening, once the sun sets, I become a wolf, and duly comport myself as a wolf does."

"You're going to eat me, then," snarled Lisel, irritated out of all attempts to placate.

"Eat you? Hardly necessary. The forest is bursting with game. I won't say I never tasted human meat, but I wouldn't stoop to devouring a blood relation. Enough is enough. Besides, I had the opportunity last night, don't you think, when you swooned away on the stairs not fifty feet from me. Of course, it was almost dawn, and I *had* dined, but to rip out your throat would have been the work only of a moment. Thereafter we might have stored you in the cold larder against a lean winter."

*"How dare you try to frighten me in this way!"* screamed Lisel in a paroxysm of rage.

Beautiful was coming back with a silver tray. On the tray rested a plate of biscuits and a decanter of the finest cut glass containing a golden drink.

"You note, Beautiful," said Madame Anna, "I like this wretched granddaughter of mine. She's very like me."

"Does that dwarf know you are a *werewolf?*" demanded Lisel, with baleful irony.

"Who else lets me in and out at night? But all my servants know, just as my other folk know, in the forest."

"You're disgusting," said Lisel.

"Tut, I shall disinherit you. Don't you want my fortune any more?"

Beautiful set down the tray on a small table between them and began to pour the liqueur, smooth as honey, into two tiny crystal goblets.

Lisel watched. She remembered the nasty dishes of raw meat—part of Anna's game of werewolfery—and the drinking of water, but no wine. Lisel smirked, thinking she had caught the Matriarch out. She kept still and accepted the glass from Beautiful, who, while she remained seated, was a mere inch taller than she.

"I toast you," said Anna, raising her glass to Lisel. "Your health and your joy." She sipped. A strange look came into her strange eyes. "We have," she said, "a brief winter afternoon before us. There is just the time to tell you what you should be told."

"Why bother with me? I'm disinherited."

"Hardly. Taste the liqueur. You will enjoy it."

"I'm surprised that you did, Grandmère."

"Don't be," said Anna with asperity. "This wine is special to this place. We make it from a flower which grows here. A little yellow flower that comes in the spring, or sometimes, even in the winter. There is a difference then, of course. Do you recall the flower of my escutcheon? It is the self-same one."

Lisel sipped the liqueur. She had had a fleeting fancy it might be drugged or tampered with in some way, but both drinks had come from the decanter. Besides, what would be the point? The Matriarch valued an audience. The wine was pleasing, fragrant and, rather than sweet as Lisel had anticipated, tart. The flower which grew in winter was plainly another demented tale.

Relaxed, Lisel leant back in her chair. She gazed at the flames in the wide hearth. Her mad grandmother began to speak to her in a quiet, floating voice, and Lisel saw pictures form in the fire. Pictures of Anna, and of the château, and of darkness itself. . . .

❊ 4

How young Anna looked. She was in her twenties. She wore a scarlet gown and a scarlet cloak lined with pale fur and heavy brocade. It resembled Lisel's cloak but had a different clasp. Snow melted on the shoulders of the cloak, and Anna held her slender hands to the fire on the hearth. Free of the hood, her hair, like marvelously tarnished ivory, was piled on her head, and there was a yellow flower in it. She wore ruby eardrops. She looked just like Lisel, or Lisel as she would become in six years or seven.

Someone called. It was more a roar than a call, as if a great beast came trampling into the château. He was a big man, dark, all darkness, his features hidden in a black beard, black hair—more, in a sort of swirling miasmic cloud, a kind of psychic smoke: Anna's hatred and fear. He bellowed for liquor and a servant came running with a jug and cup. The man, Anna's husband, cuffed the servant aside, grabbing the jug as he did so. He strode to Anna, spun her about, grabbed her face in his hand as he had grabbed the jug. He leaned to her as if to kiss her, but he did not kiss, he merely stared. She had steeled herself not to shrink from him, so much was evident. His eyes, roving over her to find some overt trace of distaste or fright, suddenly found instead the yellow flower. He vented a powerful oath. His paw flung up and wrenched the flower free. He slung it in the fire and spat after it.

"You stupid bitch," he growled at her. "Where did you come on that?"

"It's only a flower."

"Not only a flower. Answer me, where? Or do I strike you?"

"Several of them are growing near the gate, beside the wall; and in the forest. I saw them when I was riding."

The man shouted again for his servant. He told him to take a fellow and go out. They must locate the flowers and burn them.

"Another superstition?" Anna asked. Her husband hit her across the head so she staggered and caught the mantel to steady herself.

"*Yes*," he sneered, "another one. Now come upstairs."

Anna said, "Please excuse me, sir, I am not well today."

He said in a low and smiling voice:

"Do as I say, or you'll be worse."

The fire flared on the swirl of her bloody cloak as she moved to obey him.

And the image changed. There was a bedroom, fluttering with lamplight. Anna was perhaps thirty-five or -six, but she looked older. She lay in bed, soaked in sweat, uttering hoarse low cries or sometimes preventing herself from crying. She was in labor. The child was difficult. There were other women about the bed. One muttered to her neighbor that it was beyond her how the master had ever come to sire a child, since he got his pleasure another way, and the poor lady's body gave evidence of how. Then Anna screamed. Someone bent over her. There was a peculiar muttering among the women, as if they attended at some holy ceremony.

And another image came. Anna was seated in a shawl of gilded hair. She held a baby on her lap and was playing with it in an intense, quite silent way. As her hair shifted: traceries became momentarily visible over her bare shoulders and arms, horrible traceries left by a lash.

"Let me take the child," said a voice, and one of the women from the former scene appeared. She lifted the baby from Anna's lap, and Anna let the baby go, only holding her arms and hands in such a way that she touched it to the last second. The other woman was older than Anna, a peasant dressed smartly for service in the château. "You mustn't fret yourself," she said.

"But I can't suckle her," said Anna. "I wanted to."

"There's another can do that," said the woman. "Rest yourself. Rest while he is away." When she said "he" there could be no doubt of the one to whom she referred.

"Then, I'll rest," said Anna. She reclined on pillows, wincing slightly as her back made contact with the fine soft silk. "Tell me about the flowers again. The yellow flowers."

The woman showed her teeth as she rocked the baby. For an instant her face was just like a wolf's.

"You're not afraid," she said. "*He* is. But it's always been here. The wolf-magic. It's part of the Wolfland. Wherever wolves have been, you can find the wolf-magic. Somewhere. In a stream or a cave, or in a patch of ground. The château has it. That's why the flowers grow here. Yes, I'll tell you, then, it's simple. If any eat the flowers, then they receive the gift. It comes from the spirit, the wolfwoman, or maybe she's a goddess, an old goddess left over from the beginning of things, before Christ came to save us all. She has the head of a wolf and yellow hair. You swallow the flowers, and you call her, and she comes, and she gives it you. And then it's yours, till you die."

"And then what? Payment?" said Anna dreamily. "Hell?"

"Maybe."

The image faded gently. Suddenly there was another which was not gentle, a parody of the scene before. Staring light showed the bedchamber. The man, his shadow-face smoldering, clutched Anna's baby in his hands. The baby shrieked; he swung it to and fro as if to smash it on some handy piece of furniture. Anna stood in her nightdress. She held a whip out to him.

"Beat me," she said. "Please beat me. I want you to. Put down the child and beat me. It would be so easy to hurt her, and so soon over, she's so small. But I'm stronger. You can hurt me much more. See how vulnerable and afraid I am. Beat *me*."

Then, with a snarl he tossed the child onto the bed where it lay wailing. He took the whip and caught Anna by her pale hair—

There was snow blowing like torn paper, everywhere. In the midst of it a servant woman, and a child perhaps a year old with soft dark hair, were seated in a carriage. Anna looked at them, then stepped away. A door slammed, horses broke into a gallop. Anna remained standing in the snow storm.

No picture came. A man's voice thundered: "Where? Where did you send the thing? It's mine, I sired it. My property. *Where?*"

But the only reply he got was moans of pain. She would not tell him, and did not. He nearly killed her that time.

Now it is night, but a black night bleached with whiteness, for a full moon is up above the tops of the winter pines.

Anna is poised, motionless, in a glade of the wild northern forest. She wears the scarlet cloak, but the moon has drained its color. The snow sparkles, the trees are umbrellas of diamond, somber only

at their undersides. The moon slaps the world with light. Anna has
been singing, or chanting something, and though it can no longer be heard, the dew of it lies heavy over the ground. Something is drawn there, too, in the snow, a circle, and another shape inside it. A fire has been kindled nearby, but now it has burned low and has a curious bluish tinge to it. All at once a wind begins to come through the forest. But it is not wind, not even storm. It is the soul of the forest, the spirit of the Wolfland.

Anna goes to her knees. She is afraid, but it is a new fear, an exulting fear. The stalks of the flowers whose heads she has eaten lie under her knees, and she raises her face like a dish to the moonlight.

The pines groan. They bend. Branches snap and snow showers down from them. The creature of the forest is coming, nearer and nearer. It is a huge single wing, or an enormous engine. Everything breaks and sways before it, even the moonlight, and darkness fills the glade. And out of the darkness Something whirls. It is difficult to see, to be sure—a glimpse of gold, two eyes like dots of lava seven feet in the air, a grey jaw, hung breasts which have hair growing on them, the long hand which is not a hand, lifting—and then every wolf in the forest seems to give tongue, and the darkness ebbs away.

Anna lies on her face. She is weeping. With terror. With—

It is night again, and the man of the house is coming home.

He swaggers, full of local beer and eager to get to his wife. He was angry, a short while since, because his carriage, which was to have waited for him outside the inn, had mysteriously vanished. There will be men to curse and brutalize in the courtyard before he goes up to his beloved Anna, a prelude to his final act with her. He finds her a challenge, his wife. She seems able to withstand so much, looking at him proudly with horror in her eyes. It would bore him to break her. He likes the fact he cannot, or thinks he does. And tonight he has some good news. One of the paid men has brought word of their child. She is discovered at last. She can be brought home to the château to her father's care. She is two years old now. Strong and healthy. Yes, good news indeed.

They had known better in the village than to tell him he should beware on the forest track. He is not anxious about wolves, the distance being less than a mile, and he has his pistol. Besides, he organized a wolf hunt last month and cleared quite a few of the brutes off his land. The area about the château has been silent for many nights. Even Anna went walking without a servant—though he had not approved of that and had taught her a lesson. (Sometimes it occurs to him that she enjoys his lessons as much as he enjoys delivering them, for she seems constantly to seek out new ways to vex him.)

He is about a quarter of a mile from the château now, and here a small clearing opens off on both sides of the track. It is the night after the full moon, and her disc, an almost perfect round, glares down on the clearing from the pine tops. Anna's husband dislikes the clearing. He had forgotten he would have to go through it, for generally he is mounted or in the carriage when he passes the spot. There is some old superstition about the place. He hates it, just as he hates the stinking yellow flowers that grew in it before he burned them out. Why does he hate them? The woman who nursed him told him something and it frightened him, long ago. Well, no matter. He walks more quickly.

How quiet it is, how still. The whole night like a pane of black-white silence. He can hardly hear his own noisy footfalls. There is a disturbance in the snow, over there, a mark like a circle.

Then he realizes something is behind him. He is not sure how he realizes, for it is quite soundless. He stops, and turns, and sees a great and ghostly wolf a few feet from him on the track.

In a way, it is almost a relief to see the wolf. It is alone, and it is a natural thing. Somehow he had half expected something unnatural. He draws his pistol, readies it, points it at the wolf. He is a fine shot. He already visualizes lugging the bloody carcass, a trophy, into the house. He pulls the trigger.

A barren click. He is surprised. He tries again. Another click. It comes to him that his servant has emptied the chamber of bullets. He sees a vision of the park gates a quarter of a mile away, and he turns immediately and runs toward them.

Ten seconds later a warm and living weight crashes against his back, and he falls screaming, screaming before the pain even begins. When the pain does begin, he is unable to scream for very long, but he does his best. The final thing he sees through the haze of his own blood, which has splashed up into his eyes, and the tears of agony and the enclosing of a most atrocious death, are the eyes of the wolf, gleaming coolly back at him. He knows they are the eyes of Anna. And that it is Anna who then tears out his throat.

The small crystal goblet slipped out of Lisel's hand, empty, and broke on the floor. Lisel started. Dazed, she looked away from the fire, to Anna the Matriarch.

Had Lisel been asleep and dreaming? What an unpleasant dream.

Or had it been so unpleasant? Lisel became aware her teeth were clenched in spiteful gladness, as if on a bone. If Anna had told her the truth, that man—that *thing*—had deserved it all. To be betrayed by his servants, and by his wife, and to perish in the fangs of a wolf. A werewolf.

Grandmother and granddaughter confronted each other a second, with identical expressions of smiling and abstracted malice. Lisel suddenly flushed, smoothed her face, and looked down. There had been something in the drink after all.

"I don't think this at all nice," said Lisel.

"Nice isn't the word," Anna agreed. Beautiful reclined at her feet, and she stroked his hair. Across the big room, the stained-glass window was thickening richly to opacity. The sun must be near to going down.

"*If* it's the truth," said Lisel primly, "you will go to Hell."

"Oh? Don't you think me justified? He'd have killed your mother at the very least. *You* would never have been born."

Lisel reviewed this hypothetical omission. It carried some weight.

"You should have appealed for help."

"To whom? The marriage vow is a chain that may not be broken. If I had left him, he would have traced me, as he did the child. No law supports a wife. I could only kill him."

"I don't believe you killed him as you say you did."

"Don't you, m'mselle? Well, never mind. Once the sun has set, you'll see it happen before your eyes." Lisel stared and opened her mouth to remonstrate. Anna added gently: "And, I am afraid, not to myself alone."

Aside from all reasoning and the training of a short lifetime, Lisel felt the stranglehold of pure terror fasten on her. She rose and squealed: "What do you mean?"

"I mean," said Anna, "that the liqueur you drank is made from the same yellow flowers I ate to give me the power of transmogrification. I mean that the wolf-magic, once invoked, becomes hereditary, yet dormant. I mean that what the goddess of the Wolfland conveys must indeed be paid for at the hour of death—unless another will take up the gift."

Lisel, not properly understanding, not properly believing, began to shriek wildly. Anna came to her feet. She crossed to Lisel and shook the shrieks out of her, and when she was dumb, thrust her back in the chair.

"Now sit, fool, and be quiet. I've put nothing on you that was not already yours. Look in a mirror. Look at your hair and your eyes and your beautiful teeth. Haven't you always preferred the night to the day, staying up till the morning, lying abed till noon? Don't you love the cold forest? Doesn't the howl of the wolf thrill you through with fearful delight? And why else should the Wolfland accord you an escort, a pack of wolves running by you on the road. Do you think you'd have survived if you'd not been one of their kind, too?"

Lisel wept, stamping her foot. She could not have said at all what she felt. She tried to think of her father and the ballrooms of the city. She tried to consider if she credited magic.

"Now listen to me," snapped Anna, and Lisel muted her sobs just enough to catch the words. "Tonight is full moon, and the anniversary of that night, years ago, when I made my pact with the wolf goddess of the north. I have good cause to suspect I shan't live out this year. Therefore, tonight is the last chance I have to render you in my place into her charge. That frees me from her, do you see? Once you have swallowed the flowers, once she has acknowledged you, you belong to her. At death, I escape her sovereignty, which would otherwise bind me forever to the earth in wolf form, phantom form. A bargain: you save me. But you too can make your escape, when the time comes. Bear a child. You will be mistress here. You can command any man to serve you, and you're tolerable enough the service won't be unwilling. My own child, your mother, was not like me at all. I could not bring her to live with me, once I had the power. I was troubled as to how I should wean her to it. But she died, and in you I saw the mark from the first hour. You are fit to take my place. Your child can take yours."

"You're hateful!" shrieked Lisel. She had the wish to laugh.

But someone was flinging open the doors of the hall. The cinnamon light streamed through and fell into the fire and faded it. Another fire, like antique bronze, was quenching itself among the pines. The dying of the sun.

Anna moved toward the doors and straight out onto the snow. She stood a moment, tall and amazing on the peculiar sky. She seemed a figment of the land itself, and maybe she was.

"Come!" she barked. Then turned and walked away across the park.

All the servants seemed to have gathered like bats in the hall. They were silent, but they looked at Lisel. Her heart struck her over and over. She did not know what she felt or if she believed.

Then a wolf sang in the forest. She lifted her head. She suddenly
knew frost and running and black stillness, and a platinum moon,
red feasts and wild hymnings, lovers with quicksilver eyes and the
race of the ice wind and stars smashed under the hard soles of her
four feet. A huge white ballroom opened before her, and the champagne of the air filled her mouth.

Beautiful had knelt and was kissing the hem of her red cloak.
She patted his head absently, and the gathering of the servants
sighed.

Presumably, as Anna's heiress, she might be expected to live on
in the forest, in the château which would be hers. She could even
visit the city, providing she was home by sunset.

The wolf howled again, filling her veins with light, raising the
hair along her scalp.

Lisel tossed her head. Of course, it was all a lot of nonsense.

She hastened out through the doors and over the winter park
and followed her grandmother away into the Wolfland.

# ❉ 36 ❉

## Not So
## Little Red
## Riding Hood

## By Anne Sharpe

## (1985)

IT WAS HER MOTHER, not Scarlet, who was in the habit of saying that in November, night arrived in one sudden bound to land on your shoulders and overpower you with blackness. Women in particular were vulnerable then.

But Scarlet was not fanciful or concerned that dusk had fallen. As her strides opened out her red cape, she did not pull it closer. Treading crisply on unnoticed twigs, her eyes followed the rooks' ungainly flop into high nests on the tops of oak trees. Each bird harshly squawked out a place for itself before settling down fussily for the night. Scarlet smiled. The laden basket under her arm did not drag her down. It helped her to pace her step as the wide sway-ing umbrella of the fir trees gradually welcomed her to itself.

A shadow fell. The wolf whistle was so soft and low that she took it for yet another innocent sylvan preparation for rest. She could not join in, even had she been invited. She had to hurry on, so she promptly ignored and forgot about it. But he, the man in the per-fectly cut grey suit, would most definitely not be ignored. He stepped out fully and confidently into her path. He leant against the tallest fir, folded his arms and smiled, knowing at least that his front teeth were perfect. Then he wedged his right foot in front of her, in line with the knotted tree root, casually, slowly, as if his mind were elsewhere. The *Irish Times* under his elbow carefully brushed her waist. At that, Scarlet skipped abruptly to the side to pass.

He allowed his eyes to look hurt but not puzzled. They would have been puzzled if this had not happened before. But this wasn't the first time that a girl in a brilliant scarlet cape had led him on. Sometimes it seemed to him that every day of his life women paraded briefly in front of him before letting him down with a bang. At least, to give himself due credit, he had not given up on the entire sex yet.

But Scarlet's peace of mind was now disturbed. The stride had broken into an undignified scurry through the now unwelcoming wood. The wood enclosed her within an embrace of its own. Her breath tightened her body as with a lace. She heard bare branches smack like whips above her head and watched the woody fragments flutter slowly to the ground.

The man in grey took some time to decide the next step. It was that he should become a natural spirit of the wood, back to nature and all that. So he became a spirited animal in its true element swinging down from the branch of a large oak in her path. Scarlet smelt the faint scent of Brut first before she saw the display. But then, standing and smiling, he did not want her to think that he was merely animal. In fact, he went to some pains to dispel any impression of physical over-exuberance. He made quite a show of dusting down his jacket and straightening his collar. He flicked back his tinted hair with carefully manicured nails. Then he busied himself to make an even smaller knot of his tie, a hard little obstacle to everything, and nothing. He was ready. Matters were taking their course.

"I hope I didn't startle you."

Scarlet was still recovering from the shock of seeing a large creature emerge from an oak. She first cast around for her fiercest curse but then settled for irony instead.

"Of course not. What would make you think such a thing?"

He was a little disappointed but soon cheered up.

"Tell you what," he said, "you look a bit tired and uptight with all that running in the dark. What's a nice girl like you doing in a place like this anyway? How about a bite to eat and then a good film."

He paused to give himself time to smile ingratiatingly at her, but she had gone. Now she was just another fleck in the expansive darkness—not a word of thanks, not even a smile. He raged. He wanted to uproot the tree from which he had swung and hurl it at the sky. He wanted not just the wood but the whole universe to

*Les Contes de Perrault,* **Paris, 1928. Illustrator Lucien Boucher.**

know how he had been abused. As a gentleman, he had offered a courteous invitation, but as the card passed from his hand to hers, she had crumbled it to shreds and then simply vanished.

He brought himself slowly up to his full height and threw his head back. But he saw nothing of Scarlet or the wood, nor did he hear the rooks cawing. He ran as he had never run before, as if he were used to fourfootedness. With an unerring instinct, he headed straight for the grandmother's cottage and slunk behind a nearby shrub to wait.

Scarlet was herself again. Striding ahead with the laden basket, she was planning the meal ahead and humming over a new recipe for lentil soup. She had clearly forgotten him already, as if he had been one of life's daily irritants. Black rage bit further into his throat. He decided at once that he would make sure that she never forgot him. His body became sheeted steel from which his limbs extended as grappling hooks. He was the last invincible warrior with the ultimate weapon. As he began to grapple, he smiled.

Scarlet said nothing but looked slightly irritated. The task was almost too easy for a karate black belt. But casually and in a leisurely manner, she moved forward to deal him an eye gouge first and then a kick to the groin. Before she could reach for the nerve center, the solar plexus, it was all over. He had crumbled to pieces and was whimpering for mercy. She flicked him out of her way with her boot and he was grateful for the disdainful, disappearing step.

Scarlet proceeded up her grandmother's path and the man heard the door open to the question "Had a good day, dear?" and saw Scarlet shrug in answer. When he was able he loped for the lights of the nearest pub, deciding to drown the memory of Scarlet in his pints. It was best for both of them that way really.

# ❊ 37 ❊

## *The Waiting Wolf*

### *By Gwen Strauss*

### (1990)

F IRST, I SAW HER FEET—
beneath a red pointed cloak
head bent forward
parting the woods,
one foot placed straight
in front of the other.

Then, came her scent.
I was meant to stalk her
smooth, not a twig snaps.
It is the only way I know;
I showed her flowers—
white dead-nettle, nightshade,
devil's bit, wood anemone.

I might not have gone further,
but then nothing ever remains
innocent in the woods.

When she told me about Grandmother,
I sickened. She placed herself on my path,
practically spilling her basket of breads and jams.

**Perrault's Complete Fairy Tales,** New York: Dodd, Mead & Co. Illustrator W. Heath Robinson.

Waiting in this old lady's ruffled bed,
I am all calculation. I have gone this far—
dressed in Grandmother's lace panties,
flannel nightgown and cap,
puffs of breath beneath the sheet
lift and fall. I can see my heart tick.
Slightly. Slightly.

These are small lies for a wolf,
but strangely heavy in my belly like stones.
I will forget them as soon as I have her,
still, at this moment I do not like myself.

When she crawls into Grandma's bed,
will she pull me close, thinking:
*This is my grandmother whom I love?*

She will have the youngest skin
I have ever touched, her fingers unfurling
like fiddle heads in spring.

My matted fur will smell to her of forest
moss at night. She'll wonder about my ears,
large, pointed, soft as felt,
my eyes red as her cloak,
my leather nose on her belly.

But perhaps she has known who I am since the first,
since we took the other path
through the woods.

# ❃ 38 ❃

## *Roja and Leopold*
## *By Sally Miller Gearhart*
## (1990)

O NCE UPON A TIME, in a bedroom community of Silicon Valley, there lived a career woman who was just beginning to make her way in the business world. Through her meditation, her chanting, her networking, and her hard work, she had manifested for herself many friends, many acquaintances, and scores of contacts. Her name was Constance.

Constance no longer had a husband, for he had deserted her years before when she was more vulnerable and less murderous. Her job paid better every year. Her social life was that of a very swinging single. Every day she felt herself growing wiser, more experienced. Her learning curve was steep, her savvy increased in direct proportion to her ambition, and she was stashing away every other paycheck in flexible mutual funds.

However, Constance did have two crosses to bear. One was her daughter, a strong, independent little girl whom we shall call Roja. Roja was a cross to her mother because a) Constance had never wanted children—she had borne Roja because her sensitivity group had helped her uncover deeply buried (and unfortunately very temporary) maternal feelings—and b) Roja didn't give a tinker's damn for Constance either, wishing only to spend her time with her girlfriend or her grandmother, both of whom could think laterally and had alternative views of everything, from consumerism and politics to lifestyle and religion.

331

Constance's second cross was Roja's grandmother, known as Geraldine to all her bridge and skydiving partners and to the small band of subversive activists who met weekly to plot the liberation of abused nonhuman animals. Geraldine was a burden to Constance because she was dying of cancer. Geraldine knew she was dying, had said her good-byes to the world, and was ready to go. Constance, however, felt it her duty to consult with doctors, who kept coming up with miraculous new life-prolonging drugs and surgical techniques.

All Geraldine wanted to do was die, preferably at the hands of a large ferocious tiger so the animal nations could get back some of the meat they had been providing humans for so long. And all Constance wanted to do was keep her conscience clear so nobody could say she hadn't tried everything to save her mother. All the doctors wanted to do was practice more heroic measures on Geraldine's body.

So, in her tiny house in the great forest that bordered her daughter's condominium, Geraldine lived on, long past her desire to do so. She was under the care of a top-of-the-line robot nurse whose switch she managed to keep on "Off" most of the time and whose mechanism she was constantly manipulating in the vain effort to heist some barbiturates or commandeer a razor blade.

But Geraldine had never been simply a single-issue activist, nor was she now, well into her nineties. And so, though she constantly scoured the premises for the available means of suicide, she also searched diligently for clues to a great universal healing that she was convinced lurked just beneath the surface of every violet petal, just under the reflection on the back of every puddle in the sun, just between the cracks in the wooden floor, or in the interstices between the spider's web and the dust motes that it sifted. She called the object of her search the "Fallen Threads," or whatever-it-was-that-had-once-held-things-together-in-a-kind-of-empathy-or-mutual-understanding.

She had dreams about broken paths, dammed-up or disconnected rivers, chain ends lying limp for lack of a link, gold rings with a segment of themselves removed, but most of all she dreamed of tattered strings of cotton and wool that swayed in the breeze and reached across an abyss in the effort to weave together again with partner wisps that were swaying and reaching from the other side. Sometimes they touched, sometimes even strained beyond to fold themselves together in the genesis of a slender strand, only to be torn apart once more.

Sometimes, in her waking hours, Geraldine could feel the presence of the lost Threads. Sometimes when she breathed with the
frog or swooped with the housefly, she seemed to fall into a pocket
of their presence, where she was surrounded by them and they
called to her. "Here we are! Just over here!" Her eyes could never
move fast enough, and her touch was always too clumsy. She could
not catch them, and when she tried, she was catapulted out of the
pocket. The best she could do was listen.

And then she could feel the Threads at work, reaching and
binding, twining and winding, almost mending a break, almost
reweaving a strand, then . . . Snap! They were gone, broken again.
Forced apart by some coolness, some distancing, an interference, a
consciousness somewhere that stepped between the doer and the
done-to, between the tool and that which was to be changed by
the tool.

So Geraldine kept looking for the Threads, opening herself to
the creatures in whose presence those Threads seemed to dwell,
trying to learn to be very still and listen. She listened while the
Threads struggled to reweave themselves into a tiny fragment of a
tapestry severed from itself.

Thus you could see the old woman most any time of day or night,
standing stock still by her window. You'd never guess she was slipping inside the skin of a wandering vole or a tall-eared jackbunny.
Or sometimes she would be examining the snail slime on a holly-
hock bloom or squatting under the dewdrops on the pea vines or
scrutinizing splinters of starlight and muttering, "I wonder if that's
them?" The only one who ever helped her look for the Threads was
her buddy, Roja, who would visit every week or so. The two of
them, listening together, could sit smack-dab in the middle of a
sow bug and take up no room at all. And there they could feel the
Threads at work, feel them reaching and weaving. She was a good
one, that girl. Better than her mother. Nature's always best skipping a generation, Geraldine decided.

Geraldine's daughter Constance, to her credit, was never hypo-
critical about the vast distances that separated her from her mother. Instead of visiting Geraldine herself, she had early on adopted
the custom of sending gifts of fancy (and some pretty degenerate)
edibles to the old woman. Every Sunday she packed up a wonderful
basket of finger foods, breads, chips, dips, nuts, Hostess Ho-Hos
and other sweets, all to be carried through the woods by Roja. This
ritual served two purposes for Constance: Grandma Geraldine got a

gift of filial affection, and the kid was out of her hair for a whole night. Constance usually went to a singles' bar and cruised.

Roja loved to visit her grandmother. The hike itself was a healthy one, filled with flowers, trees, birds, and breezes that often conspired to delay her until sunset. Further, she loved Geraldine herself, the songs they sang, the Threads they searched for, the games they played with n-dimensional analysis and word jumbles and the *Wall Street Journal*. Then, after tucking in the old woman for a sweet sleep, she would skip her way farther into the forest to stay overnight with her friend and lover, Ermendina, who lived and worked and had her being just a bit beyond Grandma's house.

One Sunday at high noon, burdened only by her jam-packed, food-filled, North Face rucksack, Roja skipped her way to Grandma's house, humming one of those heavy-metal ditties and thinking about her girlfriend, Ermendina, who was working day shift at the hospital. She wasn't paying much attention to the path and was surprised when a large figure suddenly loomed before her.

Now this large figure was none other than Leopold the Wolf, actually the most unhappy wolf in the whole consolidated pack that roamed the streets and parks of Silicon Valley. Leopold was unhappy because he was a closet vegetarian. The thought of devouring flesh repelled him.

Fully aware that the unexamined life is not worth living, he had long ago conducted a careful self-analysis of his family constellation and his early puphood in the effort to locate the cause of his abnormality. He now knew that his vegetarianism stemmed from the circumstances of his first home in the north where he, the last-weaned of his sisters and brothers, had been orphaned to the care of one of the tundra's most highly sophisticated wolf packs, a pack that had eschewed the nomadic life and the insecurity of the immediate kill and opted instead for a fixed pastoral society. In this case, the pack had rapidly reached that dangerous stage in any society's development when it needs must deal with the storage of surplus flesh.

And Leopold had seen for himself the atrocities of those factory farms. Though he had been but a pup, he had been sickened by the sight of those captured and imprisoned animals, and particularly the human animals, all being fattened for the pack's food. He was particularly sensitive to the humans because he had had one for a pet until it was slaughtered at the age of two. In fact, the only thing worse for him than the sight of the humans so cramped together there in the enlarged warrens, unable to move, had been his witness of their ultimate slaughter.

He was deeply troubled by his internal contradictions. He believed in Nature, Red In Tooth And Claw, believed in the necessity of the chase and the hunt, believed these things to be inherent in wolf being. But the pack's cruelty in this mass imprisonment and slaughter of beings so much like himself seemed an unnecessary indignity, an abrogation of rights, an atrocity. He recalled vividly how in protest he nearly starved until he discovered that he could be nourished, as many other animals were, by prairie grass and meadow fronds.

Secretly, he was glad when that renegade pastoral society had failed and he and friends had made their perilous way south. But Leopold never forgot his months on the tundra, and the memory of those months rendered even hunting impossible for him. He had lived since then as an impostor, under a thin veil of hypocrisy. But at least, he reminded himself, his honor was untarnished, his escutcheon unblemished, for in his heart he was at peace as a vegetarian. He had made his pact with the nations of the Earthfreed, swearing never to take the lives of their members, and with the nations of the Earthbound, thanking them for their provision of his sustenance and always revering them.

Still, Leopold the Wolf had to spend extensive time foraging for food and learning to grind herbs and berries between his large canine teeth. He spent, it seemed, the remainder of his time concealing his abnormality from other wolves, becoming a master storyteller over the years as he deflected inquiries about where he had been and why he never appeared to have any fresh blood dripping from his muzzle.

On this sunny day in the Silicon Valley Forest, his secret was perilously close to being discovered by his pack, because by this time they knew him well, and since they were animals of long and appreciative memory, they recalled his every variation on each of the thirty-seven basic plots. He was, very simply, running out of stories. Soon he would have to show evidence that he had Made A Kill. Soon he would have to forsake the fields and gardens where bloomed those tasty essences and behave as a real wolf should, preying upon and devouring, for instance, little girls who skipped alone through the forest.

"And where are you going?" he growled in his deepest voice to Roja.

*Little Red Riding Hood,* **New York: Platt & Munk, ca. 1925. Illustrator Eulalie.**

"Oh!" she said, frightened. "I'm just on my way to Grandma's house to bring her food."

"How wonderfully quaint," breathed Leopold, measuring Roja's throat from a three-quarter angle as he had seen his fellows do. "And, pray, my pretty, where does your grandmother live?" he added, nagged by the suspicion that he was uttering some oft-spoken script.

Roja suddenly felt as if she had fallen into a pocket of Threads. She was somehow in kinship with this great beast, though not identical with him as she and Geraldine sometimes were with the sow bugs. She wanted to fall upon him and stroke him.

Instead she tried to listen to the Threads even as she answered, "Only a mile or so over yonder." Then, because the feeling escaped her and because she felt socially inept, she blurted, "Want to play gin?" She extended the well-worn deck of cards she and Ermendina always carried to music festivals.

Leopold was taken off guard by her offer, and to center himself he did a quick energy-run, concentrating on the yellow chakra. Roja had spread out her hooded cape on the soft earth and was cutting for deal. She pushed a Ho-Ho toward him.

Leopold struggled to take charge of the situation. "No. I don't do gin," he said. "And I thought you were taking that food to your grandmother."

"I am, but she won't care if we eat it. She's dying. Or trying to. If she can keep them from reconnecting her tubes, she thinks she can starve by Solstice."

"Really," said Leopold. He sat tailor-fashion beside the girl, suddenly more interested than ever in pursuing this fortunate encounter. "Tell me about your grandmother," he said, taking a giant swig from the Pepsi Roja offered him.

"Well, I love the old lady a lot." Roja said, munching on chilled beansprouts. "But I wish she could die."

"You want your grandmother to die?" Leopold asked, shocked.

"Ummmmm. She's longing for it and it just won't happen. I'd miss her, of course, but I'd be very happy for her."

And so it went. For the better part of the afternoon, the two strangers shared stories about their families and friends, their hopes and dreams, their self-hatred and their fears, though Leopold resisted telling her of his greatest shame. He revealed instead that he was a seventeenth-century buff, and Roja played some ancient ballads for him on her harmonica. He sang in a soft baritone that charmed not only Roja but the juncos and cardinals as well.

When the sun dropped into late afternoon, Leopold realized he must get on with the task of Making A Kill. And certainly this little girl could not qualify as A Kill. He felt he had established too much connection with her. Perhaps he was even feeling the presence of the Threads she had told him about. Besides, as she talked, a plan had begun to evolve in his mind, a plan so audacious he felt sure he could never carry it off. And yet, he was eager to dare its accomplishment.

He said good-bye to her and assured her they could meet again the next Sunday, though he secretly knew he would be seeing her much sooner than that. He was finding himself quite reluctant to part from her, for they had struck a warm and immediate friendship. His paw touched her hand in a moment of interspecies understanding, and they went their separate ways.

"Friendship, friendship, just a wonderful blendship," sang Roja, as she skipped through the woods with the remnants of her gifts to Grandma. "Reach out and touch someone," sang the wolf, as he raced down the ravine and over the shortcut to Geraldine's house.

Leopold sped straight to Geraldine's bedside where he found her in deep meditation trying unsuccessfully to convince her tenacious heart that it was time to blow this popsicle shop. When he explained that he had come to liberate her from this Vale of Sorrow, Geraldine flung her arms around him and, momentarily confused about her identity, licked his face and panted. The Threads were very close by in that moment. The Threads were, in fact, in an apoplexy of touching and weaving.

Thus the two ruffians schemed together, speedily and gleefully, about how he, Leopold, could ease her, Geraldine, into oblivion and how she, Geraldine, could help him, Leopold, look like a blood-drenched carnivore. They decided that Leopold would pick one of those terrifying woman-in-danger plots that Hitchcock was so good at, condense it for this special occasion, and simply scare Geraldine to death—or exhaust her—with his rendition of it.

"But you got to get my blood now, Sonny, 'cause they tell me it don't flow after you go."

Gentle Leopold was horrified. He shuddered and grew pale. "Now? Now, before—"

"Druantia, deliver me from Sensitive Males!" grumped the old woman. "Now just swipe that syringe from Bessie Bluecross over there," she said, pointing to the inert robot, "and you can drain my venous line into that special tube yonder. 'Twon't hurt me a bit."

It was at that moment that the whole enterprise almost floundered, for Leopold, as we know, had no stomach for blood. But finally, with his hand over his eyes and peeping between claws only enough to get the job done, he did as Geraldine directed. To his undying amazement, the old woman smiled dreamily all the while.

"Take all you need," she urged. "In fact, take a little extra for another day." She began humming a Billie Holiday classic. "This is not a Peak Experience, but it's sure better than I thought it would be."

Leopold triumphed. With blood a-plenty at his disposal, he managed to gather himself together and settled himself on the bed, making as much of a lap as he could for the old woman to sit upon. He wrapped his furry arms about her and rocked her forward and back, around and around, while he spun out an old-fashioned tale of suspense and terror.

As he talked, she found herself more and more aware of the Threads, of their presence below and above her, around and over her. And he did indeed tell a good story, Geraldine decided.

"My friend Lollie would love that part," she murmured, "the part about how the crone decides to take karate." She imagined herself in a crisp white gi with her black belt modestly circling her waist.

"Yes," crooned Leopold, allowing that cue to point his narrative down an unexpected path. "She stayed often at the dojo, even after others had gone home, working in front of the mirror, shaping her ki-flow into whatever weapon she willed it to be. On this particular night, she deliberately planned to stay late because she was part of a cunning trap that the Shirley Temple Gang was setting for the Wrinkle Killer, the madman who had terrorized them and the city for months now, isolating and murdering old women. This might be the evening when he would fall for their bait. She was ready."

The wolf's voice took on an ominously normal quality. What little blood still rode through Geraldine's veins was chilled to a snail's pace. "It was very late that night," he was saying, "when she went back for one last kata and forty final first-form kicks. Her teacher had called to her as she left, 'Door is locked, Gerry!' and she had called back, 'Thanks!' And now the dojo was quiet."

Geraldine stirred slightly in the arms of the wolf. Her eyes were closed, her heart pumping slow but still strongly. She was filled with an enormous sense of well-being even as she thrilled to the coming of the inevitable. Leopold spoke now sotto voce, barely above a tense whisper. "As she made her precise recovery from her twelfth kick, she thought she caught a flash of movement in the far corner of the wide mirror. . . . "

Geraldine's heart sped a little faster. Leopold continued.

"There? There it was again! She disciplined herself to continue the exercise, showing no trace of having noticed. As she extended ki through her high foot she allowed herself a glance at the corner of the mirror. By the door of the dojo, behind her and far to the left, was a long deep shadow that should not have been there. She swallowed and inhaled, pushing protective ki out into her aura."

In Leopold's arms, Geraldine clenched her upright fists and positioned them perpendicular to her body. The wolf's voice grew tense. "She returned her clenched fists to her alert posture and emitted a controlled ki-ay as she delivered her next kick. The shadow was still there, unmoving. When she executed her thirty-fifth kick, she saw that it had disappeared, presumably into the darkened change-room area. 'Be ready, girls!' she muttered toward Mamie Carter and the band of old women that she hoped were waiting in the basement, 'I think we've got our man.'"

Geraldine's heart was pounding now. "What a way to go!" she thought. "Like a hero!" The Threads were right there with her, weaving themselves together with the rhythm of her heart. Her chest rose high and fell low, over and over again as she rested in the embrace of the master raconteur.

He was telling now of the moment in the dressing room when the woman turned, and the Wrinkle Killer dodged behind a stack of mats. Then, of the moment when she let him know she knew he was pursuing her. The swift rush for the stairs, the running downward, downward, three flights, four flights, down to the first floor and on toward the basement.

"She heard the door above her slam and at that same moment the stairwell was plunged into blackness. She froze. There was no sound, only her own rapid breathing. She pulled in her ki, forcing herself to breathe steadily. Where was he? Was he coming silently through the darkness? Was he only inches away? Then she heard it, the slow shuffle. Once. Twice. High above her. Moving toward her, faster now with his increasingly more certain footing."

Geraldine, tense in Leopold's arms, gasped and emitted a soft cry. She was suddenly aware that she could no longer hear Leopold's words, that she was hearing now the sounds, feeling now the textures, that were in his mind. If there had been light in the stairwell, she would be seeing the pictures in his mind.

The dark figure was chasing her now, her, Geraldine, in a white gi with a black belt, chasing her, Geraldine, down the stairs from the dojo toward the cellar. She stood there on the lightless landing, drawing him toward her, willing him to scuttle faster and faster down the cement steps to where she waited.

She was ready. But not ready enough. She felt rather than saw his leap from the landing just above her, into the air. She lifted her hands in a block, but he landed full-weight upon her, knocking her backward and down the last flight of stairs. A knife-like pain shot through her arm. She forced her knee into a crevice between their bodies and flung him over her head.

Before she was erect on her knees to defend, she took his foot full under her jaw and went reeling against the wall. His fist followed her, lifting her upright as it plunged deep into her nose and cheek. Her head was full of agonizing light. She could hardly breathe, and the thunder of the blood in her ears drowned out her scream. But she had his wrist now at a control angle. He winced. He would be completely at her mercy and literally on his knees the second she chose to put the torque to that flabby wrist joint. She grinned in the darkness, enjoying his grunts and wheezes. She knew his strength, knew her one good hand with that simple wrist torque was all that stood between her and her certain death.

And that reminded her.

She waited until she heard the shouts of the Shirley Temple Gang and the burst of ancient energy that flooded through the basement door. Then she calmly dropped the man's hand and deposited him in the hands of the old women. She hoped he could see her enigmatic smile. She lay back on a thick blanket of Threads.

"Thank you, Leopold!" she whispered and drew her last breath.

Leopold felt the frail bundle that he held in his arms contract into a suddenly closer embrace. He held her close, riding with her on the cradle of Threads. He waited for a long moment. Then he sighed and reverently carried her from the bed to the closet.

Compelled either by the desire to tease Roja, his new-found friend, or by that unarticulable sense of grim mythos he had felt off and on all day, he donned Geraldine's gown and her bedcap and crawled into her bed, feigning as best he could the demeanor of the old woman. He chuckled as he thought of how much Roja would appreciate this game of impostorship. He finally heard her knocking on the cottage door. Clearly she had been dawdling again, visiting with ants and bluebirds while he waited here with this surprise.

"Come in!" he crooned.

Unsuspecting, Roja bounced to the bedside to greet her grandmother. She politely hid her opinion that the old girl was looking quite robust today and instead began hauling out Fritos, dips, and what was left of the Ho-Hos, for their mutual consumption. She was at the point of telling Geraldine about the wonderful wolf she had met in the forest when she noticed the pointed ears emerging from her grandma's nightcap.

"Why Grandma," she said. "what big ears you have!"

"The better to hear you with, my dear," sighed the wolf.

"And Grandma, what big eyes!"

"The better to see you with as well."

"And oh," said Roja, feigning fear, "your teeth! Your teeth, Grandma, are very large! Do such teeth run in the family? Will I have teeth like that when I grow up?"

At that Leopold flung off his costume and stood split naked on the bed like the righteous self-respecting wolf that he was. "I am not your grandmother!" he shouted.

Roja was stunned, then as she realized what had transpired, delighted. The wolf took her by the hand and led her to Geraldine, and while the two of them dressed the old woman's body in a sheet that looked like a white gi, he explained to Roja all that had happened.

They performed a gentle ritual of gratitude and rejoicing over the body of Geraldine. Then, with immaculate skill and dispatch, they smeared her blood that he had drawn earlier generously all over Leopold, particularly over his paws and chops, until he looked like the fiercest of monster hunters, still digesting his Kill.

In the dusk, the two friends embraced, being careful to keep the blood off Roja's cape, and swore to meet again, not only to renew their ties of kinship but also to provide Leopold with other sources of blood for his charade: Roja's girlfriend, Ermendina, knew hundreds of folks eager to find such a quick and easy death. The wolf need never again fear the pressure of his peers, and indeed, he howled like the leader of the pack as he streaked across the parks and freeways to rejoin his kin.

Nearby, a woodsman, unaware of his brush with an alternate destiny, hummed an environmental tune as he dialogued with his trees and reflected upon the sweet sameness of his daily routine.

Roja made things look as if Geraldine had died in her sleep, then kissed her grandmother's cool cheek. She decided it was time to run away from home. She frolicked her way to Ermendina's to embark on a life of increasingly intense love and lust which was later documented by Shere Hite in *The Turn-of-the-Century Report*.

Constance, at last blissfully relieved of both her mother and her daughter, fulfilled the deep longing she had only recently discovered to follow a beautiful guru whose U.S. visit had changed her life. Over the next fifteen years, she sent occasional postcards from India to her daughter and Ermendina.

Everyone, from the juncos in the trees to the peaceful wolf inhaling luscious-smelling berry blossoms in the field behind the shopping mall, lived (and died) happily ever after.

# Epilogue:
## ❧ Reviewing and Re-Framing ❧
## Little Red Riding Hood

DURING THE LAST TEN YEARS there has been a large number of new intriguing versions of *Little Red Riding Hood* including plays, films, records, and advertisements that have appeared and will continue to appear. Obviously, this tale is still the most popular and certainly the most provocative fairy tale in the Western world. Why? Simply put, because it raises issues about gender identity, sexuality, violence, and the civilizing process in a unique and succinct symbolic form that children and adults can understand on different levels. All the issues raised in this tale are crucial for establishing principles of social justice and gender equality that have not been satisfactorily practiced in Western societies and are thus continually re-addressed in different versions of *Little Red Riding Hood*.

For instance, if we take several of the more recent versions from the United States, England, France, and Germany, texts and illustrations that will bring us up to date about the ongoing trials and tribulations of *Little Red Riding Hood*, we shall see how the tale is still closely connected to shifts in social and political attitudes toward gender identity and rape.

In Ireland, several women who participated in a Women in Community Publishing course produced several interesting feminist revisions of classical fairy tales in *Rapunzel's Revenge: Fairytales for Feminists* (1985).[1] Among them was Carol Lanigan's "All the Better to See You," in which a grandmother debunks her granddaughter Rosa's heroic act of saving her and reveals how Rosa actually neglects the sprightly old woman. Another tale, "Not So Little Red Riding Hood" by Anne Sharpe depicts a young woman named Scarlet, who uses karate to thwart a man seeking to molest her in the woods. Both tales rely on comic, ironic reversals to demonstrate the

343

capacity of young and old women to take care of themselves. In contrast to the humor of these tales, the American poet Gwen Strauss is more pessimistic in "The Waiting Wolf" (1990) and tries to grasp the nature of the male psyche by revealing how the wolf deftly rationalizes his rapacious appetite. In France, Yvette Métral adapted a Spanish tale by M. Company and R. Capdevila in a book entitled *Les Trois Petites Soeurs et le Petit Chaperon Rouge* (1987) in which a vain Little Red Riding Hood and three mischievous sisters make fools of the wolf and a witch. Another comical version is *Le Petit Chaperon Vert* (1989) by Grégoire Solotareff and Nadja. Here a courageous girl named Little Green Riding Hood exposes Little Red Riding Hood as a liar who makes up stories about wolves.

Of course, there are the traditional books in France that confuse the Grimm version with the Perrault version such as *Le Petit Chaperon Rouge* (1984) illustrated by Pascal Trigaux. As usual the hunter saves the grateful Little Red Riding Hood and her grandmother in the end. Such is the case in the book *Rotkäppchen* by the Austrian illustrator Lisbeth Zwerger that reiterates the well-known message by the Grimms that little girls should never wander alone off the path into the forest when their mothers tell them not to. Or, as the American illustrator Trina Schart Hyman puts it in her *Little Red Riding Hood* (1983), that is, puts it into the mouth of the naive girl after her rescue by the hunter, "I will never wander off the forest path again, as long as I live. I should have kept my promise to my mother."[2] For the most part, the traditional illustrated books for children, such as *The Little Red Riding Hood Rebus Book* (1987) by Ann Morris with pictures by Ljiljana Rylands and *Little Red Riding Hood* (1985) written by Rebecca Heller and illustrated by Marsha Winborn, duplicate the same scenes and plot of the Grimm version about the fortunate girl, who is rescued from the wolf's belly by a fatherly hunter and learns to take the straight path through life.

The more innovative books are either parodies, tragedies, adaptations of foreign tales, or provocative experiments. For instance, Della Rowland's upside down book or two books incorporate *The Wolf's Tale* (1991) in which the wolf exonerates himself and escapes from the hunter, and *Little Red Riding Hood*, in which he is killed as a predator. Beni Montresor's illustrated *Little Red Riding Hood* (1991) is a faithful but highly erotic rendition of Perrault's tragic version and reminiscent of Gustav Doré's artistic work. Ed Young's *Lon Po Po: A Red-Riding Hood Story from China* (1989) is a fascinating adaptation of a Chinese story about a young peasant girl who protects her sisters and kills a wolf threatening their home. Sarah Moon's harrowing if not ominous photographs in *Little Red Riding Hood* (1983) are used in an experimental way to bring out the violence that was actually behind Perrault's 17th-century text and continues to be behind the narrative today. Of course, mention must be made of Sally Miller Gearhart's *Roja and Leopold* (1990) when talking about innovative approaches. In her tale, which takes place in Silicon Valley, we learn that Constance, a divorced businesswoman whose social life was that of a very swinging single has two crosses to bear:

❄ 345 ❄

*Epilogue:
Reviewing
and
Re-Framing
Little Red
Riding
Hood*

> One was her daughter, a strong independent little girl whom we shall call Roja. Roja was a cross to her mother because a) Constance had never wanted children—she had borne Roja because her sensitivity group had helped her uncover deeply buried (and unfortunately very temporary) maternal feelings— and b) Roja didn't give a tinker's damn for Constance either, wishing only to spend her time with her girlfriend or her grandmother, both of whom could think laterally and had alternative views of everything, from consumerism and politics to lifestyle and religion.
>
> Constance's second cross was Roja's grandmother, known as Geraldine to all her bridge and skydiving partners and to the small band of subversive activists who met weekly to plot the liberation of abused nonhuman animals. Geraldine was a burden to Constance because she was dying of cancer. Geraldine knew she was dying, had said her good-byes to the world, and was ready to go. Constance, however, felt it her duty to consult with doctors, who kept coming up with miraculous new life-prolonging drugs and surgical techniques.[3]

Roja seeks to help her grandmother by finding a wolf named Leopold, who must prove his manhood to other wolves by eating a human even though he is a vegetarian. In the end, they succeed in helping Geraldine die in peace. Then Roja goes off to live with her lover Ermendina; Leopold resumes inhaling luscious smelling berry blossoms and eating fruit and vegetables. And Constance, "blissfully relieved of both her mother and her daughter, fulfilled the deep longing she had only recently discovered to follow a beautiful guru whose U.S. visit had changed her life."[4]

A strange story, to be sure. But could it be, perhaps, that it marks a shift in the rhetoric of violence in and about *Little Red Riding Hood* as we approach the 21st century? I am not so certain, and in an attempt to answer this question, I want to shift the focus away from the textual study that was the basis of my book *The Trials and*

*Tribulations of Little Red Riding Hood* and analyze the illustrations which in many cases are as important or even more important for conveying notions of sexuality and violence than are the texts themselves.

Since a complete re-examination of the illustrations would require another book, I would like to review and re-frame the story through a historical selection of illustrations from the 19th century to the present to show how certain underlying sexist notions remain prevalent if not dominant in the *contested* portrayal of Little Red Riding Hood's fate. Before re-examining some key illustrations of the standard *Red Riding Hood* texts, however, I would like once more to summarize my arguments about the socio-psychological implications of the changes made by Perrault and the Grimm Brothers. Here it is important to refamiliarize ourselves with the rendition of the oral tale as it was probably disseminated in the French countryside during the late Middle Ages, before Charles Perrault refined and polished it according to his own taste and the conventions of French high society in King Louis XIV's time.[5]

### The Story of Grandmother

There was a woman who had made some bread. She said to her daughter:

"Go carry this hot loaf and bottle of milk to your granny."

So the little girl departed. At the crossway she met *bzou*, the werewolf, who said to her:

"Where are you going?"

"I'm taking this hot loaf and a bottle of milk to my granny."

"What path are you taking," said the werewolf, "the path of needles or the path of pins?"

"The path of needles," the little girl said.

"All right, then I'll take the path of pins."

The little girl entertained herself by gathering needles. Meanwhile the werewolf arrived at the grandmother's house, killed her, put some of her meat in the cupboard and a bottle of her blood on the shelf. The little girl arrived and knocked at the door.

"Push the door," said the werewolf, "It's barred by a piece of wet straw."

"Good day, Granny. I've brought you a hot loaf of bread and a bottle of milk."

"Put it in the cupboard, my child. Take some of the meat which is inside and the bottle of wine on the shelf."

After she had eaten, there was a little cat which said: "Phooey! . . . A slut is she who eats the flesh and drinks the blood of her granny."

❀ 347 ❀

*Epilogue:*
*Reviewing*
*and*
*Re-Framing*
*Little Red*
*Riding*
*Hood*

FIGURE 1. **Original artwork by Catherine Orenstein, 1990.**

"Undress yourself, my child," the werewolf said, "and come lie down beside me."

"Where should I put my apron?"

"Throw it into the fire, my child, you won't be needing it anymore."

And each time she asked where she should put all her other clothes, the bodice, the dress, the petticoat, and the long stockings, the wolf responded:

"Throw them into the fire, my child, you won't be needing them anymore."

When she laid herself down in the bed, the little girl said:

"Oh, Granny, how hairy you are!"

"The better to keep myself warm, my child!"

"Oh, Granny, what big nails you have!"

"The better to scratch me with, my child!"

"Oh, Granny, what big shoulders you have!"

"The better to carry the firewood, my child!"

"Oh, Granny, what big ears you have!"

"The better to hear you with, my child!"

"Oh, Granny, what big nostrils you have!"
"The better to snuff my tobacco with, my child!"
"Oh, Granny, what a big mouth you have!"
"The better to eat you with, my child!"
"Oh, Granny, I've got to go badly. Let me go outside."
"Do it in bed, my child!"
"Oh, no, Granny, I want to go outside."
"All right, but make it quick."

The werewolf attached a woollen rope to her foot and let her go outside.

When the little girl was outside, she tied the end of the rope to a plum tree in the courtyard. The werewolf became impatient and said: "Are you making a load out there? Are you making a load?"

When he realized that nobody was answering him, he jumped out of bed and saw that the little girl had escaped. He followed her but arrived at her house just at the moment she entered.[6]

It is obvious from this oral tale that the narrative perspective is sympathetic to a young peasant girl (age uncertain) who learns to cope with the world around her. She is shrewd, brave, tough, and independent. Evidence indicates she was probably undergoing a social ritual connected to sewing communities:[7] the maturing young woman proves she can handle needles, replace an older woman, and contend with the opposite sex. In 1697 Charles Perrault revised the oral tale to make it the literary standardbearer for good Christian upbringing. Moreover, his fear of women and his own sexual drives are incorporated in his *new* literary version, which also reflects general male attitudes about women, portrayed as eager to be seduced or raped. In this regard, Perrault began a series of literary transformations which have caused nothing but trouble for the female object of male desire and have also reflected the crippling aspect of male desire itself.

What are the significant changes he made? First, she is topped with a *red* hat, a *chaperon*,[8] making her into a type of bourgeois girl tainted with sin, since red, like the scarlet letter A, recalls the devil and heresy. Second, she is spoiled, negligent, and naive. Third, she speaks to a wolf in the woods—rather dumb on her part—and makes a type of contract with him: she accepts a wager which, it is implied, she wants to lose. Fourth, she plays right into the wolf's hands and is too stupid to trick him. Fifth, she is swallowed or raped like her grandmother. Sixth, there is no salvation, simply an ironic moral in verse which warns little girls to beware of strangers, otherwise they will deservedly suffer the consequences. Sex is obviously sinful. Playful intercourse outside of marriage is likened to rape, which is primarily the result of the little girl's irresponsible acts.

❧ 349 ❧
Epilogue:
Reviewing
and
Re-Framing
Little Red
Riding
Hood

In 1812, the Grimm Brothers delivered the second classic version of *Little Red Riding Hood*, based on Perrault's narrative, which had already become widely known through printed editions and oral transmission by people from different social classes. The Grimms made further alterations worth noting. Here the mother plays a more significant role by warning Little Red Riding Hood not to stray from the path through the woods. Little Red Riding Hood is more or less incited by the wolf to enjoy nature and to pick flowers. Her choice symbolizes her agreement with a devilish creature whom she has already directed to her grandmother. Instead of being raped to death, both grandma and granddaughter are saved by a male hunter or gamekeeper who polices the woods. Only a strong male figure can rescue a girl from herself and her lustful desires.

The Perrault and the Grimm versions became *the* classical stories of Little Red Riding Hood and have served as the models for numerous writers of both sexes throughout the world who have either amplified, distorted, or disputed the facts about the little girl's rape, though I suspect that the sexual motif has been dominant in the minds of most writers. Of course, lest eyebrows be raised too high, most literary critics have tended to shun the thought of rape and the manner in which the girl is made to feel responsible for an atrocious act. However, there have been numerous psychoanalytically oriented critics—mainly German, of course—"brave" enough to discuss the sexual nature of the story.

For instance, commenting on the Grimm version, Erich Fromm maintains: "This fairy tale, in which the main figures are three generations of women (the huntsmen at the end is the conventional father figure without real weight), speaks of the male-female conflict; it is a story of triumph by man-hating women, ending with their victory, exactly the opposite of the Oedipus myth, which lets the male emerge victorious from this battle."[9]

Bruno Bettelheim views the tale differently:

> Deviating from the straight path in defiance of mother and superego was temporarily necessary for the young girl, to gain a higher state of personality organization. Her experience convinced her of the dangers of giving into her oedipal desires. It is much better, she learns, not to rebel against the mother, nor to try to seduce or permit herself to be seduced by the as yet dan-

gerous aspects of the male. Much better, despite one's ambivalent desires, to settle for a while longer for the protection the
father provides when he is not seen in his seductive aspects. She
has learned that it is better to build father and mother, and their
values, deeper and in more adult ways into one's superego, to
become able to deal with life's dangers.[10]

My difficulty with such "enlightening" interpretations by two of
the foremost German and Austrian psychoanalysts of the 20th century is that they fail to take into account that the tale which they
treat is *not* an ancient and anonymous folk tale reflecting "universal" psychic operations of men and women, but rather it is the product of gifted male European writers, who projected their needs and
values onto the actions of fictitious characters within a socially con-
ventionalized genre.[11] Certainly the psychic condition of the creators of these tales needs some explanation before one deals with
the psychoanalytical implications of their creations. Moreover,
Fromm and Bettelheim are totally unconscious of their own male
biases. They feel more compelled to prove their theoretical assumptions about the Oedipal or non-Oedipal features of the story than to
comprehend the historical derivation of the texts and the possible
psychological designation in terms of the changing socio-genetic
civilizing process. Their response to the text can be contrasted with
Susan Brownmiller's reaction in her book *Against Our Will*:

> Rape seeps into our childhood consciousness by impercepti-
> ble degrees. Even before we learn to read we have become
> indoctrinated into a victim mentality. Fairy tales are full of a
> vague dread, a catastrophe that seems to befall only little girls.
> Sweet, feminine Little Red Riding Hood is off to visit her dear
> old grandmother in the woods. The wolf lurks in the shadows,
> contemplating a tender morsel. Red Riding Hood and her
> grandmother, we learn, are equally defenseless before the male
> wolf's strength and cunning. His big eyes, his big hands, his big
> teeth—"The better to see you, the better to catch you, to eat
> you, my dear." The wolf swallows both females with no sign of a
> struggle. But enter the huntsman—he will right this egregious
> wrong. The kindly huntsman's strength and cunning are superi-
> or to the wolf's. With the twist of a knife Red Riding Hood and
> her grandmother are rescued from inside the wolf's stomach.
> "Oh, it was so dark in there," Red Riding Hood whimpers. "I
> will never again wander off into the forest as long as I live. . . . "
>
> *Red Riding Hood is* a parable of rape. There are frightening
> male figures abroad in the *woods*—we call them wolves, among
> other names—and females are helpless before them. Better stick
> close to the path, better not be adventurous. If you are lucky, a
> *good friendly* male may be able to save you from certain disaster.[12]

❀ 351 ❀

*Epilogue:
Reviewing
and
Re-Framing
Little Red
Riding
Hood*

After commenting on her own youthful fantasies of rape, which recall poster images relating to World War I (Belgium's rape by the Hun) and concentration camp victims of Fascism, Brownmiller makes the following points about male myths of rape, and she implies that *Little Red Riding Hood* can be considered under this aspect: (1) they tend to make women willing participants in their own defeat; (2) they obscure the true nature of rape by implying that women *want* to be raped; (3) they assert the supreme rightness of male power either as offender or protector.

In my opinion Brownmiller's comments on male attitudes toward women and rape shed more light on the historical development of the *Little Red Riding Hood* story and the debate concerning its essence than the male psychoanalytic point of view which has either repressed the notion of imposed rape—that is, the rape which Perrault imposed on the folk version—or redressed it in a seemingly positive guise. The history of *Little Red Riding Hood*'s textual development has already revealed to what extent Fromm, Bettelheim and other critics have twisted the sexual signs to reaffirm conventional male attitudes toward women: the girl is guilty because of her natural inclinations and disobedience. However, by re-examining the major illustrations of the tale and their signs, we may be able to see other features of the tale noted by Brownmiller—features obscured by a male screening process. I want to work from the texts and illustrations themselves to understand their referential systems. What do the signs refer to within the illustrations? How do they reinforce particular aspects of the literary text? Which text? What is the reference point or signified which the components or signifiers of an image are addressing?

My comments about the illustrations to the Perrault and Grimm versions of *Little Red Riding Hood* are not about an isolated case. All the most popular, classical fairy tales from *Cinderella* to *Snow White* have been illustrated basically in a sexist manner, whether the pictures have been drawn by a male or female hand. By sexist I mean that the signs center around male power and rationalize male domination as a norm. Thus the history of standard *Little Red Riding Hood* illustrations shares a great deal in common with that of other illustrated fairy tales, and there are several generalizations about fairy-tale illustrations which must be made before dealing exclusively with the intriguing scenes of the little girl and the wolf.

The earliest illustrations of fairy tales, dating back to the eighteenth century, were largely black and white woodcuts.[13] Since the

FIGURE 2. *Little Red Riding Hood,* New York: McLoughlin, c. 1885.
Illustrator unknown.

**In the illustrations 2–5, the warning, the image of the temperate
mother trying to temper the potentially rebellious or free-spirited
daughter is standard fare in the picture books of the last two
centuries.**

market for such illustrations in Europe did not really develop until
the 19th century, when fairy tales for children became more
acceptable in middle-class homes, the real beginning of fairy-tale
illustrations in the Western world—and I am dealing mainly with
France, Germany, Great Britain, and the United States—is ap-
proximately 1800, and it is not really until the 1820s, 1830s, and
1840s that prominent illustrators such as Thomas Bewick, Ludwig
Grimm, George Cruikshank, Ludwig Richter, and Gustave Doré

❧ 353 ❧

*Epilogue:*
*Reviewing*
*and*
*Re-Framing*
*Little Red*
*Riding*
*Hood*

FIGURE 3. *Le Petit Chaperon Rouge,* Paris: Editions Ruyant, 1979. Illustrator M. Fauron. Reprint of a 1900 edition.

FIGURE 4. *Little Red Riding Hood*, Racine, Wisconsin: Whitman, 1952.
Illustrator Doris Stolberg.

turned their hands to illustrating fairy tales. Here again it is important to note that all the pioneers of fairy-tale pictures were men.
The industry of design and engraving was controlled by men. Or, in
other words, male illustrators were the interpreters or mediators of
the fairy-tale texts, and they projected their sexual phantasies
through the images they composed.

Throughout the 19th century the primary audience for illustrated fairy-tale books was the middle class and the aristocracy. No
illustrator drew a picture without first taking adult censors and conventions of socialization and the Christian religion into account.
In short, the lines laid down by the pen had already been laid down
in mind and society before the image came to be printed. Only the
subtle variation of the lines leave telltale marks of rebellion and
subversion by individual needs and dreams. Though the illustrators
offered their images primarily to the wealthy because the cost of
picture books made them prohibitive for the masses, there were
broadsides, penny books, and chapbooks which were mass produced by the mid-19th century. Thus, the advances in technology

✵ 355 ✵

Epilogue:
Reviewing
and
Re-Framing
Little Red
Riding
Hood

FIGURE 5. *Little Red Riding Hood*, Retold by Rebecca Heller, New York: Golden Book, 1985. Illustrator Marsha Winborn.

enabled the fairy-tale illustrations to reach all social classes. And, the early black and white woodcuts with their sharply-drawn simple lines yielded gradually to colorful prints with subtly drawn characters and scenes. For each one of the classical fairy tales, there are thousands of illustrated books. And yet, despite this enormous quantity, most are duplications or slightly varied images of *standardized characters* and scenes which have prevailed over the years. This is no accident.

In the case of *Little Red Riding Hood* one could almost talk about a "conspiracy." There are three major scenes which almost invariably accompany the text, whether it be the Perrault or Grimm version: (1) the mother with a raised finger addressing her daughter. Generally speaking, the pictures of both the Perrault and Grimm versions have the mother instruct and warn the girl, even though the warning is not explicitly stated in the Perrault text. However, in the minds of the illustrators the girl is already guilty before a crime is committed. She is made responsible for whatever may happen. (2) Little Red Riding Hood's encounter with the wolf as a type of pact or seduction scene. The girl is rarely afraid of the wolf, despite his large size and animal appearance. The viewer must ask him/herself on some level whether she is stupid. Does she want to be violated? Is she asking for something? Is she leading him on? We shall return to these questions. (3) The wolf violating Little Red Riding Hood as punishment according to the strict Perrault version or the stalwart hunter/father saving Little Red Riding Hood according to the more lenient Grimm version. The dreadful punishment scene generally represents the consequence of Little Red Riding Hood's illicit desires and designs. Generally speaking it is preceded by Little Red Riding Hood in bed smiling at the wolf. The more prudish version of the Brothers Grimm does not call for Little Red Riding Hood to strip—and there are striptease scenes—and get into bed. She is simply gobbled up by the wolf. And, she owes her salvation and life to a male who is likened to a father figure. Explicit in these illustrations is that a girl receives her identity through a man, and that without male protection she will destroy herself and reap chaos in the world outside.

During the course of the past two centuries, these illustrations have been varied extensively, and there have been some radical changes, such as Thurber's illustration of the girl who shoots the wolf with a pistol or the Liverpool feminist group's depiction of the girl and her grandmother slaying the wolf. But, for the most part, the traditional images have prevailed and continue to be circulated by a culture industry primarily interested in making profits by gambling with our subliminal sexual phantasies and reinforcing male notions of rape. The underlying question in the images depicting the male/female encounter, whether it be in magazines, books, films, advertisements, or cartoons, concerns women's use of their sexual powers to attain supreme gratification through male sexual prowess. As every reader/viewer subconsciously knows, Little Red Riding Hood is not really sent into the woods to visit grandma but to meet the wolf and to explore her own sexual cravings and social rules of conduct. Therefore, the most significant encounter is with the wolf because it is here that *she acts* upon her desire to indulge in sexual intercourse with the wolf, and most illustrations imply that she willingly makes a bargain with the wolf, or, in male terms, "she asks to be raped."

The wiles of Red Riding Hood are many, or to be more exact, the iconic projections of illustrators reveal a great deal about the semiotic means of fairy-tale illustrations which serve to corroborate male notions about sexuality and rape. Here I should like to focus on several illustrations selected from well over 500 that recurred with significant regularity in similar shape. Not only do they suggest that Little Red Riding Hood is guilty for her own rape, but they also reveal a curious *ambivalence* about male phantasies which needs more explanation.

Perhaps the most famous engravings of *Little Red Riding Hood* are those by Gustave Doré (1832–1883), who illustrated Perrault's fairy tales in 1862. His images or imaginings were so striking that they were used in other editions soon after. For example, they appeared in Tom Hood's *A Fairy Realm* (1864) and Morris Hartmann's *Märchen nach Perrault* (1869). By the end of the 19th century, they were known throughout the Western world, and Doré's portrayal of Red Riding Hood meeting the wolf has undoubtedly influenced numerous other illustrators and continues to frame the manner in which we see Red Riding Hood's encounter with the wolf.

To explore the ideological connotations of Doré's and others' illustrations, a semiotic approach can be useful. Here the image or sign needs to be broken down into signifiers (the striking features of the major figures) and signifieds (the concepts to which the signifiers allude). By doing this we can move toward a comprehension of the whole sign or image. In the case of a fairy-tale illustration it is important to bear in mind that the signifiers in the image refer to each other and to the text in order to create a sensory impression. It is up to us as viewers/readers to convey ultimate meaning upon the patterns, and we do this in a conscious and unconscious manner but always within a socio-historical context which has already framed the way we receive signals about sex and sexuality. As Bill Nichols has remarked in *Ideology and the Image*: "Images are always particularized representations, a way of seeing is built in (since a way of seeing built them) and hence connotation is built in."[14]

In Doré's illustration [Figure 6] it seems to me that the more expressive aspects of the image are: the longing if not seductive look of Little Red Riding Hood as she peers into the eyes of the wolf and her faint smile; the enormous size of the powerful wolf who looks down into the eyes of the girl in a non-threatening manner; the proximity of wolf and girl who appear to be touching and to be totally absorbed in an intimate *tête-à-tête*. It is almost as if the viewer were an intruder who chances to come upon an assignation of two lovers in the woods. Certainly the viewer is invited to gaze voyeuristically upon a familiar world and to confirm meaning that seems always to have been there. What then is this meaning?

The signifiers point to seduction, intimacy, and power. Doré stresses the desire of the girl and wolf for one another. But, by

❋ 357 ❋

*Epilogue:
Reviewing
and
Re-Framing
Little Red
Riding
Hood*

FIGURE 19. *Les Contes de Perrault,* Paris: J. Hetzel, 1862. Illustrator Gustave Doré.

revealing the full face of the girl and her apparent seductive glance, Doré also suggests that it is primarily she who is asking for it. And, what is *it?* In this case it is an immense wolf or phallus, a male creature, who in his animal state represents both the girl's own libidinal drives *and* the voracious appetite of males, whose desire is allegedly to dominate and violate women, to lead them off the straight path—and naturally it is all women's secret desire to be misled. The erotic display in Doré's illustration indicates a transgression of society's rules of sexual behavior and sexuality while at the same time it confirms what we suppose to be true about both women *and men:* women want men to rape them; men are powerful but weak beasts who cannot help themselves when tempted by alluring female creatures. Since the sexes prey upon one another and cause their own destruction in nature as opposed to society, then another implicit message is that there can be no "true" love, certainly no Christian love, in sexual intercourse practiced outside of the institution of marriage. Only when sexual behavior is domestically ordered as in the person of the mother and the father at the beginning and end of the fairy tale can sex assume its "proper" reproductive function in society.

The central scene of the encounter between girl and wolf in the chain of signification is the crucial one in all illustrated *Red Riding Hood* books, for it is the scene of transgression. As we have seen, the first standard image always indicates domestic order and tranquillity in the person of the stern but caring mother. The last scene either represents the punishment as a result of the transgression underlined by Perrault's *moralité,* which we should not forget:

> From this story one learns that children,
> Especially young lasses,
> Pretty, courteous and well-bred,
> Do very wrong to listen to strangers,
> And it is not an unheard thing
> If the Wolf is thereby provided with his dinner.
> I say Wolf, for all wolves
> Are not of the same sort;
> There is one kind with an amenable disposition
> Neither noisy nor hateful, nor angry,
> But tame, obliging and gentle,
> Following the young maids
> In the streets, even into their homes.
> Alas! who does not know that these gentle wolves
> Are of all such creatures the most dangerous![15]

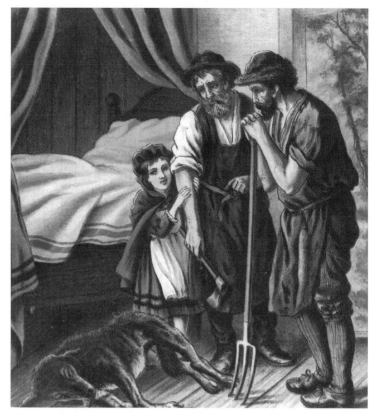

FIGURE 7. *Little Red Riding Hood*, New York: McLoughlin, c. 1880.
Illustrator unknown.

**In the illustrations 7–11, there is generally a domestic resolution
with the hunter/father treated as a hero in twentieth-century illustrations, although some still show the girl being mauled and eaten.**

Or, the last scene represents the restoration of domestic order by
a strong male figure as in the Grimm version or a Grimm variant.
In Doré's illustration it is obvious that the girl will become completely tainted by sin since she has stopped to talk to this strange
creature. Given the enormous size of the wolf, the viewer must ask
why the little girl is not afraid of the beast? Certainly any smart
peasant girl would have run from this gigantic wolf. Any self-
respecting bourgeois girl would have avoided the company of such
a hairy monster. But here, Little Red Riding Hood apparently seeks

❊ 361 ❊

*Epilogue:
Reviewing
and
Re-Framing
Little Red
Riding
Hood*

FIGURE 8. *Little Red Riding Hood,* New York: Platt & Munk, c. 1925.
Illustrator Eulalie.

his acquaintance, and the shadow of the wolf begins to cover her.

It is within this shadow that we may be able to locate the ambivalence of male desire. That is, it is possible to interpret Little
Red Riding Hood's desire for the wolf as a desire for the other, or a
general quest for self-identification. She seeks to know herself in a
social context, gazes into the wolf's eyes to see a mirror reflection of
who she might be, a confirmation of her feelings. She wants to
establish contact with her unconscious and discover what she is
lacking. By recognizing the wolf outside of her as part of herself, just
as the wolf seeks the female in himself, she can become at one with
herself. The woods are the natural setting for the fulfillment of
desire. The conventions of society are no longer present. The self
can explore its possibilities and undergo symbolic exchanges with
nature inside and outside the self. If we follow this line of thought,
the formation of this scene (girl meeting wolf) by Doré demonstrates *his* unconscious desire to free himself of social restraints in a
symbolic exchange with the other, and he also recognizes the mutual desire of the other. Yet, as much as Doré *desired* to depict the pleasure of recognition through a sexual symbolic exchange, he probably identified more with the wolf, and thus there is an indication in
his illustration that the wolf seeks to *dominate* with his gaze which

FIGURE 9. *The Gingerbread Boy, Little Red Riding Hood, and the House that Jack Built,* Racine, Wisconsin: Whitman, 1945. Illustrators Hilda Miloche and Wilma Kane.

would cancel out mutuality. The text of the tale dictated the wolf's gaze as phallic domination—a point which I shall discuss later in reference to Jacques Lacan—and the conventions of society reinforced such male desire during Doré's time. In addition, the look or gaze of Little Red Riding Hood appears to invite the wolf's gaze/desire, and therefore, she incriminates herself in his act. Implicit in her gaze is that she may be leading him on—to granny's house, to a

❀ 363 ❀

*Epilogue:*
*Reviewing*
*and*
*Re-Framing*
*Little Red*
*Riding*
*Hood*

FIGURE 10. *Little Red Riding Hood,* Racine, Wisconsin: Whitman, 1952. Illustrator Doris Stolberg.

bed, to be dominated. She tells him the way, the path to the house. But where is she actually leading him? Why?

Already influenced by other illustrations and the text, Doré's own illustration stamped many of the configurations of the late 19th-century images of the encounter between girl and wolf.[16] In England there were numerous illustrated books of fairy tales which reflected and embellished Doré's work. For instance, Raphael Tuck and Sons had a studio of artists who pursued Doré's lines and helped Tuck become one of the main distributors of fairy tales in England, France, Germany, the United States, and Canada. The illustrators are unknown, but they all maintained a particular style, as if one hand drew each scene, so that everything could be attributed to Father Tuck, the name under which most of the fairy-tale books were distributed. One scene, reminiscent of the Doré illustration [Figure 12], reveals Red Riding Hood on the right smiling and looking down at the wolf. She is intended to be doll-like, cor-

FIGURE 18. *Le Petit Chaperon Rouge,* Toulouse: Tobaggan-Magazine, 1984. Illustrator Pascal Trigaux.

responding to the Victorian image of children, especially young girls,[17] and the colors are bright pastels. But the girl is more than sweet and virginal. Again she glances seductively at the wolf, ready to accommodate him. Of course, some changes have been made. The wolf comes from the left and is much smaller than the girl. In fact, he looks more like a friendly dog with his left paw raised, almost begging to have a bone. His head is tilted, and his tongue forms a smile with his open jaws. The diminution of dog and girl was typical of Victorian illustrations, for upper-class children were considered fragile and sensitive.[18] Their sexuality had to be adorned in a way which might not disturb them. Nevertheless, the innuendos in this scene are clear.

❄ 365 ❄

*Epilogue:*
*Reviewing*
*and*
*Re-Framing*
*Little Red*
*Riding*
*Hood*

FIGURE 12. *Friends from Fairyland,* London: Raphael Tuck & Sons, c. 1880. Illustrator unknown.

In the illustrations 12–20, the encounter between girl and wolf, there is always a seductive gazing.

In the history of *Little Red Riding Hood* illustrations each nation has cultivated particular characteristics which can be traced in the signifiers of the encounter between girl and wolf. Obviously the Doré influence can be found more often in France, where illustrators have expressed a tendency to be more erotic and playful than the German, British, and American artists, who are more restrained and puritanical. For example, another French book which appeared in 1905 reveals Little Red Riding Hood and the wolf as if they were going on a picnic together [Figure 13]. The intimacy is clear: it is almost as if they were one. The girl's flirtatious smile is matched by the friendly gaze of the wolf, who is more like a companion than a stranger. Unlike the doll-like portrayals in America and England, the French illustrations tend to show a more fully-developed young girl, one approaching puberty. Both the girl and the wolf are oblivious of the woods around them. They only have eyes for each other. In my study of the literary texts, I demonstrated that the wolf and the girl were essentially one and the same figure in the minds of the writers, for the little girl was a potential witch with her red hat—witches, evil fairies, and Jews wore red hats in the oral stories which circulated in the late Middle Ages up through the 19th century—and the wolf, whose ancestor was the werewolf, was an accomplice of the devil. The encounter in the woods, a meeting place of witches and the haunting place of werewolves, is an asocial act. The meeting of the eyes (the I's), the touching bodies and linked shadows form an apparent oneness, an agreement. Here the anonymous illustrator softens the erotic nature of the scene which is more striking in Doré's illustration. Nevertheless, the smile of Little Red Riding Hood is more than just friendly.

Eye contact and knowing smiles are extremely important in the girl/wolf encounter. The gifted illustrated Walter Crane (1845–1915), who, like Doré, left his imprint on future illustrators, raised the wolf on his hind legs and dressed him in peasant clothes. Crane was by no means the first to elevate and to anthropomorphize the wolf. There were Dutch, French, and German broadsheets which depicted the wolf as soldier or farmer by the mid-19th century. Crane was, however, one of the first to present this scene in a toy book with color and strong ink lines emphasizing the intimate nature of the encounter. Here [Figure 14] Little Red Riding Hood is in her teens, and with her raised eyebrows and stiff upper lip she is not as seductive as some of her "sisters." Nevertheless, she gazes into

❦ 367 ❦

*Epilogue:*
*Reviewing*
*and*
*Re-Framing*
*Little Red*
*Riding*
*Hood*

FIGURE 13. *Le Petit Chaperon Rouge,* Paris: Emile Guérin, c. 1905.
Illustrator unknown.

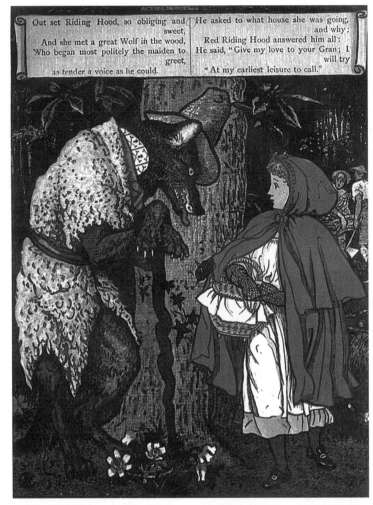

Out set Riding Hood, so obliging and
sweet,
And she met a great Wolf in the wood,
Who began most politely the maiden to
greet,
as tender a voice as he could.

He asked to what house she was going,
and why;
Red Riding Hood answered him all:
He said, "Give my love to your Gran; I
will try
"At my earliest leisure to call."

FIGURE 14. Walter Crane Toy Books, *Little Red Riding Hood,* London: George Routledge, 1870. Illustrator Walter Crane.

his eyes, which are practically on the same plane as hers, while he leans on his cane and addresses her in a friendly way. It is as though he were standing on a corner waiting for her to come by. Here there is a clear separation of the figures, emphasized by the straight stick which keeps them apart. Also, in the background we see some woodcutters, the social guardians of morality, who guarantee that the girl and wolf will behave themselves. This is why the eye con-

❀ 369 ❀

*Epilogue:
Reviewing
and
Re-Framing
Little Red
Riding
Hood*

FIGURE 15. *Little Red Riding Hood,* New York: Sam'l Gabriel Sons, c. 1939. Illustrator unknown.

tact is important, for they must exchange signals. The wolf must know where to go to meet her. He seeks to absorb her in his gaze.

An American version of the Grimms' tale, published in 1939, reflects the continued influence of Crane [Figure 15]. The eyes of the young girl and wolf are on the same plane. The figures are separated, but the wolf leans in an intimate way while the girl gazes straight into his eyes. Dressed in overalls, the wolf is obviously an American farmer, and the apple-pie complexion of the girl suggests the sweetness of innocent American girls, who use their innocence as a means of seduction.

Innocence and naiveté are generally associated with coyness and stupidity by male illustrators. For instance, another Father Tuck

FIGURE 16. Father Tuck's Fairy Tale Series, *Little Red Riding Hood*, London: Raphael Tuck & Sons, c. 1880. Illustrator unknown.

illustration [Figure 16] reflects a characteristic male attitude toward women. Although the wolf is only saying "good morning" to the girl, she acts as if she were being propositioned. With her index finger in her mouth and her eyes rolled to the right, she gives the impression of a coquette playing hard to get. Unlike most depictions of this scene, this one shows her facing the viewers while cocking her head toward the wolf. Though she is apparently avoiding eye contact with the wolf, she is also enticing him. The wolf is a debonair gentleman with top hat and cane, and there is something comical about his appearance in the woods. His courteous

❈ 371 ❈

*Epilogue:*
*Reviewing*
*and*
*Re-Framing*
*Little Red*
*Riding*
*Hood*

FIGURE 17. *Le Petit Chaperon Rouge,* Toulouse: Tobaggan-Magazine, 1984. Illustrator Pascal Trigaux.

and stately manner is in contrast to the naiveté of the little girl. One is compelled to ask who is pretending more, the wolf or the girl? Who is leading whom on?

Johnny Gruelle's depiction of the same type of naive lass is somewhat different, but not much. Famous as the creator of Raggedy Ann and Raggedy Andy, Gruelle illustrated the complete Grimms' fairy tales in a most unusual manner. Here Little Red Riding Hood plays again at being dumb, while the chevalier wolf makes his intentions obvious by licking his chops. Characteristic of American illustrations in the 20th century, and to a certain extent of most traditional ones in Europe after World War I, there is a tendency to make Little Red Riding Hood more babylike and infantile and to suggest the comical side of the encounter, as

FIGURE 18. *The Gingerbread Boy, Little Red Riding Hood, and the House that Jack Built,* Racine, Wisconsin: Whitman, 1945. Illustrators Hilda Miloche and Wilma Kane.

though it were all in good clean fun because we know how it will turn out in the end, that is, if we believe the Brothers Grimm, whose version is the most prevalent in the world.

More typical than Gruelle's illustration, which still has a strong hint of the erotic in the meeting of girl and wolf, is the prudish illustration by Hilda Miloche and Wilma Kane [Figure 18]. The girl appears to be impressed by the polite manners of the wolf, whose top hat recalls the Father Tuck illustration. The girl and wolf have been "desexed" in true Walt Disney fashion. As usual, the wolf is without genitals, and the apple-cheeked girl is more like a kewpie doll than a real living person. The eye contact remains, and the girl

❈ 373 ❈

*Epilogue:*
*Reviewing*
*and*
*Re-Framing*
*Little Red*
*Riding*
*Hood*

FIGURE 11. *Le Petit Chaperon Rouge,* Chatellerault: René Touret, c. 1950. Illustrator Thomen.

FIGURE 12. C. Perrault, *Cappuccetto Rosso,* Milan: Malpiero, c. 1980.
Illustrator A. D'Agnosi.

❄ 375 ❄

*Epilogue:
Reviewing
and
Re-Framing
Little Red
Riding
Hood*

is apparently interested in what the wolf has to say. But, as in all the illustrations, it is what is unsaid that is best understood by the viewer/reader. The words and images stimulate the imagination, refer to notions and concepts, rules and conventions, preconditioned thoughts about sexual behavior and sex roles.

The history of the pictures which illustrate the traditional versions of *Little Red Riding Hood* by Perrault and the Brothers Grimm reveal a kind of cleansing process, a gradual censorization, which is geared to eliminate the sexual connotations of the tales. Whereas the experimental storytellers and illustrators have consciously highlighted the notion of rape to parody and criticize it from different points of view, the conservative re-tellers and illustrators of the Perrault and Grimm narratives want to avoid the issue. Intimacy, seduction, and violation are made comical so as not to upset the delicate sensitivity of young readers and the keen sense of propriety of their watchdog parents. For the most part the wolf will be fully dressed and caricatured, even to the point of appearing as naive and stupid as the little girl. He is not allowed to eat the grandmother who either hides in a closet or runs into town. Nor is he allowed to put his paws on Little Red Riding Hood, who is invariably saved by a father/hunter. Nevertheless, the implications of the signals remain. It is the dumb girl who causes a "near rape." Men are natural victims of temptation, as the Adam and Eve myth suggested long ago, and generally will behave if fed and clothed properly. Only the domesticated models of mother and father are worth emulating— those strongly structured, well-composed, self-confident figures of law and order.

Ironically, the portrayals of the wolf and the girl were more erotic and sensual in the 19th century and early part of the 20th century than they are today. Michel Foucault has suggested that the Victorians were more obsessed and interested in sex than we believe.[19] That is, given the proliferation of discourses around sexuality which began in the 19th century, Foucault calls into question the very notion of repression. Certainly, in the case of *Little Red Riding Hood*, writers and illustrators were not afraid to make sex the major subject of their discourses. Historically speaking the traditional 19th-century depictions of the encounter between girl and wolf bear out Foucault's assertions: they reveal a deep longing for sexual satisfaction, a pursuit of natural inclinations against conformity to a social code. The bodies of girl and wolf are closer, more intimate, more lifelike than images which originate after World War II. In fact, 20th-century images are marked by a growing alienation: the girl and wolf keep more distance; they are afraid of sex and their bodies; they are clean and sterile, more like wooden cartoon figures or advertising props for good housekeeping.

All this is not to say that 19th-century Europeans and Americans were more emancipated in their sexual attitudes than contemporary Europeans and Americans. Rather, it seems to me that the growing rationalization of society and increased division of labor and more subtle forms of discipline and punishment first generated an intensified discussion about the body and sexuality in the 19th century. The question concerned control and use of the body, the instrumentalization for greater productivity, domination of inner and outer nature within the prescriptions of capitalist industrialization and the Protestant ethos. Thus, rules for sexual conduct and the definition of sexual roles had to be established firmly in the minds of children and adults. Since the enjoyment of extramarital sex could interfere with production and schooling in the 19th century, the sexual act, which had already been more or less equated with sin by the Church, had to be repeatedly associated with irresponsibility, chaos, and violation. Such a process had already begun in an organized way in the late Middle Ages, and the Perrault text was an outcome of such male rationalization of Christian thought. In the male imagination it was the woman who was devious, sinful, and subversive; her sexual appetite interfered with male institutionalized relations; she was an instigator, in league with the devil, that is, with wolves or male heretics, who represented sexual play, amusement, gathering flowers in the woods. So, by the 19th century Little Red Riding Hood and the wolf had become primarily responsible for the violation of bodies, for chaos, disorder, and sin. At the same time, there is an undercurrent in the images of the 19th century of a secret longing by the male illustrators to become part of a union of girl and wolf, to enjoy the bodies, to celebrate the eye contact. Since the encounter is the central scene in the chain of signification illustrating the texts, the illustrator could express his or her contradictory desires.

The illustrators of fairy-tale books in the 19th century were also influenced by market conditions. As it became cheaper to produce illustrated books, broadsheets, chapbooks, penny books, and toy books, children became more a target audience—and these were also children who began to have more leisure time and were becoming better educated in all social classes. By the turn of the century, publishers sought mainly profit from this new market, and production for children—which meant production for adult surveyors of children—demanded that the producers pay respect to decent taste and sexual codes, at least in outward form. If *Little Red Riding Hood* was to be marketed in France, Germany, America, Canada, and England, as Raphael Tuck and Sons did, then she had to entice buyers by subscribing to male notions of sexual seduction, rape, punishment, and salvation.

As I have already remarked, the major change during the 19th century, if one can call it a real change, has been marked by increased sanitization and standardization of the text and pictures. International conglomerates have worked together since 1945 to package *Little Red Riding Hood* as a standard commodity to bring profits and to convey male notions about sexuality, specifically about the violation of the body for which women are deemed responsible. The nationality or sex of the illustrator no longer plays a major role since the deviation from the normal "desexed" girl and wolf will not be tolerated. For example, the Golden Book publishers, which circulate *Little Red Riding Hood* in the thousands throughout the U.S. in supermarkets, drugstores, candystores, and bookstores, have transformed *Little Red Riding Hood* into a sterile tale of chastity.[20] The discourse about the body reflects a greater fear of and alienation from the body than ever before. Unlike the Victorians, we are no longer sexually curious, rather sexually controlled and defensive. The nonviolence depicted in the illustrations continues to violate minds with implicit messages about the stupidity and culpability of little girls. For instance, the Walt Disney Corporation and Peter Pan Company have produced a record set with text and pictures for little boys and girls to follow the story with music.[21] Naturally, they have cleaned up the act and reduced the girl's incrimination so that the tale has become insipid, totally devoid of erotic tension. Yet, the girl is made to feel that she has done something wrong. *She is* the one who should not talk to strangers. Better to be catatonic, than to be adventurous. Control is of essence today.

Ultimately, the male phantasies of Perrault and the Brothers Grimm can be traced to their socially induced desire and need for control—control of women, control of their own sexual libido, control of their fear of women and loss of virility. That their controlling interests are still reinforced and influential through variant texts and illustrations of *Little Red Riding Hood* in society today is an indication that we are still witnessing an antagonistic struggle of the sexes in all forms of socialization, in which men are still trying to dominate women. In one of the major theoretical books to deal with male phantasies in the last fifty years, Klaus Theweleit has remarked:

> The apparent rearing of children to become chaste achieves its opposite by creating a stored-up lecherousness, the installation of an unfulfilled deed as a permanent condition. The boy is sexualized. His need is directed toward woman, it is supposed to be directed right toward the woman. All images, hopes, wishes, plans, which the growing boy has, are supposed to come together, to be concentrated and fixed on the conquest of this one object—the woman, and this object woman is represented in codified form by a woman of the family.
>
> The growing boy is trained along these lines and during puberty is trained to structure his whole existence almost insanely according to a fictitious before/after scheme: "After I have first had a woman for just once, *the* woman, then. . . . " Decisive here is this "then" which appears to stand for everything: then the guilt will disappear, the fears, the insecurities, the feelings of inferiority, then life will begin, I'll be strong, I'll be able to conquer the father or leave him, my talents will unfold; She will belong to me and I'll protect her. . . .
>
> The "meaning of life" is produced from this longed-for salvation, and, since it does not occur, since salvation stems from a false direction of the wish, the crucial question about the meaning of life (thought of as being able to be accomplished in *one* act) does not stop.[22]

In endeavoring to comprehend how unresolved sexual needs contributed to the development of a Fascist mentality and male brutality in Germany, Theweleit touches on fundamental questions regarding male upbringing and male phantasies in Western society as a whole, questions which are connected to the fairy tale about Little Red Riding Hood and its reception. What is played out in the narrative of *Little Red Riding Hood* is the deep longing of males to possess their own bodies/mothers/sisters, to touch the wild unformed urges in themselves, to possess them—and then, the frustration which comes from the realization that the desire cannot be fulfilled. The frustration often leads to an act of violence, an insistence that the desire be fulfilled at all costs. Here the notions of Jacques Lacan about masculine and feminine sexuality[23] can be further helpful in explaining the psychological signification of the constellation formed by girl and wolf. As is well known, Lacan attributed a great deal of importance to the gaze in the development of human sexuality. For him, seeing is desire, and the eye functions as a kind of phallus. However, the eye cannot clearly see its object of desire, and in the case of male desire, the female object of desire is an illusion created by the male unconscious. Or, in other words, the male desire for woman expressed in the gaze is auto-erotic and involves the male's desire to have his own identity reconfirmed in a mirror image. As Larysa Mykyta explains in her essay entitled "Lacan, Literature and the Look,"

❀ 379 ❀
Epilogue:
Reviewing
and
Re-Framing
Little Red
Riding
Hood

> the sexual triumph of the male passes through the eye, through the contemplation of the woman. Seeing the woman ensures the satisfaction of wanting to be seen, of having one's desire recognized, and thus comes back to the original aim of the scopic drive. Woman is repressed as subject and desired as object in order to efface the gaze of the Other, the gaze that would destroy the illusion of reciprocity and one-ness that the process of seeing usually supports. The female object does not look, does not have its own point of view; rather it is erected as an image of the phallus sustaining male desires.[24]

In the case of the *Little Red Riding Hood* illustrations and the classical texts by Perrault and the Grimms, the girl in the encounter with the wolf gazes but really does not gaze, for she is the image of male desire. She is projected by the authors Perrault and Grimm and generally by male illustrators as an object without a will of her own. The gaze of the wolf will consume her and is intended to dominate and eliminate her. The gaze of the wolf is a phallic mode of interpreting the world and is an attempt to gain what is lacking through imposition and force. Thus, the positioning of the wolf involves a movement toward convincing the girl that he is what she wants, and her role is basically one intended to mirror his desire. In such an inscribed and prescribed male discourse, the feminine other has no choice. Her identity will be violated and fully absorbed by male desire either as wolf or gamekeeper.

If *Little Red Riding Hood*, the text as well as the key illustrations, is seen in the light of Lacan's psychoanalytic theories as a conservative male phantasy conditioned by socio-cultural conventions, then the fairy tale as a whole does little to reduce the possibility for violence and brutality in our society. If anything, it perpetuates sexual notions which contribute to our frustration and aggression. As long as we are encouraged to point our fingers at Little Red Riding Hood as willing conspirator in her own downfall and assign male guardians of law and order to kill the wolf, our minds and bodies will be prevented from grasping the fundamental issues of sexuality that are at stake in the story and in our lives.

Fortunately, as a result of the women's movement and continual struggles against sexism during the past twenty years, our eyes have been opened and made more receptive to a re-framing of Little Red Riding Hood's story. Despite the apparent increase in violence against women in Western societies, there are signs that the encouragement to point the finger at Little Red Riding Hood has waned. That is, the increase in violence may be paradoxically due to the great frustration men feel in the reduction of inducements to violate women and the resistance on the part of women to play out the role of Little Red Riding Hood according to male prescriptions. If we return to the question I posed at the beginning of this epilogue—whether there has been a turning point in the rhetoric of violence in and about *Little Red Riding Hood*—I could perhaps point to an earlier turning point than Sally Miller Gearhart's story of 1990, namely to Olga Broumas's "Little Red Riding Hood" of 1977 or Angela Carter's *The Company of Wolves* of 1979. Broumas makes a defiant statement for gay rights while Carter's eroticized version of *Little Red Riding Hood* reappropriates the folk tradition of the peasant girl who outsmarts the werewolf in her depiction of a young girl overcoming sadomasochism and taking charge of her own sexuality.[25] Since the publication of Broumas's poem and Carter's tale, the feminist impulse in literary versions as seen in the works of Tanith Lee, Anne Sharpe, and Gwen Strauss, not to mention the delightfully subversive and urbanized adaptation, *Ruby* (1990) by Michael Emberly, has become stronger and is indicative of an *intensification* in the struggle over the rhetoric of violence, perhaps not so much a shift.

In 1988 the Hungarian director Marta Meszaros, while finishing her Canadian-Hungarian production of *Little Red Ridinghood, Year 2000*, stated in an interview, "I think all my films are about little girls who try to get to the other side of the forest unscathed."[26] In 1992, the young German playwright/actress, Cordula Nossek, performed a play in Berlin on a raised bed with the title *The Hunter Wolfgang or Wolf Rolf: What Little Red Riding Hood Always Wanted to Know about Sex*, in which a young girl's desire to be on top of sex and to express her sexual needs is enacted with humor and enlightenment.[27] These narrative strategies used by women are intended to undermine the dominant male discourse that does violence to women's bodies, and they are fortunately multiplying in western societies. When James Thurber wrote at the end of his 1939 version of *Little Red Riding Hood* that it is not so easy to fool little girls nowadays as it used to be, he implied it was necessary for girls to resort to violence to protect themselves. However, the hope in the best of the more recent re-framings of the Red Riding Hood story, as Angela Carter and Sally Miller Gearhart demonstrate, is that women do not have to reproduce the violence of men to change the rhetoric of violence.

# ❊ *Notes* ❊

1. Attic Press has also published three other delightful books of feminist fairy tales: *Ms. Muffet and Others* (1986), *Mad and Bad Fairies* (1987), and *Sweeping Beauties* (1989).

2. Trina Schart Hyman, *Little Red Riding Hood* (New York: Holiday House, 1983), last page of an unpaginated book.

3. Sally Miller Gearhart, "Roja and Leopold" in *And a Deer's Ear, Eagle's Song, and Bear's Grace: Animals and Women*, Ed. Theresa Corrigan and Stephanie Hoppe (Pittsburgh: Cleis Press, 1990), pp. 136–37.

4. *Ibid.*, p. 147.

5. Cf. Dorothy Thelander, "Mother Goose and Her Goslings: The France of Louis XIV as Seen through the Fairy Tale," *The Journal of Modern History* 54 (September 1982), 467–96 and my chapter "Setting Standards for Civilization through Fairy Tales" in *Fairy Tales and the Art of Subversion* (New York: Routledge, 1983), pp. 13–44.

6. See Paul Delarue, "Les contes merveilleux de Perrault et la tradition populaire," *Bulletin folklorique de l'Ile-de-France* (1951), 221–8, 251–60, 283–91; (1953), 511–71.

7. See Yvonne Verdier, "Grands-mères, si vous saviez: le Petit Chaperon Rouge dans la tradition orale," *Cahiers de littérature orale* 4 (1978), 17–55.

8. There are numerous theories about the *chaperon rouge*. One of the more interesting interpretations is to be found in Hans T. Siepe's article "Rotkäppchen einmal anders. Ein Märchen für den Französis-

chunterricht," *Der fremdsprachliche Unterricht* 65 (1983), 1–9. Siepe points out that the term *grand chaperon* designated an older woman who was supposed to escort young girls from the upper class as chaperone in the English sense of the word. The fact that Little Red Riding Hood only has a "little chaperon" indicates that she did not have enough protection. Whatever the case may be, the chaperon transforms the peasant girl into a bourgeois type, and the color red, which may suggest menstruation, was a clear symbol of her sin. See also Bernadette Bricout, "L'aiguille et l'epingle" in *La 'Bibliotheque bleue' nel Seicento o della Letteratura per il popole*, eds. P.A. Jannini, G. Dotoli and P. Carile, 4 (1981), pp. 45–58.

9. Erich Fromm, *The Forgotten Language* (New York: Grove Press, 1957), p. 241.

10. Bruno Bettelheim, *The Uses of Enchantment: The Meaning and Importance of Fairy Tales* (New York: Knopf, 1976), p. 181.

11. For a different critique of Fromm and Bettelheim that is most perceptive and sheds new light on the possibilities of psychoanalysis and folklore, see Alan Dundes "Interpreting 'Little Red Riding Hood' Psychoanalytically" in *Little Red Riding Hood: A Casebook* (Madison: University of Wisconsin Press, 1989), pp. 192–236.

12. Susan Brownmiller, *Men, Women and Rape* (New York: Bantam, 1976), pp. 243–44.

13. See David Bland, *A History of Book Illustration* (London: Faber & Faber, 1958) and Percy Muir, *Victorian Illustrated Books* (London: Batsford, 1971).

14. Bill Nichols, *Ideology and the Image* (Bloomington, Indiana: Indiana University Press, 1981), p. 47. See also John Berger, *Ways of Seeing* (Harmondsworth: Penguin, 1972).

15. I have purposely taken this quotation from a book that has had seven printings since 1961, *Perrault's Complete Fairy Tales*, Trs. A.E. Johnson and others (Harmondsworth: Kestrel/Penguin, 1982), p. 77. Illustrations by W. Heath Robinson.

16. In America Doré's illustrations have been mainly reprinted in *Perrault's Fairy Tales* (New York: Dover, 1969). The Dover books are inexpensive, and therefore the illustrations are easily accessible to the public. Moreover, Dover has not been the only publisher to make use of the Doré illustrations.

17. Cf. Peter Coveney, *The Image of Childhood* (Harmondsworth: Penguin, 1967).

18. Cf. Marion Lochhead, *Their First Ten Years. Victorian Childhood* (London: John Murray, 1956).

19. Michel Foucault, *The History of Sexuality* (New York: Pantheon, 1978), p. 49. "We must therefore abandon the hypothesis that modern indus-

❀ 383 ❀

*Epilogue:*
*Reviewing*
*and*
*Re-Framing*
*Little Red*
*Riding*
*Hood*

trial societies ushered in an age of increased sexual repression. We have not only witnessed a visible explosion of unorthodox sexualities; but—and this is the important point—deployment quite different from the law, even if it is locally dependent on procedures of prohibition, has ensured, through a network of interconnecting mechanisms, the proliferation of specific pleasures and the multiplication of disparate sexualities. It is said that no society has been more prudish (Foucault is referring to Victorian society, J.Z.); never have the agencies of power taken such care to feign ignorance of the thing they prohibited, as if they were determined to have nothing to do with it. But it is the opposite that has become apparent, at least after a general review of the facts: never have there existed more centers of power; never more attention manifested and verbalized; never more circular contacts and linkages; never more sites where the intensity of pleasures and the persistency of power catch hold, only to spread elsewhere."

20. The same development can be traced in other Western countries. Cf. the Ladybird Easy Reading Books in England. In particular, see *Little Red Riding Hood*, retold by Vera Southgate with illustrations by Eric Winter (Loughborough: Ladybird Books, 1972).

21. The recording industry has also had a great impact on the market. See *Little Red Riding Hood*, Six More Favourite Stories Played by the Robin Lucas Children's Theatre, London: BiBi Music, BBM82.

22. Klaus Theweleit, *Männer Phantasien* (Frankfurt am Main: Roter Stern, 1977), pp. 478–79.

23. See Jacques Lacan, *Feminine Sexuality*, Eds. Juliet Mitchell and Jacqueline Rose (New York: Norton, 1983).

24. Larysa, Mykyta, "Lacan, Literature and the Look," *SubStance* 39 (1983), 54.

25. For an excellent essay that deals with Carter's political critique of pornography and sadomasochism, see Robin Ann Sheets, "Pornography, Fairy Tales, and Feminism: Angela Carter's 'The Bloody Chamber,'" in *Forbidden History*, Ed. John C. Fout (Chicago: University of Chicago Press, 1992), pp. 335–360.

26. Gerald Peary, "Little Red Ridinghood," *Sight and Sound* 57 (Summer 1988), 150.

27. See Iris Brennberger, ""Ein Wolf für gewisse Stunden," *Der Tagesspiegel* (June 29, 1992), 10.

# ❅ Notes on Authors ❅

BARING-GOULD, SABINE (1834–1924). English novelist and writer of hymns and religious works. He also wrote a great deal about folklore, including a study of werewolves, and books for children. Among his most famous hymns, "Onward Christian Soldiers" is the best known.

BAYLEY, FREDERICK W.N.(1808–1853). English writer, poet, and journalist. Aside from writing travel books, he was the author of *Comic Nursery Rhymes* (1846), which contains adaptations of *Blue Beard* and *Little Red Riding Hood*.

BROUMAS, OLGA (1949). Greek-American poet. Born in Syros Greece, Broumas moved to the United States in 1968 and studied at the Universities of Pennyvania and Oregon. Her first book in English was *Caritas* (1976) followed by *Beginning with O* (1977), which contains "Little Red Riding Hood." Since then she has published three volumes of poetry, *Pastoral Jazz* (1983), *Black Holes, Black Stockings* (1985), and *Perpetua* (1989) and translated from the Greek two volumes of poetry by Nobel Laureate Odysseas Elytis.

CAMI, PIERRE (1884–1958). French dramatist, critic, librettist, and screenplay writer. He studied theater at the Conservatoire de Paris and soon made a name for himself as a playwright with a flair for fantasy and irony. The titles of his first two important collections, *Pour lire sous la douche* (*For Reading Under the Shower*, 1913) and *L'Homme à la tête d'épingle* (*The Man With the Head of a Pin*, 1914), indicate his bizarre sense of humor. Cami wrote well over 40 books including songs, operettas, vaudeville revues, screenplays, and radio programs. *Little Green Riding Hood* (1914) was one of his early parodies of the fairy-tale genre.

CARTER, ANGELA (1940–1992). English novelist and short-story writer. She specialized in fantasy and Gothic fiction with such works as *The Magic Toy Shop* (1967), *The Infernal Desire Machines of Doctor Hoffman* (1972), *Nights at the Circus* (1984), and *Wise Children* (1991). She also produced several collections of stories, *Heroes and Villains* (1969), *The Bloody Chamber* (1979), which includes "The Company of Wolves," and *Fireworks* (1984). Her strong interest in folklore was manifested in her translation of *The Fairy Tales of Charles Perrault*

(1979) and *The Virago Book of Fairy Tales* (1990), and she also wrote a significant feminist study dealing with pornography entitled *The Sadeian Woman* (1979).

DAUDET, ALPHONSE (1840–97). French novelist and dramatist. One of the most popular novelists of France in the 19th century, Daudet was known for his realistic style and gentle humor. Like Dickens he had a great deal of sympathy for the common people and exposed the hypocrisy of charlatans and mean-spirited people. His major works are *Tartarin of Tarascon* (1872), *The Nabob* (1877), *Sapho* (1884), and *Tartarin on the Alps* (1885). *The Romance of Red Riding Hood* (1864) is a rare work by Daudet and was published early in his career with several other dramatic sketches.

DE LA MARE, WALTER (1873–1956). English poet, novelist, essayist, and writer of fantasies and tales for children. Known chiefly as a lyrical poet, De La Mare also wrote remarkable short stories and fairy tales that evoked a sense of the strange and otherworldly. He published over 50 volumes of prose and poetry, and among his more notable works are *Songs of Childhood* (1909), *Memoirs of a Midget* (1921), *Broomsticks* (1925), *Told Again* (1927), *The Lord and the Fish* (1933), *Memory and Other Poems* (1938), *The Scarecrow* (1945), and *Collected Stories for Children* (1947).

DUMAS, PHILIPPE (1940). French co-author of *Le Petit Chaperon Bleu Marine* in *Contes à l'envers* (1977). He has written and illustrated numerous other books such as *Histoire d'Edouard* (1976), *La petite géante* (1978), and a series of narratives about a girl named Laura.

FETSCHER, IRING (1922). German professor of political science and journalist. Aside from numerous scholarly books, he has published two mock collections of fairy tales entitled *Wer hat Dornröschen wachgeküßt? Ein Märchen-Verwirrbuch* (1972), which contains "Little Redhead and the Wolf," and *Der Nulltarif der Wichtelmänner* (1982).

GEARHART, SALLY MILLER (1931) American writer, professor, and activist for animal rights, lesbian/gay and women's rights, and in Central America solidarity work. She is the author of *The Wanderground: Stories of the Hill Women* (1979) and *A Feminist Tarot* (with Susan Rennie). In addition, she has appeared in two films, *The Life and Times of Harvey Milk* and *The Word Is Out*.

GMELIN, O. F. (1932). German filmmaker, director, and writer of children's books. Aside from his anti-sexist collection of tales *Märchen für tapfere Mädchen* (1978), illustrated by Doris Lerche, he has also written a critical study of children's books *Böses kommt aus Kinderbüchern* (1972).

GRIMM, JACOB (1785–1863) and WILHELM (1786–1859). German folklorists and linguists. Their collection *Kinder- und Hausmärchen* (published in two volumes in 1812 and 1815), literally, *Children's and Household Tales*, is perhaps the most famous anthology of folk and fairy tales in the world. In addition the Grimm Brothers collaborated on numerous projects dealing with myths, legends, and ballads, and they conceived the first modern dictionary of German.

GROSS, MILT (1895–1953) American cartoonist and humorist. He created cartoons for the *New York Evening Journal*, the *New York Tribune*, and the *New York World*. Among his best-known humorous works are *Nize Baby* (1926) and *Famous Fimales from Heestory* (1928).

GRÜN, MAX VON DER (1926). German novelist and writer for radio and television. He is known chiefly for books and stories dealing with a working-class milieu and exposing racism and prejudice in Germany. Among his better known works are *Irrlicht und Feuer* (1963), *Zwei Briefe an Popischiel* (1968), *Flächenbrand* (1979), and *Die Lawine* (1986).

LEE, TANITH (1947). Educated at Croydon Art School outside London, she began writing fairy tales and science fiction during the 1970s and is considered one of the leading writers of fantasy in Great Britain today. She has written two outstanding works for young readers, *The Dragon Hoard* (1971) and *Princess Hynchatti and Some Other Surprises* (1972), and among her best fantasy and science fiction works for adults are: *The Birthgrave* (1975), *The Quest for the White Witch* (1979), *Electric Forest* (1979), *The Gorgon and Other Beastly Tales* (1985), *Women as Demons* (1989), and *Blood of Roses* (1990). "Wolfland" appeared in *Red as Blood or Tales from the Grimmer Sisters* (1983), an innovative collection of traditional fairy tales written from a feminist perspective.

MARELLE, CHARLES. French folklorist and writer of miscellaneous works. He is known chiefly for his collection of folk stories in *Affenschwanz* (1880).

MEINERT, ANNELIESE (1902). German author of "Rotkappchen '65" (1965).

MERSEYSIDE FAIRY STORY COLLECTIVE (AUDREY ACKROYD, MARGE BEN-TOVIM, CATHERINE MEREDITH, ANNE NEVILLE). Formed in 1972, this English women's liberation group from Liverpool has written political and feminist adaptations of *Red Riding Hood*, *The Swineherd*, and *Snow White*.

MI, CHIANG. Chinese writer and illustrator of *Goldflower and the Bear*. (1979).

MILLS, ALFRED (1776–1833). American historian and author of *Ye True Hystorie of Little Red Riding Hood* published in *Nast's Illustrated Almanac* (1872). Mills was chiefly known as the author of *Pictures of Roman History* (1809), *Costumes of Different Nations* (1811), and *Pictures of Grecian History* (1812).

MOISSARD, BORIS (1940). French co-author of *Le Petit Chaperon Bleu Marine* in *Contes á l'envers* (1977). He has written another book in collaboration with Philippe Dumas, entitled *Aventures du vantard* (1979).

PERRAULT, CHARLES (1628–1703). French poet, essayist, and administrator. His most famous work is the collection of fairy tales entitled *Histoires ou Contes du temps passé* (1697), in which he created the literary figure of Little Red Riding Hood. One of the leading poets and intellectuals during the reign of Louis XIV, Perrault also played a significant role in the "Querelle des Anciens et des Modernes" against Racine and Boileau.

PHILLIPS, HARRY IRVING (1887–1965). American columnist and writer of miscellaneous works. He developed a column for the *New York Sun*, contributed to popular magazines, and wrote such humorous books as *On White or Rye* (1941).

RINGELNATZ, JOACHIM (pseudonym of HANS BÖTTICHER, 1883–1934). German poet, illustrator, and writer. He is best known for his satirical works, *Turngedichte* (1920), *Kuddel Daddeldu* (1923), and *Gedichte dreier Jahre* (1932).

RODARI, GIANNI (1920–1982). Italian journalist and writer of children's books. Rodari was one of the foremost innovators of the fairy-tale tradition in Italy and wrote an important pedagogical and theoretical study about fairy tales. Among his notable works in English are *Benfara's Toyshop* (1970) and *Tales Told by a Machine* (1976).

SAMBER, ROBERT. English author of the first known translation of Perrault's *Little Red Riding Hood*, which was published in *Histories, or Tales of Past Times* (1729). Samber translated numerous other Latin, French, and Italian works during the 18th century.

SEXTON, ANNE (1928–1974). American poet. One of the foremost contemporary poets in America, her important books are *To Bedlam and Part Way Back* (1960), *All My Pretty Ones* (1962) and *Live and Die* (1967). She adapted several Grimms' fairy tales and set them to verse in *Transformations* (1972).

SHARPE, ANNE (pseudonym for Frances Molloy, d. 1992). Irish novelist and short-story writer. Born in Derry, Molloy lived in England for over eighteen years and published many short stories in various magazines and anthologies. Her first novel, *No Mate for Maggie* (1985), was highly acclaimed, and she contributed "Not So Little Red Riding Hood" to *Rapunzel's Revenge: Fairytales for Feminists* in 1985.

SOMERVILLE, EDITH ANNA ŒNONE (1858–1949). Irish novelist and writer of miscellaneous works. She is best known for the novels she wrote with her cousin Florence Martin under the names "Somerville and Ross." Two important works are *The Real Charlotte* (1894) and *Some Experiences of an Irish R.M.* (1899).

STODDARD, RICHARD HENRY (1825–1903). American lyric poet and journalist. His most significant works include *Songs of Summer* (1856), *Abraham Lincoln: A Horatian Ode* (1865), and *Poems* (1880).

STORR, CATHERINE (1913). English writer of children's books, novelist, and playwright. She began writing as a practicing physician and published three volumes of "Clever Polly Books" from 1952–1980. "Little Polly Riding Hood" appeared in *Clever Polly and the Stupid Wolf* (1955). Among Storr's other remarkable books for children are *The Chinese Egg* (1975), *The Painter and the Fish* (1975), *Androcles and the Lion* (1987), *Daljit and the Unqualified Wizard* (1989), and *Last Stories of Polly and the Wolf* (1990).

STRAUSS, GWEN. American poet. She attended Wheelock College in Boston and received an M.A. in elementary education. After working in schools, she began writing poetry and short stories for children. Her tales and poems have appeared in various literary journals. "The Waiting Wolf" and other intriguing fairy-tale poems were published in *Trail of Stones* (1990), and her second book, *The Night Shimmy*, was published in 1991.

TIECK, LUDWIG (1773–1853). German poet, novelist, and playwright. One of the foremost members of the romantic school, Tieck is known mainly for his unusual fairy tales such as *Der blonde Eckbert* (1776) and *Der Runenberg* (1802). He also adapted fairy tales for the stage, including *Der gestiefelte Kater* (1797) and *Leben und Tod des kleinen Rotkäppchens* (1800).

THURBER, JAMES (1894–1961). American illustrator, journalist, and short-story writer. He achieved fame through his humorous stories and parodies, which include *Is Sex Necessary?* (1929), *The Owl in the Attic and Other Perplexities* (1931), *Fables for Our Time* (1939), and *Men, Women, and Dogs* (1943).

UNGERER, TOMI (pseudonym of JEAN THOMAS, 1931). American-French illustrator, graphic artist, and writer of children's books. Known for his wry and provocative humor, Ungerer created the "Mellops" series in 1957, and some of his other unusual works include *Zeralda's Ogre* (1967), *The Beasts of Monsieur Racine* (1973), *Allumette* (1974), *Babylon* (1979), and *No Kiss for Mother* (1991). His version of "Little Red Riding Hood" appeared in *A Storybook* (1974).

WIEMER, RUDOLF OTTO (1905). German writer of children's books and plays, teacher, and puppeteer. Among his best-known works are *Der gute Räuber Willibald und seine sieben Abenteuer* (1965), *Das Pferd, das in die Schule kam und andere heitere Geschichten* (1970), *Der Kaiser und der kleine Mann* (1972), *Sehnsucht der Krokodile* (1985), and *Schilfwasser* (1987).

# Bibliography
❄ *of Little Red Riding Hood Texts* ❄

THIS BIBLIOGRAPHY IS A chronological list of the major literary texts in English, French, German, and Italian, and it also includes a few examples of folk versions. For additional bibliographies, consult Harry B. Weiss, *Little Red Riding Hood: A Terror Tale of the Nursery* (Trenton, N.J.: Privately Printed, 1939); Hans Ritz, *Die Geschichte vom Rotkäppchen* (Emstal: Muriverlag, 1981); Wolfgang Mieder, "Survival Forms of 'Little Red Riding Hood' in Modern Society," *International Folklore Review* 2 (1982), 23–41; and Elisabeth and Richard Waldmann, *Wo hinaus so früh, Rotkäppchen? Veränderungen eines europäischen Märchens*. Zurich: Schweizerisches Jugendbuch-Institut, 1985.

## SEVENTEENTH CENTURY

1697 Perrault, Charles. "Le Petit Chaperon Rouge." In *Histoires du temps passé: Avec des Moralitez*. Paris: Fleuron.

## EIGHTEENTH CENTURY

1729 Samber, Robert. "The Little Red Riding-Hood." In *Histories, or Tales of Past Times*. London.

1790 "Rothkäppchen." In *Die Blaue Bibliothek*, vol. 1. Gotha: Ettingersche.

1796 "The Story of Little Red Riding Hood." In *The House That Jack Built*. Boston: James White.

## NINETEENTH CENTURY

1800 Tieck, Ludwig. *Leben und Tod des kleinen Rotkäppchens: Eine Tragödie* In *Schriften*, vol. 2. Berlin: Reimer. Translated as *The Life and Death of Little Red Ridinghood: A Tragedy*, adapted from the German by Jane Browning Smith. London: Groombridge, 1852.

1801 "The Wolf-King, or Little Red-Riding-Hood." In *Tales of Terror*. London: Bulmer.

1812 Grimm, Die Brüder (Jacob and Wilhelm). "Rotkappchen." In *Kinder- und Hausmärchen*. Berlin: Realschulbuchhandlung.

1821 *The History of Little Red Riding-Hood*. 2d American Ed. Philadelphia: Mary Charles.

1823 Legrand, Armand, Junien Champeaux, and Auguste Gombault. *Le Petit Chaperon Rouge. Conte en Action, Melé de Couplets*. Paris: Duvernois.

1830 Penny Books of J. Kendrew. *The Entertaining Story of Little Red Riding Hood*. York: J . Kendrew .

1831 Boieldieu, François Adrien. *Le Petit Chaperon Rouge: Opéra-féerie, en trois actes et en prose de M. Théaulon*. Paris: C. Ballard, 1818. Translated as *The Little Red Riding Hood*. Trs. W. F. F. Baltimore: E. J. Coale.

1840 Holting, Gustav. *Das kleine Rotkäppchen*. Berlin: Winckelmann.

1845 Summerly, Felix. *The Traditional Faery Tales of Little Red Riding Hood, Beauty and the Beast & Jack and the Bean Stalk*. London: Joseph Cundall.

1846 Bayley, F. W. N. *Little Red Riding Hood*. London: Orr.

1853 Bechstein, Ludwig. "Rotkäppchen." In *Ludwig Bechsteins Märchenbuch*. Leipzig: Wigand.

1859 Bridgeman, J. V., and H. Sutherland Edwards. *Little Red Riding Hood: Or, Harlequin and the Wolf in Granny's Clothing*. London: Chapman.

1862 Daudet, Alphonse. *Le Roman du Chaperon Rouge*. Paris: Michel Lévy.

1863 Craik, Dinah Maria. "Little-Red-Riding-Hood." In *The Fairy Book*. London: Macmillan.

1863 Very, Lydia Louisa Anna. *Red Riding Hood*. Boston: Prang.

1864 Stoddard, Richard Henry. *The Story of Little Red Riding Hood*. New York: James G. Gregory.

1865 Hood, Tom. "Little Red Riding Hood." In *Fairy Realm: A Collection of the Favourite Old Tales Told in Verse*. London: Ward, Lock, and Tyler.

1866 Walter Crane's Toy Books. *Little Red Riding Hood*. London: Routledge.

1867 Thackeray, Miss (Anne I. Ritchie). *Little Red Riding Hood*. Boston: Loring.

1869 Hartmann, Moritz. "Das Rothkäppchen." In *Märchen nach Perrault*. Stuttgart: Halberger.

1870 Gibb's Good Child's Picture Library. *Little Red Riding Hood*. Glasgow: Gibb.

1872 Mills, Alfred. "Ye True Hystorie of Little Red Riding Hood." In *Nast's Illustrated Almanac 1872*. New York: Harper.

1875 Cooper, George, and Harrison Millard. "Little Red Riding-Hood: An Operetta for Juveniles." In Harrison Millard, *Silver Threads of Song for School and Home*. New York: S. T. Gordon.

1880 Siewert, Ernst. *Rotkäppchen: Ein Kindermärchen in drei Akten*. Berlin: Schreiber.

1882 Childe-Pemberton, Harriet. "All my Doing; or, Red Riding-Hood over again." In *The Fairy Tales of Every Day*. London: Society for Promoting Christian Knowledge.

1885 Blum, Ernest, and Raoul Toché. *Le Petit Chaperon Rouge: Opérette en trois actes et quatre tableaux (Musique de Gaston Serpette)*. Paris: Choudens.

1888 Baneux, E. *Le Petit Chaperon Rouge*. Paris: Librairie Théatrale.

1888 Marelle, Charles. "La Veritable Histoire du Petit Chaperon d'or." In *Affenschwanz. Variantes orales de Contes populaires et étrangers*. Braunschweig: Westermann.

1890 Father Tuck's Fairy Tale Series. *Little Red Riding-Hood*. New York: Tuck.

1894 Baring-Gould, Sabine. "Little Red Riding-Hood." In *A Book of Fairy Tales*. London: Methuen.

1894 Baring-Gould, Sabine. *Fairy Tales from Grimm*. London: Wells Gardner & Darton.

1895 Rhys, Grace. *Little Red Riding Hood and the History of Tom Thumb*. Banbury Series. London: J. M. Dent.

1895 Star Rhymes. *The Story of Little Red Riding Hood*. Star Soap Rhymes. Zanesville, Ohio: Schultz.

1898 Baldwin, James. "Little Red Riding Hood." In *Fairy Stories and Fables*. New York: American Book Company.


TWENTIETH CENTURY

1900 Riley, James Whitcomb. "Red Riding-Hood." In *Home-Folks*. New York: Century.

1900 *Red Riding Hood* (in verse). New York: Merimack Reprint, 1979.

1903 The Mother Goose Series. *Little Red Riding-Hood and Other Stories*. New York: A. L. Burt.

1907 Rhys, Ernest. "Little Red Riding-Hood." In *Fairy Gold: A Book of English Fairy Tales*. London: J. M. Dent.

1914 Mathieu, Émilie. *Le Nouveau Chaperon Rouge*. Paris: Deselée, DeBrouwer.

1914 Cami, Pierre. "Le Petit Chaperon vert." In *L'Homme à la tête d'épingle*. Paris: Flammarion.

1916 Riley, James Whitcomb. "Maymie's Story of Red Riding Hood." In *The Complete Works of James Whitcomb Riley*. Vol. 7. New York: Harper.

1920 Thomason, Caroline. *Red Riding Hood: A Play for Children in Three Scenes*. Philadelphia: Penn.

1922 Guyot, Charles. "La Petite Fille du Chaperon Rouge." In *Le Printemps d'autres contes du bon vieux temps*. Paris: L'Edition d'Art.

1922 Piper, Walter, ed. *Little Folks Red Riding Hood and Other Stories*. New York: Platt & Munk.

1923 Ringelnatz, Joachim. "Kuttel Daddeldu erzählt seinen Kindern das Märchen vom Rotkäppchen." In *Kuttel Daddeldu*. Munich: Wolff.

1923 Lichtenberger, André. *Le Petit Chaperon Vert suivi d'autres contes*. Paris: G. Crès.

1925 Gandéra, Félix, and Claude Gével. *Le Petit Chaperon Rouge: Comédie en un acte (en vers)*. Paris: Librairie Theatrale.

1926 Gross, Milt. "Sturry from Rad Ridink Hoot." In *Nize Baby*. New York: Doran.

1926 Bouliech, Julien. *Le Petit Chaperon Rouge en vers*. Paris: Editions de la Revue Litteraire et Artistique.

1927 de la Mare, Walter. "Red Riding Hood." In *Told Again: Traditional Tales told by Walter De La Mare*. Oxford: Basil Blackwell.

1929 Gruelle, Johnny. "All about Red Riding Hood." In *The All About Story Book*. New York: Cupples & Leon.

1934 Somerville, Edith Anna Œnone. "Little Red Riding-Hood." In *The Fairies Return, or New Tales for Old*. London: Peter Davies.

1934 Walt Disney Studios. *The Big Bad Wolf and Little Red Riding Hood*. Toronto: Musson Book Company.

1934 Noury, Pierre. *Les contes de Perrault*. Paris: Flammarion.

1937 Link, Ulrich. "Rotkäppchen." Fasching ed. of the *Münchner Neueste Nachrichten*. Reprinted in the *Süddeutsche Zeitung*, 22 (February, 1952).

1939 Thurber, James. "The Girl and the Wolf." In *Fables for Our Time and Famous Poems*. New York: Harper.

1939 Linenette Series. *Little Red Riding Hood*. New York: Gabriel.

1940 Phillips, H. I. "Little Red Riding Hood as a Dictator Would Tell It." *Collier's* 105 (January 20), p. 16.

1944 *The Gingerbread Boy, Little Red Riding Hood, and The House That Jack Built*, illustrated by Hilda Miloche and Wilma Kane. Racine, Wisconsin: Whitman.

1946 De Heriz, Patrick. "Little Red Riding Hood." In *Fairy Tales with a Twist*. London: Peter Lunn.

1946 Arvel, Pierre. *Le Petit Chaperon Rouge: Pièce en Trois Actes*. Paris: Lescot.

1948 Jones, Elizabeth Orton. *Little Red Riding Hood*. New York: Golden Press.

1948 Bal, Jean-Claude. *Le Petit Chaperon Rouge: Adaption scénique*. Villefranche: Cep Beaujolais.

1951 Richard, Raymond. *Le Petit Chaperon Rouge et les 7 Nains: Féerie musicale*. Paris.

1952 Colmont, Marie. *Marlaguette*. Paris: Flammarion.

1953 Carryl, Guy Wetmore. "Red Riding Hood." In *The Home Book of Verse*. New York: Holt, Rinehart, and Winston.

1955 Storr, Catherine. "Little Polly Riding Hood." In *Clever Polly and the Stupid Wolf*. London: Faber & Faber.

1959 Landrová, Divica, and Novotny. *Rotkäppchen*. Prague: Artia Prag.

1965 Chang, Isabelle C. "The Chinese Red Riding Hoods." In *Chinese Fairy Tales*. New York: Crown.

1965 Meinert, Anneliese. "Rotkäppchen, '65." *Frankfurter Rundschau* (September 6). Reprinted in Lutz Röhrich. *Gebärden—Metapher-Parodie*. Düsseldorf: Schwann, 1967.

1966 Bruna, Dick. *Dick Bruna's Little Red Riding Hood*. Chicago: Follett.

1967 Wells, Joel. "Little Red Riding Hood." In *Grim Fairy Tales for Adults*. New York: Macmillan.

1967 Hogrogian, Nonny. *The Renowned History of Little Red Riding Hood*. New York: Crowell.

1967 Rouger, Gilbert, ed. *Contes de Perrault*. Paris: Garnier.

1968 Pincus, Harriet. *Little Red Riding Hood*. New York: Harcourt Brace Jovanovich.

1968 *The Story of Little Red Riding Hood*. Chicago: Encyclopedia Britannica Corp.

1968 Merrill, Jean. *Red Riding*. New York: Pantheon.

1970 Weigle, Oscar. *Little Red Riding Hood*, pictures by T. Izawa and S. Hijikata. New York: Grosset & Dunlap.

1970 Londeix, Georges. *Le Petit Chaperon Rouge*. Paris: Éditions de L'Herne.

1971 Zupan, Vitomil. "A Fairy Tale." *Literary Review*. 14:298.

1971 Jacintho, Rogue. *The Big Bad Wolf Reincarnate*. Trs. Evelyn Morales and S.J. Haddad. Rio, Brazil: Federacao Brasileira.

1971 Sexton, Anne. "Red Riding Hood." In *Transformations*. Boston: Houghton Mifflin.

1972 Janosch. "Das elektrische Rotkäppchen." In *Janosch erzählt Grimm's Märchen*. Weinheim: Beltz & Gelberg.

1972 Regniers, Beatrice Schenk de. *Red Riding Hood*. New York: Atheneum.

1972 Fetscher, Iring. "Rotschöpfchen und der Wolf." In *Wer hat Dornröschen wachgeküßt? Das Märchen-Verwirrbuch*. Hamburg: Classen.

1972 Merseyside Fairy Story Collective (Audrey Ackroyd, Marge Ben-Tovim, Catherine Meredith, and Anne Neville). *Red Riding Hood*. Liverpool: Fairy Story Collective.

1973 Rodari, Gianni. "Little Green Riding Hood." *Cricket* 1:17–19.

1973 Cullivier, M. *Un Nouveau Petit Chaperon Rouge. Sylvain et Sylvette*. Nr. 29. Illustr. J.-L. Pesch. Paris: Fleurus.

1973 Sklarew, Myra. "Red Riding Hood at the Acropolis." *Carolina Quarterly* 24:42–43.

1974 Grün, Max von der. "Rotkappchen." In *Bilderbogengeschichten— Märchen, Sagen, Abenteuer*, ed. Jochen Jung. Munich: Heinz Moos.

1974 A Tell-A-Tale Book. *Little Red Riding Hood*. Racine, Wisconsin: Western.

1974 Ungerer, Tomi. "Little Red Riding Hood." In *A Storybook*. New York: Franklin Watts.

1974 Galdone, Paul. *Little Red Riding Hood*. New York: McGraw-Hill.

1974 Hope, A.D. "Coup de Grâce." In *Poetry, Past and Present*, Ed. Frank Brady and Martin Price. New York: Harcourt, Brace, Jovanovich.

1976 Wiemer, Rudolf Otto. "Der alte Wolf." In *Neues vom Rumpelstilzchen und andere Märchen von 43 Autoren*, Ed. Hans-Joachim Gelberg. Weinheim: Beltz & Gelberg.

1977 Broumas, Olga. "Little Red Riding Hood." In *Beginning with O*. New Haven: Yale University Press.

1977 Schädlich, Hans Joachim. "Kriminalmärchen." In *Versuchte Nähe*. Reinbek bei Hamburg: Rowohlt.

1977 Dumas, Philippe, and Boris Moissard. "Le Petit Chaperon Bleu Marine." In *Contes à l'envers*. Paris: l'école des loisirs.

1978 Imagerie Pellerin. "Le Petit Chaperon Rouge," Imagerie d'Epinal, Nr. 1099. In *Contes de Fées*. Reprint of 19th-century Images d'Epinal. Epinal: Pellerin.

1978 Gmelin, O. F. "Rotkäppchen." In Doris Lerche and O. F. Gmelin, *Märchen für tapfere Mädchen*. Giessen: Schlot.

1978 Ross, Tony. *Little Red Riding Hood*. Garden City: Doubleday.

1979 Loumaye, Jacqueline. *L'histoire VRAIE du PETIT CHAPERON ROUGE de sa Mère-grand et du grand mechant Loup*. Brussels: Louis Musin.

1979 Watts, Mabel. *Little Red Riding Hood.* 10th ptg. Racine: Golden Press.

1979 Ainsworth, Ruth. *Little Red Riding Hood.* New York: Banner Press.

1979 Carter, Angela. "The Company of Wolves." In *The Bloody Chamber.* New York: Harper & Row.

1979 Mi, Chiang. *Goldflower and the Bear.* People's Republic of China.

1980 Derrydale Series. *Red Riding Hood.* New York: Crown.

1980 Kassajep, Margaret. "Rotkäppchen mit Sturzhelm." In *"Deutsche Märchen" frisch getrimmt.* Dachau: ASIS.

1981 Munari, Bruno and Enrica Agostinelli. *Cappuccetto Rosso Verde Giallo Blue Bianco.* Torino: Einaudi.

1982 Hay, Sara Henderson. "The Grandmother." In *Story Hour.* Fayetteville: University of Arkansas Press.

1982 Dahl, Roald. "Little Red Riding Hood and the Wolf." In *Revolting Rhymes.* London: Jonathan Cape.

1983 Lee, Tanith. "Wolfland." In *Red as Blood, Or Tales from the Sisters Grimmer.* New York: DAW Books.

1983 Perrault, Charles. *Little Red Riding Hood.* Illustr. Sarah Moon. Mankato, Minnesota: Creative Education.

1983 Rühmkorf, Peter. "Rotkäppchen under der Wolfspelz." In *Der Hüter des Misthaufens. Aufgeklärte Märchen.* Reinbek: Rowohlt.

1983 Grimm, Brüder. *Rotkäppchen.* Illustr. Lisbeth Zwerger. Salzburg: Neugebauer.

1983 Hyman, Trina Schart. *Little Red Riding Hood.* New York: Holiday House.

1984 Yolen, Jane. "Happy Dens, or A Day in the Old Wolves Home." In *Elsewhere.* Vol. III. New York: Ace Fantasy.

1984 Claus, Uta and Rolf Kutschera. "Ein Typ erzählt Rotkäppchen." In *Total Tote Hose: 12 bockstarke Märchen.* Frankfurt am Main: Eichborn.

1984 *Le Petit Chaperon Rouge.* Illustr. Pascal Trigaux. Toulouse: Tobaggan-Magazine.

1985 Lanigan, Carol. "All The Better To See You." In *Rapunzel's Revenge: Fairytales for Feminists.* Dublin: Attic Press.

1985 Sharpe, Anne. "Not So Little Red Riding Hood." In *Rapunzel's Revenge: Fairytales for Feminists.* Dublin: Attic Press.

1985 Heller, Rebecca. *Little Red Riding Hood.* Illustr. Marsha Winborn. New York: A Golden Book.

1985 Mansk, Izaak. *Rotkapuze.* Düsseldorf: Marion von Schröder.

1985 Garbe, Burckhard and Gisela. "Rotkäppchen oder: Wolf bleibt Wolf." In *Der gestiefelte Kater: Grimms Märchen umerzählt.* Göttingen: sage und schreibe.

1986 Hayes, Sarah. *Little Red Riding Hood*. New York: Derrydale.

1987 Morris, Ann. *The Little Red Riding Hood Rebus Book*. New York: Franklin Watts.

1987 Marshall, James. *Red Riding Hood*. New York: Dial.

1987 Company, M. and R. Capdevila. *Les Trois Petites Soeurs et le petit Chaperon Rouge*. Adapt. Yvette Métral. Paris: Nathan.

1988 Sondheim, Stephen and James Lapine. *Into the Woods*. Adapt. and illustr. Hudson Talbott. New York: Crown.

1989 Young, Ed. *Lon Po Po: A Red-Riding Hood Story from China*. New York: Philomel.

1989 Solotareff, Grégoire. *Le Petit Chaperon Vert*. Paris: l'école des loisirs.

1989 Crump, Fred. *Little Red Riding Hood*. Nashville: Winston-Derek.

1990 Strauss, Gwen. "The Waiting Wolf." In *Trail of Stones*. London: Julia MacRae Books.

1990 Gearhart, Sally Miller. "Roja and Leopold." In *And a Deer's Ear, Eagle's Song, and Bear's Grace: Animals and Women*, Ed. Theresa Corrigan and Stephanie Hoppe. Pittsburgh: Cleis.

1990 Emberley, Michael, *Ruby*. Boston: Little Brown.

1991 Montresor, Beni. *Little Red Riding Hood*. New York: Doubleday.

1991 Rowland, Della. *Little Red Riding Hood and the Wolf's Tale*. New York: Birch Lane Press.

1992 Scieszka, Jon and Lane Smith. "Little Red Running Shorts." In *The Stinky Cheese Man and other Fairy Stupid Tales*. New York: Viking.

### Folk Versions

1889 Abrousset, M. and M. Daumas. "A South African Red Riding-Hood." In Sir James Frazier, "A South African Red Riding-Hood," *Folklore Journal*, 7:167–168.

1953 A. Millien et P. Delarue, *Contes du Nivernais et du Morvan*, Paris: Érasme.

1957 Delarue, Paul. "Le Petit Chaperon Rouge." In *Le Conte Populaire Français*, vol.1. Paris: Érasme.

1959 *Versions populaires Haut-Alpines des Contes de Perrault*. Gap: Ribaud Frères.

1971 Joisten, Charles. *Contes Populaires du Dauphiné*, vol. 1. Grenoble: Publications du Musée Dauphinois.

# ❦ *General Bibliography* ❦

Addy, Sidney Oldall. *Folk Tales and Superstitions*. London: Nutt, 1895.

L'Ancre, Pierre de. *L'Incrédulité et mescréance du sortilège pleinement convaincue*. Paris, 1622.

Ariès, Philippe. *Centuries of Childhood: A Social History of Family Life*. New York: Knopf, 1962.

_____. "At the Point of Origin." *Yale French Studies* 43 (1969): 15–23.

Barchilon, Jacques, and Henry Petit. *The Authentic Mother Goose Fairy Tales and Nursery Rhymes*. Denver: Swallow, 1960.

Barchilon, Jacques. *Le Conte Merveilleux Français de 1690 à 1790*. Paris: Champion, 1975 .

Baring-Gould, Sabine. *The Book of Were-Wolves: Being an Account of a Terrible Superstition*. London: Smith, Elder, 1865.

Becker, Gabriele, Silvia Bovenschen, Helmut Brackert, Sigrid Brauner, Ines Brenner, Gisela Morgenthal, Klaus Schneller, Angelika Tummler. *Aus der Zeit der Verzweiflung: Zur Genese und Aktualität des Hexenbildes*. Frankfurt am Main: Suhrkamp, 1977.

Berger, John. *Ways of Seeing*. Harmondsworth: Penguin, 1972.

Berne, Eric. *What Do You Say After You Say Hello?* New York: Grove Press, 1972.

Bettelheim, Bruno. *The Uses of Enchantment: The Meaning and Importance of Fairy Tales*. New York: Knopf, 1976.

Bland, David. *A History of Book Illustration*. London: Faber & Faber, 1958.

Bottigheimer, Ruth B., ed. *Fairy Tales and Society: Illusion, Allusion, and Paradigm*. Philadelphia: University of Pennsylvania Press, 1986.

_____. *Grimms' Bad Girls and Bold Boys: The Moral and Social Vision of the Tales*. New Haven: Yale University Press, 1987.

Boucher, François. *20,000 Years of Fashion*. New York: Abrams, 1958.

Bremond, Claude. "Les bons récompensés et les méchants punis: Morphologie du conte merveilleux français." In *Semiotique narrative et textuelle*, Ed. Claude Chabiol. Paris: Larousse, 1973, pp. 96–121.

Brennberger, Iris. "Ein Wolf für gewisse Stunden." *Der Tagesspiegel* (June 29, 1992): 10.

Bricout, Bernadette. "Les Deux Chemins du Petit Chaperon Rouge." In *Frontières du contes*, Ed. James Austin. Paris: Centre National de la Recherche Scientifique, 1982, pp. 47–54.

Brownmiller, Susan. *Against Our Will: Men, Women and Rape*. New York: Bantam, 1976.

Bülow, Werner von. *Märchendeutungen durch Runen: Die Geheimsprache der deutschen Märchen*. Hellerau bei Dresden: Hakenkreuz-Verlag, 1925.

Burns, Lee. "Red Riding Hood." *Children's Literature* 1 (1972): 30–36.

Calvetti, Anselmo. "Tracce di Riti di Iniziazione nelle Fiabe di Cappuccetto Rosso e delle tre Ochine." *Lares* 46 (1980): 487–96.

Chorover, Stephan. *From Genesis to Genocide: The Meaning of Human Nature and the Power of Behavior Control*. Cambridge: MIT Press, 1979.

Coffin, Tristram Potter. *The Female Hero in Folklore and Legend*. New York: Seabury, 1975.

Corten, Irina H. "Evgenii Shvarts as an Adapter of Hans Christian Andersen and Charles Perrault." *Russian Review* 37 (1978): 51–67.

Coveney, Peter. *The Image of Childhood*. Harmondsworth: Penguin, 1967.

Darnton, Robert. *The Great Cat Massacre and Other Episodes in French Cultural History*. New York: Basic Books, 1984.

Delarue, Paul. "Les contes merveilleux de Perrault et la tradition populaire." *Bulletin folklorique de l'Ile-de-France* (1951): 221–28, 251–60, 283–91; (1953): 511–17.

————, Ed. *The Borzoi Book of French Folk Tales*. Trs. Austin E. Fife. New York: Knopf, 1956.

————. "Le Petit Chaperon Rouge." In *Le Conte Populaire Français*, vol. 1. Paris: Érasme, 1957. Pp. 373–83.

Deulin, Charles. *Les Contes de Ma Mère l'Oye avant Perrault*. Paris: E. Dentu, 1879.

Doderer, Klaus, and Helmut Müller, Eds. *Das Bilderbuch*. Weinheim: Beltz, 1973.

Duerr, Hans Peter. *Traumzeit: Über die Grenze zwischen Wildnis und Zivilisation*. Frankfurt am Main: Syndikat, 1978.

Duncker, Patricia. "Re-Imagining the Fairy Tale: Angela Carter's Bloody Chambers." *Literature and History* 10 (Spring 1984): 3–14.

Dundes, Alan, Ed. *Little Red Riding Hood: A Casebook*. Madison: University of Wisconsin Press, 1989.

Dworkin, Andrea. *Woman Hating*. New York: Dutton, 1974.

Eberhard, Wolfram. "The Story of Grandaunt Tiger." *Taiwanese Folktales* 1 (1970): 14–17; 27–76; 91–5.

Elias, Norbert. *Über den Prozeß der Zivilisation*, 2 vols. Frankfurt am Main: Suhrkamp, 1977. English ed., *The Civilizing Process*, Trs. Edmund Jephcott. New York: Urizen, 1978.

Farrer, Claire R., Ed. *Women and Folklore*. Austin: University of Texas Press, 1975.

Favret, Jeanne. "Sorcières et Lumières." *Critique* 27 (1971): 351–76.

Foucault, Michel. *Discipline and Punish: The Birth of the Prison*. New York: Pantheon, 1978.

_____. *The History of Sexuality*. New York: Pantheon, 1978.

Fout, John C., Ed. *Forbidden History: The State, Society, and the Regulation of Sexuality in Modern Europe*. Chicago: University of Chicago Press, 1992.

Freeman, Jo., Ed. *Women: A Feminist Perspective*. 3rd ed. Palo Alto: Mayfield, 1984.

Fromm, Erich. *The Forgotten Language: An Introduction to the Understanding of Dreams, Fairy Tales and Myths*. New York: Grove Press, 1951.

Frost, Brian J., Ed. *Book of the Werewolf*. London: Sphere Books, 1973.

Gennep, A. van. "Remarques sur l'Imagerie populaire." *Revue d'Ethnographie et de Sociologie* 2 (1911): 26–50.

Habermas, Jürgen. *Legitimation Crisis*, Trs. Thomas McCarthy. Boston: Beacon, 1975.

Hagen, Rolf. "Perraults Märchen und die Brüder Grimm." *Zeitschrift für Deutsche Philologie* 74 (1955): 392–410.

Hanks, Carole, and D. T. Hanks. "Perrault's 'Little Red Riding Hood': Victim of Revision." *Children's Literature* 7 (1978): 68–77.

Henssen, Gottfried. "Deutsche Schreckmarchen und ihre europäischen Anverwandten." *Zeitschrift für Volkskunde* 51 (1953): 84–97.

Hermann, Horst. *Ketzer in Deutschland*. Cologne: Kiepenheuer & Witsch, 1978.

Hertz, Wilhelm. *Der Werwolf*. Stuttgart: Kroner, 1862.

Heurck, E. van, and G. J. Boekenoogen. *Histoire de l'Imagerie populaire flammande et ses rapports avec les imageries étrangères*. Brussels: G. van Oest, 1910.

Holbek, Bengt. *Interpretation of Fairy Tales: Danish Folklore in a European Perspective*. Helsinki: Academia Scientarium Fennica, 1987.

Honegger, Claudia. *Die Hexen der Neuzeit: Studien zur Sozialgeschichte eines kulturellen Deutungsmusters*. Frankfurt am Main: Suhrkamp, 1978.

Husson, Hyacinthe. *La chaine traditionelle*. Paris: Franck, 1874.

Jacoby, Michael. *Warus, vagr. 'Verbrecher' 'Wolf.'* Uppsala: Almqvist & Wiksell, 1974.

Jäger, Hans-Wolf. "Trägt Rotkäppchen eine Jakobiner-Mütze? Über mutmassliche Konnotate bei Tieck und Grimm." In *Literatursoziologie*, *vol.* 2, Ed. Joachim Bark. Stuttgart: Kohlhammer, 1974, pp. 159–80.

Jones, Steven Swann. "On Analyzing Fairy Tales: 'Little Red Riding Hood' Revisited." *Western Folklore* 46 (1987): 97–106.

_____. "Response to Oring." *Western Folklore* 46 (1987): 112–14.

Kast, Verena. *Märchen als Therapie*. Olten: Walter-Verlag, 1986.

Köhler, Carl. *A History of Costume*, Trs. Alexander K. Dallas. London: Harrap, 1928.

Kühleborn, Heinrich E. *Rotkäppchen und die Wölfe: Von Märchenfälschern und Landschaftszerstörern*. Frankfurt am Main: Fischer, 1982.

Lacan, Jacques. *Feminine Sexuality*. Ed. Juliet Mitchell and Jacqueline Rose. New York: Norton, 1983.

Lang, Andrew. *Myth, Ritual and Religion*. London: Longmans, Green, 1887.

Laruccia, Victor. "Little Red Riding Hood's Metacommentary: Paradoxical Injunction, Semiotics and Behavior." *Modern Language Notes* 90 (1975): 517–34.

_____. "Progress, Perrault and Fairy Tales: Ideology and Semiotics." Ph.D. diss., University of California at San Diego, 1975.

Leiss, William. *The Domination of Nature*. Boston: Beacon, 1972.

Leubushcher, Rudolf. *Ueber die Wehrwölfe und Thierverwandlungen im Mittelalter*. Berlin: Reimer, 1850.

Linnig, Franz. *Deutsche Mythen-Märchen: Beitrag zur Erklärung der Grimmschen Kinder- und Hausmärchen*. Paderborn: Schoningh, 1883.

Lochhead, Marion. *Their First Ten Years. Victorian Childhood*. London: John Murray, 1956.

Londeix, Georges. *Le Petit Chaperon rouge*. Paris: L'Herne, 1970.

Macfarlane, Alan. *Witchcraft in Tudor and Stuart England*. London: Routledge & Kegan Paul, 1970.

Majewski, Henry. *The Preromantic Imagination of L.-S. Mercier*. New York: Humanities Press, 1971.

Mallet, Carl-Heinz. *Kennen Sie Kinder?* Hamburg: Hoffmann und Campe, 1980.

Mandrou, Robert. *Magistrats et sorciers en France au XVIIe siècle*. Paris: Plon, 1968.

Middleton, Christopher. "Sexual Divisions in Feudalism." *New Left Review* 113–114 (1979): 147–68.

Mieder, Wolfgang, Ed. *Grimms Märchen modern*. Stuttgart: Reclam, 1979.

_____. "Survival Forms of 'Little Red Riding Hood' in Modern Society." *International Folklore Review* 2 (1982): 23–41.

_____. *Tradition and Innovation in Folk Literature*. Hanover: University Press of New England, 1987.

Mistler, Jean, François Blaudez, and André Jacquemin. *Épinal et l'imagerie populaire*. Paris: Hachette, 1961.

Mourey, Lilyane. *Introduction aux contes de Grimm et de Perrault*. Paris: Minard, 1978.

Müller, Konrad. *Die Werwolfsage*. Karlsruhe: Macklotsche Verlag 1937.

Muir, Percy. *Victorian Illustrated Books*. London: Batsford, 1971.

Mykyta, Larysa. "Lacan, Literature and the Look." *SubStance* 39 (1983): 49–57.

Newall, Venetia, Ed. *The Witch Figure*. London: Routledge & Kegan Paul, 1973.

Nichols, Bill. *Ideology and the Image*. Bloomington: University of Indiana Press, 1981.

O'Donnell, Elliott. *Werwolves*. London: Methuen, 1912.

Oring, Elliott. "On the Meanings of Mother Goose." *Western Folklore* 46 (1987): 106–11.

Peary, Gerald. " Little Red Ridinghood." *Sight and Sound* 57 (Summer 1988): 150.

Planché, James Robinson. *Encyclopedia of Costume*, vol. I. London: Chatto & Windus, 1876.

Prestl, Josef. *Märchen als Lebensdichtung*. Munich: Hueber, 1938.

Pusey, W.W. *Louis-Sebastien Mercier in Germany: His Vogue and Influence in the Eighteenth Century*. New York: Columbia University Press, 1939.

Reich, Wilhelm. *The Sexual Revolution*. rev. ed., Trs. Theodore P. Wolfe. New York: Farrar, Straus & Giroux. 1970.

_____. *Sex-Pol Essays, 1929–1934*, Trs. Anna Bostock, Tom DuBose, and Lee Baxandall. New York: Vintage, 1972.

Ritz, Hans. *Die Geschichte vom Rotkäppchen. Ursprünge, Analysen, Parodien eines Märchens*. Emstal: Muriverlag, 1981.

_____. *Bilder vom Rotkäppchen*. Munich: Heyne, 1986.

Robinson, Paul A. *The Freudian Left*. New York: Harper, 1969.

Röhrich, Lutz. "Zwölfmal Rotkäppchen." In *Gebärden—Metapher—Parodie*. Düsseldorf: Schwann, 1967, pp. 130–52.

Rölleke, Heinz, ed. *Die älteste Märchensammlung der Brüder Grimm*. Cologny—Genève: Fondation Martin Bodmer, 1975.

Rouger, Gilbert, Ed. *Contes de Perrault*. Paris: Garnier, 1967.

Rumpf, Marianne. "Rotkäppchen: Eine vergleichende Märchenuntersuchung." Ph. D. diss., University of Göttingen, 1951.

_____. "Ursprung und Entstehung von Warn- und Schreckmärchen." *F.F. Communications* 160 (1955): 3–16.

_____. "Caterinella: Ein italienisches Warnmärchen." *Fabula* 1 (1957): 76–84.

Russell, Jeffrey Burton. *Witchcraft in the Middle Ages*. Ithaca: Cornell University Press, 1972.

Saintyves, P. *Les Contes de Perrault et les récits parallèles*. Paris: E. Nourry, 1923.

Scherf, Walter. "Anmerkungen" and "Nachwort." In Ludwig Bechstein, *Sämtliche Märchen*. Darmstadt: Wissenschaftliche Buchgesellschaft, 1970.

Schödel, Siegfried, Ed. *Märchenanalysen*. Stuttgart: Reclam, 1977.

Schoof, Wilhelm. *Zur Entstehungsgeschichte der Grimmschen Märchen*. Hamburg: Hauswedell, 1959.

Schott, Georg. *Weisagung und Erfüllung im Deutschen Volksmärchen*. Munich: Wiechmann, 1925.

Sheets, Robin Ann. "Pornography, Fairy Tales, and Feminism: Angela Carter's 'The Bloody Chamber.'" In *Forbidden History: The State, Society, and the Regulation of Sexuality in Modern Europe*. Ed. John C. Fout. Chicago: University of Chicago Press, 1992, pp. 335–59.

Soriano, Marc. *Les Contes de Perrault: Culture savante et traditions populaires*. Paris: Gallimard, 1968.

_____. "Le petit chaperon rouge." *Nouvelle Revue Française* 16 (1968): 429–43.

_____. "From Tales of Warning to Formulettes: The Oral Tradition in French Children's Literature." *Yale French Studies* 43 (1969): 24–43.

Storer, Mary Elizabeth. *La Mode des contes de fées*. Paris: Champion, 1928.

Stone, Kay. "Things Walt Disney Never Told Us." In *Women and Folklore*, Ed. Claire R. Farrer. Austin: University of Texas Press, 1975, pp. 42–50.

Summers, Montague. *The Werewolf*. Hyde Park: University Books, 1966.

Tatar, Maria M. *The Hard Facts of the Grimms' Fairy Tales*. Princeton: Princeton University Press, 1987.

Tawney, R. H. *Religion and the Rise of Capitalism*. New York: Harcourt, Brace, 1926.

Tenèze, Marie-Louise, Ed. *Approches de nos traditions orales*. Paris: Maisonneuve et Larose, 1970.

Tesdorpf, Paul. *Beiträge zur Würdigung Charles Perraults und seiner Märchen*. Stuttgart: Kohlhammer, 1910.

Thelander, Dorothy. "Mother Goose and Her Goslings: The France of Louis XIV as Seen through the Fairy Tale." *The Journal of Modern History* 54 (September 1982): 467–96.

Theweleit, Klaus. *Männer Phantasien*. Frankfurt am Main: Verlag Roter Stern, 1977.

Thomas, Keith. *Religion and the Decline of Magic*. London: Weidenfeld & Nicolson, 1970.

Trevor-Roper, H. R. "The European Witch-Craze of the Sixteenth and Seventeenth Centuries." In *Religion, the Reformation and Social Change*. London: Macmillan, 1967, pp. 90–192.

Velay-Vallantin, Catherine. *L'histoire des contes*. Paris: Fayard, 1992.

_____. *La fille en garçon*. Carcassonne: Garae/Hesiode, 1992.

Velten, H. V. "The Influence of Charles Perrault's *Contes de ma Mère L'Oie* on German Folklore." *Germanic Review* 5 (1930): 4–18.

Verdier, Yvonne. "Grands-mères, si vous saviez; Le Petit Chaperon Rouge dans la tradition orale." *Cahiers de la littérature orale* 4 (1978): 17–55.

_____. "Le Petit Chaperon Rouge dans la tradition orale." *Le débat* 3 (July-August, 1980): 31–61.

Veszy-Wagner, Lilla. "Little Red Riding Hoods on the Couch." *Psychoanalytic Forum* 1 (1966): 400–15.

Viergutz, Rudolf F. *Von der Weisheit unserer Märchen*. Berlin: Widukind, 1942.

Waldmann, Elisabeth and Richard. *Wo hinaus so früh, Rotkäppchen? Veränderungen eines europäischen Märchens*. Zurich: Schweizerisches Jugendbuch-Institut, 1985.

Weber, Max. *The Protestant Ethic and the Spirit of Capitalism*, Trs. Talcott Parsons. New. York: Scribner, 1958.

Weiss, Harry B. *Little Red Riding Hood: A Terror Tale of the Nursery*. Trenton: Privately Printed, 1939.

_____. *A Forgotten Version of Little Red Riding Hood*. New York: New York Public Library, 1950.

Wichelhaus, Barbara. "Märchentext-Märchenbild: Eine semiotische Untersuchung." *Semiosis* 3–4 (1985): 62–71.

Wolfzettel, Friedrich. "Märchenmoral und Leseerwartung am Beispiel des Rotkäppchenstoffes." In *Text-Leser-Bedeutung: Untersuchungen zur Interaktion von Text und Leser*, ed. Herbert Grabes. Grossen-Linden: Hoffmann, 1977, pp. 157–75.

Yearsley, Macleod. *The Folklore of Fairy Tales*. London: Watts, 1924.

Zipes, Jack. *Breaking the Magic Spell: Radical Theories of Folk and Fairy Tales*. London: Heinemann, 1979; and Austin: Univ. of Texas, 1979.

_____. *Fairy Tales and the Art of Subversion*. London: Heinemann, 1983; and New York: Routledge, 1983.

_____. *Don't Bet on the Prince: Contemporary Feminist Fairy Tales in North America and England*. New York: Routledge, 1986.

_____. *The Brothers Grimm: From Enchanted Forests to the Modern World*. New York: Routledge, 1988.

# ❀ *Copyrights* ❀